PLANNING EFFECTIVE INSTRUCTION FOR STUDENTS WITH LEARNING AND BEHAVIOR PROBLEMS

Rebecca B. Evers
Winthrop University

Sue S. Spencer
Winthrop University

Boston   Columbus   Indianapolis   New York   San Francisco   Upper Saddle River
Amsterdam   Cape Town   Dubai   London   Madrid   Milan   Munich   Paris   Montreal   Toronto
Delhi   Mexico City   Sao Paulo   Sydney   Hong Kong   Seoul   Singapore   Taipei   Tokyo

Vice President and Editor in Chief: Jeffery W. Johnston
Executive Editor: Ann Castel Davis
Editorial Assistant: Penny Burleson
Vice President, Director of Marketing: Quinn Perkson
Marketing Manager: Erica De Luca
Marketing Assistant: Drew Jameson
Production Manager: Kathy Sleys
Creative Director: Jayne Conte
Cover Designer: Bruce Kenselaar

Photo Coordinator: Sandra Schaefer
Cover Art: © Gideon Mendel/CORBIS All Rights Reserved
Full-Service Project Management/Composition: Mohinder Singh/Aptara®, Inc.
Printer/Binder/Cover Printer: R. R. Donnelley & Sons, Inc.
Text Font: Palatino

Credits and acknowledgments borrowed from other sources and reproduced, with permission, in this textbook appear on appropriate page within text.

Every effort has been made to provide accurate and current Internet information in this book. However, the Internet and information posted on it are constantly changing, so it is inevitable that some of the Internet addresses listed in this textbook will change.

Photo Credits: Index Open, pp. 1, 243; Katelyn Metzger/Merrill, p. 27; T. Lindfors/Lindfors Photography, pp. 55, 100, 217; Bob Daemmrich Photography, Inc., pp. 75, 119, 302; Creatas, p. 153; Anthony Magnacca/Merrill, pp. 179, 268.

Library of Congress Cataloging-in-Publication Data
Evers, Rebecca B.
   Planning effective instruction for students with learning and behavior problems/
Rebecca B. Evers, Sue S. Spencer.
      p. cm.
   ISBN-13: 978-0-205-54319-9
   ISBN-10: 0-205-54319-7
   1. Learning disabled children—Education—United States.   2. Problem children—
Education—United States.   3. Curriculum planning—United States.
4. Remedial teaching—United States.   I. Spencer, Sue S.   II. Title.
   LC4705.E84 2011
   371.90973—dc22

                                                           2009037722

10 9 8 7 6 5 4 3 2 1

www.pearsonhighered.com

ISBN 13: 978-0-205-54319-9
ISBN 10:   0-205-54319-7

PREFACE

PURPOSE

Understanding of the complex factors underlying the academic and social/emotional problems experienced by students and teachers is enhanced by our summary of theoretical, conceptual, psychological, methodological, and instructional issues associated with the often-complex task of teaching students with diverse learning needs in inclusive settings. We guide prospective teachers to understand how individuals learn, how and why learning occurs or does not occur, and how both students and teachers can utilize research-based methods to facilitate the learning process. We utilize the principles of Universal Design for Learning, metacognitive and cognitive strategies, and project-based learning to identify potential barriers to learning and simplify instructional decision making.

- To promote an understanding of the principles recommended by research and standards set forth by professional organizations for inclusive education across content and grade levels
- To prepare teachers to use a variety of best practices in diverse classrooms where students may differ in culture, language, ability, income, and other important areas

AUDIENCE

This text was written to present relevant information to pre-service and in-service special and general education teachers who are preparing to teach in diverse and inclusive classrooms. Our goal is to provide a source of information on practical and proven research-based methods and materials. We recognize that many children with disabilities are educated primarily in the general education classroom, and we support co-teaching and collaborative instructional models in all content areas. We believe this text can assist all educators and parents as they prepare their students for learning, living, and working in the 21st century.

ORGANIZATION

The beginning of the text focuses on the laws and mandates that affect the work of all education professionals. In these first three chapters, we provide a brief overview of education laws and other mandates, identify the students found in diverse classrooms and discuss the implications of their learning needs, and emphasize the need for collaborative relationships among all education professionals, families, and community agencies.

The middle portion of the text contains the pedagogy we suggest for teaching in today's classroom. Here we present assessments for planning, teaching, and managing behavior. The chapter on using assessment for planning and teaching includes practical ways to design accessible assessments using Universal Design. This chapter includes selecting appropriate accommodations for assessment as well the why and how for teaching study and test-taking skills. The chapter on using assessment for managing behavior is based on the three tiers of the positive behavior support and intervention model. Practical suggestions for supporting appropriate behavior are offered for each of the tiers—conducting Functional Behavior Assessment, implementing Behavior Intervention Plans, and teaching cognitive strategies for learning appropriate behavior. In the next four chapters, we define and explain how use metacognitive strategies, Universal Design for Learning, technology, and project-based learning to support the learning needs of diverse students with an emphasis on teaching students with learning problems and other unique needs.

In the final three chapters, we focus on the important basic skills of reading, writing, and mathematics. In each of these chapters, we explain the prevalence, causes, and characteristics of problems students experience in learning these skills. Then we present research-based teaching practices for each of these content areas with examples for using the LEARNS strategy to meet the unique needs of all learners.

STRENGTHS

Throughout the book, we:

- Offer practical and realistic approaches to planning, teaching, assessing, and managing behavior in inclusive settings.
- Integrate planning strategies using Universal Design for Learning and LEARNS to support planning for teaching that meets students' learning needs.
- Emphasize teaching strategies, methods, and materials based on sound principles and research data that assert effectiveness.
- Provide supports for teachers and pre-service teachers as they facilitate learning for students who vary in background, language, ability, and other characteristics.

ACKNOWLEDGMENTS

Writing the first edition of a book can be a trying experience, except when you have the help and support of Ann Castel Davis, Sheryl Langner, and Penny Burleson at Merrill/Pearson, true professionals with the patience of saints.

A special thanks to our friends and colleagues who shared their expertise by writing chapters for this book. Dr. Lisa Harris from Winthrop University authored Chapter 9 on project-based learning, and Dr. Mary Little from the University of Central Florida and Dr. Brad Witzel from Winthrop University co-authored Chapter 12, on teaching mathematics.

We also want to thank all of our university students who have given us feedback and encouragement during the writing of this text. But special thanks to our graduate assistants, Kimberly Cook, Kyle Rippey, Brian Martin, and Gwen Troxell, who were an invaluable support team as they made copies, found and checked references, and otherwise got us what we needed when we needed it. Finally, we are grateful to our friend Virginia Wagoner, who as a graduate student did whatever we asked and as a friend continued her support throughout this process.

A special thank-you to the following reviewers for their helpful suggestions: Joyce Bergin, Armstrong Atlantic State University; Gerlinde Beckers, Louisiana State University; Nettye Brazil, University of Louisville; James Burton, Marshall University; Walter Cegalka, St. Thomas University; Helen Dainty, Tennessee Tech University; Anne Gallagos, New Mexico State University; Joan Henley, Arkansas State University; Jan Janz, University of New Orleans; Mike Kelly, Dominican University; Mei-Ling Li, Eastern Illinois University; Paulette Mills, Washington State University; Teshami Reid, California State University, Northridge; Craig Rice, Providence College; Tamar Riley, Florida Memorial College; Cathy Shea, Indiana University Southeast; and Elizabeth Were, Pensacola Junior College.

BRIEF CONTENTS

CONTENTS

Introduction

After reading this chapter, you will be able to:

1. Discuss the setting demands found in most public school classrooms and suggest implications for students with exceptional needs

2. Discuss the instructional demands found in most public school classrooms and suggest implications for students with exceptional needs

3. Elaborate on the reasoning for using the teaching strategies and methods suggested in this book

4. Identify the primary legislation that determines service delivery to children and youth with identified disabilities and other learning needs

5. Explain how each of the four major legislative acts (IDEIA-04, Section 504, ADA, and NCLB) contributes to meeting the needs of a majority of students with disabilities and exceptional needs

6. Discuss the educational implications of the legislative acts protecting students who are English speakers of other languages, highly mobile, or homeless
7. Explain how students with disabilities can benefit from opportunities offered in the legislation for occupational and career programs

C hildren in the United States are required to attend school until they reach a state-mandated minimum age, usually 16 years of age. Federal and state laws, legislative acts of Congress, and Supreme Court decisions mandate that all students receive instruction that provides equal opportunity to learn and subsequently meet state curriculum standards and pass standardized assessments to demonstrate that learning. The emphasis on all students, including students with disabilities and other special needs, meeting state curriculum standards by attending general education classes has increased in recent years; however, at the same time, support services and instructional programs offered outside the general classroom have decreased. As a result of this increased emphasis on inclusion, all teachers must be prepared to work with a variety of students with unique individual needs.

In the past, educators could generally expect that most students in their classrooms would look, learn, and behave pretty much as they themselves did. In today's classrooms, though, growing diversity in terms of students' daily lives, belief systems, and values often presents a totally different picture (McEwan, 2000). Further, teachers should expect to find students achieving on three to five different grade levels in most classrooms. This means that even without students who have stated disabilities, teachers cannot use a one-size-fits-all curriculum to meet the unique needs of every child.

WHO ARE THE STUDENTS WE SERVE?

In Chapter 2, we will describe in detail the characteristics of students who have specific disabilities that meet guidelines for special education services as well as other exceptionalities, such as students who are culturally and linguistically diverse, at risk for school failure, and gifted and talented. Most likely, some students in your classroom may fit into more than one of the categories, such as a student who has a specific learning disability in addition to being gifted or talented or culturally and linguistically diverse. The typical public school classroom, whether a general or special education setting, will have students who:

1. Are racially diverse: In 2006, 55.9 percent of students were Caucasian, 16.9 percent were Black, 20.5 percent were Hispanic, 4.5 percent were Asian/Pacific Islander, and 1.2 percent were American Indian/Alaska Native (School Data Direct, 2008).
2. Live in poverty: 40.9 percent of the nation's K–12 students received free or reduced-price lunch in 2006 (Center for Public Education, 2007).
3. Speak a language other than Standard English: Students who are ELL constituted 8.5 percent of the nation's K–12 students in 2006 (U.S. Census Bureau, 2008).
4. Live in diverse family groups: In 2003, 68 percent of elementary and high school students lived in two-parent families, 23 percent lived with a mother only, and 5 percent lived with a father only (U.S. Census Bureau, 2008).

5. Have a disability: In 2006, 13 percent of all students had a diagnosed disability (School Data Direct, 2008).
6. Will be gifted: While no specific data is collected on the number of gifted students in public schools, the National Association for Gifted Children estimates that approximately 6 percent of students are gifted (National Association for Gifted Children, 2008).
7. May have difficulty with basic reading skills: While national reading scores have risen when assessed at both the fourth and eighth grades, students who are eligible for free or reduced-price lunch continue to score lower than their peers who are not eligible for subsidized lunch (National Center for Education Statistics, 2007b). Further, the gaps in reading achievement between Caucasian–Black and Caucasian–Hispanic students have not significantly decreased since 1992 (National Center for Education Statistics, 2007b).
8. May have difficulty with basic mathematics skills: As with reading, national mathematic scores have risen as assessed in both fourth and eighth grades. Further, students who are eligible for free or reduced-price lunch continue to score lower than their peers who are not eligible for subsidized lunch (National Center for Education Statistics, 2007a). Further, the gaps in mathematic achievement between Caucasian–Black and Caucasian–Hispanic students have not significantly decreased since 1992 (National Center for Education Statistics, 2007a).
9. Will be students with other exceptional needs: At any point in time you may have students who have special needs due to a change in family conditions—for example, temporary illness, divorce, death of a family member, or homelessness may cause a change in a student's academic performance or behavior.

These conditions will affect how students feel about themselves and their abilities to achieve in academic tasks.

Take a moment to recall the class you liked best as a student and where you felt most competent; then recall the class you remember as a struggle because you felt incompetent or unable to meet expectations. Chances are three factors affected your perceptions in both classes: the setting (environment) and instructional (curriculum and teaching methods used) demands of the classroom, as well as knowledge of your own strengths and weaknesses as a student. In the next section, we will examine the setting and instructional demands found in most public school classrooms.

SETTING DEMANDS

While we all have been students, we may not have recognized or been aware of the setting demands we were required to meet. As teachers, however, we must be keenly aware of these demands and how they will affect the students we teach. If we take the time to examine what happens in most elementary classrooms, for example, we will see a very busy place, and to the untrained eye the classroom might even look chaotic. Weinstein and Mignano (2003) offered the following vivid description of the complex environment found in the elementary classroom. Teachers and students are placed in *contradictory* roles. Students are asked to be cooperative by sharing and working harmoniously with peers, but within minutes they may be placed in a competitive situation of working against peers for special privileges or prizes from the treasure chest. Teachers ask students not to talk during seatwork or independent practice but often arrange desks so that students are seated directly next to or across from one another to be ready for times when they want students to work in groups.

Students and teachers work together in a *multidimensional* situation as well, where a broad range of events take place (Weinstein & Mignano, 2003). Teachers would like to be viewed as helping and caring by giving each student individual attention, but they also are called upon to maintain a schedule of teaching tasks, evaluate student performance, and manage student behavior, such as attending to students' collective and individual educational needs in addition to taking attendance, completing required paperwork, collecting money for field trips or lunch, settling disagreements among students, offering counsel to students with problems, and communicating with parents.

Further, these various activities may be taking place *simultaneously* (Weinstein & Mignano, 2003). That is, at any given moment, some students may be participating in reading groups with the teacher, while others are working at computers, in cooperative learning groups, or alone at their desks. The teacher must attend simultaneously to the reading group and all the other activities taking place around the room. At the same time, the teacher must be ready to respond *immediately* (Weinstein & Mignano, 2003) to any problems that arise in the other groups, inappropriate behavior of students at the computers, or straying attention of students in any of the activities. Despite the teacher's careful planning on any given day, the *unpredictable* may happen—student disputes, visits from the principal or other school officials, fire drills, sudden storms that send students back from recess early, or even serious events that send students home early.

As teachers and students work within these classrooms, both groups exist in the public eye and suffer from a *lack of privacy* (Weinstein & Mignano, 2003), since all behavior can be observed by others around them. Students spend the entire day watching the teacher's movements, body language, and reactions to students' responses and behaviors. As a result, teachers must try to keep their feelings private by avoiding movements or facial expressions that might betray their inner feelings or be misinterpreted by students. Students also lack privacy. Even if the teacher misses off-task behaviors or decides to let a mistaken answer go by, there is always a peer who notices. Students cannot hide even the smallest event; it is very difficult to have a private conversation with the teacher, ask for additional assistance, avoid sharing a poor grade on an assignment, or conceal a mistake.

Finally, every class builds a collective *history* (Weinstein & Mignano, 2003) of past events. This history lives in the memory of each student and the history of who has been disciplined, won the most prizes, had a fight, earned both good and poor grades, or whose parent has been called. This history may follow students from grade to grade and sometimes on to middle and high school. This gives the teacher yet another task of helping to build a positive history for this group of students.

Secondary classrooms share the same characteristics of being contradictory, multidimensional, unpredictable, simultaneous, public, immediate, and remembered (Weinstein, 2003), but there are some differences (Bender, 2004). For example, by the time students reach secondary school, they are expected to be independent and responsible but are also expected to follow, without question, the teacher's rules and directions. Due to differences in the organization of the day, students must remember when and where classes meet, and during short passing periods breaks students must remember which books and materials to retrieve from their lockers for the next class or even several classes (Bender, 2004). Other differences include the time constraints of semesters rather than a year, time limitations of individual class periods, and larger numbers of students (often 90+ compared to the 25 or fewer for early childhood and elementary classes) across a number of classes. These differences found in secondary schools can make it more difficult for teachers to know their students well. Problems experienced by beginning teachers may be attributed to their lack of understanding of the complexity in their classrooms (Weinstein & Mignano, 2003). In addition, students with exceptional learning needs (ELN) and other diverse characteristics may experience difficulty with setting demands without support and specific instructions regarding how to meet teacher, school, and peer expectations for behavior.

It is important to remember that these setting demands construct the environment where teaching and learning must take place and may be overlooked. Therefore, understanding that (a) teacher and student roles are contradictory, (b) many classroom tasks are multidimensional, (c) numerous events are unpredictable, (d) happen simultaneously in a (e) public space (f) requiring the teacher's immediate attention, and (g) are part of a collective history is essential for managing and teaching in today's diverse and complex classroom. Finally, it is important to note that delivering and receiving instruction within classrooms such as those described above imposes another set of demands, described in the following section.

INSTRUCTIONAL DEMANDS

At the elementary level, teachers generally structure their lessons around small-group, whole-class, and individual-instructional activities using a variety of methods, which include lectures, demonstrations, class discussions, role-plays, and field trips (Bender, 2004). Student placement in groups varies depending on the activity to be completed, so students may work in several types of groups each day. For example, reading groups will most likely be homogenous, containing students with similar skill levels, whereas a group assigned to complete a social studies project may contain students with varying skill levels. Teachers use a variety of instructional materials, such as commercial children's literature, grade-level texts for academic content with accompanying workbooks, and teacher-made and technology-based materials.

In contrast, secondary-level teachers use a narrower range of instructional methods, generally lecturing to the whole class using a textbook as the basis for class discussions and assignments. While teachers may be willing to offer assistance to students who are having difficulty, generally students are required to seek out the teacher and independently request help (Bender, 2004). Specific content areas, such as occupational skills courses or the performing arts, offer more hands-on activities and may provide for more individual student–teacher interaction during class time. However, secondary teachers are mindful of the need to teach the content so that students can meet graduation requirements and pass standardized content exams such as the national Advanced Placement and state mandated End-of-Course (EOC) and exit exams. They feel pressured to keep up the pace of instruction to cover content within the allotted time of a semester or year. Teachers expect students to have independent study skills and the prerequisite content knowledge required to attain new skills and knowledge. In addition, they expect students to organize course materials, listen to lectures and demonstrations, take notes, participate in class activities and discussions, complete assignments, and study independently for exams (Mastropieri & Scruggs, 2001).

As students progress through elementary and middle school they must master the academic skills and strategies required to achieve success in rigorous content-area classes and meet those realities noted in Table 1.1. Deshler and Schumaker note that a performance gap exists for most secondary students with high incidence disabilities and that as this gap increases over time students become disengaged and discouraged as the student realizes she can not meet the requirements for graduation (Deshler & Schumaker, 2006) which can lead to unsatisfactory ends such as dropping out. To change this trend, teachers at all levels must use research-based interventions and teaching materials to prepare students to meet the ultimate demands of secondary education and adult life after school.

In this book we will discuss models of instruction designed to increase access to the curriculum using research-based methods known to be effective for students with diverse and exceptional needs by supporting the academic achievement of all learners.

MODELS OF INSTRUCTION

In this section we will highlight five instructional methods that have been shown to be effective in inclusive classrooms and should be the foundation for meeting the needs of students in a diverse classroom. These are teaching metacognitive and cognitive skills, using Universal Design for Learning (UDL) in planning lessons, providing authentic Project-Based Learning (PBL) experiences, integrating technology into teaching and learning, and using collaboration and co-teaching when planning and delivering instruction.

Metacognitive and Cognitive Skills and Knowledge

Schools, districts, and state education agencies that are working to implement the requirements of No Child Left Behind (NCLB) as well as state accountability systems are seeking ways to help and support students who struggle to learn the standard curriculum given the setting and instructional demands found in most classrooms. Metacognitive and cognitive strategy instruction offers an effective method for helping students become self-directed learners.

The Metacognitive Framework for Learning presented in Chapter 6 provides teachers and students a common language and framework from which to both access and deliver academic content and social skills instruction. The instructional methods and cognitive theory upon which this model is based promote the acquisition, maintenance, and generalization of both content knowledge and metacognitive and cognitive strategy knowledge and skills (Borkowski, 1992; Flavell, Miller, & Miller, 2002; Hartman & Sternberg, 1993; Spencer & Logan, 2005). Last, empirical evidence suggests that metacognitive knowledge instruction can not only increase student achievement as required by NCLB standards, but it can foster the development of traits described as desirable by teachers, business leaders, and educational administrators (Anderman, 2004; Bouffard, & Couture, 2003; Harlen & Crick, 2003; Ngeow & Kong, 2001; Nichols, Jones, & Hancock, 2003; Palmer & Wehmeyer, 2003). The metacognitive model presented in this book is designed to help P–12 students develop and apply metacognitive knowledge. Teachers need to provide students with explicit instruction in metacognitive and cognitive knowledge and strategies because students with exceptional learning needs (ELN) often lack this type of knowledge. This metacognitive model provides P–12 students and their teachers with an effective way of learning content material.

TABLE 1.1 Realities of Secondary Schools

Realities	Description
1. Pressure to cover large amounts of content	• Because secondary teachers see themselves as "content experts" whose role is to disseminate information to meet standards and assessment and to prepare students for postsecondary settings, they believe that lecture is the most efficient way to accomplish their goals. • An information explosion in content areas causes stress and a sense of urgency in teachers to cover more in less time.
2. Complexity of content-area textbooks	• Texts are written under the assumption that students know how to access information from the written word. • Many texts are written beyond the grade level where they are used, are poorly organized, and not user-friendly. • Texts are often characterized as "encyclopedic" and lacking depth. • Texts are densely packed with facts, names, and details that may obscure meaning.
3. Significant academic diversity	• Classrooms have become more diverse in recent years, but content teachers do not believe it is their responsibility to teach students how to learn the content. • Teachers lack time and knowledge to consider student differences when planning.
4. Limited opportunities for academic interactions	• Teachers see students for limited periods of time and primarily only in classroom setting. • It is difficult for teachers to become familiar with individual students' strengths and needs. • Within the context of the secondary class period there is less time available for monitoring learning and adjusting lesson plans.
5. Instruction geared to achieving students	• The focus of content classes is generally on the achieving students, thus the lower-level students are often left behind and feel disconnected.
6. Limited time for planning and teaching	• The demands of grading, conferences, and other teacher duties mean that teachers must plan on their own time.
7. Limited opportunities for collegial study, planning, or teaching	• Teachers have little common time that would allow opportunities for collaboration, conversation about teaching, or sharing of resources. • Teachers may not have sufficient support or problem-solving sessions for implementation of new methods presented at in-service workshops.

Sources: Bender (2004); Deshler, Ellis, & Lenz (1996); Thousand, Rosenberg, Bishop, & Villa (1997).

Universal Design for Learning (UDL)

When teachers adopt UDL they make fundamental shifts in their thinking, planning, and teaching in four ways. First, they understand that students with ELN fall along a continuum of learner differences just as all students do. Second, they understand that teachers should be adjusting for learner differences among all students, not just those with exceptional needs. Third, they understand that instructional materials used to teach any curriculum should be varied and diverse rather than centering on a single textbook. Finally, they understand that instead of remediating students or asking them to change, the curriculum should be made flexible to accommodate learner differences found in all students.

The goal of UDL and the teachers who use it is to provide alternatives to make the curriculum accessible and appropriate for individuals with different backgrounds, abilities, and disabilities, but these teachers also understand that *universal* in *Universal Design* does not mean that there is one solution for everyone. Rather, teachers who use UDL know the unique nature of each learner and the need to accommodate differences, create learning experiences that suit the learner, and maximize his or her ability to progress (Rose & Meyer, 2002).

All educators must know how to enhance curriculum features that are not already in place to meet the needs of any student in their classroom, whether an exceptionality is present or not. When teachers do not use general education curriculum materials and standards because the curriculum as it is presented in texts and commercial teaching materials does not match some students' exceptional needs, they may be doing students a disservice by alternating or changing curricula so that it is not sufficiently challenging and thereby inadvertently undermining a student's ability to successfully meet general education standards (Ellis, 1997; King-Sears, 2001; Pugach & Warger, 2001; Thousand, Rosenberg, Bishop, & Villa, 1997).

UDL presents the opportunity for curriculum-centered dialogue between general and special educators that allows them to discuss the appropriateness and quality of the curriculum for all students. Curriculum-centered dialogues have the potential both to increase the degree to which teaching methods and instructional materials meet the needs of students from various racial, ethnic, cultural, linguistic, and socioeconomic backgrounds and to support students with exceptional needs (Pugach & Warger, 2001). Technology and digital materials offer one path to an accessible curriculum (Rose & Meyer, 2002). UDL teaching methods incorporate any technology that will support student learning based on the belief that all students can benefit from technology that is integrated into classroom activities.

Integrating Technology to Provide Access to the Curriculum

When writing about using technology to provide equal access to learning experiences for all students, French (2002) stated that "providing equal access to educational opportunities is simply the right thing to do" (p. 1). The presence of technology in public school classrooms is seen as the equalizer of the 21st century (Flippo, Inge, & Barcus, 1995; cited in Cavanaugh, 2002). Parsad and Jones (2005) noted that by the fall of 2003 nearly 100% of the schools in the United States had access to the Internet, and 93% of classrooms were connected to the Internet. Through the use of technology already present in many U.S. public classrooms, students with ELN can decrease their isolation and increase their success in the general classroom (Cavanaugh, 2002).

No doubt a large number of the readers of this text belong to a group of students known as the Millennial Generation (Millennials)—persons born after 1982 and have grown up so exposed to and comfortable with technologies of all types that it is seemingly transparent to them (Peterson-Karlan & Parette, 2005). As a result, students with disabilities who also are Millennials may expect to use technology as part of their educational experience. Unfortunately, Millennial students report being dissatisfied with the level of comfort with technology demonstrated by their teachers versus their own preferences to use technology (Peterson-Karlan & Parette, 2005). Furthermore, data collected for the U.S. Department of Education (Parsad & Jones, 2005) note growing discrepancies in student preferences for and skills in technology use and what schools are providing. This is an issue teachers must address if they want to provide equal access for all students in their classrooms. Therefore, being familiar with and being able to integrate technologies, including assistive technology, into their planning and delivery of accessible learning experiences for all is vital.

Project-Based Learning

With this teaching method, learning is made relevant and useful to students by establishing connections to life outside the classroom, addressing real-world concerns, and developing skills needed in adult living situations. Learning of content takes place in authentic moments of the process, rather than in isolation. PBL focuses on student investigations, either in groups or individually, guided by state curriculum standards and teacher expertise. When students participate in PBL they become active learners, rather than passive learners of the teacher's understanding of a topic. When PBL is used, students are engaged in learning activities that are long term, interdisciplinary, student centered, and integrated with real-world issues. Teachers are engaged as the coach, facilitator, and co-learner. Students' projects can be shared with an authentic audience who has a mutual interest in the information presented, such as peers, teachers, parents, mentors, and the community at large. The powerful instructional principles of differentiating and scaffolding instruction and facilitating socially constructed knowledge (Ellis, 2000) will be discussed in Chapter 9.

Collaborative Teaching

Tutoring, basic skills instruction, and homework completion are often the primary activities occurring in special education resource rooms and inclusion classes, particularly at the secondary level. Despite its widespread use, the use of tutoring interventions in inclusive secondary classes has shown mixed results. Co-teaching, on the other hand, has been associated with positive outcomes for students with disabilities (Mastropieri & Scruggs, 2001). In addition, data reveal a high level of teacher satisfaction with this collaborative effort (Mastropieri & Scruggs, 2001).

Henley, Ramsey, and Algozzine (2002) noted that general education teachers often refer students with unique needs to be evaluated for a disability in hopes that special education services will help students meet general education requirements. However, the very act of referral can have a negative effect on students and their families, who may feel they are being rejected, as well as on the relationship between the general and special educators. For example, when the student is not eligible for special education services, the general education teacher can feel helpless and without support for the problems a difficult student might present. If a true co-teaching relationship exists, however, the special educator can support all students within a classroom who need help and provide the general educator with the support needed to implement strategies and teaching methods that will improve academic achievement. We advocate the use of collaboration and co-teaching as effective practices that support implementation of cognitive and metacognitive strategy use, development of problem-solving skills, and curriculum design and modification using UDL and assistive technology.

LAWS AND REGULATIONS THAT MANDATE PROGRAMS AND SERVICES FOR STUDENTS WITH DIVERSE NEEDS

This section provides a review for readers who have prior knowledge while offering an overview to readers who have little or no prior knowledge of the laws and legislative acts that inform teaching of students with ELN in the United States, including students who are not served by special education programs. Specifically, we will cover legislation that provides protections, educational services, accommodations, and specific programs for children and youth who are in special education programs. Several legislative acts and laws are also described that offer protection to students who have exceptional needs but who are not eligible for special education services, including students with needs due to cultural and linguistic differences or environmental circumstances. Finally, we will address legislation that supports occupational education for students with ELN.

We will begin with the No Child Left Behind Act (NCLB Act), because this act, which encompasses all P–12 public education, has a number of important provisions that directly affect the educational experience of students with disabilities and their teachers. We will explain each of those provisions and discuss possible implications for children with disabilities and other exceptional needs.

No Child Left Behind Act (NCLB)

When passed by Congress in 2001, the NCLB Act (U.S. Department of Education, n.d.) replaced the Elementary and Secondary Education Act (ESEA). This landmark act requires that schools bring all students to proficiency in reading and math by the 2013–2014 school year. Indeed, the stated purpose of NCLB is to "ensure that all children have a fair, equal, and significant opportunity to obtain a high-quality education. . . ." (20 U.S.C. §6301). In fact, accountability has been referred to as the foundation of NCLB (Simpson, LaCava, & Graner, 2004). Thus, five provisions of NCLB address school accountability. The first provision, accountability through adequate yearly progress (AYP), requires schools to assess students annually to demonstrate progress. Schools are allowed to report scores of diverse students in subgroups such as ethnicity, income level, disability, and English language speakers of other languages; however, each group must make adequate yearly progress toward proficiency. Failure to demonstrate AYP for any subgroup has consequences for a school that will then be deemed a *failed school*.

What does NCLB mean for students with special needs and their teachers? The Council for Exceptional Children (CEC; 2004a) stated that the "enactment of NCLB has significant implications for special education policy and practice mainly in the areas of school accountability and personnel certification/licensure issues" (p. 6). The implications of these two issues are explained in the following paragraphs.

ACCOUNTABILITY   The requirements for demonstrating that all students make AYP toward meeting standards and goals are likely to have two significant implications for students with disabilities, their teachers, and their schools. First, schools are required to show AYP toward meeting the goal of 100% proficiency in reading and math for all students, in Grades 3 through 8, within 12 years. Since *all children* now includes children with disabilities, their scores will help determine a school's compliance with the NCLB accountability clause. While it is still unclear exactly what this means, CEC (2004b) suggests that most likely local schools will feel pressured to ensure that students with disabilities are exposed to the general curriculum in order to meet content standards. According to CEC (2004b), this will have the direct effect of increasing the linkage of IEP goals to content standards.

A second implication for accountability relates to the use of accommodations during test taking. According to NCLB, students with disabilities may take the tests in any one of four ways that meet their individual needs (National Association of Protection and Advocacy Systems, 2004):

Option 1: Students with ELN are assessed in the same manner as other students.

Option 2: Students with ELN are assessed with approved accommodations or modifications.

Option 3: Students with ELN are given an alternate assessment that is based on the same achievement standards as the regular assessment.

Option 4: Students with ELN are given an alternate assessment based on different achievement standards—for example, basing the assessment on a life skills curriculum rather than an academic one.

However, a student may be counted as participating in a state assessment *only* if his or her test score is counted in the statewide accountability system. One reason that a student's score might be eliminated or determined to be invalid is that accommodations used during assessment were not allowable. For this reason you must be aware of regulations within your state regarding accommodations considered reliable and valid; that is, listed on the state's approved accommodations list.

The second provision, accountability through highly qualified teachers, requires that all teachers of core academic subjects are appropriately certified to teach the subject(s). This provision includes paraprofessionals who are required to meet minimum qualification standards. This provision is based on the educational research that links the achievement of students to the quality of their teachers (Simpson et al., 2004).

PERSONNEL CERTIFICATION/LICENSURE   Originally, NCLB required states to develop a plan for ensuring that all teachers be highly qualified by the end of the 2005–2006 school year, but this date was recently extended until 2007 by the secretary of education (Simpson et al., 2004). The term *highly qualified* is defined as requiring that all teachers:

1. Have obtained full state certification as a teacher or passed the state teacher licensing examination and hold a license to teach in the state and do not have certification or licensure requirements waived on an emergency, temporary, or provisional basis.
2. Hold a minimum of a bachelor's degree.
3. Have demonstrated subject area competence in each of the academic subjects in which the teacher teaches, in a manner determined by the state.

All public school teachers who teach a core academic subject, whether new hires or veteran teachers with advance degrees, must meet these standards. At this time, this regulation is being interpreted to mean that *all teachers* includes special education teachers. This means that special education teachers must hold dual certification in special education and the core subject area(s) they teach. The *core academic subjects* include English, reading or language arts, mathematics, science, foreign languages, civics and government, economics, arts, history, and geography.

The third provision, use of scientifically researched practices (SRP), promotes the use of effective teaching methods based on scientific research. To be considered as SRP, these teaching methods must meet rigorous standards, have been shown to lead to positive results, and have been subject to rigorous peer review. Simpson and colleagues (2004) described the controversy surrounding the choice of randomized experimental group design as the preferred standard of scientific evidence. In general, however, the idea that teachers should use well-documented effective teaching practices is viewed as a positive step toward improving the academic success of all students, including those with ELN.

The fourth provision, expanded options for parents, encourages parents to become more involved with their child's education. For example, expanded parental rights to their student's assessment data and school or school district report cards are included in NCLB. Report cards describe school's overall effectiveness and progress toward meeting AYP. If parents, based on such information, determine that their child is attending a school deemed as a failing school, they have the option of moving their child to another school and requesting supplemental services.

The fifth provision, increased school district control and flexibility, allows schools that are meeting NCLB standards to use federal dollars for a variety of programs, such as increased technology resources, professional development for teachers and support staff, and drug-free, bully-free school programs. Thus, schools are able to provide increased educational opportunities to their students based on local interests, unique needs, and other considerations.

While there remains some uncertainty and controversy about NCLB, there is little doubt that it has the potential for having a significant impact on student learning and achievement. As you begin or continue your teaching career, you may wish to examine how the NCLB programs, procedures, and results in your state and school district will affect your teaching and career options. This information is available from your state's board of education and local school report cards.

Individuals with Disabilities Education Improvement Act-04

On December 3, 2004, President George W. Bush signed the reauthorized Individuals with Disabilities Education Improvement Act (IDEIA) of 2004 to become IDEA-04. See Table 1.2 for details regarding new provisions and changes to IDEA-97 that have direct implications for teachers and support staff in public schools. These topics include definitions of highly qualified special educators and other school personnel based on requirements of NCLB, changes to the evaluation process, and allocation of funds to support low achieving students who do not have disabilities.

These provisions of IDEA-04 will have a direct impact on teacher certification requirements, evaluation for determination of and continuing eligibility of students,

TABLE 1.2 Changes and New Provisions for IDEA-04

Teacher qualifications	• Highly qualified teachers should be fully licensed in special education and competent in the curriculum of the subject areas in which they teach. (See discussion under NCLB Act.) • All educators and related services providers, such as paraprofessionals, should meet state standards for highly qualified personnel.
Early intervention services	• Allows IDEA funds to be used for services to help students who have not been identified with disabilities; including additional academic and behavior supports to help the students succeed in the general education setting.
Evaluation	• Establishes a timeline of 60 days from parental consent to completion of the evaluation process. • Schools cannot ask for dispute resolution to override parents' refusal to consent for special education/related services. • When parental consent is refused, schools are not responsible to provide free, appropriate public education (FAPE) or develop an IEP [Individualized Education Program]. • Revaluations may not occur more than once a year unless agreed to by all parties, but must occur at least once every three years unless all parties agree that it is unnecessary. • Removes the native language requirements but states that evaluations should be offered in the language and format most likely to yield accurate information on what the child knows and the academic, developmental and functional levels. • Provides new provisions for summaries of academic achievement, functional performance, and recommendations for assisting the individual in meeting their postsecondary goals.
Learning disabilities	• Removes the requirement to use a discrepancy model when identifying a suspected learning disability. • Allows evaluation team to use "response-to-treatment" (response to a scientific, research-based intervention) as a part of the evaluation process for LD.
IEP	• Removes the requirement for benchmarks and short-term objectives. • Revises the requirements for parental reporting. Now requires descriptions in the IEP of how the student's progress towards meeting the annual goals will be measured and when reports on progress will be provided. • Removes the specific age requirements for including transition goals in IEPs. New provision requires a statement of measurable postsecondary goals based on age-appropriate transition assessment related to training, education, employment, and, if appropriate, independent living skills.
IEP: Team attendance	• New provisions state that when parents and local education agency (LEA) agree 　○ A team member may be excused if his or her related service or content area is not being modified or discussed. 　○ A team member may be excused, even if his or her related service or content area is being discussed, if written input for the development of the IEP has been provided prior to the meeting.

(continued)

TABLE 1.2 Changes and New Provisions for IDEA-04 (*continued*)

Students transferring into new settings	• As students move from special education early childhood programs, schools must consider recommendations in the family service plan. • When a student enters from another LEA, either from within the state or from another state, the previous IEP and related services provided must be honored while the receiving LEA evaluates the student and develops a new IEP.
Change in the IEP	• Parties may agree not to hold a meeting to make changes, but to develop a written document to amend or modify the current IEP.

Discipline	• This new provision to give schools the right to consider special circumstances for each case when deciding to change a placement because the student with a disability has violated the code of conduct.
	• This changes the wording related to the length of time a student may be removed to an alternative setting without a hearing from 45 days to 45 school days.
	• Schools may remove a student to an interim setting who has inflicted serious bodily injury to another person without a hearing.
	• New criteria for determining whether a behavior was a manifestation of a student's disability now state
	  ○ "if the conduct in question was caused by, or had a direct and substantial relationship to, the child's disability; or
	  ○ if the conduct in question was the direct result of the LEA's failure to implement the IEP" [CEC, 2004b, p. 19–20].
	• Protections for students who are not yet eligible under IDEA require that the parents must put their concerns regarding child's need for special education services in writing so that LEA has knowledge of the child's need.
	• If parent refuses special education services or if the evaluation team determines no disability exists, then the school is not required to consider any disability during proceedings to change placement.
	• The definition of "substantial evidence" was deleted from the new bill.

Procedural safeguards	• Complaints must be submitted no more than two years from persons should have or did know about the issues being disputed. • The complaining party must submit a due process complaint notice before filing a complaint. • Allows for mediation process to be requested prior to filing a complaint. • Creates a new dispute resolution process called "resolution session" which must convene prior to a due process hearing unless all parties agree otherwise. • Resolutions sessions must be conducted within 15 days of the request for a hearing and the compliant must be resolved within 30 days of the request OR a due process hearing may occur. • A decision made by a hearing officer must be based on substantive grounds as to whether or not the child received FAPE [Free Appropriate Public Education]. This includes, if procedural errors impeded the student's right to FAPE, significantly impeded the parent's opportunity to participate, sor caused deprivation of educational benefits. • Parties have 90 days from the hearing officer's decision to bring civil action.

Note: This table contains the changes and new provisions viewed as important to or of interest to public school teachers, both special and general educators.

Source: From Council for Exceptional Children (2004b).

development of Individualized Education Programs (IEP), methods used to determine a learning disability, discipline of students with ELN, and procedural safeguards.

The Rehabilitation Act Amendments of 1973 (Section 504)

When students do not qualify for special education services under IDEA-04, they may be protected by Section 504 of the Rehabilitation Act Amendments of 1973. These are students who do not require support for their learning needs but need other types of accommodations, such as a student with attention-deficit hyperactivity disorder (ADHD) or one who uses a wheelchair. Public schools are included in legislation that prohibits agencies receiving federal funds from discriminating against persons who have physical and mental impairments. Provisions of this legislation require schools to follow procedures similar to IDEA to identify and provide accommodations for students with special needs but not special education.

The Rehabilitation Act Amendments were among the civil rights legislation in the United States. For many years this legislation was underutilized by schools because they assumed that they had only to comply with the special education laws (i.e., Pub. L. No. 94-142 and later IDEA-97). More recently, Section 504 has provided protection and services to a variety of students that are not served under IDEA. To receive protection or service under Section 504, a person must be otherwise qualified to take a class, belong to a school club, or participate in any other school activity but is hampered by or denied participation because of a disability (Rosenfeld, 1999; Smith, 2002). For example, if a student who is a wheelchair user is able to sing well enough to belong to the mixed chorus, he or she may not be denied participation because accommodations for a wheelchair are necessary. Here the disability does not automatically make the student eligible for special education services but allows for protection from discrimination and eligibility for accommodations under Section 504. See Figure 1.1 for definitions and criteria for determining eligibility under Section 504.

Since students with Section 504 plans should not need and rarely receive the extensive services given students with IEPs, general education teachers are the primary provider of instruction and accommodations for these students. In some cases special educators may be involved in developing the 504 plan based on their expertise with students who have ELN. In addition, a school nurse, social worker, and psychologist may collaborate with the general educator. How students are selected, what format is used for the 504 plan, and who does the monitoring for compliance are all local decisions. Thus, each district must establish its own procedures for referral, evaluation, determination of eligibility, accommodations, reevaluation, and monitoring compliance. One drawback to this freedom is a lack of uniformity that may affect families that are mobile. As they move and change school districts, the services provided for a child change depending on how a school district implements IDEA, Section 504, or the level of support may be different (see Figure 1.2 for more information).

Americans with Disabilities Act of 1990 (ADA)

The Americans with Disabilities Act (ADA) prohibits discrimination on the basis of disability in employment, state and local government, public accommodations, commercial facilities, transportation, and telecommunications. Protection from discrimination

Definitions found in Section 504 Amendments

The three sections of the Amendments that define the term disability, who is eligible for services, and what services should be provided are important to all teachers. First, Section 504, 29 U.S.C. §794, states that:

> "No otherwise qualified individual with a disability in the United States, as defined in section 7(20), shall, solely by reason of her or his disability, be excluded from the participation in, be denied the benefits of, or be subjected to discrimination under any program or activity receiving Federal financial assistance. . . ."

Further, Section 504, 29 U.S.C. §705(B), states that a person is considered to have a physical or mental impairment if the person:

> "(a) has a physical or mental impairment which substantially limits one or more of such person's major life activities, (b) has a record of such an impairment, or (c) is regarded as having such an impairment."

Finally, Section 504, 34 C.F.R. §104.33(b)(1), states that a free, appropriate public education is defined as:

> "the provision of regular or special education and related aids and services that . . . are designed to meet individual educational needs of persons with disabilities as adequately as the needs of persons without disabilities are met and . . . are based upon adherence to specified procedures."

Eligible Criteria

Students who may be eligible for accommodations under Section 504 include
- Students who have attention deficit–hyperactive disorder
- Students who are addicted to substances such as drugs and alcohol but are no longer using illegal substances
- Students who have temporary medical conditions that may require homebound services or hospitalization
- Students with long-lasting or serious medical conditions such as cancer, organ transplants, or communicable diseases such as AIDS
- Students with health problems such as allergies, asthma, cardiac conditions, or epilepsy• Students with orthopedic or other physical conditions but who are not eligible for special education services
- Students with learning disabilities, attention deficit–hyperactive disorder, or low IQ scores who do not meet eligibility requirements for special education

FIGURE 1.1 Section 504
Sources: Office of Education and Civil Rights. (n.d.); Wright & Wright (2004).

under ADA is provided if a person has a disability or has a relationship or association with an individual with a disability. Section 12132 of ADA uses the same definition of disability as Section 504: a person who has a physical or mental impairment that substantially limits one or more major life activities, a person who has a history or record of such impairment, or a person who is perceived by others as having such impairment (U.S. Department of Justice, 2002). And just as Section 504 does not specifically name all the impairments that are covered, neither does ADA. The decision about what impairments may be eligible for accommodations is left to employers, which may

1. Section 504 requires removal of barriers to participation in educational programs. IDEA requires provision of remedial programs and other services.
2. Section 504 has a broad definition of a disability as a condition that limits major life activities. IDEA requires that students fall under a specific category of disability that limits ability to benefit from educational programs and requires special education to achieve benefits from educational programs.
3. Section 504 assumes that general education teachers are the educators responsible for providing instruction and recommended accommodations for students. IDEA assumes that a team of service providers will collaborate to meet the needs of students with IEPs.
4. Section 504 requires schools to undertake additional expenditures but provides no additional funding. IDEA does provide LEAs with additional funds.
5. Section 504 has no age restrictions so that persons are protected from birth to death. IDEA services and protections are restricted by age eligibility to attend a public school until age 21.

FIGURE 1.2 Distinctions Between Section 504 and IDEA
Sources: Rosenfeld (1999); Smith (2002).

mean that some employees will not be given appropriate accommodations or make it necessary to take issues to the legal system.

The provisions governing public schools are found in Title II of ADA, which covers responsibilities of state and local governments regardless of size or acceptance of federal funding. Therefore, state and local governments, which include public schools, are required to give persons with disabilities equal opportunities to benefit from their programs, services, and activities (e.g., public education, employment, transportation, recreation, and health care). Based on these requirements, public schools must provide fully accessible buildings and classrooms, not only for students who need such accommodations but for all persons who have business in the building, such as family members of enrolled students (U.S. Department of Justice, 2002). If a building cannot be altered to meet the ADA requirements, programs must be relocated. An additional requirement is that schools must communicate effectively with people who have hearing, vision, or speech disabilities. This may mean translating written communications into Braille for guardians who have visual impairments or providing a sign language interpreter for parents with hearing impairments. Schools are not required to assume undue financial and administrative burdens, but they are required to make reasonable modifications to policies, practices, and procedures to avoid discrimination.

The Americans with Disabilities Act and Section 504 are seen as virtually identical by the Office of Civil Rights, which is responsible for compliance oversight. The primary difference between these two acts is that Section 504 is limited to agencies and organizations who receive federal funds, whereas the ADA applies to the much broader arena of public places and spaces.

Assistive Technology Act of 2004 (H.R. 4278)

On October 25, 2004, President Bush signed the Assistive Technology Act of 2004 (ATA), which provides federal funding to 50 states and six territories. The first ATA, passed in 1988, provided funds for 10 years, so that states could establish infrastructures for administering assistive technology resources. Each state has established a statewide AT project that makes resources available to persons with disabilities, their caregivers, and the professionals who work with them. (To find the AT project in your state, see the list of resources in the Appendix.)

The reauthorized act changed the priority to increasing access to needed devices for individuals with disabilities. States are now required to spend the bulk of their grants on services to directly help individuals. Grant funds must be spent in one of two ways:

a. Use 60 percent of assistive technology fund on direct aid programs, including reutilization, demonstration programs, alternative financing, and device loan programs,

b. OR use 70 percent of grant funds on direct aid programs, but states are given full discretion on how to allocate funds for at least two, but up to four of the programs listed in option A. (Boehner, 2004, p. 2)

In addition, the act requires states to submit applications for funding with detailed descriptions of planned programs and measurable goals. Further, states must evaluate the effectiveness of their activities and provide an annual report to Congress. As an educator, you should be familiar with your state's AT project and with how it can support students' access to and use of AT to improve their learning in your classroom.

The legislation outlined above determines how children are educated in the United States, provides specific educational benefits and access to educational materials and facilities, defines how teachers and other educational professionals are qualified, and protects these rights for all children. In addition, there is legislation to provide for and protect the educational rights of other students with special needs, such as students who are gifted or talented, homeless or highly mobile, and English speakers of other languages.

LEGISLATIVE SUPPORTS FOR STUDENTS WITH OTHER SPECIAL NEEDS

Legislative acts that include entitlement provisions for students who are gifted or talented, homeless or highly mobile, and English speakers of other languages are important to educators, and particularly for special educators. Entitlement provisions within laws give a person rights to benefits specified especially by that law. For example, students with disabilities may qualify for additional protections and services because they are English speakers of other languages (ESOL). Further special circumstances surrounding these students, such as homelessness, may occur after students are placed in special education programs and therefore have implications on the delivery of special education services.

Gifted and Talented

Students who are gifted and talented can be found in all cultural and socioeconomic groups. Therefore, Congress has passed and recently reauthorized an act that provides funds for research and demonstration projects. Target populations are those who are gifted and talented *and* who are economically disadvantaged, have limited English proficiency, or have disabilities. The Jacob K. Javits Gifted and Talented Students Education Act of 1989 provided federal grant funding for scientifically based research, demonstration projects, innovative strategies, and similar activities designed to build and enhance the ability of elementary and secondary schools to meet the special educational needs of gifted and talented students. The major emphasis of the program was on serving students traditionally underrepresented in gifted and talented programs and to reduce the achievement gap of those students. Underrepresented students include students from minority groups determined by factors such as race, low socioeconomic status, or disabilities.

Congress reauthorized the Jacob K. Javits Gifted and Talented Students Education Act as Title V, Part D, Subpart 6, of the No Child Left Behind Act of 2001 to support education of gifted and talented students. This portion of NCLB reauthorizes the U.S. Department of Education to continue funding grants, providing leadership, and sponsoring a national research center on the education of gifted and talented students.

One program established with Javits funds is the National Research Center on the Gifted and Talented, located at the University of Connecticut, in collaboration with the University of Virginia, Yale University, and Columbia University. The center serves as a resource for teachers and schools looking for effective ways to identify and help gifted and talented students from populations traditionally underserved and underrepresented in gifted and talented programs (see the resource list in the Appendix).

English Speakers of Other Languages (ESOL)

No Child Left Behind, in the 2001 reauthorization of the ESEA, authorized programs for students who are limited English proficient (LEP) or are immigrants under Title III, known as the English Language Acquisition, Language Enhancement, and Academic Achievement Act.

The purposes of this part of NCLB are to help ensure that students who are LEP, including immigrant children and youth, attain English proficiency, develop high levels of academic attainment in English, and meet the same standards as *all* students are expected to meet in the core academic subjects. Further, school districts are required to develop and sustain high-quality language instruction educational programs and use research-based methods when teaching students who are LEP or immigrants. Further, states are required to promote parental and community participation in language instruction programs for the parents and communities of limited English proficient children. The NCLB regulations hold state educational agencies, local educational agencies, and schools accountable for demonstrated improvements in the English proficiency of students who are LEP each school year.

Several questions remain about the impact of NCLB's accountability requirements of annual yearly progress as it relates to students who are ESOL. The act currently requires that students be tested in English after they have been in school for 3 years. Ortiz (cited in Chamberlain, 2004) noted that some of these students, particularly from low-incidence language groups, are at considerable disadvantage if the assessments are available only in English. That is, if assessments are provided only in English, a student's ability to succeed is directly related to his or her ability to function in English, not academic competency for the task. This is especially true if teachers are not allowed to explain directions or unfamiliar terminology. In addition, Ortiz (in Chamberlain, 2004) noted that accommodations and modifications known to be effective in assessment

Homeless children and youths are those who

- lack a fixed, regular, and adequate nighttime residence, including children and youths who share housing with other persons due to loss of housing, economic hardship, or a similar reason;
- are living in motels, hotels, trailer parks, or camping grounds due to the lack of alternative adequate accommodations;
- are living in emergency or transitional shelters;
- are abandoned in hospitals;
- are awaiting foster care splacement;
- have a primary nighttime residence that is a public or private place not designed for or ordinarily used as a regular sleeping accommodation for human beings; for example, persons who are living in cars, parks, public spaces, abandoned buildings, substandard housing, bus or train stations, or similar settings; or
- are migratory children who qualify as homeless

FIGURE 1.3 Definition of Homelessness
Source: National Coalition for the Homeless (n.d.).

situations with students who are ESOL and also have a disability have not been determined. Therefore, since we do not have effective accommodations or appropriate language modifications, students' assessment results may not accurately record student's actual academic achievements. As a teacher you should seek out and be familiar with procedures used in your school district for assessment of students with ESOL.

Children Who Are Homeless or Highly Mobile

The Stewart B. McKinney Homeless Assistance Act (Pub. L. No. 100-77), now known as the McKinney-Vento Act, was signed into law by President Ronald Reagan on July 22, 1987. This act is the first and only major federal legislative response to homelessness. The McKinney Act originally consisted of 15 programs providing a range of services to homeless people, including emergency shelter, transitional housing, job training, primary health care, education, and some permanent housing. Title VII of the McKinney Act has implications for schools and teachers by authorizing education and job training programs, including the Education of Homeless Children and Youth Program.

The primary purpose of the educational provisions is to ensure that children who are homeless can continue their education. Figure 1.3 provides the definition used to determine homelessness for children of school age. Prior to this bill, when students did not have a legal residence within a particular school district, they could be dropped from the district's attendance rolls. According to McKinney, schools must either continue students' education in the school of origin or enroll them in a public school where non-homeless students who live in the district attend (Sec. 722). This means students are allowed to continue attending the school where they were when they became homeless. Students who become homeless in between academic years are able to return to their school of origin for the following academic year (Sec. 722).

In 2001, the act was reauthorized and renamed as McKinney-Vento Act. New requirements include provisions that allow students to remain in the school of origin for the duration of their homelessness, and if students become permanently housed during the academic year, they are entitled to stay in the school of origin for the remainder of the academic year (Sec. 722). Additional provisions require written notifications to parents and rights to appeal school district decisions.

This section has outlined the major points of legislation (IDEA-04, Section 504, NCLB, and ADA) that protects and serves students with disabilities as well as legislation that ensures protection for students with other exceptional needs, such as giftedness, homelessness, and language differences. In addition to these regulations, Congress has provided special legislation to cover occupational and career education. While occupational and career programs in public schools are open to all students, several of these acts have provisions for specific special populations. We will look at these provisions in the next section of this chapter.

LEGISLATION THAT SUPPORTS OCCUPATIONAL EDUCATION FOR STUDENTS WITH EXCEPTIONAL LEARNING NEEDS

The Perkins Vocational and Applied Technology Education Act of 1990

This act, which amended previous Perkins Acts, reflects efforts to improve the quality of vocational programs in general and to provide services to special populations. The educational focus shifts from teaching job-specific skills to integration of vocational and academic skills, leading to the reform known as the Tech-Prep.

The last reauthorization of the Perkins Vocational and Applied Technology Education Act in 1998 contains two major changes from the 1990 act. First, set-aside funding for students with special needs is gone, and local school districts must set and meet performance standards for these programs, but Tech-Prep remained intact, if not stronger, because separate funding was incorporated into the reauthorization.

Originally, implementation of Tech-Prep required an extensive reorganization of vocational programs to meet the requirement that programs deliver academic and job-related information to students in curricula that are clearly related to the workplace (Green & Weaver, 1994).

The Tech-Prep curriculum is competency based, stressing assessment of the competencies needed by workers in realistic settings, including (a) basic skills (e.g., reading, writing, arithmetic, listening, speaking), (b) thinking skills (e.g., creativity, decision making, problem solving, reasoning, the ability to visualize abstract information), and (c) personal qualities (e.g., responsibility, self-esteem, sociability, self-management, integrity). Another requirement of Tech-Prep programs is that the number of years students are enrolled in secondary and postsecondary vocational or technical programs must be combined (e.g., 2 + 2 = 2 years of secondary and 2 years of postsecondary training; 4 + 2 = 4 years of secondary and 2 years of postsecondary training) to provide a smooth transition with continuity of curricula between secondary and technical or community colleges. For example, a secondary student who took either 2 or 4 years of Transportation Technology would be transitioned into a 2-year automotive program at a community college.

Tech-Prep programs present positive opportunities for students with disabilities if the curriculum consistently offered to *all* students contains (a) a common core of math, communication, and science; (b) an emphasis on transition from school to postsecondary settings; (c) opportunities for career planning; and (d) connections between school years and the future. At the same time, however, these programs may present problems for students with disabilities. Target students suggested for Tech-Prep classes are the middle quartiles of the typical high school student body, and target occupations are midrange jobs that require education and training beyond high school (Schell & Babich, 1993). There is a possibility that Tech-Prep classes may become so academically oriented that students with exceptional learning needs are likely to encounter failure. However, the educational and job-training benefits have been shown to benefit students with disabilities (Hughes, Bailey, & Karp, 2002), and school personnel should seek placements in Tech-Prep classes for students with exceptional needs when appropriate.

The School-to-Work Opportunities Act (STWOA)

This act, signed into law on May 4, 1994, and sunsetted (the act's authority ended) in October 2002, was not written solely for students with special needs but also to increase students' awareness of career opportunities. The act offered states initial seed money to plan, implement, and establish STOWA programs for all students in public schools. When the act was discontinued, the intent was that states would continue the programs under their own budgets.

STWOA was intended to serve all students and was an effort to increase opportunities for youth to prepare for careers that were not traditional for their race, gender, or disability. Therefore, *all students* refers to male and female students from a variety of backgrounds and circumstances, including disadvantaged youth; persons with diverse racial, ethnic, or cultural backgrounds (e.g., American Indian, Alaskan Natives, and Native Hawaiians); students with disabilities; and others with special needs, such as English language learners, children of migrant workers, youth at risk of dropping out, and academically gifted or talented students (Evers, 2009).

One purpose of the act was to establish school-to-work transition systems that enabled all youth to identify potential careers and move into the workplace (Council for Exceptional Children, 1994). Funding was provided to programs such as Tech-Prep, career academies, school-to-apprenticeship programs, cooperative education, youth apprenticeship, and business–education partnerships. These programs were required to include school-based and work-based learning components as well as guidance and counseling, workplace mentoring, technical assistance for employers, and coordination with employers.

The Workforce Investment Act (WIA; Pub. L. No. 105-220)

Enacted in 1998 (American Federation of State, County, and Municipal Employees, n.d.), WIA requires that state programs—including employment services, unemployment insurance, vocational rehabilitation, adult education, welfare-to-work, and postsecondary vocational education—be coordinated. Further, the Rehabilitation Act Amendments of 1998 are included in the WIA to integrate all federal, state, and local programs into a comprehensive training act.

A primary purpose was to create a customer-friendly training system. This one-stop delivery system provides all employment-related and training services at one physical site, supplemented by additional sites and technological networks as necessary. Services include (a) job training, (b) adult education, (c) amendments to Wagner-Peyser and related acts, (d) amendments to the Vocational Rehabilitation Act, and (e) general provisions. Note that WIA does not include vocational education available in public schools that is covered by other legislation. All youth between the ages of 14 and 21 who meet one or more of the six barriers to successful workforce entry are eligible for services. The barriers include (a) school dropout; (b) basic literacy skills deficiency; (c) homeless, runaway, or foster child; (d) pregnant or a parent; (e) an offender; or (f) need help completing an educational program or securing and holding a job (American Federation of State, County, and Municipal Employees, n.d.). Further, specific sections of the act note individuals with disabilities as members of the target populations. With this in mind, school personnel who work with students to implement transition plans should be familiar with their local WIA youth programs and how to access services in order to inform students and families of the postsecondary services available to them, especially for those students who exit school without graduating.

Summary

The diverse classrooms found in most public schools today create many challenges for teachers who must meet a variety of unique individual needs. In addition, the growing emphasis on standards-based curriculum and accountability for student learning has further increased pressures for teachers. Finally, the instructional and setting demands found in today's classrooms may be quite different from the ones most teachers experienced as children. Given these realities, using effective teaching practices becomes vitally important for the success of both teachers and students. Educators need planning and teaching practices that are also cost and time efficient, or they may resort to low-level or no accommodations for differences among students. Students indicate that they want to be challenged with engaging classroom activities that are related to their perceived educational goals and have purpose for their lives; offering metacognitive strategies and project-based learning experiences in a UDL classroom employing co-teaching methods can offer challenges while supporting individual needs.

Students with exceptional learning needs have protections and assurances provided by a variety of legislative acts. In fact, acts such as No Child Left Behind, Section 504, IDEA-04, ADA, and Perkins mandate that students with all types of exceptional needs have full access to educational settings and resources. These rights include having highly qualified teachers, participating in the assessment process, and receiving remedial or special education services to enhance and support their learning experiences. When students are in elementary school, teachers and parents have program and placement choices; however, at the secondary level those choices increase and often determine postsecondary transition paths. Finally, the graduation outcomes for students with exceptional needs continue to be of concern to families, educators, and administrators. The increasing standards for high school graduation and exit exams can be barriers to obtaining a high school diploma or to even finishing high school.

As you think about what you have read in the chapter, consider that while we have laws to mandate what we *must* do, only families, students, and educators can determine what we *should* do. The purpose of this book is to provide information about planning and instructional practices that will allow teachers to provide effective and efficient instruction to a diverse population of students. The practices explained and illustrated in this book will provide teachers with methods that can be implemented in any classroom, curriculum, and content area.

References

American Federation of State, County, and Municipal Employees, AFL-CIO (n.d.). *The workforce investment act*. Retrieved on January 3, 2003, from http://www.afscme.org/pol-leg/wiahome.htm: Author.

Anderman, L. H. (2004). Student motivation across subject-area domains. *Journal of Educational Research, 97*(6), 283–285.

Bender, W. (2004). *Learning disabilities: Characteristics, identification, and teaching strategies* (4th ed.). Boston: Allyn & Bacon.

Boehner, J. (2004). *Bill summary: Assistive technology act of 2004*. Washington, DC: House Education & the Workforce Committee. Retrieved on December 12, 2004, from http://edworkforce.house.gov/issues/108th/education/at/billsummary.htm

Borkowski, J. G. (1992). Metacognitive theory: A framework for teaching literacy, writing, and math skills. *Journal of Learning Disabilities, 25,* 253–257.

Bouffard, T., & Couture, N. (2003). Motivational profile and academic achievement among students enrolled in different school tracks. *Educational Studies, 29*(1), 19–38.

Cavanaugh, T. (2002). The need for assistive technology in educational technology. *Educational Technology Review, 10*(1). Retrieved February 3, 2005, from http://aace.org/pubs/etr/issue2/cavanaugh.cfm

Center for Public Education (2007). *The United States of education: A guide to our changing demographics and their implications for public schools*. Retrieved December 28, 2008, from http://www.centerforpubliceducation.org/site/c.kjJXJ5MPIwE/b.3567939/k.E55/The_United_States_of_education_A_guide_to_our_changing_demographics_and_their_implications_for_public_schools.htm#race

Chamberlain, S. (2004). An interview with Asa G. Hilliard, III, and Aba A Ortiz: The effects of No Child Left Behind on diverse learners. *Intervention in School and Clinic, 40*(2), 96–105.

Council for Exceptional Children. (1994). *Summary of the School-to-Work Opportunities Act*. Reston, VA: Author.

Council for Exceptional Children. (2004a). *No Child Left Behind Act of 2001: Reauthorization of the Elementary and Secondary Education Act: A technical assistance resource*. Retrieved on December 29, 2004, from http://www.cec.sped.org/pp/OverviewNCLB.pdf

Council for Exceptional Children. (2004b). *The new IDEA: CEC's summary of significant issues*. Arlington, VA: Author. Retrieved January 6, 2009, from http://www.cec.sped.org/Content/NavigationMenu/PolicyAdvocacy/IDEAResources/CEC_Summary_of_Selected_IDEA_Reauthorization_Issues.pdf

Deshler, D. D., Ellis, E. S., & Lenz, B. K. (1996) *Teaching adolescents with learning disabilities: Strategies and methods* (2nd ed.). Denver, CO: Love

Deshler, D., & Schumaker, J. B. (2006). *Teaching adolescents with disabilities: Accessing the general education curriculum*. Thousand Oaks, CA: Corwin Press.

Ellis, E. (1997). Watering up the curriculum for adolescents with learning disabilities: Goals of knowledge dimension. *Remedial and Special Education, 18*(6), 326–346.

Ellis, E. (2000). *Project-based learning strategies for differentiating instruction*. Tuscaloosa, AL: Masterminds.

Evers, R. B. (2009). Developing career and occupational skills in students with learning disabilities. In G. Blalock, J. R. Patton, P. Kolar, & D. Bassett (Eds.), *Transition and students with learning disabilities: Facilitating the movement from school to adult life* (2nd ed.) Austin, TX: Don Hammill Institute.

Flavell, J. H., Miller, P. H., & Miller, S. A. (2002). *Cognitive development* (4th ed.) Upper Saddle River, NJ: Prentice Hall.

French, D. (2002). Editorial on accessibility: An integral part of online learning. *Educational Technology Review, 10*(1). Retrieved February 3, 2005, from http://aace.org/pubs/etr/issue2/french-ed.cfm

Green, J. E., & Weaver, R. A. (1994). *Tech Prep: A strategy for school reform*. Bloomington, IN: Phi Delta Kappa Educational Foundation.

Harlen, W., & Crick, R. D. (2003). Testing and motivation for learning. *Assessment in Education, 10*(2), 169–207.

Hartman, H. J., & Sternberg, R. J. (1993). A broad BACEIS for improving thinking. *Instructional Science, 21*(5), 400–425.

Henley, M., Ramsey, R., & Algozzine, R. (2002). *Characteristics of and strategies for teaching students with mild disabilities.* Boston: Allyn & Bacon.

Hughes, K. L., Bailey, T. R., & Karp, M. M. (2002). School-to-work: Making a difference in education. *Phi Delta Kappan, 84*(4), 272–279.

King-Sears, M. E. (2001). Three steps for gaining access to the general education curriculum for learner with disabilities. *Intervention in School and Clinic, 37*(2), 87–76.

Mastropieri, M. A., & Scruggs, T. E., (2001). Promoting inclusion in secondary classrooms. *Learning Disability Quarterly, 24,* 265–274.

McEwan, B. (2000). *The art of classroom management: Effective practices for building equitable learning communities.* Upper Saddle River, NJ: Merrill/Pearson Education.

National Association for Gifted Children. (2008). *Frequently asked questions.* Retrieved December 28, 2008, from http://www.nagc.org/index2.aspx?id=548

National Association of Protection and Advocacy Systems. (2004). *Children with disabilities under No Child Left Behind: Myths and realities.* Retrieved December 5, 2004, from http://www.wrightslaw.com/nclb/info/myths.realities.napas.htm

National Center for Education Statistics. (2007a). *Nation's Report Card: Mathematics 2007.* Retrieved on December 5, 2008, from http://nces.ed.gov/pubsearch/pubsinfo.asp?pubid = 2007494

National Center for Education Statistics. (2007b). *Nation's Report Card: Reading 2007.* Retrieved on December 5, 2008, from http:// nces.ed.gov/pubsearch/pubsinfo.asp?pubid = 2007496

Ngeow, K., & Kong, Y. (2001). *Learning to learn: Preparing teachers and students for problem-based learning.* Bloomington, IN: ERIC Clearinghouse on Reading, English, and Communication. (ERIC Document Reproduction Service No. ED457524)

Nichols, W. D., Jones, J. P., & Hancock, D. R. (2003). Teachers' influence on goal orientation: Exploring the relationship between eighth graders' goal orientation, their emotional development, their perceptions of learning, and their teachers' instructional strategies. *Reading Psychology, 24*(1), 57–85.

Office of Education and Civil Rights. (n.d.). *Protecting children with disabilities: Frequently asked questions about Section 504 and the education of children with disabilities.* Retrieved December 28, 2004, from http://www.ed.gov/about/offices/list/ocr/504faq.html

Palmer, S. B., & Wehmeyer, M. L. (2003). Promoting self-determination in early elementary school: Teaching self-regulated problem-solving and goal-setting skills. *Remedial and Special Education, 24*(2), 115–126.

Parsad, B., & Jones, J. (2005). *Internet access in U.S. public schools and classrooms: 1994–2003* (NCES 2005–015). Washington, DC: U.S. Department of Education. National Center for Education Statistics.

Peterson-Karlan, G. R., & Parette, P. (2005). Millennial students with mild disabilities and emerging assistive technology trends. *Journal of Special Education Technology, 20*(4), 27–38.

Pugach, M. C., & Warger, C. L. (2001). Curriculum matters: Raising expectations for students with disabilities. *Remedial and Special Education, 22*(4), 194–196, 213.

Rose, D. H., & Meyer, A. (2002). *Teaching every student in the digital age: Universal design for learning.* Alexandria, VA: Association for Supervision and Curriculum Development.

Rosenfeld, S. J. (1999). Section 504 and IDEA: Basic similarities and differences. Washington, DC: *LDOnLine.* Retrieved December 28, 2004, from http://www.ldonline.org/ld_indepth/legal_legislative/edlaw504.html

Schell, J. W., & Babich, A. M. (1993). Tech-Prep and the development of higher-order thinking skills among learners with special needs. *Journal for Vocational and Special Needs Education, 16*(1), 6–13.

School Data Direct (2008). *School Environment.* Retrieved on December 28, 2008, from http://www.schooldatadirect.org/app/data/q/stid=1036196/llid=162/stllid=676/locid=1036195/catid=1015/secid=4570/compid=859/stype=

Simpson, R., LaCava, P. G., & Graner, P. S. (2004). The No Child Left Behind Act: Challenges and implications for educators. *Intervention in School and Clinic, 40*(2), 67–75.

Smith, T. E. C. (2002). Section 504: What teachers need to know. *Intervention in School and Clinic, 37*(5), 259–266.

Spencer, S. S., & Logan, K. R. (2005). Improving students with learning disabilities ability to acquire and generalize a vocabulary learning strategy. *Learning Disabilities: A Multidisciplinary Journal, 13,* 87–94.

Thousand, J., Rosenberg, R. L., Bishop, K., & Villa, R. (1997). The evolution of secondary inclusion. *Remedial and Special Education, 18*(5), 270–284.

U.S. Census Bureau. (2008). *School enrollment—Social and economic characteristics of students: October 2003.* Retrieved December 28, 2008, from http://www.census.gov/prod/2008pubs/p20-559.pdf

U. S. Department of Education (n.d.). *No Child Left Behind Act.* Retrieved on August 28, 2009, from http://www.ed.gov/nclb/landing.jhtml

U.S. Department of Justice. (2002). *A guide to disability rights laws.* Washington, DC: Author.

Weinstein, C. S. (2003). *Secondary classroom management: Lessons from research and practice* (2nd ed.). Boston: McGraw-Hill.

Weinstein, C. S., & Mignano, A. J. (2003). *Elementary classroom management: Lessons from research and practice* (3rd ed.). Boston: McGraw-Hill.

Wright, P., & Wright, P. (2004). The Rehabilitation Act of 1973 (29 U.S.C., Chapter 16) *Wrightslaw: Special education law.* Hartfield, VA: Harbor House Law Press.

Characteristics of Learners with High-Incidence Disabilities and Other Exceptional Needs

After reading this chapter, you will be able to:

1. Define and identify high-incidence disabilities and other special needs

2. Discuss the characteristics, prevalence, and etiology of students with exceptional learning needs

3. Describe the effects of disabilities and other special needs on student learning

4. Discuss the effects of disabilities and other special needs on social–emotional development

5. Delineate the social–emotional issues facing students with disabilities and other special needs

RATIONALE

This chapter provides a review of the definitions and characteristics of students with high-incidence disabilities and exceptional needs. The assumption is that most readers are familiar with the topic through previous coursework or other experiences. Those requiring background information or wishing to expand on their knowledge are referred to the resources in the Appendix.

In the following sections we will review the federal definitions of the various disabilities and make note of any changes that resulted when, on December 3, 2004, President Bush signed the Individuals with Disabilities Education Improvement Act of 2004 (IDEA) into law. As mentioned, not all conditions and exceptional needs noted in the high-incidence category are recognized under IDEA and therefore have no federally recognized definition. In those instances, or in situations where the definitions of professional organizations are more widely accepted, those definitions will be used.

Because each disability grouped under the umbrella term *high-incidence disabilities* manifests differently, characteristics specific to a given disability are reiterated with particular emphasis on those traits that might directly influence academic and/or social outcomes. Last, causal factors as they relate to each are discussed.

STUDENTS WITH HIGH-INCIDENCE DISABILITIES: WHO ARE THEY?

Today's classrooms in the United States are crowded, complex, and potentially chaotic. For example, the average range of student performance in a typical classroom exceeds five grade levels (Jenkins, Jewell, Leceister, Jenkins, & Troutner, 1990). This means that the typical fourth-grade general educator can expect to teach students who perform at first-, second-, third-, fourth-, fifth-, and sixth-grade levels. In addition, class sizes average 23 students for elementary schools and 25 for high schools (Bracey, 1999). These classrooms are heterogeneous in terms of race/ethnicity, academic ability, and achievement.

Meet Ms. Lee's Class

Take, for example, the fourth-grade classroom of Kim Lee. Similar to other classrooms across the country, her class is diverse in terms of racial/ethnic composition: 12 students are European American, 6 are African American, 5 are Latino, and 2 are Asian American. Of those 25 students, 4 receive extra "basic skills instruction," 4 qualify for enrichment, 1 has autism, 2 have attention-deficit hyperactivity disorder (ADHD), 3 are identified as having a specific learning disability, 1 is identified as being mildly mentally retarded, and 2 students are classified as emotionally disturbed. Kim's classroom exemplifies the school district's policy and the federal mandate under IDEA of including students with disabilities to the greatest degree possible in the general education classroom. As a result, her classroom is a mixture of students with high-incidence disabilities, students with other special learning needs, and those who learn typically.

WHAT ARE HIGH-INCIDENCE DISABILITIES?

The high-incidence category comprises of developmental disabilities such as specific learning disabilities (SLD), speech and language impairments (SLI), emotional disturbance (ED), and mild mental retardation (MMI). Attention deficit–hyperactivity disorder

(ADHD) is also included in the group even though it is not specifically recognized under IDEA. This is because (a) there is compelling evidence that ADHD and LD often co-occur, (b) students with SLD make up approximately 50% of the students who receive special education services, and (c) students with ADHD frequently require special education services under the Other Health Impaired category (President's Commission on Excellence in Special Education, 2002).

High-incidence disabilities are widely regarded as variations on typical development that interfere significantly with school performance and adaptive functions. While students in this group are often difficult to distinguish from their peers without disabilities, they exhibit a combination of behavioral, social, and academic problems that place them at risk academically and socially. Students in this category account for 90% of all students served under IDEA, and most of them receive their education in the general education classroom.

SPECIFIC LEARNING DISABILITIES (SLD)

Definition

According to IDEIA (2004), a specific learning disability (SLD) is:

> . . . a disorder in one or more of the basic psychological processes involved in understanding or in using language, spoken or written, that may manifest itself in an imperfect ability to listen, think, speak, read, write, spell, or do mathematical calculations, including conditions such as perceptual disabilities, brain injury, minimal brain dysfunction, dyslexia, and developmental aphasia.

Learning disabilities do not include "learning problems that are primarily the result of visual, hearing, or motor disabilities, of mental retardation, of emotional disturbance, or of environmental, cultural, or economic disadvantage" (34 Code of Federal Regulations §300.7(c)(10), found in IDEIA, 2004).

While the definition itself was not altered in the 2004 reauthorization of IDEA, the following change in how states may determine the existence of an SLD was instituted and marked the first such change since the law was passed nearly 30 years ago. The addition reads as follows:

> . . . when determining whether a child has a specific learning disability as defined in section 602(29), a local educational agency shall not be required to take into consideration whether a child has a severe discrepancy between achievement and intellectual ability in oral expression, listening comprehension, written expression, basic reading skill, reading comprehension, mathematical calculation, or mathematical reasoning. (B) ADDITIONAL AUTHORITY- In determining whether a child has a specific learning disability, a local educational agency may use a process that determines if the child responds to scientific, research-based intervention as a part of the evaluation procedures described in paragraphs (2) and (3).

This new language results from longstanding dissatisfaction with the IQ-achievement discrepancy formula that has historically been used to identify SLD. Thus, decades of research suggests that the discrepancy model does not reliably discriminate against children with learning disabilities from generally low-achieving children (Swanson, 2000). Research further points out that this model essentially requires waiting for a child to fail before services are provided, thereby acting as an obstacle to the provision of services. In addition, the National Research Council has offered evidence in a recent study that much of the testing used in the IQ discrepancy model is culturally biased (Case, Speece, & Molloy, 2003; Kaloi, 2004).

What does this new language mean to the field of learning disabilities? It means in part that students who are suspected of having a learning disability will not have to fall significantly behind academically before they are eligible to receive research-based intervention, as was the case when using the discrepancy model. The law further supports enactment of the law by providing funds for early intervention services that could include students at risk for learning disabilities.

The model most often cited as satisfying the new language in this law is the "response-to-intervention" (RTI) model (Kaloi, 2004). The RTI model targets children in the early grades who are having academic difficulty and provides for the delivery of research-based interventions designed to ameliorate the students' problems before they are at risk for academic failure. If a student does not respond favorably to the intervention, he is a candidate for further evaluation and special education eligibility.

Proponents of the RTI model believe it provides teachers with a framework within which to assess the child's needs and inform instructional decisions while ensuring that students do not suffer as they wait for formal evaluation. By using the RTI model, teachers also reduce the risk of misidentifying students for special education who only needed early support and assistance to ensure academic progress.

Prevalence

One out of every five people in the United States is thought to have a learning disability. Of students ages 6 through 21, approximately 3 million have some form of a learning disability and receive special education services in school (the majority of these students receive these services in the general education classroom). Reinforcing the idea of high incidence, over half of all children who receive special education do so because they have a learning disability (U.S. Department of Education, 2002).

Etiology

Neurological research indicates that learning disabilities are caused by genetic and/or neurobiological factors that alter brain structure and functioning in a manner that affects one or more psychological processes related to learning. Recent research has found that variations in the following areas of the brain may contribute to learning disabilities: the planum temporale, medial geniculate nuclei, perisylvian regions, frontal cortex, parietal operculum, inferior parietal lobe, temporal gyrus, corpus callosum, insular region, angular gyrus, occipital–striatal region, and the brainstem reticular activating system (National Institute of Mental Health, 2004). Take, for example, the planum temporale, a language-related area found in both sides of the brain. In people with dyslexia, the two structures were found to be equal in size. In people who are not dyslexic, however, the left planum temporale was noticeably larger. Some scientists believe dyslexia may be related to such differences (National Institute of Mental Health, 2004). Although the specific genes responsible for these structural and functional abnormalities remain unknown, molecular geneticists have identified several chromosomes that contribute to specific reading problems such as single-word reading, phonological and orthographic processing, and phoneme awareness (Fisher, Francks, Marlow, MacPhie, & Newbury, 2002).

Additional research suggests other possible causes of learning disabilities, including injury, childhood illness, exposure to toxins, prenatal complications, perinatal oxygen depravation, or traumatic brain injury. These disorders are not due primarily to hearing and/or vision problems, socioeconomic factors, cultural or linguistic differences, lack of motivation, or ineffective teaching, although these factors may exacerbate the problems associated with the disabilities. Learning disabilities may coexist with various conditions, including attentional, behavioral, and emotional disorders, sensory impairments, and other medical conditions.

Educational Characteristics of Students with SLD

Learning disabilities exist on a continuum of severity that ranges from mild to severe. While SLD is a lifelong condition, the manner in which it manifests across an individual's lifetime may vary, depending largely on the interaction between the person's strengths and needs and the demands of a given environment.

Many of the difficulties students with learning disabilities encounter in academic settings stem from their poor information-processing abilities and metacognitive deficits, which make learning in the typical manner problematic. In addition, individuals with learning disabilities may have difficulty with the acquisition and use of:

- oral language (e.g., listening, speaking, understanding);
- reading (e.g., decoding, phonetic knowledge, word recognition, comprehension of subject area textbooks);
- written language (e.g., slow learning of the correspondence of sound to letter, consistent errors in reading or spelling, difficulty remembering basic sight words, inability to retell a story in sequence, difficulty summarizing);
- mathematics (e.g., computation, problem solving, confusion over math signs, trouble with place value, difficulty remembering the steps of mathematic operations such as long division);
- problem solving (e.g., setting goals, strategy use);
- social skills (e.g., group work, easily frustrated, mood swings, tendency to misinterpret behavior of peers and/or adults);
- attention (e.g., perseveration, difficulty staying on task, difficulty finishing on time);
- motor skills (e.g., clumsiness, poor balance, difficulty copying from the board, poor handwriting);
- organizational skills (e.g., time management, sequencing, poor concept of direction). (Mercer, 1997)

During the elementary school years, learning problems become obvious as disabilities interfere with increasingly complex demands. As children progress through elementary school they may begin to have trouble in learning academic material, and emotional and/or social skills may become problematic. Less severe learning disabilities often go undetected until secondary school, where increased academic demands coupled with the expectation for independence at the middle and senior high school level may cause them to become apparent (Mercer & Pullen, 2005). Social skills proficiencies begin to change at this age also. Inappropriate or poor social skills may lead to undesirable changes in peer relationships and discipline problems. As a result, students with learning disabilities may experience increased frustration and poor self-concepts, which can lead to depression and/or inappropriate classroom behaviors.

ATTENTION DEFICIT–HYPERACTIVITY DISORDER (ADHD)

Attention deficit–hyperactivity disorder (ADHD) is one of the most frequently cited disorders affecting school-aged children. The core symptoms of ADHD include developmentally inappropriate levels of inattention, hyperactivity, and impulsivity. Children with ADHD have impaired functioning across settings, including home, school, and in relationships with peers. These characteristics are persistent, typically continuing through adolescence and adulthood (Forness & Kavale, 2001).

Definition

As mentioned, IDEA does not specify a separate category for attention deficit–hyperactivity disorder, and for that reason, there is no federal definition for the disorder. The definition most often referred to when identifying and describing ADHD is found in the *Diagnostic* and Statistical Manual of Mental Disorders (American Psychological Association [APA], 2000). Three subtypes of ADHD are recognized. These are the predominantly hyperactive–impulsive type (does not show significant inattention); predominantly inattentive type (does not show significant hyperactive–impulsive behavior), sometimes called ADD; and combined type (displays both inattentive and hyperactive–impulsive symptoms).

According to the DSM-IV-TR, six or more of the following characteristics of inattention must have been present for at least 6 months to a point that is disruptive and inappropriate for developmental level to be diagnosed with ADHD:

Inattention

1. Often does not give close attention to details or makes careless mistakes in schoolwork, work, or other activities.
2. Often has trouble keeping attention on tasks or play activities.
3. Often does not seem to listen when spoken to directly.
4. Often does not follow instructions and fails to finish schoolwork, chores, or duties in the workplace (not due to oppositional behavior or failure to understand instructions).
5. Often has trouble organizing activities.
6. Often avoids, dislikes, or doesn't want to do things that take a lot of mental effort for a long period of time (such as schoolwork or homework).
7. Often loses things needed for tasks and activities (e.g. toys, school assignments, pencils, books, or tools).
8. Often is easily distracted by extraneous stimuli.
9. Often is forgetful in daily activities.
10. Six or more of the following symptoms of hyperactivity-impulsivity have been present for at least 6 months to an extent that is disruptive and inappropriate for developmental level:

Hyperactivity

1. Often fidgets with hands or feet or squirms in seat.
2. Often gets up from seat when remaining seated is expected.
3. Often runs about or climbs when and where it is not appropriate.
4. Often has trouble playing or enjoying leisure activities quietly.
5. Often is "on the go" or often acts as if "driven by a motor".
6. Often talks excessively.

Impulsivity

1. Often blurts out answers before questions have been finished.
2. Often has trouble waiting one's turn.
3. Often interrupts or intrudes on others (e.g., butts into conversations or games). (p. 92)

In addition, these characteristics that are present before the age of 7 must be evidenced in two or more settings (e.g., at school/work and at home). There must also be clear evidence of significant impairment in social, school, or work functioning. To be diagnosed as having ADHD the characteristics are not better accounted for by another mental disorder (e.g., mood disorder, anxiety disorder, dissociative disorder, or a personality disorder).

Remember, a diagnosis of ADHD does not automatically qualify a student for special education. The child must be assessed and found eligible by the public school's multidisciplinary team to qualify for services. Students with ADHD may be eligible to receive services under the "specific learning disability" category, since attention problems may be the cause of significant academic difficulties; in fact, LD and ADHD can co-occur at a rate of 20% to 30%. Students may qualify as "emotionally disturbed" if their social or emotional behaviors negatively affect their ability to learn. Or they can be considered "other health impaired" if they have limited strength, vitality, or alertness (including increased attention to environmental stimuli that results in limited concentration in the educational setting) and the ADHD adversely affects their educational performance.

If the student does not qualify for special education, services may be provided under Section 504 of the Rehabilitation Act, which prohibits discrimination based on disability. For this to happen, a school's 504 team has to agree that, in a comparison to the average child with no disability, a student has an impairment that "substantially limits one or more major life activities."

Prevalence

ADHD is one of the most commonly diagnosed behavioral disorders of childhood, estimated to affect 3 to 7 out of every 100 school-aged children, or over 2 million children (American Psychiatric Association, 2004). This means that in a classroom of 25 to 30 children, it is likely that at least one will have ADHD.

ADHD is diagnosed more frequently in boys than in girls. In fact, the boy/girl ratio is as high as 5:1 (American Academy of Pediatrics, 2000). Based on those numbers, it is logical to assume that ADHD may be underdiagnosed in girls (APA, 2000). Research suggests that boys display more externalizing behaviors in the classroom, including ADHD symptoms, than do girls, which could account for the differences (Biederman, Faraone, Keenan, Knee, & Tsuang, 1990).

Etiology

Research is being conducted in an effort to identify better ways to treat, and perhaps someday prevent, ADHD. Although the precise cause is unknown, evidence indicates that ADHD does not stem from the home environment but from biological causes. The fact that ADHD runs in families supports the likelihood that the disorder is caused by genetic influences. Studies indicate that 25% of close relatives in the families of children with ADHD also have ADHD, whereas the rate is about 5% in the general population (Abikoff, et al., 2002; National Institute of Mental Health, 2004). More specifically, approximately 14% to 40% of children who have ADHD have a parent with ADHD (Abikoff, et al., 2002). Additionally, if a child has ADHD, there is 15% to 25% likelihood that a sibling also has ADHD (Faraone, Biederman, & Spencer, 2002). The exact number of genes involved and their contribution to the disorder is not known (Faraone et al., 2002). What is known is that the genes involved in ADHD affect the neurotransmitters, receptors, and/or transporters for dopamine and norepinephrine (Comings, 2001).

ADHD has been found to co-occur with other genetically based disorders, disabilities, and/or conditions such as bipolar disorder, learning disabilities, conduct disorder, oppositional defiant disorder, Tourette's syndrome, anxiety disorder, and depression.

Educational Characteristics of Students with ADHD

ADHD does not negatively affect intelligence. So what makes these children function so differently in our classrooms? Why are they often impulsive, distracted, and hyperactive? The answer is that, unlike their peers, they lack the ability to self-regulate. Self-regulation or self-control comes naturally to most, but in students with ADHD this function is impaired because of neurological abnormalities. As a result, 90% of students with ADHD are underachievers and half are held back at least once. About 20% have reading difficulties, and 60% have serious handwriting problems. Experts are focusing on deficits in "executive functions" in the brain as the key to understanding ADHD behaviors (Fisher, Barkley, Smallish, & Fletcher, 2005; Weyandt, 2005). Such impaired executive functions may manifest in the classroom as the following:

INABILITY TO HOLD INFORMATION IN SHORT-TERM MEMORY   Many experts believe that an essential feature in ADHD, as well as in LD, is impaired working, or short-term, memory. People with ADHD are unable to "hold" groups of sentences and images in their mind until they can extract organized thoughts from them. Therefore, they are not necessarily inattentive but unable to remember a full explanation (such as a homework assignment) or unable to complete processes that require remembering sequences, such as model building. In general, children with ADHD are often attracted to activities that do not tax this working memory or produce distractions (e.g., television, computer games, or active individual sports). For children with ADHD there are no differences in long-term memory compared with other children.

IMPAIRED ORGANIZATION AND PLANNING SKILLS   Inattention and distractibility make organization problematic for students with ADHD. Therefore, they often have difficulty being on time and planning the correct amount of time to complete tasks. In addition, these students often have problems organizing materials such as notebooks, assignments, and bringing the necessary materials to class. Also, even if they manage to bring what they need to class, they may have trouble finding it at the right moment.

COGNITIVE AND METACOGNITIVE STRATEGY USE If they do establish a goal, students with ADHD may have difficulty using them to guide behavior, such as selecting strategies, monitoring, modifying, and evaluating tasks. As a result, they often experience problems working independently, beginning tasks, and completing tasks and as a result become easily frustrated.

DISTRACTIBILITY Children with ADHD are usually distracted and made inattentive by an overstimulating environment or by situations that place unusually heavy demands on them. For example, in large classrooms, it may be difficult for them to filter out the many stimuli, and thus they appear distracted as they try to attend to them all. Situations that are repetitive, effortful, uninteresting, and usually not the child's choice may also be problematic. When classroom situations do not provide immediate, frequent, predictable, and meaningful payoffs or rewards for completion, children with ADHD struggle even more. Conversely, they can exhibit a kind of "super concentration" to a highly stimulating activity (such as a video game or a highly specific interest). In such instances, they may become over-attentive, so absorbed in a project that they cannot modify the direction of their attention.

HYPERACTIVITY Students with ADHD may also be hyperactive and lack the ability to control their need to fidget and move about the classroom. Following classroom rules, routines, and procedures can be very difficult. Out-of-seat behaviors, jumping from task to task, and a general need to be in constant motion can cause problems.

IMPULSIVITY If present, impulsivity may manifest as an inability to delay gratification. What is really happening is an inability to impose self-control due to impaired executive processing capabilities. That is, if students think something, they must do it or say it. As a result, they interrupt often, talk incessantly, or intrude upon other students' games or activities. It is important to remember that it is neurological factors that dictate this behavior; the students are not trying purposely to be difficult.

MILD MENTAL RETARDATION (MMR)

Definition

By definition, a student must have subaverage intelligence to be classified as having mental retardation. Subaverage intelligence is defined as two or more standard deviations from the mean of an individualized intelligence, such as the *Stanford Binet IV* or the *Wechsler Intelligence Scale for Children* (3rd ed.; WISC-III). The mean of the most frequently used intelligence tests is 100 with a standard deviation of 15, therefore a student would have to score 70 or below to be considered for eligibility for MMR.

The American Association on Mental Retardation (AAMR) recognizes the following definition, provided by the International Statistical Classification of Diseases and Related Health Problems (ICD–10), of mild mental retardation:

> . . . approximate IQ range of 50 to 69 (in adults mental age from 9 to under 12 years) likely to result in some learning difficulties in school. Many adults will be able to work and maintain good social relationships and contribute to society (2002, p. 109).

Although one must have subaverage intelligence to be identified as having mental retardation, the degree to which the disability affects academic and social success varies as a function of students' levels of intelligence, adaptive skills deficits, and setting demands.

Prevalence

Approximately 10.6% of students receiving services under IDEA have mental retardation. Of these, 85% are considered to have mild mental retardation. Persons with MMR account for 7.5% of people with retardation, while those classified as severely or profoundly retarded account for 3.5% (Field & Sanchez, 1999). Thus, when general and special education teachers encounter students with mental retardation, chances are their cognitive limitations will be relatively mild.

Etiology

Mental retardation can have both biological and environmental determinants that lead to atypical neurological and behavioral development. Most cases of mental retardation occur prenatally, however, and are the result of genetic abnormalities (AAMR, 2002). This is particularly true in the case of severe mental retardation (defined as an IQ of 50 or less), where up to 60% of cases can be attributed to genetic causes, making it the most common cause of severe mental retardation (AAMR, 2002).

People with mild mental retardation (defined as an IQ between 50 and 75), on the other hand, are not as likely to inherit mental retardation. The most common genetically transmitted forms of mild mental retardation include Down syndrome (a chromosomal disorder) and fragile X syndrome (a single-gene disorder) (AAMR, 2002; Moser, 1995). Environmental factors unrelated to genetics that can lead to mental retardation include maternal drug use, toxins, nutritional deficiencies, and poverty.

Characteristics of Students with Mild Mental Retardation

Physically most students with mild mental retardation do not differ from their nondisabled peers. However, by definition, they are performing at an intellectual level below that of their peers and are inefficient learners. The cognitive development of individuals with MR can be considered from two different theoretical perspectives. For example, some view the cognitive development of individuals with MR as being qualitatively different from that of individuals who are not mentally retarded. This perspective, the developmental position, contends that cognitive development for the child with mild mental retardation is similar to that of a child who is not mentally retarded (AAMR, 2002; Beirne-Smith, Ittenbach, & Patton, 2002). From this perspective, children with mild mental retardation develop cognitively just as nondisabled children do. That is, they go through the same developmental stages, in the same sequence, but at a slower rate. The main difference from children who are not mentally retarded lies in the level of functioning they are ultimately capable of attaining (Beirne-Smith et al., 2002). From the perspective of those who espouse this model, children with mental retardation experience academic difficulty because they are presented with tasks beyond their ability level. As a result, proponents recommend that educational programming utilize traditional teaching methods, making instructional decisions based on the students' mental age (Beirne-Smith et al., 2002; Ellis & Dulany, 1991).

Alternatively, some researchers view the cognitive development of individuals with mental retardation as quantitatively different from that of children who are not mentally retarded. Thus, they contend that individuals with mental retardation do not just develop the ability to process information more slowly, but they process it differently compared to individuals who are not mentally retarded (Ellis & Dulany, 1991). For teachers of students with mild mental retardation, the implications of such a view are that these students require unique teaching methods and materials to ameliorate the effects of their disability (Beirne-Smith et al., 2002).

Several areas within the learning process pose academic difficulties for students with mild mental retardation, including attending, cognitive and metacognitive strategy use, memory, transfer, and generalization of information learned in one setting to another (AAMR, 2002; Beirne-Smith et al., 2002; Borkowski, Peck, & Damberg, 1983). These may manifest in the classroom in the following ways.

ATTENDING   Students with mild mental retardation may have difficulty identifying and attending to the relevant or salient features of an academic task and must, therefore, be specifically taught how to do so. This group of students also finds parallel thought problematic wherein an individual must be able to consider several aspects of an academic task at the same time (Zeaman & House, 1979). For example, a science project that has multiple steps or a sheet of math problems of more than one type can cause difficulty.

MEMORY   Students with mild mental retardation have considerable difficulty with some aspects of memory. For example, whereas they recall information from long-term memory about as well as someone who is not mentally retarded (Beirne-Smith et al., 2002; Belmont, & Butterfield, 1977), short-term memory, where information is held for a few seconds, minutes, or hours, is problematic (Beirne-Smith et al., 2002; Borkowski et al., 1983). These memory problems are thought to be metacognitive in nature (Brown, 1987; Sternberg & Spear, 1985). These problems manifest as an impaired ability to automatically attend to salient details (Beirne-Smith et al., 2002) and choosing a strategy for organizing the information so it can be efficiently input into long-term memory (Borkowski et al., 1983; Raymond, 2000).

METACOGNITIVE AND COGNITIVE STRATEGY USE   Students with mild mental retardation are generally inactive learners who do not know how to process information automatically as their nondisabled peers do. They have trouble with inputting information, storing it, and then retrieving it for use in an academic setting. This implies that they will have trouble using cognitive and metacognitive strategies to direct their learning. That is, they will have difficulty working independently because they do not know how to go about setting goals, beginning a task, deciding what strategy to use to get the job done, or how to monitor their progress toward successful task completion (Brown, 1987; Sternberg & Spear, 1985). These students also have difficulty transferring what was learned in one setting to another setting with similar task demands (Belmont & Butterfield, 1977).

EMOTIONAL DISTURBANCE (ED) AND EMOTIONAL AND BEHAVIORAL DISORDERS (E/BD)

All children engage in inappropriate behavior; it is to be expected. It may even be developmentally appropriate, for example, for a teenager to be defiant, understandable for a child whose grandmother died to be withdrawn, or predictable for a student to withdraw when having to face an academic task at which she has been unsuccessful in the past. These behaviors are usually not severe or intense and are usually only temporary. Therefore, they are not a cause for concern for parents or teachers.

Students with ED or E/BD, on the other hand, demonstrate problem behavior on a consistent basis that is much more severe, intense, and of longer duration. For students with ED or E/BD, their inappropriate behaviors (a) are chronic, (b) significantly interfere with academic achievement, and (c) inhibit their ability to establish and maintain appropriate social relationships across settings such as home, school, and community (Colarusso & O'Rourke, 2003; Hallahan & Kaufman, 2003; Turnbull, Shank, Turnbull, & Smith, 2003).

Definition

Multiple definitions of ED and related terms (E/BD) are being used to describe a heterogeneous population of students with significant behavioral challenges (Colarusso & O'Rourke, 2003). The two most frequently used definitions are the federal definition of an emotional disturbance as found in IDEA 2004 and the one proposed by the National Special Education and Mental Health Coalition.

The IDEA definition of *emotional disturbance* is as follows:

(i) The term "emotional disturbance" means a condition exhibiting one or more of the following characteristics over a long period of time and to a marked degree, which adversely affect educational performance:
- An inability to learn which cannot be explained by intellectual, sensory, or other health factors.
- An inability to build or maintain satisfactory interpersonal relationships with peers and teachers.
- Inappropriate types of behavior or feelings under normal circumstances.
- A general, pervasive mood of unhappiness or depression.
- A tendency to develop physical symptoms or fears associated with personal or school problems.

(ii) The term includes children who are schizophrenic. The term does not include children who are socially maladjusted, unless it is determined that they are seriously emotionally disturbed. (Part 300(A), 300.8(c))

Some researchers and professionals believe the IDEA definition inhibits the provision of services to students who need them in two notable ways. First, language in the IDEA definition serves to exclude students identified as socially maladjusted, which seems contradictory to section (B) of the definition. Second, the definition raises concerns regarding the eligibility team's ability to measure accurately and objectively what is meant by "a marked degree" and "a long period of time."

Dissatisfaction with the IDEA (2004) definition led to the formation of the National Special Education and Mental Health Coalition. The goal of this multidisciplinary group representing over 40 mental health, family, education, and advocacy organizations was to generate a definition to replace the IDEA definition of ED.

The definition proposed by the coalition refers to emotional or behavioral disorders (E/BD) as a disability characterized by behavioral or emotional responses in school programs that are significantly different from age, cultural, or ethnic norms to the extent that these responses adversely affect students' educational performances, including academic, social, or vocational skills. These responses are more than a temporary expected response to stressful events in the environment; they are consistently exhibited in at least two different settings, one of which is school related. The behaviors are unresponsive to direct intervention by general education teachers, or the condition of the child is such that general education interventions would be insufficient. This definition provides for ED/E/BD to coexist with other disabilities (Hallahan & Kaufman, 2003). The 2004 reauthorization of IDEA did not modify the original federal definition; nonetheless, controversy regarding the definition continues.

Prevalence

Approximately 473,000 youth in the United States are receiving special education and related services under the category of emotional disturbance (U.S. Department of Education, 2002). This figure represents a 2% increase from the previous year and a 20% increase from 10 years ago (U.S. Department of Education, 2002). Of the students being served for ED/E/BD, boys outnumber girls at a ratio of about 5:1 (Hallahan & Kaufman, 2003).

Students with ED/E/BD frequently experience academic difficulties that result in lower grades, more failing grades, greater retention rates, and a greater likelihood of dropping out of school (Locke & Fuchs, 1995). About 50% of students with ED/E/BD drop out of school; therefore, as a group, they have lower employment levels and subaverage employment histories (U.S. Department of Education, 1998). Poor academic performance has also been associated with the onset, frequency, and persistence of delinquency (Hallahan & Kaufman, 2003).

Etiology

The cause of ED/E/BD is frequently unknown and is often the result of multiple factors contributing to the manifestation of maladaptive patterns of behavior (Coleman & Webber, 2001). Specifically, research points to biological and environmental factors as being the two primary causes of behavioral disorders (Hallahan & Kaufman, 2003). Biological causes are either organic—that is, genetic—or acquired adventitiously after birth. Behavior problems of the type associated with behavior disorders typically begin at a young age and persist across time into adulthood. Research suggests they are a function of biochemical imbalances, neurological abnormalities, genetic predisposition, physiological factors, injury, or illness.

Several environmental factors have been found to contribute to the development of ED/E/BD, including traumatic brain injury, child abuse, home environment (e.g., drugs/drug abuse in the home, poor parenting), socioeconomic status, and stress from significant losses (Kerr & Nelson, 2002). Social and behavioral theorists contend that many students with ED/E/BD behave as they do because they have learned to do so (Colarusso & O'Rourke, 2003).

Educational Characteristics of Students with ED/E/BD

Students with ED/E/BD are reported to have IQs in the average to above-average range (Coleman & Webber, 2001), but their academic performance may not reflect this due to the negative effects of their inappropriate behaviors. The student's behavior not only has an immediate effect on learning, but it also has an additive effect: Successive failures diminish the student's knowledge base, which in turn negatively affects his ability to learn new information. Soon the student is in a downward spiral of academic failure from which he cannot recover.

In addition to academic difficulty, students with ED/E/BD, also by definition, find it difficult to make and maintain social relationships. For example, they will often not work well in groups, choosing to boss others around or dominate discussions. These behaviors can lead to marginalization and social isolation. Students with behavior disorders may seek the company of younger or older students for friendship. Learning is a social activity, therefore social success in school can predict success as an adult. It becomes clear that behavior disorders can represent a significant problem for students.

According to Quay and Peterson (1987), ED/E/BD can be classified into two categories—externalizing and internalizing. Students exhibiting externalizing behaviors are difficult to miss. These students are loud, disruptive, aggressive, noncompliant, and bullying and intimidating and are regularly truant from school. Students with internalizing emotional disorders may be mistaken for model students at first because they are often shy and quiet and do not cause the teacher any problems. Nevertheless, closer inspection will reveal a student who is often anxious, depressed, dependent, helpless, possibly suicidal, and frequently victimized.

Many of the social skill deficits experienced by students with externalizing and internalizing behaviors contribute to their inability to control or manage their behaviors. For example, a student with externalizing behaviors may not have had the opportunity to observe and develop appropriate social skills because he was excluded from social and academic interactions by his peers or because there was no role model in the home from whom he could learn socially acceptable responding.

Students who have not had opportunities to develop social skills naturally may exhibit academic and social skills deficits in the following areas: reading skills, problem solving, time management, organization, perseverance, staying on task, and accepting feedback (Baker & Brightman, 1997; Coleman & Webber, 2001). Educational difficulties may arise due to the child's disregard for classroom rules, poor concentration, truancy, low self-esteem, lack of motivation, and disruptive behavior.

COMMUNICATION DISORDERS

Language affords us the means by which we communicate. Most people develop the ability to share information, thoughts, and feelings in the context of language-rich environments. Some children regardless of environmental affordances have difficulty acquiring and applying language, and ensuing problems may cause them to experience both academic and social problems. It is important to remember, however, that language problems are not atypical; most are generally developmental in nature and disappear as the child matures (Colarusso & O'Rourke, 2003).

Definition

The following two definitions are the most widely used for the purposes of determining if a communication disorder exists. The American Speech-Language-Hearing Association (ASHA) (1993) criterion used by speech and language pathologists and other related service providers to determine if a student has a communication disorder is as follows:

> . . . an impairment in the ability to receive, send, process, and comprehend concepts or verbal, nonverbal and graphic symbol systems. A communication disorder may be evident in the process of hearing, language, and/or speech. (p. 40)

A special educator, on the other hand, uses the IDEA definition for determining eligibility, related services, and research purposes. According to this definition, to be eligible for special education services a student's communication problems must be such that they are placing the student at risk for academic failure. Specifically, IDEA defines speech and language disorders as stuttering, impaired articulation, language impairment, or a voice impairment that adversely affects a child's educational performance.

Etiology

While the exact causes of communication disorders are unknown, some are thought to be illness, disease, injury to the head, genetic predisposition, or limited opportunity to learn language. They also co-occur with other disabilities, such as learning disabilities, mental retardation, hearing impairment, autism, and emotional disorders. Speech and language disorders, a subset of communication disorders, may be caused by stroke, certain drugs, faulty learning of speech sounds, dental problems, physical impairments such as cleft lip or palate, vocal abuse or misuse, hearing impairments caused by ear infections, heredity, birth defects, health problems at birth, exposure to loud noise, aging, and tumors (National Information Center for Children and Youth with Disabilities, 2004).

Prevalence

Estimates indicate that 42 million Americans have a speech, language, or hearing disorder. In schools, students categorized as having speech and language disorders account for approximately 20% of all students receiving special education services, making it the second largest special education category disturbance (U.S. Department of Education, 2002). Communication disorders are estimated (including speech, language, and hearing disorders) to affect 1 of every 10 people in the United States (National Information Center for Children and Youth with Disabilities, 2004).

Characteristics of Students with Communications Disorders

Students with communication disorders often find reading difficult, misunderstand social cues, experience frequent absences from school, utilize poor judgement, and perform poorly on academic work (Colarusso & O'Rourke, 2003). Students with communication disorders also frequently experience social isolation, which contributes to their academic problems. Communication disorders are classified as either speech disorders or language disorders. There are two catagories of speech and language problems: receptive and expressive. Any child who has difficulty understanding language also has problems with expression, but some children have good receptive skills while being unable to formulate their thoughts and feelings into spoken language (Colarusso & O'Rourke, 2003; Gleason, 2005). For this reason, DSM-IV (APA, 1994) gives criteria for receptive and mixed expressive/receptive language disorder. Problems can occur with both receptive and expressive language at several levels: phonology (distinguishing between sounds), syntax (extracting meaning from grammatically complex sentences), semantics (differentiating word meaning), and pragmatics (using language in socially appropriate ways).

It is important to remember a student's speech is said to be disordered only when it deviates so far from the norm that it calls attention to the speaker, interferes with communication, or causes either the speaker or those listening to feel uncomfortable (Leonard, 1998). Some children are generally delayed (i.e., their development in all cognitive areas will be slower than is usual). For others, development occurs at a generally normal pace with the exception of one or more areas of speech and language (Gleason, 2005). In those instances the term *specific language impairment*, or *disorder*, is used.

Students with speech disorders have problems with producing oral language. The three most frequently cited speech disorders occur in articulation, voice, and fluency. It is important to remember atypical speech that results from cultural or dialectical differences are not considered to be disordered speech.

Articulation is the process by which sounds, syllables, and words are formed when your tongue, jaw, teeth, lips, and palate alter the air stream coming from the vocal folds (ASHA, 1993). A person with an articulation problem produces sounds, syllables, or words incorrectly so that listeners do not understand what is being said or pay more attention to the way the words sound than to what they mean. While this may sound similar to baby talk in young children, it is quite different. Articulation errors generally fall into one of three categories—omissions, substitutions, or distortions. An example of an omission is *at* for *mat* or *oo* for *shoe*. An example of a substitution is the use of *w* for *r*, which makes *rabbit* sound like *wabbit*, or the substitution of *th* for *s* so that *sun* is pronounced *thun*. When the sound is pronounced inaccurately, but sounds something like the intended sound, it is called a distortion.

Voice is the sound produced by the larynx as air passes from the lungs through the larynx (manipulated exhalation). A person manipulates the flow of air to produce sound. Voice is a problem when the pitch, loudness, or quality calls attention to itself rather than to what the speaker is saying. It is also a problem if the speaker experiences pain or discomfort when speaking or singing (ASHA, 1993). Voice is judged according to whether the pitch, loudness, and quality support communication that is suited for the situation and individual (ASHA, 1993). For example, an individual's voice may be pitched too high or too deep or too loud or too soft, or the voice quality may be too hoarse, breathy, or nasal. Sometimes a voice may seem inappropriate for an individual, such as a deep-pitched voice in a ninth-grade girl. Finally, fluency disorders are a type of speech disorder that influence the flow of speech, involving abnormal rate, rhythm, and repetitions. Children with fluency problems exhibit what are referred to as *disfluencies* in their speech (Gleason, 2005).

Fluency disorders are divided into three categories: continuity, rate, and effort (ASHA, 1993):

- *Continuity*—repetitions and fragmented speech
- *Rate*—irregular tempo, slow or fast, and jerking
- *Effort*—obvious muscular or mental effort

Two of the most common fluency disorders are *stuttering* and *chuttering*, with stuttering being the most frequently diagnosed disfluency. Stuttering appears in childhood, usually before the age of 6, and it is thought to be hereditary. There are distinct gender differences in the incidence of stuttering, with males 3 to 4 times more likely to stutter than females (Gleason, 2005).

Stuttering is characterized by breaks in the usual time sequence of utterance, repetition, and prolongation of sounds and syllables (Gleason, 2005). For example, a child will repeat words or syllables such as, "Clo-clo-clo-clo-close the window." Alternatively, he may stretch out sounds in words such as, "L-l-l-l-l-leave me alone!" or "I beeelieve I am going to be ill."

Chuttering, on the other hand, is characterized by excessive speed, disorganized sentence structure, interjections, revisions, and words collapsed or condensed, with syllables or sounds slurred or omitted (Gleason, 2005; Leonard, 1998). The condition is distinct from stuttering, although the two often co-occur. The two are different in that chuttering is attributed to disorganized speech planning; the speaker may not know what she wants to say because of processing problems such as those exhibited by students with learning disabilities. A person who stutters, on the other hand, may know what he want to say but has difficulty saying it (Gleason, 2005; Leonard, 1998).

Classroom teachers must be aware of the educational implications associated with communication disorders, including academic problems such as difficulty in learning to listen, speak, read, or write. Students with communication disorders may also experience difficulty with comprehension, problem solving, and strategy use. Finally, communication disorders can isolate students from their peers both socially and academically if not detected and treated (Gleason, 2005; Leonard, 1998).

STUDENTS AT RISK FOR ACADEMIC FAILURE

In 1953, Robert Maynard Hutchins, president of the University of Chicago, speaking on education, said, "Perhaps the greatest idea America has given to the world is the idea of education for all." Societal changes and cultural trends over the past 40-plus years have indeed positioned us to do just that. It all began with the *Brown v. Board of Education* decision in 1954 to desegregate public schools, followed by the Education of All Handicapped Children's Act of 1975, later reauthorized as the Individuals with Disabilities Education Improvement Act (2004), and culminating with the No Child Left Behind Act of 2002.

All these laws, with hundreds of pieces of supporting legislation, have sought to mandate an equal education for all. As a result, schools today serve a diverse student population. Classrooms are complex with racial, linguistic, and culturally diverse minorities and more students who are poor or have disabilities than ever before. For instance, the number of limited English proficiency (LEP) students enrolled in Grades K–12 was 2.2 million in 1990; by 2000, that number had doubled to approximately 4.4 million. Many of these students find school a challenge, and educators often struggle in an effort to meet their unique learning needs. As a result, despite legislative supports and school reform efforts, these students often "fall through the cracks," underperforming their peers to such a degree that they are at risk of academic failure.

Students may be at risk for academic failure if their appearance, language, culture, values, communities, and family structures do not match those of the dominant White culture that our public schools were originally designed to serve and support. These students may be considered culturally or educationally disadvantaged or deprived.

Historically, students at risk were primarily minorities, the poor, students whose parents were migrant workers, and immigrants for whom English was a second language (Goodlad & Keating, 1990). Recently, homeless children, children living in foster homes, and children whose families are in the military service were added to the list of students who might be at risk for academic failure (Popp, Hindman, & Stronge, 2003).

Etiology and Prevalence

Each year more and more students enter our school systems with academic and social–emotional needs that will place them at risk for academic failure (Nunn & McMahan, 2000). While there may be no one definitive factor that causes a child to be at risk for academic failure, poverty is widely recognized as one of the leading contributors to increased risks for academic and social emotional difficulty (Duncan & Brooks-Gunn, 2000). The U.S. Census Bureau reported that in 2007 there were 13.3 million U.S. children living in poverty. This is up from 11.6 million in 2000. Unfortunately, children across time continue to represent a disproportionate share of the poor in the United States (National Center for Children in Poverty, 2007; National Poverty Center, 2001).

These figures are important because when children living in poverty are compared to more affluent children, we find that poor children are 2 times more likely to repeat a grade, drop out of high school, have a learning disability, have parents with emotional or behavior problems, and experience abuse, neglect, and violent crimes (Duncan & Brooks-Gunn, 2000). In addition to environmental factors associated with poverty and academic success (e.g., access to health care, parents' education levels, and quality of parental interactions), recent research has identified another characteristic shared by many at-risk students that is also highly correlated with poverty: high mobility (Popp et al., 2003). Mobility is gaining attention in the literature because of its potential impact on student achievement.

"Highly mobile" is defined as students who move six or more times in the course of their school careers (Popp et al., 2003). Many of the students who fall into this category are also among those generally identified as at risk for academic failure (Popp et al., 2003). Students classified as highly mobile may include children who (a) are homeless; (b) come from corporate executive, military, or migrant worker families; (c) live in low socioeconomic circumstances; (d) receive special education services; (e) speak English as a second language; and (f) live in a home where there is domestic violence or abuse.

Most families move from time to time, and not all of these moves have a negative effect on student learning. Some are the result of positive career changes or promotions. Most children affected by such moves are from middle-class homes and receive the necessary support at home and school to make the transition to a new school without any academic difficulty. For other children, their moves are the result of such factors as poverty, immigration, and homelessness; these moves are more likely to have negative educational consequences (Popp, et al., 2003). Regardless of the reason for a move, research indicates that highly mobile students often underperform their more stable peers (Popp et al., 2003).

In addition to poverty, there are other environmental factors that can place students at risk for academic failure: Certain school-related factors may jeopardize a student's chance for academic success. These include teaching practices, teacher expectations, and teacher beliefs. Thus, teachers may place students at risk for academic failure when they (a) hold lower expectations for them; (b) teach remedial basic skills, deemphasizing higher-level thinking and problem solving; and (c) do not take into account students' differing learning needs when selecting, delivering, and designing instructional methods and materials.

According to Hixson (1993),

> . . . students are placed "at risk" when they experience a significant mismatch between their circumstances and needs, and the capacity or willingness of the school to accept, accommodate, and respond to them in a manner that supports and enables their maximum social, emotional, and intellectual growth and development. As the degree of mismatch increases, so does the likelihood that they will fail to either complete their elementary and secondary education, or more importantly, to benefit from it in a manner that ensures they have the knowledge, skills, and dispositions necessary to be successful in the next stage of their lives—that is, to successfully pursue post-secondary education, training, or meaningful employment and to participate in, and contribute to, the social, economic, and political life of their community and society as a whole. (p. 298)

Characteristics of Students at Risk for Academic Failure

Children who are at risk for academic failure typically have test scores that are substantially lower than those of their peers. For example, a student who is poor the first 4 years of her life may demonstrate as much as a 9-point difference on Wechsler Preschool and Primary Scale of Intelligence (WPISSI) IQ test scores at age 5 compared to peers who are not poor (Duncan & Brooks-Gunn, 2000). In general, at-risk students experience academic achievement significantly below average in areas such as reading and writing, basic math skills, test-taking skills, self-esteem, motivation, social skills, and problem-solving skills. Further, they learn more slowly than their peers do and require more assistance. Since they often do not get the necessary support at school or at home, their academic difficulties increase and build over time, making an established pattern of failure difficult to break.

EFFECTS OF DISABILITY AND EXCEPTIONAL NEEDS ON LEARNING

Students with high-incidence disorders share common characteristics concerning the ways they learn, interact with others, and relate to classroom challenges, albeit for differing reasons unique to their disabilities and/or exceptional needs. In general, many of these students have deficits in basic skills and knowledge, social and emotional skills and knowledge, problem-solving skills and knowledge, test-taking skills and knowledge and generalization. What this means for the classroom teacher is that students with high-incidence disorders tend to have limited basic math and reading knowledge, which over time is compounded, interfering with their ability to build a comprehensive knowledge base, as prior knowledge for what is being taught is, to some degree, a prerequisite to assimilate new information. Students will lack a prior knowledge base for differing reasons, but the negative outcome of not having one is the same.

Let us compare how two different types of students confront the challenge of reading a book on a topic that is too difficult for them. Students who are at risk often do not know what to do when faced with such a challenge and give up frustrated, possibly acting inappropriately in class as a result. A student who understands how to learn when faced with a similar challenge might seek to identify a book on the same topic with a lower readability level, building prior knowledge until such a point where she can read and understand the assigned book.

This illustrates one of the defining differences between good and poor students. Poor students are ineffective learners because they lack the ability to solve problems such as this one using specific strategies. Or they do have skills and strategies at their disposal, but they often use them inefficiently. For example, a student studies for a spelling test by writing the words five times each and subsequently fails the test. Rather than examining his plan, evaluating its effectiveness, and finding that it is not leading to his goal (passing the spelling test), he perseverates and continues to use this ineffective strategy on future tests even though he sees no improvement. Successful learners, on the other hand, identify their goal, in this case passing the spelling test. Then they choose a strategy that they have successfully used before, implement it, monitor its effectiveness, modify their strategy choice if necessary, and evaluate the effectiveness of their choices. If the choice is deemed effective, they will then consider other instances with similar task demands where the strategy may be useful, such as in a science or social studies class.

After repeated failures, students who are at risk become frustrated and angry and want to give up. Their self-esteem may suffer, and they falsely attribute their lack of success to a lack of ability, which often is not the case. Success evades them because they do not know how to learn using the strategies at the disposal of more successful students; they are not motivated to continue to participate in class. Learned helplessness is a common cause of failure, both academically and socially. These shared characteristics as they relate to learning and social–emotional development are listed in Table 2.1.

EFFECT OF DISABILITY AND EXCEPTIONAL NEEDS ON CHILDREN'S SOCIAL–EMOTIONAL DEVELOPMENT

Students with disabilities and exceptional needs often have difficulty in social situations that, if not remediated, may place them at risk for social failure. It begins when they are young and are not invited to parties, selected for team membership, or are functionally excluded when group work is undertaken. While painful socially, these situations are significant for other reasons.

Learning is a social activity in which people learn to solve problems and become a part of a larger support system. Learning is verbally mediated, and participation in groups is necessary to teach students to make socially appropriate decisions based on trial and error. Individuals who do not fit in are often disenfranchised and therefore are not afforded such learning opportunities.

A number of obstacles that all adolescents face test their abilities to make appropriate decisions. These include depression, suicide, teenage pregnancy, drug and alcohol abuse, sexually transmitted diseases, delinquency, and school dropout. Challenges such as these are difficult for all students; however, they are particularly challenging for students with disabilities and exceptional needs who often do not cope well without special assistance and education.

Juvenile Delinquency

In 2001 there were nearly 2.3 million arrests of juveniles, accounting for approximately 16.6% of total crimes (Office of Juvenile Justice and Delinquency Prevention, 2005). It is estimated that 30% to 50% of adjudicated juveniles have a documented

TABLE 2.1 Comparison of Learner and Social–Emotional Characteristics

Domain	Learning Disability	Mild Mental Retardation	Emotional and/or Behavioral Disorders	ADHD	Communication Disorder	At Risk
Basic Academic Skills and Knowledge	Processing deficits lead to difficulty with reading, writing, spelling, math calculation and reasoning.	Subaverage intelligence leads to deficits across all basic skills areas.	Withdrawal or inappropriate behaviors lead to expulsion, excessive absences, & noncompliant behaviors, which may affect development of basic skills.	Inattention & distractibility lead to missed information, deficits in some basic skills areas.	Impaired receptive & expressive abilities may lead to difficulty acquiring basic reading and writing skills.	Poverty, high mobility, lack of support, developmental delays may lead to difficulties acquiring basic skills.
Test-Taking Skills and Knowledge	Difficulty applying new information, memory deficits, information processing problems, poor study and test-taking strategies	Difficulty applying new information, poor study and test-taking strategies, memory deficits	Lack motivation, depressed, noncompliant oppositional, defiant, lack of prior knowledge, poor study and test-taking strategies	Lack prior knowledge, rush to finish, may not complete exam, careless mistakes, lack of study and test-taking strategies	Difficulties with expressive and receptive language interfere with ability to organize and categorize thoughts, take notes, apply knowledge, lack study and test-taking strategies	Lack of prior knowledge, learned helplessness, poor test-taking and study skills, lack of support
Social Skills and Knowledge	Misperceive social cues, facial expressions, gestures, do not learn by imitation	Do not learn from experience misrepresents target behaviors	Poor self-management, makes poor choices	Poor impulse control leads to inappropriate behaviors	Often isolated by communication problems such as stuttering, chuttering	Cultural isolation

(continued)

TABLE 2.1 *Continued*

Domain	Learning Disability	Mild Mental Retardation	Emotional and/or Behavioral Disorders	ADHD	Communication Disorder	At Risk
Emotional Skills and Knowledge	Low self-esteem, faulty attribution, lack motivation, learned helplessness	Low self-esteem, faulty attribution, lack motivation, learned helplessness	Low self-esteem, faulty attribution, lack motivation, learned helplessness	Low self-esteem, faulty attribution, lack motivation, learned helplessness	Low self-esteem, faulty attribution, lack motivation, learned helplessness	Low self-esteem, faulty attribution, lack motivation, learned helplessness
Problem Solving Skills and Knowledge	Cognitive and metacognitive strategy deficits	Cognitive and metacognitive strategy deficits	Cognitive and metacognitive strategy deficits	Cognitive and metacognitive strategy deficits	Cognitive and metacognitive strategy deficits	Cognitive and metacognitive strategy deficits
Generalization	Cognitive and metacognitive strategy deficits	Cognitive and metacognitive strategy deficits	Cognitive and metacognitive strategy deficits	Cognitive and metacognitive strategy deficits	Cognitive and metacognitive strategy deficits	Cognitive and metacognitive strategy deficits

Source: Spencer, S., & Evers, R. (2004). Unpublished course material. Center for Pedagogy, Winthrop University.

disability (National Center for Juvenile Justice, 1999), with approximately 30% to 70% of the youth in corrections and detention centers identified as having either learning, behavioral, or emotional disabilities (National Center on Education, Disability, and Juvenile Justice, 2005). While disabilities do not cause delinquency, learning and behavioral disorders place youth at greater risk for involvement with the juvenile courts and for incarceration. School failure, poorly developed social skills, and inadequate school and community supports are associated with the overrepresentation of youth with disabilities at all stages of the juvenile justice system (National Center on Education, Disability, and Juvenile Justice, 2005).

School Dropout

The world has changed; society's employment needs are intolerant of dropout rates that have not improved much over the last 10 years (National Center for Educational Statistics, 2005). According to the National Center for Educational Statistics, some 3.8 million 16–24-year-olds were listed as having dropped out or not having completed high school in October 2001. These students accounted for 10.7% of the 35.2 million 16–24-year-olds in the United States in 2001 (National Center for Educational Statistics, 2005).

A comparison of dropout rates by race/ethnicity indicate the dropout rate of Caucasians remains lower than that of Blacks; however, that difference has decreased over the past 30 years, with the majority of that change occurring during the 1980s. Since 1990, the gap between Caucasians and Blacks has remained fairly constant, but the dropout rate among Hispanic students has continued to be relatively high compared to Caucasians, Blacks, or Asians/Pacific Islanders. In 2001 for example, 43.4% of Hispanic 16–24-year-olds born outside of the United States were high school dropouts. Hispanic students born in the United States, on the other hand, were much less likely to drop out than their peers who immigrated to the United States (National Center for Educational Statistics, 2005). Regardless of when the youth or their families immigrated to the United States, Hispanic students, when compared to students of other racial/ethnic groups, were more likely to drop out of school. In contrast, the dropout rate for Asian/Pacific Islander students born in the United States was 3.6%, compared to 27.0% for Hispanic students, 10.9% for Black students, and 7.3% for Caucasian students.

One reason for these disparities may be socioeconomic status. For example, during that same year 2001, 22.7% of Blacks and 21.4% of Hispanics were reported as living in poverty for a total of 11.7% of U.S. population. By comparison, 9.9% of Caucasians and 10.2% of Asians and Pacific Islanders lived in poverty in 2001 (National Poverty Center, 2007) and their dropout rates were lower.

Given that poverty is one of the strongest predictors of academic failure and/or dropping out of school, it is not surprising to see a higher dropout rate among students from racial/ethnic groups who are also in the subgroups with higher percentages of poverty. The same goes for a correlation between disability and an increased incidence of dropping out of high school. In addition, the numbers of students with disabilities not completing high school are high. For example, the National Center for Educational Statistics (2008) reported that only 57% of students with disabilities enrolled in special education programs during the 2005–2006 school year graduated with a regular diploma. The correlation between students with disabilities and dropping out of school may in fact be more a function of their association with other risk factors, such as teenage pregnancy, suicide, substance abuse, or depression, than any specific disability.

Teenage Pregnancy

The literature (e.g., Kalmuss, Davidson, Cohall, Laraque, & Cassell, 2003) identifies four key sets of factors associated with risky sexual behaviors and pregnancy: race and ethnicity; socioeconomic status; social influences; and attitudes toward contraception, condoms, and pregnancy and safer-sex behavioral skills. Differences by race and ethnicity vary across risk behaviors and may be attributable in part to differences in socioeconomic status (National Poverty Center, 2007). As we have seen across many of the student populations discussed in this chapter, socioeconomic status can place a student at risk for social and academic failure. Socioeconomic indicators that significantly predict risky sexual behaviors and pregnancy include the adolescents having parents with low educational attainment and living in a single-parent family (Kalmuss, Davidson, Cohall, Laraque, & Cassell, 2003). Last, risky sexual behavior relates positively to teenagers who are below grade level in academic achievement.

The link between poor academic performance and high-risk sexual behaviors is well established (Kalmuss et al., 2003). Thus, research indicates that teenagers with cognitive disabilities or deficits often engage in early, unprotected sexual activity at higher rates than others do (Kalmuss et al., 2003). Cognitive deficits may cause low academic achievement, which in turn increases the likelihood of sexual risk taking. A study based on data from the National Longitudinal Survey of Youth documented a significant association between low cognitive ability and early childbearing (Kalmuss et al., 2003). The hypothesis was that practicing safe sex requires a series of skills and abilities (e.g., abstract thinking, cost–benefit analysis, delayed gratification, and behavioral control) that students with cognitive disabilities often lack. Adolescent counseling and health education curriculum and methodology typically adopt a standardized one-size-fits-all approach that does not meet the unique needs of learners with disabilities, thus placing these teenagers at a clear disadvantage.

Suicide, Depression, and Substance Abuse

Most teenagers feel depressed from time to time. However, if a depressed state lasts more than 2 weeks with no relief during the day, and if there are other signs of depression such as changes in appetite, activity level, sleep pattern, loss of interest in activities that normally give pleasure, social withdrawal, or thoughts of death or punishment, treatment from a mental health professional should be sought.

Depression and the risk for suicide may have biological as well as psychological causes. In fact, depression in people who have behavioral and emotional disorders, conduct disorders, social and communication disabilities, mental retardation, and autism are all higher than in the general population (Hollins & Currin, 1996). This may explain why individuals with intellectual disabilities are more prone to mood disorders and suicide than those without disabilities (Iacono, 2004). Children with LD and ADHD, for example, have high incidences of chronic depression and therefore are at greater risk for suicide. Altered levels of certain brain chemicals—such as serotonin, a key brain chemical involved in regulating mood—along with poor coping skills, and high levels of stress associated with lack of academic and social success could exacerbate this biological and psychological predisposition.

Substance abuse also puts teens at risk for suicidal thinking and behavior. Misuse of these substances can bring on serious depression, especially in teens prone to depression because of a disability, genetic or biological predisposition, family history, or intense life stressors. Alcohol abuse rates for people with disabilities are higher than those of the general population (National Institute for Mental Health, 2004). This is of particular concern given that suicide attempts generally occur more often when teenagers are under the influence of alcohol or drugs, an added risk factor for teenagers with disabilities. Students with ADHD, for example, are at elevated risk for alcohol and other drug abuse due to neurological factors. For teenagers with a disability such as ADHD or a learning disability, who already have an impaired ability to assess risk, make good choices, and think of solutions to problems, alcohol and drugs will further impair their judgment and exacerbate their predisposition to make poor choices. In addition to substance abuse, many students with disabilities face disability-related factors that contribute to their increased rates of depression and suicidal thoughts; these include prescribed medications, chronic medical problems, social isolation, coexisting behavioral problems, and disenfranchisement.

Summary

This chapter has reviewed a number of high-incidence disabilities and disorders. Students with these disabilities often experience a number of barriers to academic and social success. It was not the intent to provide an in-depth discussion of these topics, but it is important to be familiar with the characteristics and educational implications of the various disabilities and disorders.

As you reflect, you will no doubt note that these students are overall more alike than they are different in terms of their academic and social needs. Most of the students in the high-incidence category are at risk for academic and or social failure because they are inefficient or ineffective learners. They lack cognitive and metacognitive skills and knowledge necessary to make appropriate choice—whether it involves choosing a study strategy or electing not to participate in risky behaviors. In general, these students have an underlying inability to effectively solve academic and social problems. We will discuss in subsequent chapters how to design curriculum and choose methods and materials to meet the needs of students with these types of characteristics.

References

Abikoff, H. B., Jensen, P. S., Arnold, L. E., Hoza, B., Hechtman, L., Pollack, S., et al. (2002). Observed classroom behavior of children with ADHD: Relationship to gender and comorbidity. *Journal of Abnormal Child Psychology, 30*(4), 349. Retrieved February 2, 2005, from http://www.questia.com

American Association on Mental Retardation. (2002). *Mental retardation: Definition, classification, and systems of supports* (10th ed.) Washington, DC: Author.

American Academy of Pediatrics. (2000). Clinical practice guideline: Diagnosis and evaluation of the child with attention-deficit/hyperactivity disorder (AC0002). *Pediatrics, 105*(5), 1158–1170.

American Psychiatric Association (2004). *Teenage suicide.* Retrieved December 13, 2004, from http://www.psych.org/advocacy_policy/leg_res/apa_testimony/SENATEINDIANAFFAIRS302. cfm

American Psychological Association. (1994). *Diagnostic and statistical manual of mental disorders* (4th ed.). Washington, DC: Author.

American Psychological Association. (2000). *Diagnostic and statistical manual of mental disorders* (4th ed., revised). Washington, DC: Author.

American Speech-Language-Hearing Association. (1993). Definitions of communication disorders and variations. *ASHA, 35*(Supp. 10), 40–41.

Baker, B. L., & Brightman, A. J. (1997). *Steps to independence: Teaching everyday skills to children with special needs* (3rd ed.). Baltimore: Paul H. Brookes.

Belmont, J. M., & Butterfield, E. C. (1977). The instructional approach to developmental cognitive research. In R. V. Kail & J. W. Hasen (Eds.), *Perspectives on the development of memory and cognition* (pp. 437–481). Hillsdale, NJ: Erlbaum.

Beirne-Smith, M., Patton, J., & Ittenback, R. (2002). *Mental retardation*. Upper Saddle River, NJ: Merrill/Pearson Education.

Biederman, J., Faraone, S. V., Keenan, K., Knee, D., & Tsuang, M. F. (1990). Family–genetic and psychosocial risk factors in DSM-III attention deficit disorder. *Journal of the American Academy of Child and Adolescent Psychiatry, 29*(4), 526–533.

Borkowski, J. G., Peck, V. A., & Damberg, P. R., (1983). Attention, memory, and cognition. In J. L. Matson & J. A. Mulick (Eds.) *Handbook of mental retardation* (pp. 479–497). New York: Pergamon.

Bracey, G. W. (1999). Reducing class size: The findings, the controversy. *Phi Delta Kappan, 81*(3), 246. Retrieved February 2, 2005, from http://www.questia.com

Brown, A. L. (1987). Metacognition, executive control, self-regulation and other even more mysterious mechanisms. In R. H. Kluwe & F. E. Weinert (Eds.), *Metacognition, motivation, & learning* (pp. 65–116). Hillside, NJ: Lawrence Erlbaum.

Case, L. P., Speece, D. L., & Molloy, D. E. (2003). The validity of a response-to-instruction paradigm to identify reading disabilities: A longitudinal analysis of individual differences and contextual factors. *School Psychology Review, 32*(4), 557. Retrieved February 2, 2005, from http://www.questia.com

Colarusso, R., & O'Rourke, C. (2003). *Special education for all teachers*. Dubuque, IA: Kendall Hunt.

Coleman, M. C., & Webber, C. C. (2001). *Emotional and behavioral disorders: Theory and practice*. Boston: Allyn & Bacon.

Comings, D. E. (2001). Clinical and molecular genetics of ADHD and Tourette's syndrome. *Annals of the New York Academy of Sciences, 931*, 50–83.

Duncan, G., & Brooks-Gunn, J. (2000). Family poverty, welfare reform and child development [Special Issue]. In *Child Development, 71*(1), 188–196.

Ellis, N. R., & Dulaney, C. L. (1991). Further evidence for cognitive inertia of persons with mental retardation. *American Journal on Mental Retardation, 95*, 613–621.

Faraone S. V., Biederman J., & Spencer T. (2002). Attention-deficit/hyperactivity disorder in adults: An overview. *Biology and Psychiatry, 48*, 9–20.

Field, M. A., & Sanchez, V. A. (1999). *Equal treatment for people with mental retardation: Having and raising children*. Cambridge, MA: Harvard University Press.

Fisher, M., Barkley, R. A., Smallish, L., & Fletcher, K. (2005). Executive functioning in hyperactive children as young adults: Attention, inhibition, response perseveration, and the impact of comorbidity. *Developmental Neuropsychology, 27*(1), 107–133.

Fisher, S. E., Francks, C., Marlow, A. J., MacPhie, I. L., & Newbury, D. F. (2002). Independent genome-wide scans identify a chromosome 18 quantitative-trait locus influencing dyslexia. *Natural Genetics, 30*(1), 86–91.

Forness, S. R., & Kavale, K. A. (2001). ADHD and a return to the medical model of special education. *Education & Treatment of Children, 24*(3), 224. Retrieved February 2, 2005, from http://www.questia.com

Gleason, J. (2005). *The development of language*. Boston: Allyn & Bacon.

Goodlad, J. I., & Keating, P. (Eds.). (1990). Access to knowledge: An agenda for our nation's schools. New York: The College Entrance Examination Board.

Hallahan, D. P., & Kaufman, J. M. (2000). *Exceptional learners: Introduction to special education*. Boston: Allyn & Bacon.

Hixon, J. (1993). *Redefining the issues: Who's at risk and why*. Revision of a paper originally presented in 1983 at "Reducing the Risks," a workshop presented by the Midwest Regional Center for Drug-Free Schools and Communities. Retrieved December 22, 2004, from http://www.ncrel.org/sdrs/areas/issues/students/atrisk/at5def.htm

Hollins, S., & Curran J. (1996). *Understanding depression in people with intellectual disabilities.* Retrieved December 9, 2004, from http://www.intellectualdisability.info/walking/trainee_psych/6_depression_idhtm.htm

Hutchins, Robert M. (1953) *The University of Utopia.* Chicago: The University of Chicago Press.

Iacono, T. (2004). *Diagnosing depression in people with intellectual disabilities.* News-Medical.Net. Retrieved November 1, 2004, from http://www.news-medical.net/?id=3124

Individuals with Disabilities Education Improvement Act. (2004). Final IDEA bill posted on the Web site of the Committee for Education and the Workforce. Retrieved January 6, 2005, from http://edworkforce.house.gov/issues/108th/education/idea/conferencereport/confrept.htm

Jenkins, J., Jewell, M., Leicester, N., O'Connor, R. E., Jenkins, L., & Troutner, N. M. (1992). Accommodations for individual differences without classroom ability groups: An experiment in school restructuring. *Exceptional Children, 60*(4), 344–359.

Kalmuss, A., Davidson, A., Cohall, A., Larques, D., & Cassell, C. (2003). Preventing sexual risk behaviors and pregnancy among teenagers: Linking research and programs. *Perspectives on Sexual and Reproductive Health, 35*(2).

Kaloi, L. (2004). *IDEA04 update: Congress updates process to determine eligibility for specific learning disabilities.* National Center for Learning Disabilities. Retrieved January 15, 2005, from http://www.ld.org/newsltr/1204newsltr/1204newlang.cfm

Kerr, M. M., & Nelson, C. M. (2002). *Strategies for managing behavior problems in the classroom* (3rd ed.). Upper Saddle River, NJ: Merrill/Pearson Education.

Locke, W. R., & Fuchs, L. S. (1995). Effects of peer-mediated reading instruction on the on-task behavior and social interaction of children with behavior disorders. *Journal of Emotional and Behavioral Disorders, 3*, 92–99.

Leonard, L. B. (1998). *Children with specific language impairment.* Cambridge, MA: MIT Press.

Mercer, C. D. (1997). *Students with learning disabilities* (5th ed.). Upper Saddle River, NJ: Merrill/Pearson Education.

Mercer, C. D., & Pullen, P. C. (2005). *Students with learning disabilities* (6th ed.). Upper Saddle River, NJ: Merrill/Pearson Education.

National Center for Children in Poverty. (2007). *Reducing disparities beginning in early childhood.* Retrieved January 30, 2009, from http://www.nccp.org/publications/pub_744.html

National Center for Educational Statistics. (2008). *Student effort and educational progress.* Retrieved May 20, 2009, from http://nces.ed.gov/programs/coe/2008/section3/indicator22.asp

National Center for Juvenile Justice. (1999). *Juvenile court statistics 1999.* Retrieved January 6, 2005, from http://ncjj.servehttp.com/NCJJWebsite/whatsnew/whatsnew.htm

National Center on Education, Disability, and Juvenile Justice. (2001). *Students with disabilities in correctional facilities.* Retrieved January 13, 2005, from http://www.edjj.org/Publications/#QETA

National Institute of Mental Health. (2004). *Depression in children and adolescents.* Retrieved January 6, 2005, from http://www.nimh.nih.gov/publicat/NIMHdepchildresfact.pdf

National Institute of Mental Health. (2004). Attention deficit hyperactivity disorder. Retrieved December 13, 2004, from http://www.nimh.nih.gov/publicat/adhd.cfm#ref.

National Information Center for Children and Youth with Disabilities. (2004). *Fact sheet number 11 (FS11), January 2004.* Retrieved January 4, 2005, from www.nichcy.org/pubs/factshe/fs11txt.htm

National Poverty Center (2001). *Poverty in the United States, 2001.* Retrieved December 19, 2004, from http://www.npc.umich.edu/poverty/.

Nunn, G. D., & McMahan, K. R. (2000). "Ideal" problem solving using a collaborative effort for special needs and at-risk students. *Education, 121*(2), 305–12.

Office of Juvenile Justice and Delinquency Prevention. (2005). *Fact sheet on juvenile offenders.* Retrieved January 23, 2005, from http://ojjdp.ncjrs.org/search/topiclist.asp

Popp, P. A., Hindman, J. L., & Stronge, J. H. (2002). *Local homeless education liaison toolkit: Prepublication draft.* Greensboro, NC: National Center for Homeless Education. Retrieved January 4, 2005, from http://www.serve.org/nche

President's Commission on Excellence in Special Education. (2002). *A new era: Revitalizing special education for children and their families.* Retrieved December 22, 2004, from http://www.ed.gov/inits/commissionsboards/whspecialeducation/

Quay, H. C., & Peterson, D. R. (1987). *Manual for the revised behavior problem checklist.* Odessa, FL: Psychological Assessment Resources.

Raymond, E. B. (2000). *Learners with mild disabilities: A characteristic approach.* Boston: Allyn & Bacon.

Sternberg, R. J., & Spear, L. C. (1985). A triarchic theory of mental retardation. *International Review of Research in Mental Retardation, 13,* 310–326.

Swanson, H. L. (2000). Issues facing the field of learning disabilities. *Learning Disability Quarterly, 23*(1), 37.

Turnbull, A. P., Shank, M., Turnbull, R., & Smith, S. (2003). *Exceptional lives: Special education in today's schools.* Upper Saddle River, NJ: Merrill/ Pearson Education.

U.S. Department of Education. (1998). *Twentieth annual report to Congress on the implementation of the Individuals With Disabilities Education Act.* Washington, DC: Author. (ERIC Document Reproduction Service No. ED242 722)

U.S. Department of Education. (2002). *Twenty-fourth annual report to Congress on the implementation of the Individuals with Disabilities Education Act.* Retrieved January 9, 2005, from http://www.ed.gov/about/reports/annual/ osep/2002/index.html

Weyandt, L. L. (2005). *Executive function in children, adolescents, and adults with attention deficit hyperactivity disorder: Introduction to the special issue.* Mahwah, NJ: Lawrence Erlbaum.

Zeaman, D., & House, B. J. (1979). A review of attention theory. In N. R. Ellis (Ed.), *Handbook of mental deficiency: Psychological theory and research* (2nd ed., pp. 63–120). Hillsdale, NJ: Lawrence Erlbaum.

Chapter 3

Collaborative Problem-Solving Methods for Educators

After reading this chapter, you will be able to:

1. Discuss the role of collaboration in recent educational reform movements
2. Define collaboration, its characteristics, and provide examples of collaborative opportunities occurring in schools
3. Define collaborative teaming, discuss its purpose, and identify strategies that promote team effectiveness
4. Identify and discuss why barriers to collaboration exist
5. Discuss how collaborative teaming methods facilitate collaborative problem solving and reflective practice and promote the development of metacognitive and cognitive knowledge for students and teachers

BACKGROUND AND RATIONALE

Successful classrooms of today rely on collaborative practices to provide student services, but prior to the passage of Public Law 94-142, teachers typically worked in isolation each within their own classrooms. Segregation across most educational settings was the norm—special educators worked with special needs students in generally self-contained classrooms and general education teachers in grade level or content area classrooms. There was little interaction between special education teachers and their peers in general education classrooms (Friend & Cook, 2007). The expectation that they work together collaboratively did not exist in the past as it does now. Despite the changes, brought about by federal mandates such as IDEA and NCLB that have led to the use of more collaborative practices, general and special education teachers alike report feeling underprepared to utilize these methods (Leonard & Leonard, 2003; Welch, 1998).

In this chapter, we will discuss four key themes. First, we will define and identify the basic characteristics of collaboration. Second, we will discuss collaborative work among teachers, parents, other professionals, and students. Third, we will explain how collaborative teaching methods can increase problem-solving ability and critical thinking and promote academic and social success. Fourth, we will examine the challenges teachers encounter when working collaboratively.

EDUCATIONAL COLLABORATION DEFINED

What is educational collaboration? There are many different definitions of *educational collaboration*. West (1990) viewed collaboration as an activity requiring interactive planning or problem solving that involves two or more teams. Welch and Sheridan (1995) described collaboration as a dynamic framework that promoted interdependence, parity, and sharing between people who make decisions while working together to achieve a common goal. Friend and Cook (2007) expressed similar views of collaboration when they define it as "direct interaction between at least two co-equal parties voluntarily engaged in shared decision making as they work toward a common goal" (p. 7).

As implied in each of these definitions, collaboration cannot exist in isolation. By definition, collaboration requires people to engage in a specific process to complete a task or problem-solving activity. For example, members of an Individualized Education Program (IEP) team meet for the purpose of reviewing assessment data to determine where a student will receive educational services. This process is dynamic; it requires planning, shared problem solving, and decision making. Can you think of other examples of collaboration in schools?

Special education teachers are in collaborative situations frequently because of the nature of their jobs. For example, special education teachers work with others on large student caseloads; they arrange and plan IEP meetings that include related service providers and other professionals; they must schedule, lead, and attend numerous meetings with classroom teachers; and they work with the parents of students with disabilities and those from culturally and linguistically diverse backgrounds (Billingsley, 2004).

CHARACTERISTICS OF COLLABORATION

According to Friend and Cook (1992, 2007), there are six elements of effective collaboration:

1. Collaboration is voluntary.
2. Collaboration requires parity between individuals.
3. Collaboration is based on common goals.
4. Collaboration depends on shared responsibility for participation in decision making.
5. Individuals who collaborate share their resources.
6. Individuals who collaborate share accountability for outcomes.

Individuals Who Collaborate Do So Willingly

To be effective, collaboration must be voluntary. Legislation and administrators may mandate that teachers work together, but they cannot force them to do so. For example, a teacher can be required to attend a student support team meeting, but if this teacher does not want to be there, he or she may complain to the point that no one accomplishes anything. As this example illustrates, individuals can be compelled to attend a meeting, but that does not ensure they will contribute. This does not imply that teachers will not collaborate in situations that are mandated; it simply means they must perceive a benefit in doing so if they are to voluntarily participate. Consider this situation: Teachers are told to attend a professional development class after school. If the session covers a topic they believe is beneficial to them, they will work with the presenter to complete instructional activities or projects, but if the teachers consider the session unimportant or a waste of their time, they may not work with the presenter effectively.

Individuals Who Collaborate Are Respectful

Effective collaboration requires respect between those participating. When members of a group value each person's expertise, contribution, point of view, knowledge, and right to contribute in the decision-making process, there is parity. If one person dominates the conversation because she believes she has more experience, the power structure of the group will be a disproportionate. Most people have been in situations like this and know what happens; the other members of the group will stop contributing and let the dominant person do all the work. For example, a reading consultant is invited to attend a meeting where teachers are charged by the administration with choosing a new textbook. If the consultant is perceived as acting like the expert or dominating the group, the teachers may follow his suggestions without providing input.

Individuals Who Collaborate Share Common Goals

Members of a group do not have to share all goals, but they must share at least one common goal to be effective. It stands to reason that if a group of teachers does not perceive a common reason for their having been called together, the group may fail to achieve anything meaningful. For example, in multidisciplinary team meetings, each person may come with a personal goal—the speech therapist wants to discuss if the student's expressive language is improving, the psychologist wants to discuss the student's growth in self-esteem, and the classroom teacher wants to know if strategies learned in the resource room have positively affected the student's ability to work in groups. They also, however, have a common goal from which to work. Can you identify it?

Opinions will differ, as will philosophical orientation, but regardless of how disparate these may be, successful teams have a shared goal that serves to unite them. It is important to identify the common goals of each team early on to ensure success.

Individuals Who Collaborate Share Responsibility

When individuals agree to work with others to achieve a common goal they are also agreeing to fully participate in the activity they are undertaking and in the decision-making process. For example, suppose a team of teachers is invited to make a presentation on effective instructional strategies at an upcoming state conference. The team agrees on what needs to be done, and the work is divided according to expertise and interest. One person may take on the responsibility of constructing a PowerPoint presentation, another conducts research, and another collects examples of student work. Sometimes when the tasks are divided, each member may not appear to have equal responsibility, but the contribution is nonetheless valuable or important to the successful completion of the task.

Individuals Who Collaborate Share Resources

Sharing resources is often the motivating factor for individuals to collaborate. Teachers find it very rewarding to share expertise, materials, ideas, and even their time with colleagues. For new teachers especially, sharing resources with veteran teachers has a particularly strong appeal. Sharing resources is also helpful, since in most schools resources are scarce. For example, by pooling money the administration has allocated for new materials, a group of grade-level teachers can afford software none could afford independently. It is tremendously satisfying to share for the purpose of realizing common goals. Remember, everyone has something to contribute that will in some way support the group's ability to meet its goal.

Individuals Who Collaborate Share Accountability for Outcomes

When any task is undertaken, whether singularly or in a group, there are no guarantees as to the outcome. Take this example: A grade-level group of the teachers plan and design a new unit of instruction. Each takes responsibility for preparing a different component. One designs an in-class activity for guided practice, another takes on the responsibility of inviting a guest speaker, and someone else develops the assessment. The lesson is running smoothly until the guest speaker fails to arrive at the designated time. Luckily, this is a collaboratively taught lesson where all members of the team share responsibility for the outcome of the lesson. The team acts quickly to remedy the situation. One of the teachers has a video on the topic that will be a perfect substitute for the speaker. Collaboration saved the lesson for these teachers.

In the next section, we will discuss collaborative teaming, elaborating on select methods for facilitating effective collaboration in both general and special education settings.

COLLABORATIVE TEAMS

Collaborative teaming is a popular model for implementing school reform initiatives, professional development, school improvement, and special education programming (Friend & Cook, 2007). Teams may engage in a variety of activities that involve decision making on disparate issues such as budgetary concerns, school scheduling, and personnel. Some problems they consider are relatively insignificant and do not greatly affect the professional lives of teachers or students, such as what to include on the lunch menu, particulars of the school dress code, or selecting a fund-raising project. Other decisions, like selecting related services, hiring a paraprofessional, or referring a student for special education testing, are significantly more important, because while they affect us professionally in the short term, they may affect our students' lives forever.

Governmental guidelines provided in IDEA and NCLB, for example, are intended to increase interaction and communication among teachers, parents, and school administrators, thereby making educational decision making more effective. Those who have attempted collaboration with parents and professionals in compliance with IDEA and NCLB, however, know firsthand that the process is complex. Meaningful collaboration requires both purpose and skill beyond the information typically covered in federal and state directives. In this section, we will discuss collaborative teaming for facilitating the inclusion of students with disabilities and other students who are at risk for academic failure.

Collaborative Teaming Defined

Teacher teaming is a social arrangement defined by shared responsibility and interdependence (Sundstrom, 1999). Although there are numerous definitions of *team* in existence across many disciplines, the consensus is that teaming involves individuals working together to reach a specific goal through shared problem solving (Friend & Cook, 2007). The members of all effective teams share an overarching goal: They each engage in decision making for effecting positive educational outcomes for students. In the next section, we will discuss some of the types of collaborative teams found in educational settings.

Types of Collaborative Teams

The educational literature discusses the following types of teams (Flowers, Mertens, & Mulhall, 2000; Friend & Cook, 2007): multidisciplinary, interdisciplinary, transdisciplinary, and co-teaching. While some of these forms of teaming are new to general education teachers, many are familiar to special educators. Regardless, all teachers will be expected to participate in one or more of these teams during their professional careers. We will begin with what will be a review of teaming for some and an introduction for others.

MULTIDISCIPLINARY TEAMS   These teams are composed of members of different professions representing a number of theoretical and philosophical perspectives. IDEA-04 and its predecessor, Pub. L. 94-142, passed in 1975, specify that decisions regarding assessment, classification, placement, and the development of individualized education plans, to protect the rights of students and parents, require a group consensus. These laws are predicated upon the belief that group decisions provide safeguards against individual errors in judgment and personal or professional bias. Team members develop and implement separate plans for intervention from within their disciplines (Friend & Cook, 2007). Multidisciplinary teams may include specialists in foreign language, adaptive physical education, art therapy, or music therapy, to name a few. Since student's need determines team membership, the composition of these teams is always subject to change.

INTERDISCIPLINARY TEAMS   These teams integrate knowledge and perspectives from multiple disciplines to holistically solve problems. They are distinguished from multidisciplinary teams along three dimensions: numerical, territorial, and epistemological (Pirrie, Hamilton, & Wilson, 1999). Interdisciplinary teams reach across the traditional classroom boundaries to combine the perspectives of two or more disciplines to provide services and instruction to students. For example, teachers who teach math, science, English, and special education may work together to develop a curriculum based on the principles of Universal Design for Learning, thus ensuring that all students have equitable access to their teaching materials.

Their interaction may range from sharing ideas to full integration of theory, terminology, organization, and procedures (Pirrie, Hamilton, & Wilson, 1999). Team members work individually and together by discipline to develop goals. Ideas are shared with teammates, discussed, and synthesized, and a common goal emerges (Friend & Cook, 2007). Team members may share instructional responsibilities, but they are individually accountable for coordinating services, delivering instruction, or providing any work from their disciplinary specialties (Friend & Cook, 2007).

TRANSDISCIPLINARY TEAMS   These teams are particularly useful for planning early intervention programming for infants, toddlers, and young school-aged children with disabilities (Seery & Galentine, 1999). These teams are holistic; those participating work together to avoid fragmentation and duplication of services along disciplinary lines (McWilliam, 2000). Transdisciplinary teams are considered more integrative and collaborative than other teams (Friend & Cook, 2007). They view the child development as a part of an integrated whole, emphasizing the importance of the family as equal contributing members of the team (McWilliam, 2000; Pirrie, Hamilton, & Wilson, 1999). They monitor the developing needs of the child within the context of the family and school rather than in isolation (McWilliam, 2000; Pirrie, Hamilton, & Wilson, 1999). Communication is a key feature, and as such, each team has one designated member who, acting as a liaison for the group, communicates with the family to understand how the home environment and educational decisions affect the student (McWilliam, 2000; Pirrie, Hamilton, & Wilson, 1999).

Members of transdisciplinary teams work interactively to perform their related tasks in a process known as role release (Friend & Cook, 2007). Role release is a method in which members from one discipline train members of another to deliver interventions. This results in the sharing of professional expertise and the blending of roles (Rogers, 2001).

CO-TEACHING TEAMS   These teams originally partnered general educators and special educators to provide direct instruction to students with IEPs in inclusive settings. Today, co-teaching is becoming an increasingly common method for delivering services and differentiating instruction for all students in general education classroom. Co-teaching involves two or more equivalently credentialed educators partnering to deliver substantive instruction to diverse groups of students, including those with disabilities and other factors that place them at risk for academic failure (Friend & Pope, 2005; Pugach & Johnson, 2002). To avoid one teacher being relegated to the role of assistant to the other, establish clear expectations regarding the contribution each will make, and inform students of the equal status of each teacher.

It is important to note that most special education classrooms do have assistants, called paraeducators or volunteers (Jolly & Evans, 2005). These individuals, however, are not licensed teachers and must not be treated as such. Due to licensing and certification restrictions, paraprofessionals may not be utilized as co-teachers. In fact, according to IDEIA-04, paraeducators are expected to supply only the following services under the supervision of a licensed teacher:

- Provide one-on-one tutoring, if such tutoring is scheduled at a time when a student would not otherwise receive instruction from a teacher
- Assist with classroom management, such as organizing instructional materials
- Provide instructional assistance in a computer laboratory
- Conduct parental involvement activities
- Provide support in the library or media center
- Act as translators
- Provide instructional support services under the direct supervision of a teacher.

Remember that paraeducators are not to act as primary service providers (Dover, 2002). The professional educator retains responsibility for the management of the class, instructional design, implementation, selecting accommodations, and evaluation of student progress.

Co-Teaching Models

There are a number of co-teaching options, including one teaches and another drifts, station teaching, parallel teaching, alternative teaching, and team teaching (Friend & Bursuck, 2002).

ONE TEACHES AND ANOTHER OBSERVES OR DRIFTS (SUPPORTING THE CLASS IN A PASSIVE MANNER) This method requires little planning time, but be careful, as this method can result in one teacher becoming an assistant rather than a co-teacher. Use this method to keep students on task, provide instructional support, or check work as it is being completed. Also, it can be used in situations where one teacher does not know the curriculum very well (e.g., high school chemistry).

STATION TEACHING Two teachers divide instructional content into two different parts and takes responsibility for planning and teaching one part of it each. Students move from one station to another. It must be done with content that does not have to be presented in any specific order. A third group can be developed as an independent station, where students work together. Stations can take the entire class period or less.

PARALLEL TEACHING Two teachers jointly plan the instruction and each delivers the same instruction to a heterogeneous group comprising half of the students. This method can take advantage of teacher's different teaching styles to match with students' learning styles. Reduces teacher/student ratio by half. An adaptation can be made to present different perspectives on a topic and then use a problem-solving approach to address differing points of view.

ALTERNATIVE TEACHING   Teachers provide highly intensive instruction within the general education class. Each teacher takes responsibility for a small group. These groups can be used for pre-teaching, makeup, teaching higher-level skills, enrichment, and teaching social skills and are ideally made up of heterogeneous group of students.

TEAM TEACHING   Both teachers are responsible for planning and instruction of all students. They can alternate leading discussion. Content responsibility is divided depending on the teachers' preferences, training, and strengths. Typically, the general education teacher maintains primary responsibility for teaching the subject matter and the special education teacher takes responsibility for students who are having difficulty mastering the material. This does not have to be the case, however; in many instances, teachers who are practiced team teachers will trade roles back and forth during a lesson modeling good communication skills and collaboration for the students. Figure 3.1 depicts each of the co-teaching models.

In schools where co-teaching is practiced, instruction takes place primarily in a shared classroom or other designated spaces. This decreases the negative effects commonly associated with pullout models that move students to separate places to receive instruction (Friend & Bursuck, 2002). It does not, however, preclude students moving to

Co-Teaching Models

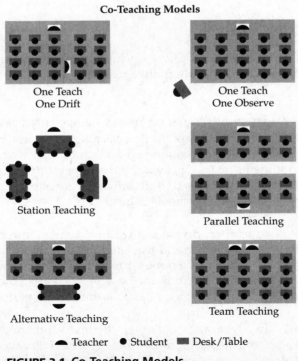

One Teach
One Drift

One Teach
One Observe

Station Teaching

Parallel Teaching

Alternative Teaching

Team Teaching

⏜ Teacher ● Student ◼ Desk/Table

FIGURE 3.1 Co-Teaching Models

other instructional locations such as a computer lab, when appropriate. With careful consideration of goals and objectives, teachers can choose the co-teaching model that best suits their individual styles, utilizes professional expertise, and includes a variety of teaching methods and materials to facilitate student learning.

METHODS FOR EFFECTIVE COLLABORATION AND PROBLEM SOLVING

Regardless of the teaming format, how members of a collaborative group choose to organize the team often dictates success or failure. In addition to professional expertise, productive collaboration requires problem-solving skill and critical thinking ability. As discussed previously, teachers may lack these important metacognitive skills, making it necessary to review the process.

Creating an Outline

Skilled decision making is made more efficient and effective when teams are guided by clearly established procedures (Snell & Janney, 2005; Thousand & Villa, 2000). Effective teams understand collaboration is process oriented. They utilize a planning process to analyze the elements of the task to determine the steps required to achieve their goals (see Figure 3.2). Many people new to teaming do not realize the importance of conducting

---

Task Analysis Worksheet

Directions: Before beginning any project, you must first conduct a task analysis. Break down the task into smaller items or objectives that once completed lead to goal attainment. Take into consideration the strengths or weakness of each person on the team relative to the task objectives. Then, based on this information, assign each team member's responsibilities.

1. Analyze and list steps needed to successfully complete the task before you. List specific steps or objectives below:
   1.
   2.
   3.
2. Note any obstacles to completing the objectives. Consider time, strengths, and weakness of the team members:
   1.
   2.
   3.
3. Brainstorm and come up with possible solutions to overcome the obstacles.
   1.
   2.
   3.
4. Choose the best option to solve the shared problem.
5. Decide who will be responsible for each of the objectives identified in Step 1.
6. Next, use this information to complete the Team Planning Worksheet.

FIGURE 3.2 Task Analysis Worksheet
Source: Spencer & Evers (2004). Unpublished course material. Center for Pedagogy, Winthrop University.

TABLE 3.1 Planning Worksheet			
Directions: Once tasks have been identified, use this planning sheet to organize collaborative projects. It focuses each person on his or her responsibility on a given task. The evaluation component provides teams a way to assesses outcomes and identifies any necessary subsequent action. This information can serve as a guide for the teams meetings.			
	Task 1	**Task 2**	**Task 3**
Identify each task on a separate line and specify exactly what must be done to successfully complete this task.			
Note who is responsible for each task.			
Record methods for accomplishing the assigned task.			
Specify when each task is to be completed.			
Evaluate outcomes and determine subsequent steps required to complete the task.			

Source: Spencer & Evers (2004). Unpublished course material. Center for Pedagogy, Winthrop University.

a task analysis of the project they are undertaking before beginning. Before undertaking any project, you must first clearly understand the requirements of the task. Begin by analyzing the task; break it down into the component parts. These individual objectives or task demands once completed lead to goal attainment. Take into consideration the strengths or weakness of each person on the team relative to the task objectives. Then, based upon this information, assign team members responsibilities.

Collaborative Planning

Teams new to working collaboratively may find that the Team Planning Worksheet (see Table 3.1) facilitates this process. The worksheet supports and extends initial efforts to plan and organize collaborative team meetings begun with the Task Analysis Worksheet (see Figure 3.2). Although teams generally form to solve common problems, they sometimes encounter difficulty implementing the process. As you will read in Chapter 6 on metacognition, problem-solving generally consists of five stages: (1) identification of the problem or goal, (2) consideration of strategies and/or resources that may lead to goal attainment, (3) deciding which options best fit the requirements of the task, and (4) monitoring and (5) modifying choices if necessary. The Team Planning Worksheet is designed to support teachers as they become more familiar with the procedure.

The worksheet focuses each person on the purpose of the meeting and moves the group individually and collectively closer to completing their shared goal. It will ensure that team members know what they are responsible for and how and when the assigned task is to be completed. The evaluation component of the Team Planning Worksheet provides teams a format for guiding and assessing members' efforts and identifies any necessary subsequent action to accomplish a given task.

Collaborative Teaming Agenda

The Team Planning Worksheet can serve as a framework from which to plan and conduct team meetings. It is particularly helpful for constructing meeting agendas, which, although valuable organizational tools, are often overlooked by novice meeting planners because they are unaware of their existence. They need to be taught the value of using an agenda to guide the collaborative process or its utility for assigning leadership roles, keeping within time constraints, note taking, and planning for subsequent meetings (Thousand & Villa, 2000).

REFLECTING ON THE COLLABORATIVE PROCESS

Professional growth and ultimately student achievement depend on a two-part process of collaborative action and reflection. Reflection supports teachers' abilities to make effective instructional decisions regarding how classroom time is spent, which materials to select, and the teaching methods most likely to bring about student achievement. Many times, due to the increasing complexity of the classroom, teachers find it helpful to seek the input of other professionals. As a part of a team, teachers can together reflect upon and analyze classroom situations, determine patterns and trends, and then make instructional outcomes.

Effective collaboration does not occur without effort. It requires communication, reflection, and sharing of both accomplishments and challenges. When evaluating a completed team project, consider how well each individual element of the collaborative process worked. For example, was communication effective? Did the each team member participate equally? If there was conflict, was it resolved to everyone's satisfaction? Decision making is an important part of the collaborative process, as is problem solving. Were these effectively managed? It is important to encourage the members of the team to reflect on these elements, using them to guide both individual and group planning.

COLLABORATION ACROSS EDUCATIONAL CONTEXTS

Each day teachers must plan how to interact effectively with others to solve student-related problems. In general, teachers find themselves involved in one or more of the following four types of collaborative contexts on a day-to-day basis: collaborating with parents, other professionals, school administrators, and university teacher education faculty.

Collaborating with Parents

In this era of increasing concern about the quality of education, legislation stipulates increased collaboration between teachers and parents. A decade of research supports these mandates, indicating that when schools and families work together to support student learning, children tend to do better in school (e.g., Marcon, 1999; Miedel & Reynolds, 1999; Sanders & Herting, 2000). Educational benefits are not limited by cultural background, educational level, or socioeconomic status. All students regardless of status can and do profit from parental involvement (Sanders & Herting, 2000; Shaver & Walls, 1998), but not all types of parental involvement have the same effect.

Family involvement linked to student learning is found to have a greater effect on achievement than are more general forms of involvement (Clark, 2002; Shaver & Walls, 1998). Most teacher-initiated parent involvement in the past has not been of this type (Epstein & Sander, 2000). Teacher-initiated communication with parents tends to be limited to the issuance of report cards and the requisite twice-a-year parent–teacher conference. Parental-initiated involvement also tends to be nonacademic, restricted to PTA meetings and fund raisers. This is often due to a number of factors, as reported by Cotton and Wikelund (2001). Minority, culturally and linguistically diverse, or low-income parents may be underrepresented in parental involvement due to:

- Lack of time or energy attributed to long hours of physical labor or working two jobs
- Concerns about their own level of education or earlier negative experiences with the educational system
- Linguistic barriers, which contribute to a lack of understanding of school materials, structure, and acceptable options for communicating with teachers and other professionals
- Perceived lack of welcome by teachers and administrators
- Assumptions of teachers and administrators that parents are not interested in their children's education

As indicated above, parents sometimes do not involve themselves because they believe they are not welcome or respected by the school staff. The 1997 National Portrait Study on parental involvement supports their beliefs. Of those responding, 38% of parents said the school had never asked how it might help them to become more involved (Datta, 1998). An additional 77% indicated that they felt teachers did not understand them and needed to learn more about encouraging involvement with them (Datta, 1998).

Highly politicized changes in educational assessment and subsequent media coverage (e.g., school report cards) have, however, begun to coalesce parents' attitudes regarding their involvement in the educational process, and their attitudes are shifting. Families of all income and education levels and ethnic and cultural groups are becoming more engaged in their children's education and the decision-making process.

This may be due in part to federal mandates such as NCLB and IDEA that expect schools to cultivate parental participation. Parents today are more aware than ever before of their rights and society's expectations for our nation's schools. Despite the federal laws and intense media scrutiny, many parents still do not exercise their rights to participate in their children's education equally. Parental involvement in the educational process varies according to factors including socioeconomic level, education, race, ethnicity, disability, and grade level of the student. Of these, poverty accounts for most of the variation. Research indicates the parents of low-performing students from high-poverty schools participate less frequently in their children's education than do their higher socioeconomic peers.

Methods for Effectively Collaborating with Parents

While there are a number of barriers to collaboration with parents, research indicates a perceived lack of mutual understanding and ineffective planning are two of the greatest (Cotton & Wikelund, 2001). Parents, it seems, believe teachers often lack an understanding of their students when they are culturally or linguistically different from themselves (Cotton & Wikelund, 2001). Professional preparation to work with culturally and ethnically diverse students usually begins in teacher preparation programs, or, absent that, professional development opportunities are provided. In addition to course content, teachers have the opportunity to teach multiethnic classes and participate in community activities or other learning experiences. Unfortunately, these experiences are often not enough to promote understanding or change teachers' attitudes toward students whose religions, customs, and languages differ from their own.

Promoting effective parent–teacher involvement begins with conversation; in addition to theory and practice, teachers must learn to talk to the families of their students. Many training programs often overlook this important fact. Conversing with parents culturally and ethnically dissimilar from themselves can clear up teachers' misperceptions and help identify values and beliefs underlying the parents' goals for their children. When teachers learn to engage parents in meaningful dialogue, mutual understanding and respect can develop, leading to increased credibility for both parties.

Below are step-by-step guidelines for developing cultural reciprocity (Harry, Rueda, & Kalyanpur, 1999). Following these guidelines—taking time to communicate and learning more about the students, their families, and yourself in the process—will lead to more effective collaborative decision making:

Step 1: Identify cultural values and beliefs behind your decision making. Imagine that you have recently recommended a student for special education services. Can you identify the values underlying your decision? What are your beliefs relative to this decision? Consider the role of nationality, culture, socioeconomic status, and professional education in shaping your beliefs.

Step 2: Share, talk to the family of the student. Find out if they share your values and beliefs. Do the family members consider special education an option, and why? Are there cultural or family reasons for their beliefs? How do their values and beliefs compare to yours?

Step 3: Acknowledge and explain any cultural basis for your decision. Explain to the family how U.S. society views special education. What values and beliefs do educators hold in reference to special education services? Explaining your views from a cultural perspective allows the family to understand the basis for your recommendation.

Step 4: Adapt your professional recommendations to accommodate the values and beliefs of the family. Collaborate with the family and work out a solution that respects their values and provides the child with the necessary support.

In addition to understanding, cultivating parental involvement requires planning. Teachers have to plan for a variety of interactions between parents, teachers, and other professionals. Ensuring that all of these meetings with parents are productive and successful requires thoughtful planning before, during, and after the meeting. Perhaps the most recognizable and common of these meetings is parent–teacher conference. Organizing and conducting these meetings is challenging, even intimidating for new teachers. Having an outline will facilitate planning, improve effectiveness, and alleviate anxiety. Working with parents can be productive and successful with thoughtful planning before, during, and after the meeting. Below are suggestions for conducting a parent conference adapted from the North Carolina Regional Educational Library (2007).

Before the meeting:
- Invite the parents and any others necessary to this discussion, determine possible meeting times and dates.
- Clearly state the purpose of the meeting, identify no more than two or three issues.

- Invite the parents to bring questions or concerns.
- Coordinate the schedules of all those involved.
- Confirm the meeting day, time, and place by phone, letter, or email.
- Collect samples of student work, folders, or other pertinent materials and organize them so that they are easily accessible.
- Review notes on academic progress, behavioral and social issues.
- If necessary, arrange for an interpreter.
- Prepare a comfortable meeting space for the meeting.

During the meeting:
- Begin the meeting on a positive note, greet everyone with a smile and handshake.
- Present specific information and materials that provide examples of the academic or behavioral issue or concern that prompted the meeting.
- Seek input from parents.
- Use active listening techniques when responding to parents.
- Taking notes can inhibit dialogue, so if you must do so keep them brief or appoint a person to take notes for the group.
- After discussing the problem together, determine a shared goal.
- Brainstorm and identify possible solutions.
- Summarize the major points, identify the items requiring action, who is responsible for each item, when the task is to be completed, and if meeting again will be necessary.
- End the meeting on a cordial note, thank everyone for his or her participation, remind him or her when and where the next meeting will be.

After the meeting:
- Take time to reflect on the meeting, read over the minutes, and make notes.
- Make any necessary phone calls or arrangements resulting from the action items noted during the meeting.
- Provide feedback to attendees in a timely fashion to ensure continued support and participation in the educational process.

Taking the time to prepare adequately for these meetings is important, because parent–teacher conferences are an opportunity to correct mistaken assumptions of parents and schools about one another's motives, intentions, and abilities. They also increase parents' abilities to serve as resources for the academic, social, and psychological development of their children. Ideally, these meetings will lead to parents acting as advocates for the school throughout the community or prompt them to further their own education, thereby providing their children with improved role models. Regardless, schools, too, must work to increase parental engagement in the educational process.

According to the National Network of Partnership Schools, parent involvement thrives when it is meaningfully integrated not only into a school's programs but also into the community. To facilitate parental participation, Epstein (2005) recommended that schools do the following:

- Help families with parenting and childrearing skills
- Communicate with families about school programs and student progress and needs

- Work to improve recruitment, training, and schedules to involve families as volunteers in school activities
- Encourage families to be involved in learning activities at home
- Include parents as participants in important school decisions
- Coordinate with businesses and agencies to provide resources and services for families, students, and the community

In addition to working with parents, educators will find it necessary and advantageous to collaborate with school-level administrators.

Collaborating with Teachers and Administrators at the School Level

Schools are composed of many workgroups. Principals routinely ask teachers to serve as members of these groups or teams who work collaboratively to make educational decisions that affect teachers and students. The most frequently cited forms of collaborative practices are faculty meetings, departmental meetings, grade-level or subject area meetings, and special education meetings (Leonard & Leonard, 2003). These meetings can be formal and frequent with prearranged times and places reserved for grade-level teams to work with teaching coaches or other professionals to plan units of instruction. Teams may also meet infrequently based on need, such as collaborating with the curriculum coordinator to select textbooks, or a year-end meeting with the school psychologist to prepare testing materials. Other meetings with school administrators are informal, in that they do not have an agreed-upon time and place, as needed teachers will seek to discuss specific concerns.

It is important to remember that each workgroup is made up of people with different roles, levels of responsibility, academic preparation and philosophies, and expectations. It is necessary that these groups function effectively if schools are to produce well-educated students. To ensure that these workgroups are efficient, they must share some common characteristics (Snell & Janney, 2005):

- Members must have a mutually agreed-upon goal.
- Members agree to share resources and expertise, acknowledging that each person in the team has something to contribute.
- Participants agree to demonstrate parity, acting as teacher and learner.
- Each member must believe that group interaction will generate ideas that may not have been created individually.

The shift to shared decision making, responsibility, and authority creates new opportunities and pressures for many school staff members. Naturally, teachers have concerns about their ability to function successfully in these collaborative endeavors in schools. It is therefore necessary for the workgroup to review their roles and responsibilities with administrators periodically.

In addition to working with teachers and administrators, it has increasingly become an expectation that educators collaborate with university teacher education faculty.

Collaborating with University Teacher Education Faculty

School and university partnerships began in the mid-1990s when the Carnegie Forum suggested their collaboration could improve teaching and learning (Burstein, Gudoski, Kretschmer, & Smith, 1999). Previously, this collaborative context did not exist formally.

Most conventional approaches to teacher education were static, focused on teacher candidates acquiring skills and knowledge from just one or two master teachers. It is increasingly the case where public schools partner with local universities to provide clinical settings much like those experienced by medical students in which pre-service teachers intern. Teacher education programs regularly ask teachers in area schools to serve as a clinical facilitators or mentors for their teacher candidates. These programs are a collegial network of teacher-led facilitators who coach and supervise pre-service university students.

The expectations for mentor teachers are many and varied. Mentor teachers serve as model teachers and as such engage in coursework, conduct research, and participate in professional development activities so that they can supervise effectively. In addition, classroom teachers who become mentor teachers often receive training to perform evaluations and plan staff development activities. They may also be expected to design and conduct workshops for teacher candidates or facilitate meetings to conduct team-building activities.

To summarize, effective mentoring requires teachers to examine their own practice and become reflective practitioners. Together with university faculty, family, school district personnel, and professional associations, mentor teachers scaffold teacher candidates as they learn to apply coursework to the everyday challenges of teaching. Unfortunately, despite participants' efforts, there will be barriers that can hamper collaborative efforts. Understanding potential barriers is the first step in removing them.

BARRIERS TO EFFECTIVE COLLABORATION

Three overarching barriers exist to creating and maintaining a professional community in which collaboration among teachers and other educational stakeholders is successful (Barton, 2005; Ware, 1994). Organizational barriers can serve to impede collaboration between administrators and teachers in several ways (Ware, 1994). The literature identifies four organizational barriers to collaborative efforts: lack of support, rapid turnover, teacher attitudes, and lack of training.

A lack of building-level support for collaboration by the principal can act as an organizational barrier. Administrative support by the principal is unfortunately frequently absent or inconsistent. Research suggests teachers' collaborative efforts most often fail due to a lack of support by the principal when it comes to scheduling common planning times for teaching teams (e.g., Leonard & Leonard, 2003; Ware, 1994). Administrators commonly identify lack of time in the school day and school year for planning and reflection as the major barrier to supporting collaboration (Leonard & Leonard, 2003). A review of the literature on collaboration indicates that support for collaborative practices is an ideal in many schools rather than a reality (e.g., Banks, 2003; Hall & Hord, 2001; Leonard & Leonard, 2003; Speck, 1999). This is despite the universal recognition by education-based associations and governmental agencies that devising new ways for teachers to work together is valuable and the data that indicate collaborative practices lead to increased academic success (Leonard & Leonard, 2003).

Rapid turnover of people in leadership positions (e.g., principals, team leaders, teaching coaches, professional development providers) is another organizational barrier to collaborative practice (Gable & Manning, 1997). Imagine how frustrating it is when teachers who have worked weekends and during school holidays in a teaching team so they will have the time to plan return to school and find they are unable to continue their collaboration due to reassignment, a resignation, or transfer (Christman, Gold, Simon, & Useem, 1997). These changes may be due to human resource policies of the school district or work rules in teachers' union contracts, which play major roles in determining the availability of time for meetings, shaping transfer, and hiring policies. Regardless of the reason, staffing turnover and team integrity can have a negative effect on teachers' attitudes toward collaboration.

Teachers' attitudes toward collaborative practices act as a third barrier to collaborative practice (e.g., Monahan, Marino, & Miller, 1996; Pugach & Johnson, 2002; Welch, 1998). As previously discussed, collaboration is considered important by many, including administrators and policy makers, who by virtue of the fact that they think it is important assume teachers will collaborate with parents and other professionals when asked. Although most teachers will embrace collaboration, research suggests they feel they are not adequately prepared to implement collaborative practices (Pugach & Johnson, 2002; Thousand & Villa, 1990; Welch, 1998). Many teachers do not believe, justifiably, that they will receive the support they need from the school, citing lack of time, materials, and technical support (Friend & Cook, 2007). Collaboration also requires that teachers accept a redefinition of their roles and responsibilities to emphasize teamwork and partnerships, moving away from the previously autonomous settings to which they were accustomed (Gable & Manning, 1997). For general education teachers, collaboration means working with specialists and special educators to learn how to manage classroom behavior, teach reading, adapt curriculum, and apply learning strategies. For special educators, collaboration means working with general education teachers and specialists to consult, diagnose, recommend, and model instructional strategies in general education classrooms.

Changes in professional expectations can conflict with teachers' attitudes, values, training, and beliefs, resulting in ambiguity, overload, and resistance to collaborative practices (Pugach & Johnson, 2002; Welch, 1998). To illustrate this point, consider research by Ryan (1999, as cited in Brownell, Adams, Sindelar, Waldron, & Vanhover, 2006); teachers across three schools were studied to determine if school restructuring designed to promote collaborative practice had an effect. Findings indicate that despite adequate supports for collaboration provided by the schools, teachers were reluctant to change practices. The researchers found that when teachers' beliefs differed from those with whom they were to collaborate, they had difficulty working together and learning from each other. When teachers view collaboration negatively, it is often because they view teaming arrangements as threats to their professional autonomy (Johnson, 2003).

Last, the lack of adequate training hampers collaboration. The misperceptions and unsubstantiated beliefs of school administrators and about teacher education programs can present a fourth barrier to collaboration. Many in charge of educational programming believe collaboration is simply the ability to get along with your peers or parents or give advice (Welch, 1998). Collaboration is frequently viewed as a matter of common sense rather than a skill to be developed requiring proficiency in problem solving, interpersonal communication, and reflective practice. Therefore, few schools or teacher education programs offer adequate coursework to teach in-service or pre-service educators these collaborative practices (Welch, 1998). When educational opportunities are presented, they are frequently integrated thematically or theoretically into other professional development coursework; few do more than address it conceptually (Cook, Smagorinsky, Fry, Konopak, & Moore, 2002).

Summary

Governmental guidelines provided in IDEIA and NCLB have served to increase interaction and communication among teachers, parents, and school administrators, thereby making educational decision making more effective. Effective training and support, along with a good attitude, make working with parents and professionals a very rewarding endeavor for all involved.

References

Banks, J. A. (2003). Multicultural education: Characteristics and goals. In J. A. Banks (Ed.), *Multicultural education: Issues and perspectives* (4th ed., pp. 3–30). New York: John Wiley and Sons.

Barton, R. (2005). Collaborating to reach NCLB goals. *Northwest Education Research Brief, 11*(1), 33–34. Retrieved June 18, 2007, from http://www.nwrel.org/nwedu/11-01/brief/

Billingsley, B. S. (2004). Special education teacher retention and attrition: A critical analysis of the research literature. *Journal of Special Education, 38*, 39–55.

Brownell, M. T., Adams, A., Sindelar, P., Waldron, N., & Vanhover, S. (2006). Learning from collaboration: The role of teacher qualities. *Exceptional Children, 72*(2), 169–175. Retrieved June 22, 2007, from www.questia.com/PM.qst?a=o&d=5013537568

Burstein, N., Gudoski, P., Kretschmer, D., & Smith, C. (1999). Redesigning teacher education as a shared responsibility of schools and universities. *Journal of Teacher Education, 50*, 106–109. Retrieved July 7, 2007, from www.questia.com/PM.qst?a=o&d=5013537568

Christman, J. B., Gold, E., Simon, E., & Useem, E. L. (1997). Reforming alone: Barriers to organizational learning in urban school change initiatives. *Journal of Students Placed at Risk, 2*, 58–82.

Clark, R. (2002). Ten hypothesis about what predicts student achievement for African American students and all other students: What the research shows. In W. R. Allen, M. B. Spencer, & S. O'Conner (Eds.), *African American education: Race, community, inequality, and achievement: A tribute to Edgar G. Epps.* Oxford, UK: Elsevier

Science. Retrieved June 27, from www.questia.com/PM.qst?a=o&d=5013537568

Cook, L., Smagorinsky, P., Fry, P., Konopak, B., & Moore, C. (2002). Problems in developing a constructivist approach to teaching: One teacher's transition from teacher preparation to teaching. *Elementary School Journal, 102*(5), 389–414.

Cotton, K., & Wikelund, K. R. (2001). Parent involvement in education. *Northwest Regional Education Laboratory School Improvement Research Series.* Retrieved June 27, 2007, from http://www.nwrel.org/scpd/sirs/3/cu6.html

Datta, A. (1998). *Family involvement in education: A national portrait.* Washington, DC: U.S. Department of Education. Retrieved June 25, 2007, from http://www.ed.gov/index.jhtml

Dover, W. F. (2002). Paraeducators: Coming to a class near you. *Creative Classroom, 17*, 60–63.

Epstein, J. L. (2005). *Developing and sustaining research-based programs of school, family, and community partnerships: Summary of five years of NNPS research.* Retrieved June 27, 2007, from http://www.csos.jhu.edu/P2000/pdf/Research%20Summary.pdf

Epstein, J. L., & Sanders, M. G. (2000). Connecting home, school and community: New directions for social research. In M. T. Hallinan (Ed.), *Handbook of the sociology of education* (pp. 285–306), New York: Kluwer Academic.

Flowers, N., Mertens, S. B., & Mulhall, P. F. (2000). How teaming influences classroom practices. *Middle School Journal, 32*, 52–59.

Friend, M., & Bursuck, W. (2002). *Including students with special needs: A practical guide for classroom teachers.* Boston: Allyn & Bacon.

Friend, M., & Cook L. (1992). *Interactions: Collaboration skills for school professionals* (pp. 6–9). New York: Longman.

Friend, M., & Cook, L. (2007). *Interactions: Collaborative skills for school professionals* (5th ed.). Boston, MA: Allyn & Bacon.

Friend, M., & Pope, K. L. (2005). Creating schools in which all students can succeed. *Kappa Delta Pi Record, 41,* 56–61.

Gable, R. A., & Manning, M. L. (1997). The role of teacher collaboration in school reform. *Childhood Education, 73,* 219–223. Retrieved June 21, 2007, from http://www.questia.com/PM.qst?a=o&d=5002237181

Hall, G., & Hord. S. (2001). *Implementing change: Patterns, principles, and potholes.* Boston: Allen & Bacon.

Harry, B., Rueda, R., & Kalyanpur, M.(1999). Cultural reciprocity in sociocultural perspective: Adapting the normalization principle for family collaboration. *Exceptional Children, 66*(1), 123–136.

Johnson, B. (2003). Teacher collaboration: Good for some, not so good for others. *Educational Studies, 29,* 337–350.

Jolly, A., & Evans, S. (2005). Teacher assistants move to the front of the class: Job embedded learning pays off in student achievement. *Journal of Staff Development, 26,* 8–13.

Leonard, L., & Leonard, P. (2003). The continuing trouble with collaboration: Teachers talk. *Current Issues in Education, 6*(15). Retrieved June 18, 2007, from http://cie.ed.asu.edu/volume 6/number15/

Marcon, R. A. (1999). Positive relationships between parent involvement and public school inner-city preschoolers' development and academic performance. *School Psychology Review, 28,* 395–412.

McWilliam, R. A. (2000). Recommended practices in interdisciplinary models. In S. Sandall, M. McLean, & B. Smith (Eds.), *DEC recommended practices for early intervention/early childhood special education* (pp. 47–54). Longmont, CO: Sopris West. Retrieved June 21, 2007, from http://www.questia.com/PM.qst?a=o&d=5001642893

Miedel, W. T., & Reynolds A. J. (1999). Parent involvement in early intervention for disadvantaged children: Does it matter? *Journal of School Psychology, 37,* 379–402.

Monahan, R. G., Marino, S. B., & Miller, R. (1996). Teacher attitudes toward inclusion: Implications for teacher education in schools. *Education, 117,* 316–320. Retrieved June 21, 2007, from http://www.questia.com/PM.qst?a=o&d=5001642893

No Child Left Behind Act. (2001). Retrieved June 3, 2007 from http://www.nochildleftbehind.gov/

North Carolina Regional Educational Library. (2007). *Tips for parent conferences.* Retrieved June 13, 2009, from http://www.learnnc.org/lp/pages/740

Pirrie, A. Hamilton, S., & Wilson, V. (1999). Multidisciplinary education: Some issues and concerns. *Educational Research, 41,* 310–314.

Pugach, M. C., & Johnson, L. J. (2002). *Collaborative practitioners, collaborative schools* (2nd ed.). Denver, CO: Love Publishing.

Rogers, S. J. (2001). Diagnosis of autism before the age of 3. In L. M. Glidden (Ed.), *International review of research in mental retardation* (vol. 23, pp. 1–31). San Diego: Academic Press. Retrieved July 1, 2007, from http://www.questia.com/PM.qst?a=o&d=5001642893

Sanders, M. G., & Herting, J. R. (2000). Gender and the effects of school, family and church support on the academic achievement of African American urban adolescents. In M. G. Sanders (Ed.), *Schooling students placed at risk: Research, policy, and practice in the education of poor and minority adolescents* (pp. 141–161). Mahwah, NJ: Lawrence Erlbaum Associates.

Seery, M. E., & Galentine, J. K. (1999). Achieving role expansion and release: Conversation strategies used by one transdisciplinary team. *Infant–Toddler Intervention: The Transdisciplinary Journal, 9,* 17–38.

Shaver, A. V., & Walls, R. T. (1998). Effect of Title I parent involvement on student reading and mathematics achievement. *Journal of Research and Development in Education, 31,* 90–97.

Snell, M. E., & Janney, R. (2005). *Collaborative teaming.* Baltimore: Paul H. Brookes

Speck, M. (1999). *The principalship: Building a learning community.* Upper Saddle River, NJ: Prentice Hall.

Sundstrom, E. (1999). *Supporting work team effectiveness: Best management practices for fostering high performance.* San Francisco: Jossey-Bass.

Thousand, J. S., & Villa, R. A. (1990). Strategies for educating learners with severe disabilities within their local home schools and communities. *Focus on Exceptional Children, 23,* 1–24.

Thousand, J. S., & Villa, R. A. (2000). *Collaborative teams: A powerful tool in school restructuring.* Baltimore: Paul H. Brookes.

Ware, L. P. (1994). Contextual barriers to collaboration. *Journal of Educational and Psychological Consultation, 5,* 340–359. Retrieved June 17, 2007, from http://ww.questia.com/PM.qst?a=o&d=77019233

Welch, M. (1998). Collaboration: Staying on the bandwagon. *Journal of Teacher Education, 49,* 26–29.

Retrieved June 21, 2007, from http://www.questia.com/PM.qst?a=o&d=5001319446

Welch, M., & Sheridan, S. M. (1995). *Educational partnerships: Serving students at risk.* Ft. Worth, TX: Harcourt Brace.

West, J. F. (1990). Educational collaboration in the restructuring of schools. *Journal of Educational and Psychological Consultation, 1,* 23–40.

Chapter 4

Using Assessment Data to Plan and Teach

After reading this chapter, you will be able to:

1. Define the purpose of assessment
2. Correlate the types of assessments with the purposes of assessment
3. Use the principles of Universal Design for Learning (UDL) to remove barriers that affect assessment
4. Select appropriate accommodations for assessment situations
5. Select appropriate learning strategies to support students during assessments
6. Select appropriate test-taking skills to support students during assessments

Prior to the 1990s, the primary purposes of assessment were to assign grades to individual students for administrative purposes, such as grade promotion, or to predict a person's ability to compete in college classes, as the SAT or ACT exams did, but in the 1990s, Goals 2000 introduced a new dimension to assessment: accountability. A decade later, the passage of No Child Left Behind (NCLB) added state accountability for student achievement to ensure that all students were participating and achieving—but most important, that students were making progress toward higher achievement rates. Under the mandates of NCLB, schools are held accountable for the educational success of every child, including those with exceptional learning needs. During the 2003–2004 school year, over 95% of students with disabilities in 41 states participated in statewide reading assessment (U.S. Government Accountability Office [USGAO], 2005). As there are over 6 million students with disabilities (13% of all students) enrolled in our public schools (USGAO, 2005), teachers should expect to have students with disabilities in their classes and to be held accountable for the educational progress of all students within their classrooms. To provide effective instruction to meet the learning needs of all students, including those with exceptional learning needs, teachers must engage in a continual cycle of assessment, planning, and instruction. This chapter will discuss the purposes and types of assessments, how to use the principles of Universal Design for Learning when constructing classroom assessments, selection of appropriate accommodations for both teacher-made and mandated state assessments, and preparing students for assessments by incorporating test-taking skills into instruction.

PURPOSES OF ASSESSMENT

We are all familiar with testing and assessment. Every reader of this text has been through years of education that included hundreds of tests and other types of assessment, but I have never met a student who honestly liked to take tests. In fact, every time I have elected to cancel a test in one of my college courses, the class has risen in a deafening cheer. This dislike of tests on the part of students who become teachers can lead to teachers who do not like to give tests. Teachers like to teach, teachers want to teach, and many of us cannot think of any other occupation that would suit us, but most of us do not like to test. Yet, as Popham (2005) reminded us, we must assess if we want to be better teachers. This is the primary reason to assess: to know what students learned and, just as important, what they did not learn; to know if the methods and materials we used or provided were helpful; and finally, to know what to do next. Assessments give us the data we need to be reflective about our teaching and the learning experiences of our students.

Certainly, that is the most important reason to assess students, but over the years organizations and agencies outside the field of education have become interested in what is happening in schools. They are particularly interested in the progress of students who are achieving at substantially lower levels, such as groups of students who are minorities, disadvantaged, or disabled (Hogan, 2007). This rise in interest for minority groups began during the civil rights movement of the 1960s and has had an impact on education. The major impact can be seen in the passage of laws that have implications for assessment of students in these minority groups. The following section is a brief overview of the laws as they relate specifically to the rise of accountability for the learning of all students. Other purposes of these laws were discussed in Chapter 1.

Laws That Related to Assessment

Each of the laws described here have increased the accountability of schools for the education of all children, including students with exceptional learning needs (ELN) (see Chapter 1 for details). The first of these laws was the Elementary and Secondary Education Act (ESEA) of 1965. Hogan (2007) noted that provisions of this act led to development of educational programs to specifically address the disparity in the education of students in minority groups. This resulted in the need to evaluate new programs to demonstrate that the needs of minority students were being met. Hogan further stated that this led to the emerging accountability movement. Other laws enacted as a result of the civil rights movement, such as the Rehabilitation Act of 1973 and the Americans with Disabilities Act of 1990, further delineated the responsibilities of the educational institutions toward minority groups and specifically those with disabilities. The No Child Left Behind Act of 2001 (NCLB) requires that all students, including those with disabilities, are assessed for their ability to meet state educational standards. In 1972, Congress passed the Education of All Handicapped Children Act (EAHC), the first legislation that specifically addressed the rights of students with disability to a free and appropriate education in public schools. The latest reauthorization of this legislation is the Individuals with Disabilities Educational Improvement Act of 2004 (IDEIA-04), which contains regulations to ensure that students with disabilities are assessed without bias in a nondiscriminatory manner. Further, within the reauthorized IDEIA-04, Section 614 (b)(6)(B) states, "In determining whether a child has a specific learning disability, a local educational agency may use a process that determines if the child responds to scientific, research-based intervention as a part of the evaluation procedures." From this statute has come a new term and concept (Kame'enui, 2007) known as Response to Intervention (RTI; defined below). Another statute of IDEIA-04 notes that if using RTI to evaluate students for learning disabilities, local educational agencies are not required to find a severe discrepancy between achievement and intellectual ability to determine the existence of a learning disability and eligibility for special education services. Since its inception, RTI has been "conspicuously and actively invoked in the current discourse of the special education and, possibly, general education communities" (Kame'enui, 2007, p. 7). In the next section, we will explain the major components of RTI and its implementation in classrooms.

RTI is designed as a multitiered process to identify and support students with learning and behavior problems (National Center for Learning Disabilities, n.d.-b). The process begins with research-based, high-quality instruction and universal screening of all students in general education classrooms. Students who struggle with any aspect of instruction are then provided with interventions at increasing levels of intensity. Progress is monitored to note student learning rates and levels of performance. Throughout this process decisions are made based on individual student responses to instructional interventions. The National Center on Learning Disabilities (n.d.-b) notes the essential components for effective implementation of RTI are (a) high-quality, scientifically based classroom instruction, (b) ongoing student assessment, (c) tiered instruction, and (d) parent involvement. Figure 4.1 provides details that illustrate how these components are infused into the RTI multitiered process.

In addition to providing a process that focuses on high-quality instruction and differentiated instruction with frequent monitoring of progress, RTI offers an opportunity

Tier 1: Primary prevention with universal interventions	• Targets all students • Is preventive and proactive • Is expected to be effective for 80% to 90% of students	• Completed in the general education classroom • Includes the universal core instructional program • Provides curriculum-based screening of all students • Includes short-term progress monitoring of "at-risk" students
Tier 2: Secondary prevention with targeted group interventions	• Targets the 5% to 10% of students who are "at-risk" • Provides a rapid response to learning needs	• Uses small-group tutoring in reading and math • Duration from 8 to 20 weeks • Provides for dual discrepancy evaluation to determine responsiveness
Tier 3: Tertiary prevention with intensive individual interventions	• Targets the 1% to 5% of students who have not responded to Tier 2 interventions • Is assessment-based • Provides high-intensity interventions	• Individualized programming and progress monitoring • Provides for a multidisciplinary evaluation • Identifies specific disability • Determines placement

FIGURE 4.1 The Three Tiers of the Response to Intervention Process

Sources: Information from Fuchs & Fuchs (2007); National Center on Learning Disabilities (n.d.-b); Sugai (n.d.).

Note: At any time during this process, a parent or guardian may request a formal evaluation. The RTI process does not negate the parental right to a timely formal evaluation.

for educators to address the disproportionate representation in special education programs of students with cultural and linguistic differences. According to Hosp and Reschly (2003) (n.d.), RTI may be able to address this disproportionality in the following ways. First, since the goal of RTI is to improve learning outcomes of all students and seeks to meet the individual learning needs of all students, the expected outcome should be met by all students, including those who are culturally or linguistically different. Second, with a focus on individual student needs, the tiered delivery will allow for more efficient delivery of instruction to like students. For example, students who are "at risk" may not arrive at the schoolhouse door with the vocabulary needed to be successful readers. Their lack of vocabulary is similar to the vocabulary needs of students who are learning English as a second language. Thus, both groups of students' learning may be addressed with similar instruction and interventions. Third, the use of reliable measures for universal screening can be used to make decisions, thus both identifying the need and bypassing any teacher bias that may exist.

In addition to the legal requirements for inclusive assessment practices, Airasian (2005) noted that there are ethical and moral issues of fairness during assessments for teachers to consider. Foremost of these is collecting and interpreting valid and reliable data for decision making. Beyond that, teachers should be careful to inform students of their expectations, teach the content to be assessed, avoid making quick judgments about student ability or stereotyping them with labels, refrain from using language that might be offensive or harmful to students from diverse backgrounds, and remove bias toward persons who are English language learners (ELL) or are culturally different. While all of these might seem like obvious civilities, if we are not aware and vigilant, classroom assessments can be skewed and will not reflect students' actual knowledge or skill levels. Furthermore, in the course of working with students, particularly students with exceptional needs, teachers have access to assessment data as well as personal data collected during assessment activities. Another of our ethical duties is to safeguard the privacy of that information and never use it to harm or bully a student. And just as important, we should recognize the limitations of the data when making critical decisions. Any assessment data are snapshots of student knowledge and skills on a given day in a given place.

ADDITIONAL PURPOSES OF ASSESSMENT   Accountability has become a major influence on how teachers view assessment and the primary purpose of assessment, but it is important that teachers understand that there are other purposes for assessment that can be useful on a daily basis and lead to increased rates of success on state accountability assessments. In the section below, we will discuss six purposes for assessing students in classrooms (Airasian, 2005; Hogan, 2007; Popham, 2005). As this list of purposes for assessment clearly demonstrates, assessment is "not just a closing activity" (Gagnon & Collay, 2001, p. 113), for a lesson or unit of instruction but is ongoing activity that should happen continuously before, during, and after instruction.

ESTABLISHING CLASSROOM EQUILIBRIUM (AIRASIAN, 2005)   Teachers make many decisions on a daily basis that are assessments used to keep order and civility in their classrooms. These decisions may include selecting rules, routines, and classroom procedures; seating students to ensure quiet work settings; sending a student who needs a break on an errand; and dealing with students who are disruptive. These decisions help to ensure that classrooms run smoothly for effective teaching and learning.

PLANNING AND CONDUCTING INSTRUCTION AND DETERMINING INSTRUCTIONAL EFFECTIVENESS (AIRASIAN, 2005; POPHAM, 2005)   As noted at the beginning of the chapter, this is one primary reason for assessment. Teachers make decisions about what content to teach and how to teach that content based not only on state standards but also on personal observations of students as they work and answer questions during class and how well students complete quizzes, in-class and homework assignments, and classroom tests. All of this information helps the teacher determine what needs to be retaught as well as what should be taught next. In addition, teachers use this information to determine the most effective teaching methods and strategies to support student learning.

DIAGNOSING STUDENT'S STRENGTHS AND WEAKNESSES AND PLACING PUPILS (AIRASIAN, 2005; POPHAM, 2005)   By diagnosing students' strengths and weaknesses, teachers can plan for placing students in appropriate reading or math groups, selecting peer partners, and assigning students for project-based learning groups. Further, after diagnosing weakness, teachers can plan for remediation in areas where students need to learn knowledge or skills for moving forward in the content and avoiding future failures. The diagnosis of student strengths will identify students who have prior knowledge and skills and allow teachers to plan enrichment activities to challenge and keep these learners engaged. Teachers often use preassessment quizzes or assignments to gather information about the entire class, but checklists and observation are also methods used for diagnosing.

PROVIDING FEEDBACK AND MOTIVATIONAL INCENTIVES (AIRASIAN, 2005; HOGAN, 2007)   Formative assessment allows teachers to check student progress during the teaching and learning process rather than waiting until the end of a lesson or unit of lessons to determine student's achievement. It can be asked during a lecture to check student's understanding at that moment, a teacher–student conference, or a homework assignment that checks students' abilities to use and apply new knowledge. Providing students with positive formative feedback can be an incentive for them to keep working on a difficult skill or long-term project. Offering opportunities for receiving formative feedback also helps students feel safe to take risks as they learn rather than feeling that all work must be done perfectly the first time. Providing formative assessment feedback to parents and guardians provides valuable information they can use to help students with homework and studying for tests and helps to avoid unpleasant surprises when grades are given.

DIAGNOSING PUPIL PROBLEMS AND DISABILITIES (AIRASIAN, 2005; HOGAN, 2007)   When teachers diagnosis student strengths and weakness, they may recognize that individual students need more remediation or enrichment than can be provided in the general education classroom. At this point, a teacher may refer the student for additional diagnosis or for placement in special education, gifted/talented, or English as Second Language (ESL) programs. Smith, Dowdy, Polloway, and Blalock (1997) noted there are five purposes for assessing students with disabilities: (1) conducting initial identification and screening, (2) determining and evaluating teaching programs and strategies, (3) determining current performance level and educational needs, (4) deciding about classification and program placement, and (5) developing the individual education program (IEP). Purposes 1–4 are also useful for determining eligibility for gifted and talented or ESL programs.

JUDGING AND GRADING ACADEMIC LEARNING AND PROGRESS (AIRASIAN, 2005; HOGAN, 2007; POPHAM, 2005)   Judging and grading student work is the most common use of classroom assignments and tests and is the primary purpose of state and district standardized assessments. When teachers assess at the end of unit or semester, they are using *summative* assessment, which provides a summation of knowledge and skills students have learned during instruction. Summative assessments can include tests, project and research reports, and portfolios of work that require students to demonstrate that they have met learning objectives and/or state standards. Typically teachers will use a combination of formative and summative assessment data to judge student achievement and assign a grade.

Regardless of their precise reasons for assessing at any given moment, teachers must continue to make judgments about student learning in a variety of ways. Meanwhile, under NCLB, teachers will be asked to prepare students for high-stakes assessments that will determine student movement to the next grade or graduation, if individual schools make the "grade," and, in some cases, if teachers and principals will keep their jobs. Both NCLB and IDEIA-04 regulations require that students with disabilities must be included in these high-stakes assessments, but can students with disabilities succeed on these tests?

Across the country, educators, administrators, and caregivers are working to help students with disabilities succeed in this new task. In the next section we will discuss some of the problem areas in assessment, explore how using UDL when constructing the initial assessment can diminish or exclude the overall effect of barriers, and describe how to construct an accessible assessment. As we have noted elsewhere in this text, even with UDL-designed teaching materials and assessment, some students remain who need additional accommodations, therefore we will explore the accommodations that are being used to support assessment experiences. On an additional note, it is not our intent in this chapter to teach you how to construct assessments that are reliable and valid or that assess higher-order thinking and learning or how to write specific test items, as those topics are far too complex for one chapter; we leave that to other texts that are devoted solely to assessment. Our intent is to provide you with information to supplement and extend what you already know or will learn, so that you can plan and design assessments that eliminate barriers for the most participants possible.

IMPEDIMENTS TO STUDENT SUCCESS ON HIGH-STAKES AND CLASSROOM ASSESSMENTS

Recently the term *high-stakes assessments* has come into use in the educational literature and around the teacher's lounge. High-stakes occur with tests that have exceptionally important consequences for individuals (Hogan, 2007). With the implementation of NCLB, tests given at the end of courses or to measure yearly progress have been termed high-stakes. This is because the results of the tests can have far-reaching implications for states, school districts, schools, teachers, and even individual students. Generally these tests fall into one of two categories, individual and large-scale tests.

- Individual high-stakes tests include exit exams that determine graduation status. Twenty-five states expected to have such requirements in place by 2009 (Cortiella, 2004). Also, at least 17 states have tests that determine eligibility for promotion to the next grade or movement to the next level of a content area (e.g., Algebra II or French III). Both of these assessments hold individual students accountable rather than the school, district, or state. Critics of exit exams cite evidence that failure may lead to dropping out of school.
- Large-scale tests include the NCLB-mandated examinations of student progress toward meeting state standards, where students are expected to show annual yearly progress (AYP). Consequences for students with ELN who fail or score poorly on AYP tests include increased likelihood that they (a) are likely to be held back in a class, (b) will drop out of school before graduation, (c) will be tracked into low-level courses that do not lead to a standard high school diploma, and (d) will not earn a high school diploma (Cortiella, 2004).

According to Cortiella (2004), five barriers generally impede success of students with disabilities on high-stakes assessments: These are encountering inadequate opportunities to learn, being placed in more restrictive settings, failing to provide reasonable accommodations, not offering remediation or offering in an ineffective manner, and relying too heavily on data from one test score (see Figure 4.2 for additional information).

In addition to the external barriers described by Cortiella (2004), students may experience barriers caused by their disability or exceptional need. These barriers inhibit the student's ability to participate successfully in the assessment. Most often these barriers limit the student's ability to demonstrate accurately his or her level of achievement in content knowledge and skills, and occasionally the barriers inhibit participation

Barrier	Reasons
1. There is an inadequate opportunity to learn because students are not exposed to subject matter included on tests.	• Few states require that IEPs address state standards. • No systematic assurance exists that IEPs align curriculum standards with instruction in special education classes. • Special educators are not familiar with their state standards.
2. More restrictive placements are used by states with high school graduation exit exams.	• States with exit exams tend to place students with exceptional learning needs (ELN) in more restrictive environments • In more restrictive settings, students have less exposure to standards-based curriculum.
3. Lack of reasonable accommodations exists, in part, because there is considerable disagreement about what accommodations are and whether their use changes the validity of the text given.	• State may limit the number and types of accommodations to a predetermined list. • Increased number of states are restricting calculator use and oral administration of tests.
4. Inadequate access to remediation may be due to high costs of providing such resources.	• Few states offer or mandate remediation for students who are ELN and fail exit or promotion exams.
5. Over-reliance on a single test score can mean that students with disabilities are negatively affected.	• States frequently make decisions based on a single assessment event, such as the exit exam.

FIGURE 4.2 External Barriers That Impede Success on High-Stakes Assessments
Source: Information from Cortiella (2004).

altogether. If teachers and other school personnel are aware of these barriers, however, assessments and assessment settings can be designed to allow all students equal opportunity to demonstrate their learning. In Figure 4.3, those barriers are linked to characteristics of specific disabilities and exceptionalities.

USING UNIVERSAL DESIGN TO CONSTRUCT ASSESSABLE ASSESSMENT FOR ALL STUDENTS

In Chapter 7 you will learn about using Universal Design for Learning to design lesson plans and classroom activities with your specific students in mind can eliminate barriers to learning. The principles of UDL can be used to design and implement effective assessment in your classroom. Further states and districts are beginning to develop large-scale assessments using the principles of UDL. In this section we will illustrate how states and districts are using ULD and how teachers can follow their leads when designing assessments for their classroom students.

Johnstone, Altman, and Thurlow (2006) stated that "the goal of universally designed assessments is to provide the most valid assessment possible for the greatest number of students, including students with disabilities" (p. 2). To create accessible

Characteristic	Disability or Exceptionality	Barriers
Physical limitations	Students with sensory disabilities, traumatic brain injury, cerebral palsy, spinal cord injury, and other similar disabilities Students with other health impairments	1. Students may not be able to hold a writing instrument, see the test, hear directions or questions presented orally, or have either the physical or mental stamina required during long testing sessions.
Poor comprehension	Perception and processing difficulties (such as found in students with learning disabilities or sensory disabilities) Underdeveloped language skills (students who are deaf, English language learners, or who are at risk due to limited exposure to language)	2. Student may not clearly understand directions or questions that are presented orally and therefore may not follow directions correctly or adequately interpret questions. 3. Written directions and questions may be too lengthy or complicated and contain unfamiliar words and phrases. 4. Reading level may be above student's ability level. 5. Questions requiring inferences, evaluation, or deductive reasoning may not be understood.
Auditory perceptual	Students with LD involving auditory perception Students with ADHD: distractible type	1. Teachers may speak too quickly and may not clearly enunciate words and syllables. 2. Students must process the spoken words and translate to written answers, a task that can be impossible for some to accomplish. 3. Even reasonable background noise, both in and outside the classroom, can be a major hurdle for these students. 4. Some students may be unable to discriminate which sounds are from the teacher and which are irrelevant to the assessment task.
Visual perception	Students with LD involving visual perception	1. If assessment information is presented on chalkboards, smart boards, or overhead transparencies to be copied, some students may not be able to accurately copy. They may transpose numbers, letters, and even words and lose their place when moving from board to paper. 2. Noting answers on a separate answer sheet can be difficult and result in correct answers being placed in the wrong answer slot.

FIGURE 4.3 Barriers Related to Specific Characteristics of a Disability or Exceptionality That Students May Encounter During Assessments

Characteristic	Disability or Exceptionality	Barriers
		3. Visual distractions on the board or near the screen may clutter their field of vision and cause confusion.
		4. Illegible or unclear copies of test materials present a deciphering difficulty to these students.
		5. Formatting that is not consistent across all multiple choice questions or presents long lists of matching items may confuse and cause students to spend too much time trying to figure out the question rather than answering it.
		6. Lengthy tests of 2–3 pages can discourage students who read slowly or need time to process questions.
		7. Some students may experience difficulty interpreting symbols and abbreviations, such as found in advanced mathematics.
		8. Visual distractions, both in and outside the classroom, can interrupt the student's concentration, such as teacher movement around the room, a classmate going to the pencil sharpener, or movement in the hallway.
Time constraints	Any or all of the disabilities and exceptionalities noted above	These students will have difficulty completing assessment at the same rate as their general education peers.
Anxiety	Any or all of the disabilities and exceptionalities noted above	Based on their previous school experiences, these students may associate test taking with failure. As a result, they may be unable to function in a traditional test setting.

FIGURE 4.3 *(Continued)*

Source: Information from Rose & Dolan (2006); Salend (2001); Wood (2006).

assessments, all students must be taken into account at the beginning stages of construction. This is the same procedure used when designing universal lesson plans, bearing in mind the full range of student abilities, interests, and cultural differences from the beginning. The overall design principles suggested by the National Center on Educational Outcomes (NCEO) researchers (Johnstone, Altman, Thurlow, & Moore, 2006) are that universally designed assessments (UDA):

1. Do not change the standard of performance. They do not change the constructs of the assessment, water down the tasks, or make them easier for some students or groups of students.

2. **Are not meant to replace accommodations.** Users of UDA should assume that common accommodations will be needed by some students with disabilities, such as extended time, changes in formats that provide large print or Braille, scheduling differences that provide for breaks during testing, or alterative responses that allow the use of scribes or word processors. The general education test should be designed to allow for these common accommodations to fit into the plan (Johnstone, Altman, & Thurlow, 2006).

3. **May benefit all students, including English language learners.** This is especially important as teachers find themselves facing classrooms with increasing numbers of students who are second language learners. Salend (2001) noted that simply translating assessments into the student's native language does not remove the cultural bias that may exist and ultimately may create new problems associated with differences in language syntax and word meanings.

Additional research conducted at NCEO by Thompson and Thurlow (2002) revealed seven elements of universally designed assessments that should be present when assessments are initially constructed. In the section below, we will discuss how the elements can be used by teachers to construct universally designed classroom assessments and tests. As you read this section, consider how these elements meet the overall design principles mentioned above.

The Seven Elements

Thompson and Thurlow (2002) asserted that very few students need alternatives to standardized state and district assessments, but they believe there is "a much larger group of students who do need changes in the regular assessment" (p. 1). Thompson and Thurlow also assert that the need for accommodations can be reduced by using UDL, which includes the seven elements of design offered in Table 4.1. A more thorough discussion of these is offered below.

ACCESSIBLE, NONBIASED ITEMS   When teachers respect the diversity of their classrooms, they want to reduce bias to a minimum as they construct tests (Johnstone, Altman, & Thurlow, 2006; Johnstone, Altman, Thurlow, & Moore, 2006). As a first step, teachers should be aware of the characteristics of the learners in their classroom—aware of exceptional learning needs, cultural differences, or other subgroups so that they can recognize the bias of potential barriers within their assessments. See Figure 4.4 for an example of a chart for collecting important demographic information during the first few days of class. In addition, teachers can give students interest inventories, write autobiographies of learning needs, and, of course, assess perquisite skills and knowledge needed for specific content areas.

INCLUSIVE ASSESSMENT POPULATION   Assessments should be given to every student in the classroom—the full range, from the gifted to those with exceptional learning needs, especially if these students are expected to participate in the state and national assessments. Each assessment activity should be developed from the start with options to remove barriers to learning for the largest number of students, and all options should be available to all students. For example: Students with dyslexia, who are ELL, and

TABLE 4.1 Seven Elements of Universally Designed Assessments

Element	Explanation
Inclusive assessment population	Tests designed for state, district, or school accountability must include every student except those in the alternate assessment, and this is reflected in assessment design and field testing procedures.
Precisely defined constructs	The specific constructs tested must be clearly defined so that all construct irrelevant cognitive, sensory, emotional, and physical barriers can be removed.
Accessible, nonbiased items	Accessibility is built into items from the beginning, and bias-review procedures ensure that quality is retained in all items.
Amenable to accommodations	The test design facilitates the use of needed accommodations (e.g., all items can be Brailled).
Simple, clear, and intuitive instructions and procedures	All instructions and procedures are simple, clear, and presented in understandable language.
Maximum readability and comprehensibility	A variety of readability and plain-language guidelines are followed (e.g., sentence length and number of difficult words are kept to a minimum) to produce readable and comprehensible text.
Maximum legibility	Characteristics that ensure easy decipherability are applied to text and to tables, figures, illustrations, and response formats.

Source: Thompson & Thurlow (2002). Reprinted with permission.

those with below-grade-level reading levels will benefit from many of the same options, such as having an audio copy of the assessment and more time.

PRECISELY DEFINED CONSTRUCTS   Well-constructed tests measure exactly what they are intended to measure (Hogan, 2007; Popham, 2005); for example, math tests should measure ability to use math facts, theorems, formulas, problem-solving ability, and so forth but should not be assessments of reading ability. "A construct is the trait or characteristic" (Hogan 2007, p. 68) we wish to measure—that is, the knowledge and skills of the students we teach. We will discuss how teachers can assure their content constructs later in this chapter, but there are also "non-construct-oriented barriers, including cognitive, sensory, emotional, and physical barriers" (Thompson & Thurlow, 2002, p. 4). In fact, Johnstone (2003) cited research that demonstrated students' performance on math tests was as limited as their ability to read well. A universally designed test should remove these barriers. For example, a read-aloud or audio copy option might be offered for the math word problems. Johnstone (2003) reported that research studies conducted from 1993 through 2000 repeatedly found that students with poor reading skills scored higher on math tests when the questions were read to them. This would eliminate the non-construct barrier of reading skills from the assessment of math skills. In another situation, on a science test with fill-in-the-blank questions, teachers could offer difficult to spell vocabulary in a word bank to all students. This would eliminate the non-construct barrier of spelling ability from the construct of science knowledge.

ID#	Identifier	Gender	Race	Parent Status	SES/ Lunch Status	Reading Level	Math Level	Language, Exceptionality or Special Need	Other

FIGURE 4.4 Form for Student Demographic Information

There are two cautionary notes when considering how to accommodate for both teacher tests and standardized tests. First, accommodations that change the construct being assessed are considered as non-standard accommodations and are therefore controversial and are generally to be avoided by teachers and school districts (National Center for Learning Disabilities [NCLD], 2007). Use of nonstandard accommodations may cause the data to be disregarded in state and school reports of AYP. Second, while generally speaking all states note the importance of using accommodations in the classroom prior to using in an assessment situation, very few states mandate a specific time period; for example, Colorado and Wyoming mandate that accommodations must be used in the classroom for at least 90 days prior to use in the assessment setting (NCLD, 2007). Regardless of what your state mandates, remember that the student should be familiar and comfortable with any accommodations used during state and district tests. Thus teachers should know which accommodations are allowed by their states and districts and use those in their classroom assessments.

AMENABLE TO ACCOMMODATIONS   Tests should be constructed so that additional accommodations can be added if they are needed by specific students. Even the best universally designed test cannot meet the needs of all students, and occasionally specific accommodations will be needed (Thompson & Thurlow, 2002). For example, a student who uses Braille to read and write will need options that include a Braille copy and a means to respond in Braille. This means that the need for this accommodation should be considered during the initial construction of the test—if there is a need to use a graphic, such as a map, chart, or photo, how will these be presented to the student who is not able to see them? The teacher might consider how the question could be asked without the map, chart, or photo or if the content could be assessed in a different way for a specific student. Additional suggestions include avoiding the use of vertical or diagonal text and removing items that distract, such as clip art, icons, and other decorative items (Johnstone, 2003). These are the ways that tests can be amenable to specific, individual accommodations.

SIMPLE, CLEAR, AND INTUITIVE INSTRUCTIONS AND PROCEDURES   Clearly every assignment, including tests, should have directions, and these directions should be understandable by the persons who are taking the test. Seems a bit simplistic, but it is not. When teachers write tests, they know precisely what they want students to do, and much of that seems obvious to them. Ah, but the teacher's intentions are not always obvious to the student, especially to students with ELN. Have you ever participated in the popular class activity of writing out the directions to a peanut butter and jelly sandwich? Did you remember to start with getting the ingredients out of their storage places? Did you remember to say "open the jar of peanut butter"? In this author's experience, those are the two most frequently forgotten directions, but without doing both of those first steps, the task is not possible. Teachers can also forget the obvious direction. Therefore, check the directions before giving the test. Teachers can conduct a test run for instructions and procedures by giving a short sample test a day or two before the real test. Then ask students to tell you about any unclear directions, procedures, or questions. This can serve as both a test run for teachers and a review for the students. A possible side effect would be the relief of some test anxiety as students will see a sample of likely questions. One part of writing

TABLE 4.2 Plain-Language Editing Strategies

Strategy	Description
Reduce excessive length.	Reduce wordiness and remove irrelevant material.
Use common words.	Eliminate unusual or low-frequency words and replace with common words (e.g., replace *utilize* with *use*).
Avoid ambiguous words.	For example, *crane* should be avoided because it could be a bird or a piece of heavy machinery.
Avoid irregularly spelled words.	Examples of irregularly spelled words are *trough* and *feign*.
Avoid proper names.	Replace proper names with simple common names such as first names.
Avoid inconsistent naming and graphic conventions.	Avoid multiple names for the same concept. Be consistent in the use of typeface.
Avoid unclear signals about how to direct attention.	Well-designed heading and graphic arrangement can convey information about the relative importance of information and order in which it should be considered.
Mark all questions.	Give an obvious graphic signal (e.g., bullet, letter, number) to indicate separate questions.

Source: Thompson & Thurlow (2002). Reprinted with permission.

simple and clear directions can be accomplished if you are aware of maximum readability issues noted below.

MAXIMUM READABILITY AND COMPREHENSIBILITY   Table 4.2 provides an overview of plain-language editing strategies that will increase the readability and comprehensibility of tests. In addition to the strategies for making tests readable and comprehensible, Johnstone (2003) added five ways that teachers can improve their tests: (1) break compound complex sentences into several shorter sentences, placing the most important facts first; (2) sequence steps in directions in exact order of events; (3) introduce one idea, fact, or process at a time; (4) if some information is important to the statement, place that at the beginning of the sentence, (e.g., time and setting); and (5) make all noun–pronoun relationships very clear. Finally, teachers should use shorter sentences, fewer words per line, and sparingly use multisyllabic words to increase readability of their classroom assessments (Johnstone, 2003).

MAXIMUM LEGIBILITY   The physical appearance of text and the shapes of letters and numbers enable people to read text easily. That is legibility, and the most legible text can be read quickly with ease and understanding (Johnstone, 2003; Thompson & Thurlow, 2002). Table 4.3 provides an overview of the characteristics of legible text. If teachers can eliminate physical features that interfere with students focus or understanding of test questions or tasks, they can lower bias (Thompson & Thurlow, 2002).

Using the principles of Universal Design to construct tests is relatively new, since UDL has been discussed and used for less than 10 years. Early research in test development, however, resulted in guidelines that remove barriers that interfered with accurately measuring the content being tested, and while using these guidelines may not

TABLE 4.3 Characteristics of Legible Text

Dimension	Characteristics of Legible Text
Contrast (degree of separation of tones in print from the background paper)	• White or glossy paper should be avoided to reduce glare. Blue paper should not be used. • Black type on matte pastel or off-white paper is most favorable for both contrast and eye strain • Avoid gray scale and shading, particularly where pertinent information is provided.
Type Size (standard measuring unit for type size is the point)	• The point sizes most often used are 10 and 12 point for documents to be read by people with excellent vision reading in good light • Fourteen-point type increases readability and can increase test scores for both students with and without disabilities, compared to 12-point type. Large print for students with vision impairments is at least 18 point. • Type size for captions, footnotes, keys, and legends need to be at least 12 point also. • Larger type sizes are most effective for young students who are learning to read and for students with visual difficulties. Large print is beneficial for reducing eye fatigue. • The relationship between readability and point size is also dependent on the typeface used.
Spacing (the amount of space between each character)	• Letters that are too close together are difficult for partially sighted readers. Spacing needs to be wide between both letters and words. • Fixed-space fonts seem to be more legible for some readers than proportional-spaced fonts.
Leading (the amount of vertical space between lines of type)	• Insufficient leading makes type blurry and gives the text a muddy look. • Increased leading, or white space between lines of type, makes a document more readable for people with low vision. • Leading should be 25–30 percent of the point (font) size for maximum readability. • Leading alone does not make a difference in readability as much as the interaction between point size, leading and line length. • Suggestions for leading in relationship to type size: • 12-point type needs between 2 and 4 points of leading. • 14-point type needs between 3 and 6 points of leading. • 16-point type needs between 4 and 6 points of leading. • 18-point type needs between 5 and 6 points of leading.

increase student achievement, we have been able to determine that their use will give teachers a more accurate picture of student learning (Haladyna, 1999; McMillan, 2000; Popham, 2005). These guidelines can help teachers make more precise measurements of student learning by removing non-construct barriers, unclear or confusing language, and bias based on physical appearance.

However, even with the use of UDL, some students will need additional accommodations to succeed on both teacher-made tests and high-stakes assessments. We will discuss accommodations that can be built into tests and additional accommodations that can be offered to students with specific needs in the next section.

TABLE 4.3 (*Continued*)

Dimension	Characteristics of Legible Text
Typeface (characters, punctuation, and symbols that share a common design)	• Standard typeface, using upper and lower case, is more readable than italic, slanted, small caps, or all caps. • Avoid font styles that are decorative or cursive. Standard serif or sans serif fonts with easily recognizable characters are recommended. • Text printed completely in capital letters is less legible than text printed completely in lowercase, or normal mixed-case text. • Italic is far less legible and is read considerably more slowly than regular lower case. • Boldface is more visible than lowercase if a change from the norm is needed.
Justification (text is either flush with left or right margins—justified—or staggered/ragged—unjustified)	• Staggered right margins are easier to see and scan than uniform or block-style right-justified margins. • Justified text is more difficult to read than unjustified text—especially for poor readers. • Justified text is also more disruptive for good readers. • A flush left/ragged right margin is the most effective format for text memory. • Unjustified text may be easier for poorer readers to understand because the uneven eye movements created in justified text can interrupt reading. • Justified lines require the distances between words to be varied. In very narrow columns, not only are there extra wide spaces between words, but also between letters within the words.
Line Length (length of the line of text; the distance between the left and right margin)	• Longer lines, in general, require larger type and more leadin. • Optimal length is 24 picas—about 4 inches. • Lines that are too long make readers weary and may also cause difficulty in locating the beginning of the next line, causing readers to lose their place. • Lines of text should be about 40–70 characters, or roughly eight to twelve words per line.
Blank Space (Space on a page that is not occupied by text or graphics)	• Use the term "blank space" rather than "white space" because the background is not always white. • Blank space anchors text on the paper. • Blank space around paragraphs and between columns of type helps increase legibility. • A general rule is to allow text to occupy only about half of a page. Too many test items per page can make items difficult to read.

Source: Thompson, Johnstone, & Thurlow (2002). Reprinted with permission.

SELECTING APPROPRIATE ACCOMMODATIONS FOR STUDENTS WHO NEED ADDITIONAL SUPPORT

When selecting accommodations for students to use in classroom activities and assessments, teachers should consider what students will be allowed to use on the state and national assessments as well. In some cases the accommodations allowed by school districts and local public schools may not match those allowed during the state and national assessments. It is imperative that teachers and school personnel be familiar with both types of accommodations and how to prepare students for all types of assessment situations.

Classroom Assessments

When administering either formative or summative classroom assessments, teachers may wish to allow the student whatever accommodations were permitted during the learning experience. This will provide a link between the learning and assessment and is especially important if the accommodation can be used on the state and national assessment. By allowing use during instruction, students with disabilities are able to practice and become proficient in using the accommodation (Thurlow, Elliott, & Ysseldyke, 2003) well before the assessment situation occurs. This eliminates the possibility that the accommodation can become a variable in the testing situation.

Upon occasion, local schools may allow assessment accommodations in classroom settings that would not ever be allowed during state and national assessments, such as retaking the test, reducing the number of answer choices, simplifying the language, providing prompts, and giving feedback. This can be problematic, as students and their families may come to expect these accommodations as the norm in other educational settings, such as higher education or during end of course and national assessments. If accommodations that are not allowed elsewhere are allowed during classroom assessments, students and their families must be informed in a clear, direct manner that such accommodations will not be allowed in all assessment situations. Table 4.4 provides a worksheet that teachers can use to interview students who need accommodations for both classroom and state assessments. Table 4.5 provides typical accommodations that can be provided for specific assessment needs.

Providing appropriate accommodations that remove barriers for students with expectation needs during any assessment situation is vital to their ability to demonstrate what they have learned. Equally important is that these students are not only prepared with academic knowledge and skills and have been given accommodations but also that they have the test-taking skills that will allow them to benefit from the accommodations and demonstrate what they have learned. In the next section we will discuss the ethics of teaching test-taking skills and the more appropriate ways to prepare students for the demands of the assessment instrument.

Teaching Strategies for Assessment

As the emphasis on accountability has risen, so has anxiety risen about student preparation for these high-stakes tests in teachers, students, parents, and school administrators. Popham (2005) noted that this anxiety has led to cheating on high-stakes tests, with unhappy results for all concerned. In this section we will discuss ways to prepare students for the testing situation.

Two guidelines provided by Popham (2005) will direct our discussion of teaching test-taking skills. The first is that "No test-preparation practice should violate the ethical norms of the educational profession" (Popham, 2005, p. 305). The second is that "No test-preparation should increase students' test scores without simultaneously increasing students' mastery of the assessment domain tested" (Popham, 2005, p. 307). Just as Popham suggested, we suggest that teachers provide students with generalized test-taking skills and practice in taking tests with varied formats. In addition, we stress that teaching students cognitive strategies for test-taking situations will provide much needed support for remembering content, formulating correct answers, and understanding the test formats. In the remainder of this section we will discuss those three test preparation methods.

TABLE 4.4 Worksheet for Selecting Appropriate Accommodations

Presentation Accommodations

Useful for students who:	Ask the student . . .	Accommodations to provide
Have print disabilities because they are not able to use standard print for learning	• Can you read and understand print directions? • Do you need directions repeated frequently? • Have you been identified as have a reading disability?	

Response Accommodations

Useful for students who:	Ask the student . . .	Accommodations to provide
Have physical, sensory or learning disabilities and have difficulty with memory, sequencings, directionality, alignment, and organization	• Can you use a pencil or other writing instrument? • Do you have a disability that affects your ability to spell? • Do you have trouble with tracking from one page to another and maintaining your place?	

Timing or Scheduling Accommodations

Useful for students who:	Ask the student . . .	Accommodations to provide
• Need more time • Cannot concentrate for extended periods • Have health-related disabilities • Fatigue easily • Need a special diet • Have other medical needs	• Can you work continuously during the entire time allocated for test administration? • Do you tire easily because of health impairments? • Do you need shorter working periods and frequent breaks?	

Setting accommodations

Useful for students who:	Ask the student . . .	Accommodations to provide
Are easily distracted in large group settings, or who concentrate best in small groups	• Are you easily distracted by others? • Do you have difficulty staying on task? • Do you have behaviors that would disrupt others?	

Source: Information from National Center for Learning Disabilities (n.d.-a).

Generalized test-taking skills are the skills necessary to prepare and study for tests. These include reading, understanding, and following written and oral directions; understanding the requirements of specific types of questions (e.g., multiple choices, matching, essay); marking answer sheets correctly; proofreading and correcting answers; managing time during the test; and controlling test anxiety. Each of these skills

TABLE 4.5 Accommodations for Specific Needs

Accommodation	Reasons	Examples
Change in assessment setting	Student may 1. Have difficulty in focusing 2. Need to use special equipment 3. Be unable to attend school 4. Need an assistant, scribe, or sign language interpreter	• Separate room • Study carrel • Special lighting • Adaptive furniture • Hospital or home setting • Computer equipment • Needs read-aloud of assessments directions and questions • Individual or small group administration
Changes in duration or organization of time	Student may 1. Need extra time due to special equipment 2. Lack stamina for long testing sessions 3. Have perceptual difficulties 4. Read slowly 5. Have difficulty in writing	• Extended time • Unlimited time • Take frequent breaks
Changes in scheduling	Student may 1. Take medication or need medical attention 2. Need to coordinate with side effects of medication 3. Lack stamina for long testing sessions 4. Be anxious or easily frustrated	• Take subtests in different order • Take over multiple days • Take test at a specific time of day
Changes in presentation	Student may 1. Have a physical or sensory disability 2. Have perceptual difficulties 3. Need assistive devices 4. Have difficulties with directions 5. Have underdeveloped language skills (e.g., deaf, ELL)	• Have directions repeated • Modified answer sheet with larger bubbles • Use large print, Braille, or read-aloud • Audio/video cassettes or CDs • Use a magnification device • Use a non-English language interpreter • Use a sign language interpreter
Changes in response mode	Student may 1. Have a physical or sensory disability 2. Have perceptual difficulties 3. Need assistive devices 4. Have difficulties with directions 5. Have underdeveloped language skills (e.g., deaf, ELL)	• May mark in test booklet • Use a scribe • Use a word processor • Use reference materials (e.g., dictionary or spell checker)

Sources: Information from Salend (2001); Thurlow (2002); Wood (2006).

can be taught within the general curriculum that is taught daily in any classroom, as illustrated in detail below.

General study skills are one of the most important skills we can teach, but we often do not teach them. As will be discussed in Chapter 6, on metacognitive strategies, teachers often make assumptions about what study skills and strategies students have learned in previous years or courses and do not realize that some of those skills are not generalized across years and courses without prompting. Listed below are ways to encourage students to use appropriate study skills.

- At the beginning of the school year, provide partially completed note-taking guides for textbook reading and lectures. As the year progresses, fade out the amount of support you give in each note-taking guide until you feel the students are ready to take notes on their own.
- Teach students how to use prompts found in their textbooks that point to important information. This would include organizational items such as headings, bold or italicized and *cue* words, charts, tables, and illustrations, and chapter summaries. Encourage students to read end-of-chapter questions prior to reading the chapter content. Prompt them to use those questions as note-taking guides.
- Support the use of graphic organizers or concept maps by providing those, when appropriate, for note-taking, answering essay questions, and organizing content to be learned. As the year progresses, fade out the provision of these devices, but require students to create their own.
- Help students organize study groups or peer partners and support those groups with class time to meet. As with other strategies mentioned above, gradually fade out your support and class time given to these groups, but continue to prompt students to meet outside of class prior to assessments.
- Teach metacognitive strategies, such as problem-solving strategies and mnemonic devices for learning and organizing information. Memory devices such as chunking and visual or keyword pictures are helpful for remembering information. Specific test-taking strategies will be discussed later in this section and in Chapter 6, where metacognitive strategies are discussed in detail. Prompt students to use those when appropriate, teach them to prompt each other in their study groups, and review or add strategies as the need arises.
- Provide as much constructive feedback about their use of the above strategies as possible. Make a point to giving credit to their use of these items when they do well on assessments. As the year progresses, ask the students to explain what helped them do well on assignments and assessments. Hopefully they will begin to attribute their success to proper use of the study skills you have taught them. If not, prompt them to do so until they are doing that independently.

General test-taking strategies that would apply to all types of questions can be taught or reviewed each time you give an assessment in class. One issue that often affects all students, but especially those with exceptional needs, is time. During the course of the school year, give timed tests so that students can become accustomed to managing their time. When you give timed tests, teach, prompt, and review these strategies.

- Teach students to note how many questions are on the test and how much time they can allot to each question. For example, if you give a test that has 30 multiple choice questions and two short answer essays and it must be completed in 45 minutes, help the students determine how much time to give to the multiple choice and how much to the essays.

- Prompt them to skip questions that are too difficult or are consuming too much time and then return to those after they have completed all questions in the section.
- Prompt them to use any cognitive strategies that they have learned; this is especially important for those students who have a strategy to calm test anxiety. These will be discussed later in this section.

Mastering test directions can be taught and then reviewed any time an assessment is given in the classroom. First, teach the vocabulary to students prior to the first assessment given in your classroom. For example, tell the students what is expected when terms such as *discuss, explain, describe, compare and contrast*, and *justify* appear in test directions. Use these words throughout the school year on your teacher-made assessments and homework assignments. Provide specific feedback with examples if students are not meeting those expectations.

Mastering test formats can be tricky for students who are not able to adjust to change quickly, but it is not ethically responsible to offer all classroom and practice tests in the same format as the high-stakes tests; rather, make sure that your students are familiar with all possible formats that they may encounter on assessments.

- During the school year offer questions in a variety of formats—multiple choice, matching, true/false, sentence completion, and essay—on each assessment given in your classroom.
- Offer these questions in a variety of page formats—single column and double column, but be sure to offer more than the one used by the high-stakes assessment. After all, the goal is to help students learn to generalize, not to teach them to be successful on a single assessment.
- Teach students how to answer these questions by giving homework or in-class work that uses a variety of questioning formats.

Taking multiple choice tests can be particularly difficult for some students. Salend (2001) suggested these strategies be taught to students:

- Demonstrate and prompt students to read the question and think of the correct answer before reading the choices.
- Explain that if choices contradict each other, most likely one of them is correct. If choices are very similar, they are most likely incorrect answers. Choices that seem absurd, contain irrelevant information, or are obviously false are incorrect.
- Teach them to look for clues in the stem, such as subject, verb, tense, and modifiers such as *a* or *an*. Check for any other clues in the stem to help select the correct answer.
- Give them practice with multiple choice questions by including some on each of your class assessments.

Using separate answer sheets can pose difficulties for all students because the possibility of getting off track if the student skips a question exists for all, but especially for students who have visual acuity and visual processing problems.

- Show students how to use a ruler or sheet of scrap paper to keep their place on the answer sheet.

- Use Scantron answer sheets or teacher-made bubble sheets regularly during your classroom tests so that students have practice with them prior to the high-stakes assessment.

Cognitive strategies that are research-based and developed specifically for test-taking situations are helpful to all students, but again offer the support during testing situations needed by many students with exceptional and diverse needs. Cognitive strategies can be useful both for remembering the content being assessed and taking specific types of tests, such as objective versus essay questions (see Table 4.6 for examples). Learning and using strategies for test taking should not be substituted for studying and learning the content, but teaching students strategies that help them remember what they have learned is particularly helpful to students with long- and short-term memory deficits.

TABLE 4.6 Examples of Test-Taking Strategies

Study	Memory	Test-Taking
Develop a study plan and schedule study sessions. There are a number of planners to print on the Learning Toolbox.	**Key Word:** designed to increase recall of vocabulary words. Selecting the key words in reading and lectures will help you by helping you remember the big ideas in your reading.	**BRAVE:** to overcome test anxiety. **B**reathe deeply. **R**elax. **A**ttitude is everything. **V**isualize yourself in your favorite place. **E**nd is in sight.
CON-AIR is designed to help students study from texts and other printed materials. **C**opy chapter headings and subheadings. **O**rganize note cards. **N**umber the cards under categories. **A**rrange the note cards in columns. **I**dentify each card's correct place. **R**eview the note cards.	**BREAK:** to help memory of information **B**reak memorizing into short periods. **R**ecite information aloud. **E**stablish mnemonics. **A**lways try to picture information in your mind. **K**ey words help.	**CRAM** and/or **PIRARTES** can help pick the right answer on objective questions. **C**over the answers. **R**ead the question carefully. **A**nswer the question without looking at the answers. **M**atch your answer to one of the given choices.
WORRY: to organize information from books and notes **W**ork with note cards from both reading and lecture notes. **O**utline main ideas covered in both reading and lecture. **R**ead note cards from reading for facts. **R**ead lecture notes for facts. **Y**es, you're ready after one more reading of your outline.	**Pegword:** useful for remembering lists of information in a specific order	**FLEAS** is useful for staying on task and getting done in the allotted time. **F**irst read the directions. **L**ook over the test. **E**asiest questions answered first. **A**nswer the questions that are worth more. **S**kip a question.

Sources: Information from Deshler, Ellis, & Lenz (1996); Minskoff, Allsopp, Minskoff, & Kyger (n.d.).

Summary

In this chapter, we have discussed why students with disabilities are included by law in high-stakes assessments. We have outlined the six additional purposes of assessment and how data from these can help teachers in their daily work of teaching. However, many students with exceptional needs face barriers to successful completion of both high-stakes and classroom assessments. Therefore, we discussed the use of UDL to construct assessable assessments for all students and thereby reduce the need for accommodations. Nevertheless, some students may still need accommodations, and we offered methods for determining and selecting appropriate accommodations. Finally, we suggested ways to support students by teaching them test-taking skills.

References

Airasian, P. W. (2005). *Classroom assessment: Concepts and applications* (5th ed.). New York: McGraw-Hill.

Cortiella, C. (2004). *Implications of high-stakes testing for students with learning disabilities.* Retrieved September 8, 2009, from http://www.greatschools.net/LD/school-learning/high-stakes-testing-learning-disabilities.gs?content = 886

Deshler, D. D., Ellis, E. S., & Lenz, B. K. (1996). *Teaching adolescents with learning disabilities: Strategies and methods.* Denver: Love Publishing.

Fuchs, L. S., & Fuchs, D. (2007). A model for implementing responsiveness to intervention. *Teaching Exceptional Children, 39*(5), 14–20.

Gagnon, G. W., & Collay, M. (2001). *Designing for learning: Six elements in constructivist classroom.* Thousand Oaks, CA: Corwin Press.

Haladyna, T. M. (1999). *Developing and validating multiple-choice test items* (2nd ed.). Mahwah, NJ: Lawrence Erlbaum Associates.

Hogan, T. P. (2007). *Educational assessment: A practical introduction.* Hoboken, NJ: Wiley and Jossey-Bass.

Hosp. J. L., & Reschly, D. J. (2003). Referral rates for intervention or assessment: A meta-analysis of racial differences. *The Journal of Special Education, 37*, 67–80.

Johnstone, C., Altman, J., Thurlow, M., & Moore, M. (2006). *Universal Design online manual.* Minneapolis: University of Minnesota, National Center on Educational Outcomes.

Johnstone, C. J. (2003). *Improving validity of large-scale tests: Universal Design and student performance* (Technical Report 37). Minneapolis: University of Minnesota, National Center on Educational Outcomes. Retrieved June 30, 2007, from http://education.umn.edu/NCEO/OnlinePubs/Technical37.htm

Johnstone, C. J., Altman, J., & Thurlow, M. (2006). *A state guide to the development of universally designed assessments.* Minneapolis: University of Minnesota, National Center on Educational Outcomes.

Kame'enui, E. J. (2007). A new paradigm: Response to Interventions. *Teaching Exceptional Children, 39*(5), 6–7.

McMillan, J. H. (2000). *Essential assessment concepts for teachers and administrators.* Thousand Oaks, CA: Corwin Press.

Minskoff, E., Allsopp, D., Minskoff, J., & Kyger, M. (n.d.). *The learning toolbox.* Web site hosted by James Madison University. Retrieved on April 21, 2008, from http://coe.jmu.edu/learningToolbox/index.html

National Center for Learning Disabilities. (n.d.-a). *No Child Left Behind: Determining appropriate assessment accommodations for students with disabilities: A parent advocacy brief from National Center for Learning Disabilities.* New York: Author. Retrieved on August 10, 2007, from http://www.ncld.org/images/stories/downloads/advocacy/accommodations.pdf

National Center for Learning Disabilities. (n.d.-b). *What is RTI?* New York: Author. Retrieved on December 26, 2008, from http://www.rtinetwork.org/Learn/What/ar/WhatIsRTIhttp://www.rtinetwork.org/Learn/What/ar/WhatIsRTI

National Center for Learning Disabilities. (2007). *State testing accommodations: A look at their value and validity.* New York: Author.

Popham, W. J. (2005). *Classroom assessment: What teachers really need to know* (4th ed.). Boston: Allyn & Bacon.

Rose, D. H., & Dolan, R. P. (2006). *Implications of Universal Design for classroom assessment.* In D. H. Rose & A. Meyer (Eds.), *A practical reader in Universal Design for Learning.* Cambridge, MA: Harvard Educational Press.

Salend, S. J. (2001). *Creating inclusive classrooms: Effective and reflective practices* (4th ed.). Upper Saddle River, NJ: Merrill/Pearson Education.

Smith, T. E. C., Dowdy, C. A., Polloway, E. A., & Blalock, G. E. (1997). *Children and adults with learning disabilities.* Boston: Allyn & Bacon.

Sugai, G. (n.d.). *School-wide positive behavior support and Response to Intervention.* New York: National Center on Learning Disabilities. Retrieved on December 15, 2008, from http://www.rtinetwork.org/Learn/Behavior/ar/Schoolwide Behavior

Thompson, S., & Thurlow, M. (2002). *Universally designed assessments: Better tests for everyone!* (Policy Directions No. 14). Minneapolis: University of Minnesota, National Center on Educational Outcomes. Retrieved June 7, 2007, from http://education.umn.edu/NCEO/OnlinePubs/Policy14.htm

Thompson, S. J., Johnstone, C. J., & Thurlow, M. L. (2002). *Universal Design applied to large scale assessments* (Synthesis Report 44). Minneapolis: University of Minnesota, National Center on Educational Outcomes. Retrieved June 26, 2007, from http://education.umn.edu/NCEO/OnlinePubs/Synthesis44.html

Thurlow, M. (2002). *Issue brief: Accommodations for student with disabilities in high school.* National Center on Secondary Education and Transition, *1*(1). Retrieved on July 14, 2007, from http://www.ncset.org/publications/viewdesc.asp?id=247

Thurlow, M. L., Elliott, J. L., & Ysseldyke, J. E. (2003). *Testing students with disabilities: Practical strategies for complying with district and state requirements* (2nd ed.). Thousand Oaks, CA: Corwin Press.

U.S. Government Accountability Office. (2005). *Most students with disabilities participated in statewide assessments, but inclusion options could be improved.* Report to the ranking minority member, Committee on Health, Education, Labor, and Pension, U.S. Senate. Washington, DC: Author. Retrieved on June 7, 2007, from http://www.gao.gov/new.items/d05618.pdf

Wood, J. W. (2006). *Teaching students in inclusive settings: Adapting and accommodating instruction* (5th ed.). Upper Saddle River, NJ: Merrill/Pearson Education.

Chapter 5

Classroom Management: Getting the Behavior You Want and Need to Teach Effectively

After reading this chapter, you will be able to:

1. Identify effective classroom management strategies by preventing inappropriate behavior, teaching skills to build social competency, and correcting behavior

2. Describe the components and procedures required to implement schoolwide and classroom positive behavior and instructional supports

3. Describe the components and procedures for conducting a Functional Behavior Assessment

4. Describe the components and procedures for developing a Behavioral Intervention Plan

5. Use cognitive strategies to teach appropriate behavior and change inappropriate behavior

For teaching and learning to occur, the classroom environment must be one that is safe and free from strife and where all students feel welcome. If this is not the case, teachers are diverted from their teaching responsibilities when they must attend to inappropriate behavior and students lose their focus as they watch their peers misbehave. Keeping and restoring order seems to take an inordinate amount of time, money, and energy (Beaton, 2001). In this chapter we will focus on classroom management that will aid prevention of unwanted and inappropriate student behavior through the use of positive behavior supports and cognitive problem-solving strategies. We will explain why teachers should teach social skills and build social competence so that students with exceptional needs can be successful in the general education classroom. Finally, for those occasions when unwanted behavior is resistant and continues to occur, we will discuss the use of Behavior Intervention Plans developed from Functional Behavior Analysis and corrective behavior measures.

WHAT IS POSITIVE BEHAVIOR AND INSTRUCTIONAL SUPPORT?

The positive behavior and instructional support (PBIS) system uses a problem-solving model to prevent inappropriate behaviors by teaching and supporting appropriate behavior (OSEP Technical Assistance Center on Positive Behavior Instructional and Supports, 2007). PBIS provides a variety of interventions that are used systematically with all students based on individual needs, and it stresses the role of environment in the development and improvement of student behavior (Sandomierski, Kincaid, & Algozzine, 2007). The key difference between PBIS and the traditional approaches to academic support and discipline is that PBIS is focused on changing the environment rather than changing individual students. Further, Functional Behavior Assessments (FBA) and Behavior Intervention Plans (BIP) (see sections later in this chapter) are important parts of the process in determining appropriate academic and behavior plans (Kerr & Nelson, 2006; LD Online, 1999). While PBIS was designed as a school-wide intervention plan, individual teachers, parents, and community groups can adapt the components to fit their settings and student needs. We will describe the components and explain how classroom teachers can adapt these to their classrooms.

Three Tiers of PBIS

The first tier of PBIS, known as the *universal* or *primary tier*, is used with all students either schoolwide or in individual classrooms (Kerr, & Nelson, 2006; OSEP Technical Assistance Center, 2007). In either case, all students are included in this tier. The most important component of this tier is a curriculum that includes the rules, expectations, and routines of daily life in the school and classroom. While this may seem obvious, researchers find that "high-quality school-wide behavioral instruction is seldom evident" (Sandomierski et al., 2007). This curriculum should be considered as equally important as the lesson plans and content being taught. Further, consistent enforcement and reinforcement of these behavioral expectations should take place in all settings, schoolwide. These measures, teaching and reinforcing, ensure that a majority of students comply and exhibit the desired behaviors and at the same time act as proactive interventions for students with problem behavior (Sandomierski et al., 2007). See Figure 5.1 for examples of actions taken at each of the three tiers in a schoolwide program.

Tier	Students included	Actions taken at this level	Implementation
Tier I: Universal or primary tier	All students in a school or individual classroom	1. Create a schoolwide leadership or behavior support team to spearhead the process. The team members should include an administrator, grade-level teachers, support staff (e.g., counselors, nurse, lead teachers), and parents. 2. Solicit active support and participation of administrators. 3. Obtain committed agreement of active support and participation from at least 80% of the staff. 4. Review or self-assess the current schoolwide discipline system. 5. Develop an action plan that is based on collaborative problem solving and decision making. 6. Determine systematic ways to collect office referral and other data on a regular basis to evaluate the effectiveness of schoolwide PBIS efforts.	Create a school or classroom environment where: a. learning and teaching is valued, and aggressive, unsafe behavior is discouraged; b. respect, responsibility, cooperation, and other highly valued character traits are taught and encouraged; c. individual difference is valued rather than criticized; d. educating students with disabilities is supported, and e. teaching fundamental skills like reading and math is maximized.
Tier II: Secondary or targeted intervention	Students for whom the universal prevention strategies have not been successful	1. Conduct a simple assessment to identify the function a problem behavior serves (FBA). 2. Develop support plans (see next column).	1. Develop individualized, assessment-based intervention strategies that include: a. teaching new skills as a replacement for problem behaviors b. rearranging the environment so that problems can be prevented and desirable behaviors can be encouraged c. monitoring, evaluating, and reassessing the plan

FIGURE 5.1 Continuum of Schoolwide Positive Behavior Instructional and Support System

Tier	Students included	Actions taken at this level	Implementation
			2. Develop and implement group interventions in which targeted students participate, such as "social skills club," "check in/check out," and Behavior Education Plans.
			3. Monitor student progress with direct observations and frequent monitoring of progress.
			4. Determine what changes might be made when the student does not make progress within a reasonable time frame.
Tier III: Tertiary prevention or intensive intervention	Students who have been resistant to previous interventions or who have serious, chronic behavior problems	1. Conduct an individual FBA to identify the function a problem behavior serves. 2. Develop individualize BIP (see next column).	1. Develop an individualized BIP that includes 　a. adjusting the environment to reduce the likelihood that problem behavior will occur 　b. teaching replacement skills and building general academic competencies 　c. apply consequences that promote positive behaviors and deter problems 　d. develop a crisis management plan to use if needed

FIGURE 5.1 (*Continued*)

Sources: Information from Kerr & Nelson (2006); OSEP Technical Assistance Center (2007); Sandomierski et al. (2007).

Sandomierski and colleagues (2007) noted that when Tier I interventions are used with fidelity, school personnel are able to identify students who may need additional support or to be moved to Tier II interventions. These students come to the attention of school personnel, as they will be the students who are referred to the principal or guidance offices.

What Should Teachers Do in Tier I?

Generally speaking, Tier I interventions might be seen as being effective management of students, classroom activities, and materials to prevent unwanted behavior and foster desired behaviors. We could think of this as the positive behavior support part of PBIS. The term "positive behavior support" covers a broad range of strategies and methods for preventing problem and inappropriate behavior in schools. These strategies share the key elements of being proactive and problem solving, preventing behavior by changing the situation, and teaching appropriate alternatives (Safran & Oswald, 2003; Turnbull, et al., 2002). Proactive teachers recognize that student behavior is influenced as much by class-room climate as by individual student qualities. In addition, proactive teachers recognize the need to inject a sense of community into their classrooms. Proactive teachers use rules and routines to teach students the behaviors that are expected and use management strategies and reinforcement contingences to help students achieve these behaviors.

When using positive behavior supports, teachers are asked to build a supporting, collaborating (cooperating), and empowering community of learners. Shaw (1992) stated that "effective community building is based on facilitating a student's sense of *inclusion, influence,* and *openness*" (cited in Obenchain & Abernathy, 2003, p. 55). How, then, do teachers build a positive community for all learners? Ten ways to create supporting, collaborating, and empowering community of learners are provided below.

1. *Create a positive list of class rules.* Rules provide standards for *acceptable behavior*. Gabel, Hester, Rock, and Hughes (2009) noted a "general consensus that rules should be necessary, reasonable, easy to understand, and enforceable" (p. 196). Using these criteria, teachers can construct or collaborate with their students to construct a list of rules. Generally avoid negatives in your rules. For example, rather than saying *Don't talk when the teacher is talking,* use *When the teacher is speaking, Stop, Watch, and Listen.*

2. *Involve the students in developing class rules.* Engage the students in discussions of appropriate behaviors everyone should have at school, then ask if a list of rules you have would work. Be willing to add or reframe rules to include their comments.

3. *Teach your rules, routines, and procedures.* Teach these as you would any other part of your curriculum; include examples and non-examples, role-play situations to determine how students should behavior, review frequently during first days of school, and revisit at the end of the first month to determine if any rules need to be added or changed with student input.

4. *Review your rules to be sure they are equitable for all students* (Brown, Paulsen, & Higgins, 2003). Be sure that all students can comply with your rules and proce-dures. For example, if a teacher has a rule that requires students to work quietly in their seats during independent practice, this may be creating conditions those stu-dents can not meet at all times. Students with a language difference may need to ask a classmate for clarification, or someone may need to sharpen a pencil, or the student with ADHD may work best while quietly verbalizing the steps of a math problem. All of these are appropriate behaviors under the circumstances, but pro-hibited by the above noted rule.

5. *Provide students with choice* (Obenchain & Abernathy, 2003). Allowing choice is empowering. The choices may be as simple as using some time during the day to read a book or finish homework, select an activity when they complete an as-signment before others, or chose to work alone or in a small group.

6. *Use alpha commands, avoid beta commands.* Alpha commands are clear, direct, and specific with few verbalizations and allow sufficient time for obedience. Beta commands tend to be vague and wordy with multiple instructions and demand immediate compliance (Maag, 2000). For example, "Andy, don't you think that a good boy would be sitting down now?" is a beta command. The alpha command would be "Andy, please sit in your seat now." The alpha command is more likely to get the response the teacher desires.

7. *Use classroom jobs* **(Obenchain & Abernathy, 2003).** Assign tasks to peer partners or small groups to teach responsibility, cooperation, and interdependence. These should be real jobs needed to keep the classroom running smoothly, such as getting out supplies for art or science activities, and should be age appropriate.

8. *Use peer partners* **(Archer, 1994).** Peer partners teach collaboration and cooperation. In addition, they build connections to the classroom by linking each student to at least one other student in the class.

9. *Learn as much as you can about your students.* Each student comes to the school setting with unique experiences and expectations. In addition, even the best students can face barriers that affect learning and behavior. You can gather valuable information through informal conversations during recess, lunch, or after-school activities. Additional information can come from autobiographies, journal prompts, etc.

10. *Use a sharing chair* **(Obenchain & Abernathy, 2003).** Based on the "author's chair" idea, the sharing chair is a place and time when individuals and small groups can bring an issue, concern, or joy to share with the larger group. This activity builds leadership skills because the students lead others in problem solving or a discussion of personal importance. The students decide when to use the sharing chair. This is not for sharing academic work unless the students chose to make it so.

In addition to the suggestions above, teachers may wish to teach students strategies for dealing with specific problem behaviors that are likely to occur in every classroom. These may include disruptions due to hurt feelings, perceived and real injustices between students, and arguments over toys, books, art supplies, and other items being used in the classroom. In addition, some students may have personal issues outside the classroom that may require attention and strategies for dealing with those problems. To address these in a proactive manner, we suggest using metacognitive and cognitive strategies we discuss at the end of this chapter.

In the diverse classrooms today's teachers see, there may be students who are not as adapted as others in social skills needed to fit into the class community. These students may require help learning the cultural social skills in a particular setting and support as they learn the behaviors expected by peers and school personnel. We suggest that explicit teaching of social skills may be needed. Whether a teacher uses a commercial social skills package or provides one-on-one instruction to students is a personal or school choice. Whatever the case may be, the use of behavioral traps may be useful in teaching and reinforcing social skills. The term *behavioral trap* was first used by Baer and Wolf in 1970 to describe "how natural contingencies of reinforcement operate to promote and maintain generalized behavior changes" (Alver & Heward, 1996, p. 285). These authors suggest that

- Teachers select powerful, irresistible reinforcers that require an easy-to-perform response already known to the student. This gets the student interested and eager to perform.

- Once engaged in the task, reinforcement received will motivate the student to acquire, extend, and maintain the targeted skills, which will be maintained over an extended period of time since the student gains continual pleasure and is not satiated.

STEPS TO CREATING A BEHAVIORAL TRAP

1. Select the student or students to "bait."
2. Interview them by engaging in conversations about
   - Interests
   - Hobbies
   - Music preferences
   - Latest movies they have seen
   - TV/movie stars, athletes, sports teams, musicians, cartoon characters, national/state/local community leaders, or others they admire
3. Observe their disruptive behaviors for clues to activities they enjoy for the possibility of turning those into "traps."
4. Ask their family and friends what the students like to do in their spare time or what outside activities their families pursue.
5. Provide sample activities to find out what most appeals to them or "hooks" them.

The list below was selected from work by Church, Gottschalk, and Leddy (2003) and is only meant to help you start thinking about ways you can "trap" students into improving their social skills, making friends, or learning to share. As you may have noticed a number of these activities will help student with academic skills as well.

A SAMPLING OF ACTIVITIES THAT MAY APPEAL TO STUDENTS OF ALL AGES

- Give the student a job that matches a target skill. For example, if the student leaves trash behind or generally makes messes, make him or her the "Class Trash Monitor" with a badge to match.
- Students could become a teacher's helper in a lower grade by reading coloring, painting, playing games; telling stories or just talking with the children; taking one or two younger children on a tour of the school or a higher level classroom; or helping set up the room for a special event.
- Students could visit the media center to discuss books on manners, social skills, friendship (or whatever the target skill is) with the specialist. The purpose is to find books that would be appropriate to share with a lower-level class. Then students would read and discuss those books with younger children.
- Students can write letters to (or email) fan clubs asking for free posters, signed photographs, or other items of interest; develop a list of questions to ask the celebrity/hero in an interview; keep records of hero's activities, latest releases, wins/loses, points scored; search the Internet for information about the sport or other activity involving the hero. Note: Student could investigate a famous person who has the same disability as theirs.
- Students can share information discovered and items acquired from the letters they wrote with students in their own class or in lower grades, start a school fan club, or organize a special day at the school to celebrate a worthy hero.

- Students could teach their favorite game(s) (board, digital, or Web-based) or sport to others by demonstrating how to play, writing directions for playing, sharing strategies, and graphing the scores of classmates.
- Students could interview classmates, make a class memory book by taking photos of class or school events and activities, interview the teacher and classmates and take their photos, interview the principal and other significant school personnel, write a class history for the year, or chronicle a class field trip, special project, or day in the life of a class pet.
- Remember the *turnaround-behavior* suggestion from "What you need to do" above? Here is an example for that procedure. If the student is a paper (or other objects) thrower: Students could research how to make a paper airplane, find good design to share, write a set of directions, explain to others, have a contest to see whose plane will fly farthest, be the judge by measuring each flight length, and award a certificate at the end.

What Should Teachers Do in Tier II?

The second tier of PBIS, known as *secondary or targeted intervention*, is used with students for whom the universal prevention strategies have not been successful because they have specific problems. At this tier, schools work with individual students or small groups to target their specific problems with evidence-based interventions and resources appropriate for the students need (Kerr & Nelson, 2006; OSEP Technical Assistance Center, 2007; Sandomierski et al., 2007). Data is collected using Functional Behavior Assessment format, teacher ratings, self-assessments, and school records such as office referrals. Interventions offered to students at the Tier II level may include individual or small group counseling, social skills instruction, or mentoring programs.

Concurrence in academic problems are common among students with behavior problems. In fact, there is evidence that behavior problems often begin because students are not doing well in academic work. Sandomierski and colleagues (2007) suggested that when students are resistant to Tier I and II PBIS, their academic achievement should be assessed. Academic support or remediation should be provided to the student before moving to Tier III interventions. Figure 5.2 offers examples of actions teachers may take at Tier I and II to teach and manage behavior of students in their specific classrooms.

What Should Teachers Do in Tier III?

The third tier of PBIS, *tertiary prevention* or *intensive intervention*, targets the students who have been resistant to previous interventions or who have serious, chronic behavior problems. During this tier, a team of school personnel delivers specific, specialized services. To develop these services and select additional interventions, more data must be collected, therefore at this point a Functional Behavior Assessment (FBA) should be conducted followed by development of a Behavior Intervention Plan (BIP) to be used in Tier III. The BIP should be implemented and the student's behavior carefully monitored. In addition, direct observations of the student by other personnel as well as teacher ratings of behavior occurrences can provide data for the team. All of this is time-consuming, but at this stage the student has been resistant to interventions, therefore additional time and resources are needed to determine a future course of action. Generally

Tier I: Universal (whole class)	Tier II: Targeted Population (selected group of students)	Tier III: Intensive Interventions (selected individuals)
Teach rules, expectations, and routines.	Review rules, expectations, and routines.	Complete a Functional Behavior Assessment (FBA).
Offer examples and non-examples of rules and expectations.	Question students about their behavior with "Is [insert name or the behavior child is doing] following the rule?" With this question, the answer should be a simple "Yes" or "No" from the student.	Plan and implement a Behavior Intervention Plan (BIP).
Practice routines until students are able to comply.	Prompt the use of appropriate behaviors.	
Offer consistent, frequent positive reinforcement for compliance and good behavior.	Provide more intensive positive reinforcement for good behavior, such as tangible rewards, stickers, or time to do a favorite activity.	
Review rules, expectations, and routines frequently, especially after long weekends and holiday breaks.	Conference with the student daily regarding behavior.	
Keep a behavior log of students who are not complying with rules, expectations, and routines. • Note teacher actions taken to change behavior and/or consequences. • Note when and why students are referred to other school personnel.	Teach student how to self-motivate, self-monitor behavior, and change inappropriate behaviors using GAME or SODAS.	

FIGURE 5.2 Suggestions for Ways Classroom Teachers Can Implement PBIS

at this point, conducting an FBA and developing and implementing a BIP can determine whether a change in behavior occurs or a student is referred for additional assessment and possible special education placement. In the next section the definition and guidelines for FBA are explained.

FUNCTIONAL BEHAVIOR ASSESSMENT

All students will from time to time have difficulty with academic and or social behaviors. It is incumbent upon the teacher to select accommodations that will remove those contextual barriers within the classroom that are impeding the student's progress. As discussed throughout this text, educational decisions should be data based. Beginning in 1997, the Individuals with Disabilities Education Act (IDEA) required local education agencies to conduct Functional Behavior Assessments (FBA) to assist teachers with making decisions about students who may need or are receiving special education services. Originally, FBAs were used only with this select group of students when their behaviors were severe enough to warrant disciplinary action—as explained above, for students who are receiving Tier III interventions. This method is not widely nor well received by general education teachers because it is seen as too complicated, too different from established discipline routines, and too time-consuming (Larson & Maag, 1998). However, as schools adopt the use of PBIS systems, FBA is recommended at the beginning of both Tiers II and III.

FBA can be a key tool for planning and developing effective supports for all students, with and without identified disabilities. FBA is an informal assessment method useful for gathering information, determining where barriers lie within the classroom, and planning interventions. Data from FBAs promote principles of Universal Design in that they assist teachers with identifying where mismatches exist between the demands of the learning environment and the needs of the student. Once teachers understand the function of a behavior, they can redesign the learning environment to eliminate potential barriers. One strong rationale for using FBA is social validity.

Purposes of FBA

A primary purpose of a FBA is to understand the purpose of a given behavior. No matter what a teacher or school administrators do to stop unwanted behavior, the student will continue it if a powerful purpose is attached to the behavior (Larson & Maag, 1998). In fact, FBA requires that teachers accept that inappropriate behavior by students has a purpose and is appropriate in some contexts (Chandler & Dahlquist, 2006; Kerr & Nelson, 2006; Larson & Maag, 1998). For example, running on the playground and soccer field is acceptable, but running in the school's hallways is not. The first may be to get away from opponents in a game and the second to get away from a task that is too difficult or unpleasant for the student. In this example, the behaviors are the same but are not similarly appropriate in both cases.

A second purpose of FBA is to find and understand the setting events or antecedents that precede behaviors, because behavior is contextually defined (Larson & Maag, 1998). Environment determines and defines behavior for all of us—if the environment is safe, pleasant, and gives us what we want, need, or desire, we are happy and behave accordingly; if the environment is unsafe, aversive, unpleasant, or punishing, we will do whatever we can to avoid it or get away from it. So it is with children and youth in schools (Chandler & Dahlquist, 2006; Kerr & Nelson, 2006; Larson & Maag, 1998).

Guidelines for Conducting FBA

Functional Behavior Assessment is a problem-solving approach to remediating learning and social behavior problems. It differs from the traditional teaching model in that the teacher looks to the environment for the source of the problem rather than assuming the problem lies within the student. FBA follows these procedural guidelines:

1. A clear and specific description of the problem behaviors. For example, May Li hits someone each day. Identify the events, times, and circumstances that predict

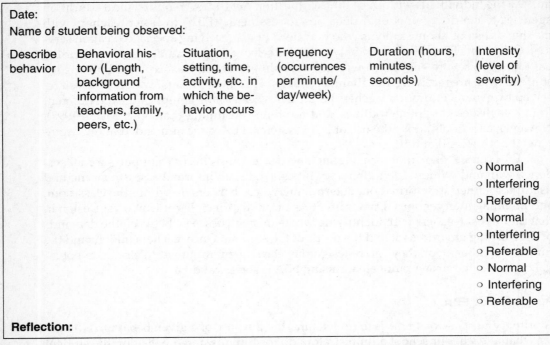

FIGURE 5.3 Positive Behavior Support and Intervention Plan: Description of Challenging Behaviors

when the behavior will occur, including the settings and times in the school day where it is evidenced. For example, May Li begins to get quiet each day about 9 a.m. She is typically talkative and participates in reading group from 8 a.m. to 9 a.m., but by 9:10, when math begins, she has hit another student and is sent to timeout. Compare these behaviors to those of peers of the same age, intelligence, and ethnicity to determine if they are significantly different from those of similar peers. Figure 5.3 provides a format for collecting such data.

2. Identify the consequences that are reinforcing or rewarding this behavior. What is maintaining the inappropriate behavior? Is the behavior to get or to avoid something (e.g., get attention or avoid a test)? What does the student gain because of this behavior? In May Li's case, when she is sent to timeout she could be avoiding the humiliation of yet another failed attempt at reading aloud in front of his classmates. Figure 5.4 provides a format for looking at the situational data collected in Figure 5.3 and analyzing this information to determine the function of the behavior.

3. Analyze the behavior and develop a hypothesis—what is reinforcing the behavior? Look for patterns in the behavior. For example, when does it occur? Are there specific times, events, people, or situations that trigger the behavior? For many students like May Li, punishment is preferable to embarrassment. Look for the function of the behavior; typically there is an academic basis. If the data support your hypothesis, design an intervention to correct the problem. For example, if the data indicated May Li was hitting to avoid math because she was unable to perform the carrying function, then your intervention would be to teach her how to carry. If correct, the intervention would terminate the inappropriate behavior.

Date:
Name of student being observed:
Identify a challenging behavior:

Situation	Behavioral characteristics	Function of the behavior
Time of day	Most likely to occur	
	Least likely to occur	
Setting	Most likely to occur	
	Least likely to occur	
Activity	Most likely to occur	
	Least likely to occur	
Other situations that trigger the behavior (changing classes, moving to the lunchroom, etc.)	Most likely to occur	
	Least likely to occur	

Reflection:

FIGURE 5.4 Positive Behavior Support and Intervention Plan: Situational and Functional Analysis

Figure 5.5 provides a format for conducting your analysis, choosing an appropriate intervention, and observing the effects of the intervention on the targeted behavior to determine if it has the desired effects. If the intervention does not have the desired effects, repeat the analysis and select another intervention.

General and special education teachers have historically used Functional Behavior Assessment differently. Special education teachers working with students who have disabilities will use FBA data to develop a Behavior Intervention Plan (BIP), a part of an Individualized Education Plan Program (IEP). This process is a part of a collaborative

Date:
Student:

Describe the behavior selected for intervention	Situation in which the behavior occurs	Choose intervention strategy: Implement and collect data on the effect of your treatment in the columns to the right	Frequency (occurrences per minute/day/week)	Duration (hours, minutes, seconds)	Intensity (level of severity)

Reflection:

FIGURE 5.5 Positive Behavior Support and Intervention Plan: Intervention Strategy

enterprise used to address the needs of students with disabilities who have a full range of problem behaviors, such as self-injury, biting, hitting, or other behaviors demonstrated by individuals with autism, mental retardation, and many developmental disabilities. Typically, teachers use FBA to address inappropriate social behaviors that can lead to suspension or other formal school action if left untreated.

General education teachers typically apply some form of functional behavior assessments for social behaviors also, but rather than using it for IEP meetings they may employ FBA as an element of a collaborative prereferral process, such as in Tier III (e.g., student support team, intervention support team, teacher support team) (Friend & Cook, 2007). Although general education teachers are not legally required to develop a formal behavior intervention plan for students without disabilities, they may use the information to generate an intervention for students who are at risk. The FBA is, therefore, a part of both general and special education teachers' assessment repertoire. When applied effectively an FBA can contribute to a reduction in false referrals and suspensions for inappropriate social behaviors and academic difficulty.

It is important to remember that many problem behaviors are often the byproduct of academic difficulty and not social skills problems at all. For example, consider a student who is not reading on grade level, who is repeatedly teased by peers when asked to read aloud. What are the student's options? School is compulsory, so what can the student do to avoid being embarrassed? Many students will choose to pick a fight or some other inappropriate behavior that will get them sent out of the room to avoid being humiliated. Teachers will usually respond to this type of repetitive inappropriate behavior with punishment. While it is true that punishment can stop unwanted behavior, can it really solve the problem? Teachers must understand the purpose of the behavior to correct it. In this example, the student could not read, which led to behaviors designed to avoid embarrassment. While it is true that punishment could stop the behavior in the short term, the underlying problem would still exist. If the student continues to have difficulty reading, it is likely that other behavioral and/or academic problems will persist. Accurately identifying the problem is the key to selecting appropriate interventions. In this case, a more appropriate choice might be reading instruction or simply having the teacher change the demands of the activity using the principles of Universal Design for Learning. Although both interventions can stop the inappropriate behavior, only one solves the problem effectively.

BEHAVIOR INTERVENTION PLANS

For educators who are working with a student who has an IEP, the BIP would be written by the IEP team, which would include the general educator and the student's family. Once a functional assessment has been completed, the team would convene to discuss a plan for intervening and changing the student's behavior. While the required elements of a BIP may vary from state to state, generally BIPs contain the following elements (Project Stay, n.d.):

- A list of student's strengths and deficits, specifically any issues that would affect targeted behavior
- Any additional information that would inform the team and impact the plan
- Detailed description of the behavior that is being targeted for change

- A statement from the FBA that describes the function of the targeted behavior
- Details of interventions previously used, including the results of how well those worked or did not work
- A measurable description of behavioral changes expected by the team, including a description of the behavior that will replace the unwanted behavior
- A description of the interventions that will be used to bring about the desired behavioral change
- A plan for assessing the effectiveness of the new intervention(s)
- A schedule for reviewing the BIP interventions, including how and when school and family will communicate
- A plan for any crisis that might arise from escalation of the student's inappropriate behaviors

The Center for Effective Collaboration and Practice (n.d.) suggests additional guidelines for BIPs. The plan should include strategies, including positive behavioral interventions and supports, program modifications, and supplementary aids or services as required to appropriately address the student's behavior. The important point here is the positive actions that can be taken to change the unwanted behavior rather than punitive actions that may stop behavior but will not make changes in behavior.

General education teachers are encouraged to consider how they might use FBAs and BIPs to solve management problems in their classrooms with students who have behavior problems but do not have an IEP. As our classrooms become more diverse, teachers are likely to have students from a variety of cultures, socioeconomic levels, and religious affiliations that have influenced each child's understanding of appropriate social behaviors and interactions with adults. Further, since all students, including those with and without IEPs, are likely to participate in special classes such as music, art, and physical education, students will work with more than one teacher whose expectations for behavior may differ from those of their primary teacher. Therefore, all teachers will need to help students understand their expectations in their classroom.

How we discipline children and youth in our schools sends powerful messages to our students. Students generally see discipline as punishment. Further, schools and teachers seldom take the time to teach problem-solving skills or strategies (Beaton, 2001). Nor do we give students the power to help other students or vent their frustrations about school environments. Beaton asked two important questions that all teachers should consider as they plan consequences for behavior in their classrooms: (1) "Do we ever step back and examine the hidden curriculum behind our disciplinary policies?" and (2) "Do we recognize what our disciplinary actions teach our young people about authority, power, and voice?" (p. 160).

In Chapter 6 we discussed the use of metacognitive and cognitive strategies to support learning of academic skills and content. These strategies can be used to teach appropriate replacement behaviors and social skills.

SOCIAL BEHAVIORS AND METACOGNITION

Constructivist and metacognitive theories provide a framework from which to understand both academic and social skills problems that lead to inappropriate classroom behaviors (e.g., Bruner, 1974; Dewey 1997a, b; Flavell, 1971, 1976, 1985; Neisser, 1967;

Piaget, 1972, 1990; Vygotsky, 1986; Vygotsky & Vygotsky, 1980). These theoretical approaches indicate individuals actively learn how to become successful in any given environment by building knowledge and skills via assimilation and accommodation of new information into previously existing schemas, thereby developing new schematic knowledge upon which the learner may act to solve problems they encounter (Huitt & Hummel, 2003).

A student's ability to make appropriate behavioral choices is heavily dependent upon prior knowledge and problem solving ability (Price & Driscoll, 1997). A comparison of students who are successful in classroom settings with unsuccessful students indicates successful learners can rely on existing schemas to interpret and react to new behavioral challenges. Many students develop social skills naturally over time. Their schema includes information regarding experiences with and exposure to a variety of social situations in and out of the classroom. They can draw upon this prior experience to solve new problems when encountered. They build a repertoire that includes perceptions of ability, attributions related to past successes and failure, strategies, and a mental problem-solving model for completing social tasks (Flavell, 1971, 1976, 1985).

Metacognitive deficiencies contribute to poor problem-solving ability. These same deficits can impair students' ability to understand how they should act in a given situation; development of plans for reaching the goal predicated on personal, task, contextual, and strategy knowledge; monitoring and modification of their thought processes related to the social problem; and evaluating situational outcomes (Flavell, 1971, 1976, 1985). Misanalysis of classroom situations and faulty attributions are common manifestations of this problem. For example, a student incorrectly thinks the other students look upon her favorably when she acts out, when in fact they only like the disruption in the class schedule. Inaccurate appraisal such as this, if not modified, can act on cumulative perceptions and lead to poor strategy choices, faulty cognitions, and the generalization of inappropriate prior experiences from the classroom to other settings (Borkowski, Carr, Rellinger, & Pressley, 1990; Flavell, 1971, 1976, 1985). You can see how some students develop behavior problems that plague them throughout their academic careers and beyond.

The ability to perform appropriately in social settings is so important that it has been noted as the defining difference in both classroom success and success after graduation. In fact, research suggests that workers who have the ability to get along with others tend to keep their jobs longer and generally become more successful. As we have learned earlier in this text, mental problem-solving models may not develop naturally or be learned at home. Unfortunately, teachers generally believe that students do learn to solve behavioral problems at home, that they learn how to make appropriate behavioral choices from their parents or through vicarious encounters in schools. As we have seen, though, parental interactions are not always of the type necessary to teach these skills, and many students for differing reasons do not learn vicariously.

Metacognitive and Cognitive Strategies for Teaching Social Skills

Misperceptions by teachers and the lack of direct social skills instruction in classrooms often culminate in behavior management difficulties. The problem is exacerbated at schools where the typical classroom management model is based on punishment and predicated upon the assumption that students know how to act but choose not to act that way. When teachers try to effect changes in student behavior with classroom management plans based on older traditional models, meaningful change seldom occurs. For example, students in elementary schools must pull out sticks for talking or a student in high school may fail because she did not follow the directions. In both of these cases, as with the teachers, it is being assumed that the child knew what to do but chose not to do it because he or she was unmotivated. As Richard Lavoie (1989) pointed out in his video *F.A.T. City: How Difficult Can This Be?*, in many instances when an individual acts inappropriately he does not know what he did wrong. His point is that the individual will have misidentified or misunderstood the problem, directions, or stimulus; it has nothing to do with motivation. If the problem is misidentified, finding the appropriate tool or solution to solve it is all but impossible.

Earlier in this text, we discussed that metacognitive strategies are useful for teaching students how to solve academic problems. Metacognitive strategies are also appropriate for teaching students how to solve their social skills problems. Both GAME and SODAS strategies are mnemonic devices for remembering the hierarchical steps of a problem-solving process. Students learn to identify the problem, make appropriate choices from among a variety of cognitive strategies, monitor the progress of the implementation of these strategies, and evaluate outcomes. GAME (Rogers & Cennamo, 1997) is designed to increase student awareness of self-regulation skills, select actions and strategies to change the problem behavior, and monitor and evaluate their progress to implementation of new behaviors. Below is a example of how a teacher might present the strategy to a student.

- *G*—In the *GOALS* section, you will think about your behavior and how you might behave differently when faced with a challenge or difficult situation. Ask yourself the following questions. What are you being asked to do? Think about what might keep you from being successful. (Note: Teachers will need to teach, model, prompt, and monitor this process.)
- *A*—In the *ACTION* section, you will decide about an action you need to take to meet your goals. What activities, strategies, or accommodations will you use to facilitate your success? (Teachers will need to teach students how to select appropriate strategies and teach those strategies to all students, so that they will know what to select when the need arises.)
- *M*—In the *MONITOR* section, you monitor your learning and reflect on whether your motivational, learning, and management strategies are leading toward goal attainment. (Teachers may need to support students when they first begin this process by prompting the monitor process.)
- *E*—In the *EVALUATE* section, you evaluate your learning and reflect on whether your strategies were successful. Can you use the same strategies in similar settings or situations?

When anyone, whether a teacher or a student, first begins to develop his or her metacognitive ability, a framework for the process can be helpful. The collaborative problem-solving strategy SODAS, outlined here, can be used by groups and individuals (such as teachers, students, and families) to develop a plan, solve a problem, or make a decision. SODAS asks the user to describe the situation, develop options, and state the disadvantages and advantages of each option. In the final step of the strategy the user selects the option with the most advantages and the least disadvantages. The letters of this mnemonic device are as follows:

Situation: Describe the problem or situation you are trying to figure out.

Options: Describe three different strategies or suggestions you can use to solve the problem you have described.

Disadvantages: are things you don't like about the options you have identified.
  • Tell at least two disadvantages for each of the options you identified.

Advantages: are things you like about the options you have identified.
  • Tell at least two advantages for each of the options you identified.

Survey the results:
  • Remember to *monitor* your progress toward the goal.
  • If the solution you chose is not working, *modify* by trying one of your other options.

It is important to remember that when students first use GAME or SODAS as well as other strategies, teachers should schedule conferences to model how to reflect and evaluate their progress. In a follow-up conference the teacher may help the students

Social Skills		
LISTEN	Bauwens & Hourcade (1989)	**L**ook. **I**dle your motor. **S**it up straight. **T**urn to me. **E**ngage your brain. **N**ow.
FAST: An interpersonal problem-solving strategy	Vaughn & Bos (2009)	**F**reeze and think! **A**lternatives? **S**olution evaluation. **T**ry it!
SLANT (a starter strategy for class participation)	Ellis (1989)	**S**it up. **L**ean forward. **A**ctivate your thinking. **N**ame key information. **T**rack the talker.
SCORE (for working in cooperative groups)	Vernon, Schumaker, & Deshler (1993)	**S**hare ideas. **C**ompliment others. **O**ffer help or encouragement. **R**ecommend changes nicely. **E**xercise self-control.

FIGURE 5.6 Examples of Mnemonic Strategies for Social Skills

evaluate their use of the strategies or the outcomes of their solutions by reminding students that they should always *evaluate* the work they did by asking and answering the following questions:

1. Did you reach your goal?
2. Are there any other situations where you can use the SODA's strategy to help you solve a problem?
3. Did you make a written list of your goals?
4. Did you congratulate yourself for doing a good job?

Figure 5.6 provides examples of strategies students may select. Teaching students how to solve problems and change their inappropriate behavior will help them learn which appropriate behaviors to use in both academic and social settings.

Summary

Bigelow, Harvey, Karp, and Miller (2001) noted that "Teachers can create classrooms that are places of hope, where students and teachers gain glimpses of the kind of society we could live in and where students learn the academic and critical skills needed to make it a reality" (p. 2). They continue: "We can teach for the society we live in, or teach for the one we want to see" (p. 4). In this chapter we have discussed ways for teachers to create those classrooms where hope lives and students are taught not just academic skills but skills that will serve them and all of us when they leave schools. Using PBIS and teaching problem-solving strategies are two research-based interventions that can teach students how our society expects them to behave and treat one another, as well as how to monitor and change their own behavior. Teachers know that classrooms with a climate where everyone is respected and treated in a positive way are classrooms where learning is able to happen.

References

Alver, S., & Heward, W. (1996). "Gotcha!": Twenty-five behavior traps guaranteed to extend our students' academic and social skills. *Intervention in School and Clinic, 31*(5), 285–289.

Archer, A. (1994). *Using peer partners*. Unpublished handout. Presentation at Annual Council for Learning Disabilities Conference on Learning Disabilities, Chicago.

Bauwens, J., & Hourcade, J. J. (1998). Hey, would you just LISTEN. *Teaching Exceptional Children, 21*(4), 61.

Beaton, J. H. (2001). Rethinking discipline. *Rethinking our classrooms: Teaching for equity and justice* (Volume 2), 160–162.

Bigelow, B., Harvey, B., Karp, S., & Miller, L. (Eds.) (2001). *Introduction. Teaching for equity and justice: Rethinking our classrooms, Volume 2*. Williston, VT: Rethinking Schools.

Borkowski, J. G., Carr, M., Rellinger, L., & Pressley, M. (1990). Self-regulated cognition: Interdependence of metacognition, attributions and self-esteem. In B. J. Jones & L. Idol (Eds.), *Dimensions of thinking and cognitive instruction* (pp. 53–92). Hillsdale, NJ: Lawrence Erlbaum Associates.

Brown, M., Paulsen, K., & Higgins, K. (2003). 20 ways to remove environmental barriers to student learning. *Intervention in School and Clinic, 39*(2), 109–112.

Bruner, J. (1974). *Toward a theory of instruction*. Cambridge, MA: Harvard University Press.

Center for Effective Collaboration and Practice. (n.d.). *Behavior planning meetings: Information for families*. Washington, DC: Author. Retrieved on March 22, 2008, from http://cecp.air.org/familybriefs/docs/BEHAVIORALMEETINGS.pdf

Chandler, L. K., & Dahlquist, C. M. (2006). *Functional Assessment: Strategies to prevent and remediate challenging behavior in school settings* (2nd ed.). Upper Saddle River, NJ: Merrill/Pearson Education.

Church, K., Gottschalk, C., & Leddy, J. (2003). 20 ways to enhance social and friendship skills. *Intervention in School and Clinic, 31*(5), 307–310.

Dewey, J. (1997a). *Experience and education.* New York: MacMillan.

Dewey, J. (1997b). *How we think.* New York: Dover.

Ellis, E. S. (1989). A metacognitive intervention for increasing class participation. *Learning Disabilities Focus, 5*(1), 36–46.

Flavell, J. H. (1971). First discussant's comments: What is memory development the development of? *Human Development, 14,* 272–278.

Flavell, J. H. (1976). Metacognitive aspects of problem solving. In L. B. Resnick (Ed.), *The nature of intelligence.* Hillsdale, NJ: Lawrence Erlbaum Associates.

Flavell, J. H. (1985). *Cognitive development* (2nd ed.). Upper Saddle River, NJ: Prentice Hall.

Friend, M., & Cook, L. (2007). *Interactions: Collaborative skills for school professionals* (5th ed.). Boston: Allyn & Bacon.

Gable, R. A., Hester, P. H., Rock, M. L., & Hughes, K. G. (2009). Back to basics: Rules, praise, ignoring, and reprimands revisited. *Intervention in School and Clinic, 44*(4), 196–205.

Huitt, W., & Hummel, J. (2003). Piaget's theory of cognitive development. *Educational Psychology Interactive.* Valdosta, GA: Valdosta State University. Retrieved July 1, 2005, from http://chiron.valdosta.edu/whuitt/col/cogsys/piaget.html

Kerr, M. M., & Nelson, C. M. (2006). *Strategies for addressing behavior problems in the classroom.* Upper Saddle River, NJ: Merrill/Pearson Education.

Larson, P. J., & Maag, J. W. (1998). Applying Functional Assessment in general education classrooms. *Intervention in School and Clinic, 19*(6), 338–349.

Lavioe, R. (1989). *How difficult can this be?: The F.A.T. City Workshop.* Washington, DC: Public Broadcasting Company.

LD Online. (1999). *Positive behavioral interventions and supports.* Author. Retrieved November 3, 2007, from http://www.ldonline.org/article/6035.

Maag, J. (2000). Managing resistance. *Intervention in School and Clinic, 35,* 131–140.

Neisser, U. (1967) *Cognitive psychology.* New York: Appleton-Century.

Obenchain, K., & Abernathy, T. (2003). 20 ways to build community and empower students. *Intervention in School and Clinic, 39*(1), 55–60.

OSEP Technical Assistance Center on Positive Behavior Intervention and Supports. (2007). *What is school-wide positive behavioral interventions & supports?* Retrieved on October 25, 2007, from http://www.pbis.org

Piaget, J. (1972). *The psychology of the child.* New York: Basic Books.

Piaget, J. (1990). *The child's conception of the world.* New York: Littlefield Adams.

Price, E., & Driscoll, M. (1997). An inquiry into the spontaneous transfer of problem-solving skill. *Contemporary Educational Psychology 22,* 472–494.

Project Stay. (n.d.). *Behavior intervention plan.* Topeka, KS: Author. Retrieved on October 25, 2007, from http://projectstay.com/pdf/BehaviorInterventionPlan.pdf

Rogers, C., & Cennamo, K. (1997). *The GAME strategy.* Unpublished course materials from FCD 1004: Virginia Tech Cyber Core Course.

Safran, S., & Oswald, K. (2003). Positive behavior supports: Can schools reshape disciplinary practices? *Exceptional Children, 69*(3), 361–373.

Sandomierski, T., Kincaid, D., & Algozzine, B. (2007). *Response to Intervention and positive behavior support: Brothers from different mothers or sisters with different misters?* OSEP Technical Assistance Center on Positive Behavior Intervention and Supports. Retrieved on January 7, 2008, from http://www.pbis.org/main.htm

Turnbull, A., Edmonson, H., Griggs, P., Wickham, D., Sailor, W., Freeman, R., Guess, D., Lassen, S., McCart, A., Park, J., Riffel, L., Turnbull, R., & Warren, J. (2002). *Exceptional Children, 68*(3), 377–402.

Vaughn, S., & Bos, C. S. (2009). Strategies for teaching students with learning and behavior problems. Upper Saddle River, NJ: Pearson.

Vernon, D. S., Schumaker, J. B. & Deshler, D. D., (1993), *The SCORE Skills: Social skills for cooperative groups.* Lawrence, KS: Edge Enterprises.

Vygotsky, L. (1986). *Thought and language.* Boston: MIT Press.

Vygotsky, L., & Vygotsky, S. (1980). *Mind in society: The development of higher psychological processes.* Cambridge, MA: Harvard University Press.

Chapter 6

A Metacognitive Model for Teaching and Learning

After reading this chapter, you will be able to:

1. Explain the importance of metacognitive skills and knowledge to academic success

2. Relate the role of metacognition in the formation and mediation of attributions, efficacious beliefs, motivation, and strategy use

3. Describe how teachers can utilize their understanding of metacognitive knowledge, skills, and strategies to create independent learners

4. Discuss methods for integrating metacognitive and cognitive strategies instruction into the curriculum

5. Compare and contrast instructional methods and materials in a metacognitive framework for learning with those of a traditional teaching model

A RATIONALE FOR UNDERSTANDING STUDENT AND TEACHER ACADEMIC DIFFICULTIES

Some suggest that although Americans are more highly educated than ever before, they are not necessarily *better* educated. Thus, "The Nation's Report Card," compiled by the National Assessment of Educational Progress (NAEP, 1996, 2005), provides evidence that many students who graduate from high school lack the basic academic literacy skills necessary to successfully complete college. This trend has not changed in any meaningful way since 1971 (U.S. Office of Educational Research and Instruction [OERI], 2002). Logan (1976) concluded that most students, including both high school and college, scored low in critical thinking. Research conducted by Keeley, Browne, and Kreutzer (1982) found that 40% to 60% of the participating seniors, when asked to read a passage and identify an example of a flaw in logic, ambiguity, or misuse of data, could not do so even when the passage contained several such errors. In 1996, NAEP data indicated that only 39% of the 17-year-old students assessed could find, understand, summarize, and explain relatively complicated information they read, while only 6% could synthesize and learn from specialized reading material.

The percentage of students graduating high school who write adequately is even lower, at 31% (NAEP, 1996), with only 2% categorized as writing well. Research further indicates that students can start an assignment but only about 83% have the skills and knowledge to finish (NAEP, 1996). A report issued by the U.S. Department of Education in March of 2002 suggests that although there have been improvements in reading and writing scores, they have not been sustainable. The long-term trend in assessment data gathered by NAEP indicates little meaningful change in students' basic reading and writing abilities since 1971 (OERI, 2002). Concerns regarding students' poor academic performance is not, however, the exclusive domain of educators. Leaders of business and industry are also noting that students graduating from our nation's schools are not adequately prepared to meet their employment needs. Specifically, they complain that many of their employees have great difficulty working independently, solving complex problems, thinking critically, and making decisions in unstructured situations (Rojewski, Schell, Reybold, & Evanciew, 2004).

Although many people have a proprietary interest in effecting student learning, educators are ultimately responsible for students' educational outcomes. To improve student learning, teachers must answer two key questions. The first and perhaps most important question requires us to define or establish the cause of the problem: Do we attribute ineffectual student outcomes to the educational system, the classroom teacher, or the student? Successfully identifying the problem leads to the next question: How do we use this knowledge to inform teaching?

To address these questions, we will utilize a metacognitive framework for learning in the belief that it provides a clearer understanding of the problems associated with student learning. This chapter consists of three sections (1) the relationship between metacognition and learning, (2) a metacognitive framework for learning, and (3) metacognition in the classroom.

In the following case study, Akeem and his teacher are engaged in a typical classroom scenario. Follow along as Akeem attempts to learn the science content his teacher is presenting. What teaching and learning strategies are Akeem and his teacher employing to facilitate learning?

Akeem, an 11th-grade student, sits attentively in his science class trying to follow the teacher's lecture on the effects of secondhand cigarette smoke on the human body. The teacher is using the analogy of a person trapped in a burning building, forced to inhale smoke for an extended period. The smoke from both the fire and the cigarette contain many harmful chemical agents—carcinogens and toxins. To illustrate her point, the teacher asks the class to recall an article she read to them on the health problems reported by firefighters and volunteers working to rescue survivors after the terrorist attack on the World Trade Center.

Akeem recalls the article, the subsequent discussion in class, and the chapter in his science textbook he studied the night before on the relevance of environmental toxins to public safety. He remembers that during the class discussion someone mentioned many workers were complaining of respiratory problems following the attack. Health officials believed these were the result of inhaling smoke and fumes from the burning buildings.

Akeem struggles to make the connection to the teacher's analogy. To his dismay, he realizes that he did not understand what he had read in the text, making listening to the discussion especially important. He tries to increase his concentration on the teacher's explanation, but he is just not interested. Further impairing his attempts to concentrate are the two students behind him whispering about college entrance exams on Saturday. The teacher's use of the cigarette-smoking analogy is acting as a distraction also; it reminds him of an acquaintance's continued attempts to get him to smoke. He worries that if he does not smoke he will be excluded from future social activities with this person and the popular group he represents; perhaps they will not mind if he chooses not to smoke and include him anyway. Thinking about what the teacher is discussing becomes even more difficult as he remembers the funeral he attended last summer. Akeem's uncle died of cancer. Akeem is worried that the chemicals used at the factory where his uncle worked caused his death. He is concerned for other family members who are still working and living near there.

Akeem decides to redouble his efforts to concentrate; he is finally able to filter out all of the distractions. He slowly realizes that maybe his mother's concerns and the conflicting feelings surrounding his new friends may be useful in understanding the teacher's lecture if he focuses his attention specifically on the two experiences as they relate to toxins in the environment. The teacher interrupts his insight by announcing a pop quiz. Akeem experiences a sinking feeling in the pit of his stomach: He knows that he did not understand the lesson, making it unlikely he will perform well on the quiz. His average for the course will undoubtedly fall to a D. He wonders if he will have the grades necessary to gain acceptance to the college he wants to attend.

If we were to analyze this scenario utilizing a metacognitive framework for learning, we would see that the student and teacher are both using metacognitive strategies to facilitate learning. The thoughts and feelings experienced by Akeem as he attempts to direct his own learning are metacognitive in nature; for example, when he acknowledges that he is not interested in the topic under discussion, when he recognizes he does not understand the material he read in the textbook or the class discussion, he is exhibiting metacognitive skill in that he is monitoring his thinking relative to the cognitive task before him. Akeem's conscious attempts to modify his thinking by blocking out distractions that are interfering with his ability to concentrate are also metacognitive, as is his plan to use his memories of past events to inform his learning. Many students, even ambitious ones, do not share Akeem's metacognitive ability (Ediger, 2005).

The teacher in the vignette is also utilizing metacognitive strategies as tools to facilitate student learning. She gives the students several examples of instances where toxins in the environment had a detrimental effect on the health of the public. She tries to establish a relationship between secondhand smoke and the potential threat of environmental toxins, issued from a variety of sources, to public safety. Metacognitively, she knows her efforts to make meaningful connections will enhance understanding and recall for most students.

Today, however, her efforts have met with mixed results. Although Akeem has begun to understand her point, it is too late for him to use his newly emerging understanding on the quiz. Research tells us her success as a teacher and Akeem's success as a student might improve if she taught the lesson using both cognitive and metacognitive strategies. How can the teacher present the information in a way that is more likely to facilitate students' understanding and recall of the concepts?

It is a widespread misperception that effort alone can improve student outcomes. Thus, it is commonly suggested that if the teacher and/or student only worked harder, we could expect a different outcome. Could it be that both teacher and student are not trying hard enough? Research suggests that simply working harder is not the answer to improving outcomes in either case. While effort is necessary to learn, effort alone is not sufficient to ensure academic success. It is only when effort is combined with the appropriate tool or cognitive strategy that an improved outcome can be expected. Unfortunately, because of underlying deficits in metacognitive knowledge and skills, teachers and students often do not choose the most appropriate tools, or if they do, they tend to use them inefficiently. As we will discuss later in this chapter, each must learn to use both metacognitive and cognitive strategies to ensure academic success. This instructional approach, more commonly referred to as teaching process and content, requires that teachers understand the process by which students learn and then use that metacognitive knowledge to plan in a way that will enable students to learn academic content.

To illustrate, let us reconsider Akeem's situation. Suppose the teacher had introduced the lesson to the class by pointing out the utility of having a PLAN (see Figure 6.1) for learning the content. She models the PLAN metacognitive framework for learning, demonstrating how students can use a graphic organizer as a tool for making abstract concepts and ideas more concrete. The graphic organizer depicts visually how the new information relates to students' prior knowledge, real-life situations, class discussions, articles they read, and what is in their textbook. Would Akeem have grasped the concepts more quickly if his teacher had taught the lesson using this instructional model? The research suggests he might have.

The metacognitive method of teaching process and content differs from methods generally adopted by teachers in that the metacognitive strategies are taught before the cognitive strategies. The metacognitive strategy then serves as a framework that supports student learning, structuring the learning process and directing tool use. In other words, metacognitive knowledge regulates and guides academic problem solving. As an instructional methodology, a metacognitive framework for learning is not widely utilized by classroom teachers. This is troubling, since metacognitive knowledge and skills are necessary components of academic literacy (Baker, 1989; Markman, 1985; Otero & Campanario, 1990; Randi, Grigorenko, & Sternberg, 2005; Spencer & Logan, 2005; Weaver, 1995).

Academic literacy refers to the knowledge, skills, and strategies that students need to ensure success across reading, writing, listening, studying, and critical-thinking

This metacognitive PLAN provides a framework from which various process options are used to access content:
 	
P Pinpoint your goal
  Precisely identify
    content/social/general objective
Picture success
Pursue confidently
L Look at your options
  List strategy or tool options
  Let experience guide choices
A Analyze progress
  Adjust if necessary
  Admit if not working & pick
  again
N Note results, refer to your goal
  Now think of other areas where this
  strategy could be used
  Note your success, attribute to appropriateness of process choice. Congratulate yourself: good choice!
	Goal
	• Science/math
	• Social studies/history
	• Music/art/theater
	• Language arts
	• Classroom management
	• Effective instruction
	
	Process Options: Teacher
	• Universal Design for Learning
	• Project-based learning
	• Strategies instruction
	• Collaboration
	
	Process Options: Student
	• Graphic organizers
	• Learning strategies
	• Social skills strategies
	• Technology

FIGURE 6.1 Metacognitive Framework for Learning

Source: Spencer, S. (2009). Unpublished course material. Center for Pedagogy, Winthrop University.

processes (Nist, 1993). For example, research indicates that children who are fluent readers display metacognition knowledge and skills relative to reading, viewing it as a problem-solving activity, and employ a variety of strategies while reading (Brenna, 1995; Randi et al., 2005). In practical terms, this means metacognitive knowledge and skills include and direct knowledge of strategies for planning one's reading and writing activities, monitoring comprehension or writing, rereading if necessary, taking notes when studying, proofreading written drafts, and modifying strategy use to improve outcomes. This is a prototypical example of how successful students learn: They learn by applying metacognitive knowledge and skills to learning academic content. Conversely, research suggests that students who are not successful lack the prerequisite metacognitive knowledge and skills necessary to become independent learners (e.g., Borkowski Carr, Rellinger, & Pressley, 1990; Borkowski & Muthukrishna, 1992; Brown, 1987; Gaskins & Elliot, 1991; Randi et al., 2005).

Earlier in this chapter, we asked that you consider two questions as you read: Why are students not learning, and what is causing the problem? You are no doubt beginning to hypothesize that many of the academic problems experienced by students in our schools are metacognitive in nature. To assist you in fully addressing these questions, the following section will provide additional insight into the construct of metacognition and its educational implications for student learning and classroom practice.

THE RELATIONSHIP BETWEEN METACOGNITION AND LEARNING

Defining Metacognition

When asked to define metacognition, most teachers and teacher candidates quickly reply that it is "thinking about thinking." When asked what that means, however, few have an answer. Defining metacognition and understanding the role it plays in learning may not be simple; however, metacognitive ability may be one of the most important factors underlying student and teacher success.

Over 30 years ago, Flavell (1971) introduced the concept of metacognition. His theory relied heavily upon constructivism; that is, what we remember are meaningfully organized events, or schemas (Flavell, 1985). As has the work of Piaget, contemporary research in cognitive psychology and information processing has contributed substantially to the base of research from which metacognitive theory has grown (e.g., Atkinson & Shiffrin, 1968; Brown, 1987; Belmont & Butterfield, 1969; Newell, Shaw, & Simon, 1958).

Flavell (1971) believed metacognition described a person's conscious ability to manage and monitor the input, storage, search, and retrieval of the contents of his or her memory, positing that metacognition functions to both monitor and regulate cognitive actions related to problem solving or goal attainment (Flavell, 1976). Drawing on the work of Piaget, he theorized that metacognitive ability begins in children at about age 6 or 7, emerging gradually in a stage-wise progression as the result of environmental affordances and maturation. As metacognitive knowledge and skills develop, the child learns to identify situations in which information deemed as potentially useful at some point in the future is consciously and purposefully stored. The child further learns to conduct deliberate, systematic searches to update this information, thereby maintaining a store of current data that are available for retrieval and application when necessary. Flavell (1976) theorized:

> Assuming cognitive development progresses typically, by adolescence children will
> have experienced six cognitive-developmental trends: (a) increases in information-
> processing capacity, (b) increases in domain-specific knowledge, (c) concrete and for-
> mal operations, (d) the ability to engage in quantitative thinking, (e) the acquisition
> of metacognitive knowledge and experiences, and (g) improvement of the cognitive
> competencies the child already possesses. (p. 1003)

He further suggested that it is during the concrete operations stage of cognitive development that the abilities of the adolescent begin to differentiate from those of the child. It is during this 7- to 11-year period that the child develops the ability to put thoughts into classes, seriating them and relating them to corresponding experiences, thoughts, and ideas—operations referred to as first-order operations or concrete operations. Flavell, Miller, and Miller (2002) suggested that:

> Metacognitively sophisticated children . . . are like busy executives, analyzing new
> problems, judging how far they are from the goal, allocating attention, selecting a
> strategy, attempting a solution, monitoring the success or failure of current perform-
> ance, and deciding whether to change to a different strategy. (p. 393)

The transformation from concrete to formal operations is complete when the child begins to formulate thoughts as propositions and then proceeds to operate further upon them, making various kinds of logical connections between them (implications, causality, junction, disjunction, etc.). Formal operations, then, are really second-order thoughts intentionally performed upon the results of prior cognitive (first order) thoughts. For example, if cognitive thoughts involve perceiving, understanding, and remembering, then metacognitive thoughts involve thinking about one's own perceiving, understanding, and remembering. As mentioned earlier, we commonly refer to this process as "thinking about thinking."

From a developmental perspective then, the research concerning metacognition indicates that the "meta" basic competencies are available to individuals from an early age (Schneider, 1998). The rate at which metacognitive knowledge and ability develops and the degree of proficiency attained vary by individual, dependent on factors such as genetics, environment, and experience. In this chapter, the focus will be on experience, in particular the effects of educational experience on metacognitive development.

HOW DOES ONE ACQUIRE METACOGNITIVE KNOWLEDGE?

Flavell (1979) suggested that metacognitive knowledge develops as a result of an individual's understanding of the learning process and the variables that affect learning. This knowledge is specific to understanding oneself as a learner, general knowledge of the learning process, and the ability to consciously use that knowledge (Flavell, Green, & Flavell, 1995). Metacognitive knowledge consists of (a) personal knowledge regarding one's own and others' thinking, (b) task knowledge requiring that different types of tasks demand different types of cognitive abilities, (c) strategy knowledge wherein one is aware that cognitive and metacognitive strategies can enhance learning and performance, and (d) an understanding that contextual or environmental knowledge can affect cognitive ability. As you read, note how the various components that make up metacognitive knowledge overlap; they are interactive and interdependent.

Personal Knowledge

Personal knowledge consists of the beliefs or knowledge an individual has regarding the process of thinking (Flavell, 1979). One can have thoughts and feelings about oneself as a learner, or make comparisons between people or groups as learners, or one can have thoughts regarding how people process information in general. The knowledge one has about oneself as a learner provides insight into personal variables that influence performance. It involves accessing information stored in long-term memory, such as recognizing what makes specific tasks easy or difficult for you, and knowledge of cognitive strategies and metacognitive strategies necessary to accomplishing those tasks. For example, we can see our case-study student Akeem demonstrating metacognitive insight. He recognizes that his inability to concentrate on the teacher's lecture is due to competing thoughts about family and friends, and he subsequently attempts to block out these thoughts. He is demonstrating personal knowledge of himself as a learner by choosing strategies to offset these factors based on this metacognitive knowledge. Knowledge of oneself as a learner develops over time. It differentiates successful students from those who face academic failure (Gaskins & Elliot, 1991).

Just as students use personal knowledge of themselves to facilitate their learning, teachers must utilize their personal metacognitive knowledge regarding how people learn in general and how student learning can vary individually and across classes if they are to ensure successful student outcomes. Consider once again the case study of Akeem. His teacher is demonstrating metacognitive ability when, recognizing that the new concepts she is introducing are difficult to comprehend, she plans to use strategies that will facilitate learning. Her plan involves using a strategy in which students relate the new information she is presenting on the effects of secondhand cigarette smoke on the human body to concepts she had previously taught; that is, the smoke-associated respiratory problems of firefighters working during the terrorist attacks on the World Trade Center. She knows that when students associate new concepts with those they have previously learned, it is easier for them to assimilate, recall, and apply new information in the future to other settings with similar task demands.

This teacher's ability to make effective strategy choices is the result of the additive effect of reflecting on how her individual students and/or groups of students learn. Flavell (1979) would have categorized the type of metacognitive knowledge exhibited by Akeem's teacher as an "understanding of the learning game." As for students, metacognitive insight such as this develops over time, via observational, experiential, and affective interactions with task, context, and strategy variables (Flavell, 1979).

Strategies Knowledge

Strategies knowledge categorically contains an individual's awareness and understanding of the mental tools available to undertake metacognitive and cognitive tasks. Both kinds of strategic knowledge are important because they positively correlate with increases in academic performance and motivational beliefs and may compensate for lack of content knowledge (Paris & Winograd, 1990). Strategic knowledge and skills can differentiate good students from those who are at risk for academic failure. Flavell (1979) made a qualified distinction between cognitive and metacognitive strategies:

> The main function of a cognitive strategy is to help you achieve the goal of whatever cognitive enterprise you are engaged in. In contrast, the main function of a metacognitive strategy is to provide you with information about the enterprise or your progress in it. (p. 106)

Cognitive strategies are the worker bees of the mind: They perform the intellectual work decided on by the metacognitive bosses. Once automatized, these strategies are referred to as skills. Examples of cognitive skills include rehearsing, inferring, comparing, predicting, and analyzing. As we mentioned earlier, although cognitive skills are important, teaching must emphasize metacognitive skills because, contrary to popular belief, while cognitive strategies are necessary, they are not sufficient to ensure learning (Sternberg, 1986a, 1986b). Table 6.1 provides suggestions for coaching students to think metacognitively. Teaching these skills is important because without the metacognitive boss skills, the cognitive strategies would lie inert in long-term memory, much as books in a library lie dormant until a reader acts upon the stored information (i.e., opens a book and reads it) to create new knowledge.

Cognitive strategies are intended only to provide students with a tool for understanding the hierarchical, stepwise order in which to perform a particular task (i.e., a means to an end); they alone do not give students the skills they need to be successful if taught independent of the metacognitive strategies (Spencer & Logan, 2005). Flavell (1979) explained the relationship as follows: "cognitive strategies are invoked to make cognitive progress, metacognitive strategies to monitor it." If there are to be any long-term benefits, cognitive strategies instruction must depend, at least in part, on training at both the metacognitive and the cognitive levels, otherwise they will sit idle in the library of one's mind.

TABLE 6.1 Cognitive Coaching

Questions to Regulate Thinking and Retrain Faulty Attributions

In your role as thinking coach, consider providing questions to prompt or guide student thinking and facilitate metacognitive development. Providing feedback to students is critical. Teach students to ask questions such as these to retrain faulty attributions, increase efficacious beliefs, motivate students to engage in learning, and promote the development of critical-thinking skills in students:

- Did I identify a goal?
- If I did not correctly identify the goal, what could I do differently to make sure I correctly identify the goal next time?
- What was my plan for successfully completing the assignment?
- Did I choose a strategy that allowed me to meet my goal? If I answered yes, where could I use this strategy with success for other assignments?
- If the strategy I chose did not work, can I identify the reasons why?
- Taking the reasons why the strategy did not work into consideration, what other strategies would have been more appropriate?
- Did I remember to monitor my progress using the strategy I chose? If yes, how did I do this? If no, how could I have done this?
- Did I remember to toss the strategy out and choose again if the strategy was not working?
- Did I remember that frustration or lack of success means that I need to toss out the tool I am using and choose again?
- Did I remember to ask for help if I wanted it?
- Did I set guidelines to determine whether I was making progressing toward my goal?
- If I was not making progress toward my goal, did I remember to make a modification to my original plan and chose another strategy? How can I remind myself to do this next time?
- Did I remember to evaluate the effectiveness of my choices to determine if this approach was successful?
- If I was successful, did I remember to remind myself my success is due to my appropriate choice of strategies or tools to get the job done?
- If I was not successful the first time, did I remind myself it is because I did not choose the appropriate tool, that all I had to do was simply choose again until I found the right one for the job?
- What did I like or not like about using the strategy?
- Is there another subject or type of assignment where you could use this strategy successfully?

Source: Spencer, S. (2009). Unpublished course material. Center for Pedagogy, Winthrop University.

Schools have included cognitive strategies instruction in their curriculum for years, but traditionally it has failed to ensure acquisition and generalization of content knowledge (Spencer & Logan, 2005). You may recall hearing students remarking, "I do not know how to do this . . ." when, in fact, the strategies or tools necessary to complete the assignment independently are within sight lying at the learning center or clearly posted on the classroom wall.

Now consider how similar this situation is to the classroom teacher who laments, "I do not know how to teach this child," when books of cognitive strategies lie within grasp on the bookshelf gathering dust, a forgotten remnant from the last professional development workshop. Students and teachers alike often have no idea how to proceed, even if the requisite tools are within their reach. In both cases, they have not acquired the metacognitive skills needed to perform a cognitive task. Everyone needs metacognitive and cognitive strategy knowledge. It enables us to regulate the flow of cognitive information and exert active control over the thought processes involved in learning (Borkowski, Carr, & Pressely, 1987; Paris & Winograd, 1990).

Metacognitive knowledge underlies students' and teachers' understanding that success, both academic and social, is dependent upon conscious, effortful behavior directed toward monitoring and modifying the variables affecting learning (Borkowski et al., 1990; Carr & Jessup, 1997; Sternberg, 1986a, 1986b). It is, therefore, of the utmost importance to understand how to develop and apply metacognitive knowledge.

As an example of how educators can develop metacognitive and cognitive knowledge in their classrooms, refer to the scenario in the previous section in which Akeem's teacher revised her teaching to include the PLAN metacognitive framework for learning (see Figure 6.1) to teach her students how to learn academic content. PLAN supports the development and application of metacognitive knowledge in that it teaches students and teachers how to plan, monitor, modify, and evaluate their learning and teaching. For example, Akeem's teacher demonstrated how students could more effectively learn the new content if they used a graphic organizer to make abstract concepts and ideas more concrete. However, the graphic organizer is but one of many cognitive strategies available. Student must learn that there are factors other than personal knowledge that influence one's strategy choices, one of which is task knowledge.

Task Knowledge

Task knowledge is metacognitive knowledge applied by learners to solve specific problems. Knowledge of task variables includes knowledge about the nature of the task as well as the type of processing demands it will place on the individual. Constructivist and metacognitive theory provide a framework from which to explain how task knowledge is developed and applied in educational contexts (e.g., Bruner, 1974; Dewey 1997a, 1997b; Flavell, 1971, 1976, 1985; Neisser, 1967; Piaget, 1972, 1990; Vygotsky, 1986; Vygotsky & Vygotsky, 1980).

These theoretical approaches indicate that we actively construct task knowledge and skills via assimilation and accommodation of new information into previously existing schemas, thereby developing new task-general and task-specific knowledge upon which we may act to solve task-related problems (Huitt & Hummel, 2003). For example, over time a student develops task knowledge relative to homework in general, math homework in particular, and more specifically math homework involving fractions in Mr. Pacheco's class, etc.

Task-associated knowledge is heavily dependent upon a metacognitive model for problem solving and prior knowledge (Price & Driscoll, 1997). A comparison of successful learners with unsuccessful learners indicates successful learners use this mental model to interpret and react to new tasks based on existing schemas. Considering that a learner's metacognitive knowledge and problem-solving ability can grow with each new experience, he or she can over time become more adept at solving academic task-related problems with each assignment, each class, and each classroom activity.

   The quality of students' individual and collective experiences with academic tasks can affect their metacognitive development and may account for the difference between successful and unsuccessful learners' ability to work independently (Flavell, 1971, 1976, 1985; Piaget, 1990). If students inaccurately interpret or do not understand task demands (i.e., the assignment), for example, they are unlikely to select appropriate strategies to complete that task successfully (Flavell, 1971, 1976, 1985; Piaget, 1990). Over time, successful learners develop more complex schema in a particular subject area, whereas unsuccessful learners over time fall behind, become frustrated, and end up being dependent on others to explain the tasks. Successful learners' schemata include information regarding experiences with the subject, including perceptions of ability, attributions related to past successes and failure, strategy knowledge, and a metacognitive problem-solving model for completing the task (Flavell, 1971, 1976, 1985). Unsuccessful learners' schemata, by comparison, do not include such information. These learners are not adept at metacognitive self-appraisal and do not understand why they cannot learn. They often falsely attribute their inability to learn to a lack of intelligence or something else outside of their control.

   Consider again our case-study student Akeem's interpretation of the situation in his science class as he heard the teacher announce a test and realized he was unprepared. He accurately appraised the task variables, considered the personal and strategy variables affecting learning, and concluded that his inability to come up with a strategy for filtering out the competing thoughts had made it impossible for him to concentrate on the teacher's lecture. As a result, he was not able to access his prior knowledge on related topics and make the connections required to understand the new concepts. Prior experience and accurate self-appraisal of the task demands led him to anticipate that he would not do well on the test; he accurately attributed his poor performance to an inability to filter out competing thoughts about family and friends. Successful learners like Akeem generally function better in any given academic domain than unsuccessful learners with no schema or an inadequate schema (Huitt & Hummel, 2003; Piaget, 1972, 1990).

   The successful learners' schemata enhance problem-solving ability by facilitating interpretation and reaction to new information, which contributes to the quality of their metacognitive problem solving. Schemata development is dependent on a student's ability to make accurate metacognitive self-appraisals. Unsuccessful learners often experience inaccuracies in metacognitive self-appraisal. This is particularly problematic because the ability to appraise one's use of cognitive knowledge and experiences is necessary to accurately identify the goal of an assignment, develop plans for reaching the goal, monitor and modify cognitive activity relative to successfully completing the task, and evaluate task outcomes (Flavell, 1971, 1976, 1985). Inaccurate self-appraisal, if not modified, can act on cumulative perceptions of strategy choice, the ability to detect and correct faulty cognitions, and the ability to generalize prior experience across tasks with similar demands (Borkowski et al., 1990; Flavell, 1971, 1976, 1985). Inaccurate appraisals can also result in faulty attributions that, if left untreated, can lead to lowered efficacious beliefs, lowered motivation, and the development of learned helplessness (Borkowski et al., 1990; Brophy, 1987).

   Students with well-developed metacognitive skills rarely make faulty attributions relative to their academic performance. Their analysis of task demands takes into consideration expectations or beliefs stemming from past successes or failures

(Borkowski et al., 1990; Brophy, 1987). This knowledge then directs their efforts as they attempt to anticipate the effect of prior knowledge on attributions, efficacious beliefs, and motivation, allowing them to act strategically. As you can see, the transformative nature of the metacognitive variables associated with learning, in particular the affective components related to faulty attributions (i.e., efficacious beliefs, motivation, learned helplessness), can determine task-related behavior (Borkowski, 1992; Borkowski et al., 1990).

Contextual or Environmental Knowledge

Contextual or environmental variables also affect students' metacognitive and cognitive knowledge, accounting for developmental and individual differences in students (Crane, 1996; Hartman & Sternberg, 1993; Paris, Newman, & Jacobs, 1985). Of interest to teachers is the role of nonacademic contexts (e.g., the home environment) and academic contexts (i.e., the classroom environment) in both student learning and teacher success. Among these variables, the quality and type of interactions between children and parents, and between students and teachers, are particularly important because these two contexts significantly affect an individual's development, retention, and transfer of metacognitive and cognitive skills and knowledge (e.g., Dickinson, 2001; Lonigan & Whitehurst, 1998; Pellegrini & Bjorklund, 1997; Stone & Conca, 1993).

It may surprise some that among nonacademic factors, parent–child interactions contribute a reported 75% to the child's intellectual development, whereas the mother's intelligence accounts for only approximately 25% of intellectual development (e.g., Crane, 1996; Dickinson, 2001; Lonigan & Whitehurst, 1998; Stone & Conca, 1993). Stone and Conca (1993) found the parent–child interactions involving children who demonstrate greater verbal intelligence were different in several ways from those involving children who demonstrated lesser degrees of verbal intelligence. For example, the parents of children who demonstrated greater verbal fluency had a greater number of conversational exchanges, used language to establish cause–effect relationships, set boundaries, provided prompts to encourage thought, provided instructions and explanations, and encouraged analysis. In comparison, the parents of the less verbally proficient children engaged in fewer conversational exchanges with their children. Their interactions were also qualitatively different in that they often provided fewer cognitive and linguistic challenges. These parents tended to have lower expectations for their children and in general were more likely to believe that children are passive recipients of knowledge (Stone & Conca, 1993).

Teachers may not find this research or its implications surprising, but many teachers are surprised at the findings of researchers examining the quantity and quality of teachers' interactions with students who are low achievers. Studies indicate trends and patterns among teacher–student interactions that mimic those of parent–child interactions (e.g., Brophy, 1992; Stone & Conca, 1993). For example, teachers tend to call on low achievers less often, allow them less time to respond, or provide them with the answer rather than provide scaffolding to elicit an improved response. Comparisons further indicate that teachers and parents alike tend to criticize low achievers more frequently when they respond incorrectly, praise them less often when they respond correctly, and provide less accurate and less detailed feedback during interactions. In general, teachers and parents provide low-achieving students with quantitatively and qualitatively different feedback as compared to high-achieving students (Stone & Conca, 1993).

This line of research contributes greatly to our ability to understand variations in students' cognitive and metacognitive knowledge and skills. The foundation for metacognitive development begins in the home, where during conversations with parents they learn how to think critically and how to use what they are learning to solve task-related problems. For example, imagine two parents watching a child building a block tower. They observe the child make a poor choice for the foundation of the tower: The size of the block the child chose is inappropriate, leading the parents to suspect the tower of blocks will become unstable and eventually fall to the floor. Parent 1 does not intercede but waits for the collapse of the tower and then uses this as an opportunity to help the child figure out why the tower fell. This parent discusses the range of options available to the child, thinking through the resultant outcomes. Parent 2 does not intercede either. However, after the tower collapses, this parent reacts very differently. This parent rushes over, scolds the child for yet another error in judgment, and then quickly demonstrates how to build a tower and walks away.

Similar scenarios occur in classrooms each day as teachers knowingly watch children make mistakes. Teachers can either perpetuate the cycle begun at home and complete the task for the student or show the student how to solve the problem for him- or herself. The teacher who understands why the student is having difficulty, and who correctly attributes the student's failure to underlying metacognitive deficits, will react very differently than the teacher who does not understand student learning. For example, two teachers announce spelling tests. One teacher suggests that students who did poorly on last week's test should study harder if they expect to pass the upcoming test. The other teacher demonstrates metacognitive insight, suggesting that anyone who did not perform well on last week's test study smarter. This means understanding that failing a test is not a sign of a lack of intelligence; it simply indicates a poor choice of study strategies. Thus, the teacher reminds the students that everyone makes a poor choice from time to time, but the trick is learning to choose the strategy that works best. Students consider a list of possible strategies as the teacher demonstrates how to make an appropriate choice.

What are the educational and societal implications? Studies indicate that many students do not have access to an environment at home or at school that is conducive to developing the metacognitive skills and knowledge necessary to ensure academic success (Langley, Wambach, Brothen, & Madyun, 2004; Nist, 1993; Pierce, 1998). Students across all grade levels and academic contexts exhibit metacognitive deficits. These deficits underlie many reading, writing, and critical-thinking problems and the affective variables that influence motivation (Pierce, 1998).

Illustrating this point, universities and colleges report growing numbers of students enrolling in developmental courses (Langley et al., 2004; Nist, 1993; Pierce, 1998). Of particular concern to the field of education, if not society, are college students who plan to teach but who have difficulty with basic academic literacy skills and deficiencies that are metacognitive in nature. The question is, will low-achieving students develop metacognitive knowledge and skills if neither parents nor teachers teach them? Principals report that teachers often do not know what to do when students fail to learn. Can teachers who do not understand how to learn effectively teach others how to learn?

METACOGNITIVE REGULATORY PROCESSES

To be an effective learner, you must efficiently operate, coordinate, and apply metacognitive and cognitive knowledge and skills. To be an effective teacher, you must be cognizant of this process and understand it well enough to teach it to others. Although there may be instances where metacognition is unconscious, it is primarily a function of effortful conscious manipulation and activation of information and processes (Fernandez-Duque, Barid, & Posner, 2000; Schunn & Dunbar, 1996).

Metacognitive processes are complex and sophisticated, exist in varying degrees of proficiency, and do not necessarily develop naturally. These skills include metacognitive activity related to planning (e.g., conflict resolution or resource allocation), monitoring (e.g., error detecting), and modifying (e.g., inhibitory control and error correction) the resources associated with cognition (Nelson & Narens, 1990; Reder & Schunn, 1996).

To illustrate these metacognitive regulatory processes, refer once again to Akeem. While listening to the teacher's lecture, Akeem lost his train of thought or failed to understand what the teacher was saying. He recognized that he has failed to comprehend, he correctly identified conflicting thoughts as the cause of the problem, but he did not correct the problem in time to pass the test. If he had had more time, would Akeem have the metacognitive skills and knowledge necessary to regulate his thinking and bring about the desired outcome? Would he have the metacognitive insight to know how to regulate his thinking about the learning task? If he had had more time, would Akeem have been able to identify the problem and construct a plan, choose a strategy to control his intrusive thoughts, monitor the effectiveness of the strategy, and modify that plan if necessary, all in time to perform well on the test? The answer is yes, because while not all students develop metacognitive knowledge naturally, they can learn it.

Students can fail to engage their metacognitive regulatory skills or experience impaired metacognitive regulatory ability due to environmental disadvantages, as previously noted (e.g., socioeconomic status, inadequate instruction, and ineffectual parental exchanges), or disability. As you will recall from Chapter 2, metacognitive and cognitive deficits, while having different causes, manifest similarly in the classroom and often place students at risk for academic failure. Students generally exhibit a limited awareness of the usefulness of specific cognitive strategies and take qualitatively different approaches to reading, math, and concept learning tasks (Ehri, Nunes, Stahl, & Willows, 2001; Torgesen, 1993; Wolf, Bowers, & Biddle, 2000). Students with metacognitive deficits may not recognize the value of strategy use and, as a result, do not use cognitive strategies even when they are available to them, or may continue to use ineffective strategies even when they prove ineffective (Gerber, 1983; Short & Ryan, 1984; Swanson, 1989; Wong, 1994). These students often do not use systematic plans for approaching problems and may have difficulty identifying relevant details (Swanson, 1989).

Students may be at risk academically because of limited flexibility—that is, they are unable to shift between strategies for reasons similar to those demonstrated by students with learning disabilities (Meltzer, 1993). For instance, a student may choose to prepare for a spelling test by writing the spelling words five times each. If the student were an inefficient learner due to metacognitive deficits, the student would not monitor, modify, or evaluate the usefulness of the study strategy and would associate poor performance with a poor strategy choice. Unfortunately, the student would not associate failure with a poor strategy choice and would inappropriately continue using a study strategy that was ineffective, this time writing the words 10 times in preparation for the next week's spelling test. This student would in all likelihood fail the test again and remain confused as to why this happened when he had studied harder the second time. Students who are ineffective learners do not realize effort alone does not provide the desired result.

Successful students, on the other hand, understand that their success is the result of pairing effort with the appropriate strategy or tool for the job; they study smarter, not harder. If you compare a student with metacognitive insight to the ineffective learner cited above you would see that the former monitors the effectiveness of the study strategy. If the strategy is not facilitating recall of the spelling words, the student will not continue to use it but will modify his choice, choosing another study strategy rather than persisting in the use of one that is not working. This student could demonstrate further metacognitive insight by choosing an alternative study strategy based on previous success with a strategy in another class that had similar testing or task demands (Meltzer, Solomon, Fenton, & Levine, 1989; Swanson, 1987, 1989; Wong, 1994).

As you are no doubt beginning to see, a lack of metacognitive and cognitive flexibility can affect the transfer of learning between academic domains and may account for poor generalization of learned strategies. Students with metacognitive deficits have insufficiently developed schemata, which impairs their ability to decode, encode, and manipulate information, which may place them at risk (Ehri et al., 2001; Torgesen, 1993; Wolf et al., 2000). Plainly put, it is difficult for these students to learn because they have a poor knowledge base to build on, or draw from, and if they had one would not know how to use it to accomplish their goals. Think of the students' knowledge base as a bank account. If the students understand learning, they make wise choices daily, learning from each task they undertake and banking that experience, like daily knowledge investments. Their knowledge base grows with each investment and can support almost any expenditure or solve any problem that arises.

Extrapolating from the banking example, consider students' knowledge base regarding academic content such as reading, and see how students without a metacognitive deficit can become more and more skilled at reading. They learn to recognize letters and words automatically, which frees them up to apply what they have learned in other classes to comprehending the text under consideration. They are in effect freeing up more and more processing capacity for comprehending the meaning of what they read (Hunt & Ellis, 1999). By comparison, students with metacognitive deficits have not learned to recognize the letters and words automatically; they must devote an inordinate amount of time and processing capacity to the decoding process itself. They are unable to draw upon metacognitive knowledge to help them solve the problem because they have had limited success with similar tasks in other settings. As a result, they have less energy available to engage in the metacognitive activity necessary to comprehend the text (Ceci, 1985; Felton & Wood, 1989; Kistner & Torgesen, 1987; McDougall, Borowsky, MacKinnon, & Hymel, 2005; Torgesen, 1993). They truly do not know what to do; they do not know how to regulate their own thinking to meet the classroom demands associated with learning. The educational implication of metacognitive deficits, regardless of the cause, is a lack of understanding of the learning process (Ceci, 1989).

Metacognitive regulatory problems can and do cause students with and without disabilities to experience academic difficulty. For example, an inability to simultaneously engage in metacognitive and cognitive thought may account for problems in coordinating the many varied cognitive processes involved in reading, writing, problem solving, and learning (e.g., perception, memory, language, strategy use, and attention) (Mazzoni & Nelson, 1998; Stone & Michaels, 1986; Swanson, 1989). Although students may not develop metacognitive knowledge naturally, they can learn it.

A METACOGNITIVE FRAMEWORK FOR LEARNING: IMPLEMENTING YOUR TEACHING PLAN

Growing numbers of students are experiencing learning problems, which makes teachers' jobs difficult. However, the job becomes less difficult when the students have similar learning problems. That is, having many students with different learning problems is far more challenging than having many students with a similar learning problem. As you will recall, metacognitive deficits explain many of the learning problems demonstrated by students in the high-incidence category; in addition, a lack of metacognitive insight accounts for many of the ineffective educational decisions teachers make.

The inability to make effective educational decisions is the most common and most disadvantageous characteristic associated with metacognitive deficits. Teachers and students who are effective learners understand that success is dependent on their ability to apply what they know. As a result, they are planful and goal oriented and choose the tools or strategies that will lead to goal attainment. Successful problem solvers periodically monitor progress toward their goal, modify their plan if necessary, and evaluate the outcome of their plan relative to improving their learning and teaching. Effective teachers and students are good problem solvers who understand the ability of well-chosen strategies to facilitate learning and educational decision making. They do not have to depend on others to solve their problems. While not everyone develops this ability naturally, it can be learned.

The PLAN strategy (see Figure 6.1) is a metacognitive strategy that both teachers and students can use to structure educational decisions, learning in the process how to become independent learners. It provides a systematic approach to teaching and learning content that combines strategic processes and metacognitive knowledge of the variables that affect learning (i.e., person, task, strategy, and context). The PLAN strategy provides students and teachers a common language, which facilitates communication and fosters a collaborative classroom environment where students and teachers can actively work together to solve academic and social problems.

Implementing the PLAN Strategy

To demonstrate how the PLAN strategy is used to guide problem solving, we will apply it to the vignette in which Akeem and his teacher are working on a science lesson. The teacher will need to make several important academic decisions before she can begin teaching the lesson.

The first decision she must make is critical: She must pinpoint her goals for herself and her students. From the case study, it appears her goal is for students to understand the relationship between secondhand smoke and the potential threat of environmental toxins from a variety of sources to public safety.

The next step in the PLAN strategy asks the teacher to look at her options. She must decide which instructional strategies or tools she will choose to meet her stated goal. We will assume this teacher is a reflective practitioner, which means she will demonstrate metacognitive insight, critical thinking, and reasoning when making her decisions. She will base her choices on knowledge of how students learn from a variety of assessments and research-based instructional methods. She will reflect on instructional methods that have worked well in the past, given similar task demands. She may also choose to collaborate with other educators before making a final decision to teach the lesson using a lecture format.

The third step in the PLAN strategy requires Akeem's teacher to analyze progress by periodically monitoring or analyzing her movement toward the goal. If she sees that the instructional methods she has chosen are not achieving the desired results, she will make another selection. Often when a teaching method is unsuccessful, teachers falsely assume they need to try harder or the student needs to try harder. Success is not a matter of effort alone; effort with the appropriate strategy or tool is what leads to successful outcomes for both students and teachers.

Let us further examine Akeem's scenario and assume he and his classmates performed poorly on the pop quiz the teacher gave. If his teacher is monitoring students' progress, the poor grades could cause her to reflect on the academic goals and methodological choices she made previously. Based on what she knows about concept development and learning, she may choose to abandon the straight lecture format she currently utilizes, choosing instead to modify her teaching methods to include the use of graphic organizers, which she knows are well researched and noted for improving students' ability to understand abstract concepts (Ellis, 2004). Upon further reflection, the teacher may choose to modify her original instructional goals and method wanting her students to develop as independent learners.

To realize her goal, Akeem's teacher could decide to abandon traditional teaching methods, choosing to discontinue her role as lecturer, simply providing information, expecting rote recall and recitation of facts. In her reconceptualized role, the teacher becomes a thinking coach, someone who acts as a facilitator working with students to construct meaning and promote critical-thinking and problem-solving skills. As a thinking coach (see Table 6.1), she would work collaboratively with students on authentic problem-solving activities that provide opportunities for developing knowledge and skills necessary to become independent learners. If Akeem's teacher chose not to monitor her progress toward her goals, she would continue teaching the content using ineffective methods, not realizing a simple methodological modification would solve her problem. She would, in effect, be dependent on others to help her solve classroom problems.

The fourth step in the PLAN strategy asks teachers and students to note the results of their educational decisions. Akeem's teacher needs to evaluate her strategy choices. Did the instructional methods she chose lead to the desired outcome? Can she employ these methods in other classes where she desires similar outcomes? Did her students develop critical-thinking skills and a greater degree of independence as learners, and are they more metacognitively aware?

Regardless of the outcome, evaluation is a necessary part of any educational plan. Choices that lead to successful outcomes and those that do not conclude successfully should be analyzed to determine utility for future situations with similar task demands. We do not always know how we got something right. Consider the computer. How often have you gotten a result and not been able to repeat it because you do not know what you did to reach the desired outcome? It is important to determine both why something went well and why it did not for future success.

Success and planful use of strategies are highly correlated; therefore, it is important for teachers to point out to students that success is dependent on making appropriate choices. Educators must emphasize the point that academic successes and/or failures are due to the educational choices we make, and nothing more. Many people who have met with repeated academic difficulty falsely attribute their lack of success to something outside their control and eventually give up in frustration. Frustration should be a signal that the choice you made is not working; the strategy is inappropriate for the task. The lesson here is rather than working harder with the same tool, work smarter. Discard a strategy that does not work and choose another.

METHODS FOR SOLVING INSTRUCTIONAL PROBLEMS

If teachers and students are to exercise control over their own learning they must understand that there is more than one way to solve a problem or complete a task. If you refer to the PLAN strategy, you will see examples of various options available to teachers and students for reaching differing goals (e.g., graphic organizers, strategic instruction). As explained earlier, students and teachers often do not consider the options available to them. Akeem's teacher chose to use graphic organizers to solve her problem. Graphic organizers are appealing for two reasons; they are well researched and have universal appeal (Ellis, 2004). Graphic organizers effectively increase learning and promote higher-order thinking across student groups (i.e., students who are gifted intellectually, students with learning disabilities, students with mild learning problems).

Graphic Organizers

Graphic organizers promote higher-order thinking skills through visual representation of concepts, visual organization of concepts, and visual depiction of the structural relationships between concepts. They affect meaningful learning by decreasing processing loads, making abstract concepts that were previously overt covert and recognizable. Graphic organizers are intended to make an abstract concept easier to understand by helping the learner organize and interpret new incoming information, and they work particularly well to develop prior knowledge. They act as a framework upon which the learner can integrate the new material into a more familiar structure. Additionally, they also facilitate the generalization of conceptual knowledge across academic domains.

Creating a graphic organizer involves the following steps:

1. Choose a text or lesson. (This strategy work equally well across content areas and grade levels where conceptual learning is emphasized.)
2. Decide what the students are to focus on while they read or listen (e.g., character analysis, cause and effect, sequences and cycles, or hierarchal analysis). This will determine the format of the graphic organizer to be used (pyramid, fishbone, story map, time line, Venn diagram, etc.)
3. Determine the detail necessary to represent the concept and/or relationship. Providing too many details in a graphic organizer may confuse students more than it clarifies ideas for them.

4. Review the graphic organizer with students. Do not assume that students will automatically understand it. Provide students with an explanation of the ideas in the graphic organizer and how they relate to one another. Explain how the graphic organizer will support their efforts to comprehend the text that they will be listening to or reading.

In summary, graphic organizers aid the development of higher-order thinking skills by teaching students to identify details and major concepts, recognize patterns, and make decisions about relationships (Ellis, 2004). They support schema development, enabling students to connect new information to existing relevant information across academic domains. Such generalization leads to an expanded knowledge base. Further, there is ample evidence that the use of graphic organizers promotes independent learning (Ellis, 2004).

Strategic Instruction

Strategic instruction is another excellent option for promoting independent learning, problem solving, and higher-order thinking. In general, a strategy is a tool, plan, or method students and teachers can use to accomplish a task. Strategies are systematic, hierarchical, stepwise progressions that when followed lead to task completion. Two types of strategies are referred to in this text—cognitive and metacognitive.

Cognitive strategies function as tools; they tend to be task specific, allowing you to manipulate information such as taking notes, asking questions, or composing a paragraph. Metacognitive strategies function to monitor tool use. Metacognitive strategies are regulatory in nature; they are strategies that a student uses when planning, monitoring, and evaluating learning or cognitive strategy performance.

Mnemonic strategies are a type of learning strategy proven by years of research to facilitate the recall of information learned in school (Mastropieri & Scruggs, 1997). For example, learning strategies help students complete academic tasks by telling them how to learn academic content. Many students have difficulty recalling information for a test or remembering vocabulary words. Mnemonic strategies work by creating meaningful connections where none exist. For learning to be effective, some type of connection must be established between the new information students are to learn and what they already know. It would be more powerful to capitalize on existing connections, but in their absence, mnemonics are very useful for helping recall of information. Keyword associations and acronyms are both examples of mnemonic strategies with which most people are familiar.

1. Keyword associations are useful for helping students learn spelling or vocabulary words. Learners are required to make a connection between the new word and a visual image they create involving a related word. The image then serves as the key to remembering the new word. For example, a student studying mathematical concepts could remember the difference between horizontal and vertical lines by picturing a horizontal line stretching across the horizon. Keyword associations work best when the student vividly pictures the association (associations that are ridiculous or unusual may aid in recall). For example, to ensure the student remembers the association for differentiating between horizontal and vertical lines, we could enhance the image by making the line stretch across a tropical horizon dotted with palm trees, sailboats, and sparkling

blue water. Keyword associations are most effective when learners generate the keyword associations themselves, rather than having them provided by a teacher or textbook. Students who experience difficulty making up their own keywords can benefit from having the teacher model the process, gradually transferring more responsibility to the learner.

 2. Acronyms are abbreviations in which each of the letters stands for the first letter in a list of words to be recalled. For example, many people are familiar with the acrostic used to remember the Great Lakes: HOMES (Huron, Ontario, Michigan, Erie, and Superior). Acrostics can also help students remember lists of words when the first letter of each word is used to form a sentence. For example, many people learned the order of the planets with the acrostic My Very Educated Mother Just Served Us Nine Pizzas (Mercury, Venus, Earth, Mars, Jupiter, Saturn, Uranus, Neptune and Pluto), and My Dear Aunt Sally has helped many students recall the proper order of mathematical operations (*m*ultiply and *d*ivide before *a*dding and *s*ubtracting). Strategies such as these support skills and knowledge development in academic areas and are important to student learning. For example, they can teach students organization, note taking, test-taking and study skills, reading comprehension, decoding, math, and writing processes.

STRATEGY SETS, INTERVENTION, AND PROGRAMS

The literature abounds with descriptions of strategy sets, strategy interventions, and strategy programs that make learners aware of what they are to do to complete specific tasks. These strategies employ acronyms to help students remember the steps they are to use when completing writing, reading, and other academic tasks. The Learning Toolbox Web site, developed by researchers at James Madison University, features strategy sets appropriate for middle and high school students. In addition to a complete array of strategies, there are assessment questionnaires students and teachers can use to identify areas of need and strategy lists that match the area of need with appropriate strategy choices. The site is interactive, providing students, parents, and teachers with step-by-step instructions and videos for supporting student learning and increasing independence—in particular, facilitating collaborative efforts, providing homework support, and improving instructional delivery. For additional information on this site, consult the appendix entry for this chapter.

 Perhaps the most widely known strategies intervention program is the Strategic Instruction Model (SIM) developed by Donald Deshler, Jeanne Schumaker, and their colleagues at the Center for Research on Learning (CRL) at the University of Kansas. Among the learning strategies developed by the CRL are word identification, paraphrasing, self-questioning, sentence writing, and vocabulary learning strategies. This model of strategies instruction is systematically delivered and embedded into core curriculum courses. The steps of SIM are as follows (Boudah & O'Neill, 1999; Schumaker & Deshler, 1992).

1. *Pretest:* Measure students' skills prior to training and obtain their commitment to learning.
2. *Describe:* Explain the steps of the strategy, where the strategy can be applied, and how the strategy will be beneficial to students.
3. *Model:* Demonstrate how to use the strategy by "thinking aloud" while applying the strategy to content material.

4. *Verbal practice:* Students memorize the strategy steps and key usage requirements.
5. *Controlled practice:* Ensure student mastery of the strategy using simplified materials in controlled settings.
6. *Grade-appropriate practice:* Ensure student mastery of the strategy in situations similar to those in the student's general education classrooms.
7. *Post-test:* Measure students' skills following training.
8. *Generalization:* Help students apply strategies in general education and nonacademic settings.

The RAP strategy (Schumaker & Deshler, 1992) is one example of a SIM strategy a teacher might employ if he or she wanted to improve students' reading comprehension. The steps of the RAP strategy are: *R*ead the paragraph; *a*sk yourself, "what are the main ideas?"; and *p*ut it in your own words.

To illustrate, suppose that at the beginning of the year, an English teacher explains that being able to paraphrase a story is important because paraphrasing helps with comprehension and is required to write reports, answer questions, and discuss ideas. The teacher shares the steps of the RAP paraphrasing strategy with students and models how to paraphrase *Romeo and Juliet* to complete different types of learning tasks. The teacher then has students participate in class activities and assignments, requiring them to practice paraphrasing text and use the information. The teacher continually evaluates and provides feedback to encourage high-quality paraphrasing. Finally, to promote generalization, the teacher suggests other academic and nonacademic areas with similar task demands where the strategy might be used (Schumaker & Deshler, 1992). Teaching for generalization is not only utilitarian but also serves to motivate students to think strategically.

Metacognitive Strategies

Metacognitive strategies direct the use of cognitive strategies. The two must therefore be used interactively, forming a pair of several strategies that are used in tandem to accomplish a learning task. For example, if a student is asked to read a book and write a report, she would use a metacognitive strategy such as SODA (see Table 6.2) to plan and monitor the use of cognitive writing strategies. The first step in writing a composition, or any task, is identifying the goal. The students asks themselves what they are being asked to do. The students plans by thinking about the audience, who will be reading what is written (e.g., what do they need or want to know), and what their expectations are. The students then consider the advantages and disadvantages of the various strategies options for completing the task and select the one most likely to lead to a successful outcome. When making their strategy choices, students consider personal, task, and strategy knowledge that will affect successful task completion, such as intent, prior knowledge of the subject, and motivation. Previous experience is also considered—which strategies have proven effective in previous learning situations with similar task demands. This information collectively informs the students' final strategy choice.

Where many students fail is they do not metacognitively monitor the implementation of their strategy choices, making modifications if necessary. Monitoring may include several mini-stages: looking back while writing to make sure they follow the outline (or deciding to abandon parts of the outline) or laying aside the composition for a day and then rereading it with a fresh eye. The student might use the COPS strategy

TABLE 6.2 SODA: Solve Problems!

When anyone, whether a teacher or a student, first begins to develop his or her metacognitive ability, a framework for the process can be helpful. The collaborative problem-solving strategy SODA (situation, options, advantages, disadvantages), outlined here, can be used by groups and individuals (such as teachers, students, and families) to develop a plan, solve a problem, or make a decision.

Situation: Describe the problem or situation you are trying to figure out.

Options: Describe three different strategies or suggestions you can use to solve the problem you have described.

1.
2.
3.

Disadvantages are things you don't like about the options you have identified.

Tell at least two disadvantages for each of the options you identified.

Option #1:
a.
b.
Option #2:
a.
b.
Option #3:
a.
b.

Advantages are things you like about the options you have identified.

Tell at least two advantages for each of the options you identified.

Option #1:
a.
b.
Option #2:
a.
b.
Option #3:
a.
b.

Review the advantages and disadvantages of the options you wrote down. Check the option that gives you the most advantages and least disadvantages.

Option #1:_____
Options #2:_____
Options #3: _____

Survey the results:

- Remember to monitor your progress toward the goal.
- If the solution you chose is not working, modify by trying one of your other options.

Always evaluate the work you did by asking:

1. Did you reach your goal?
2. Are there any other situations where you can use the SODA strategy to help you solve a problem.
3. Write them down.
4. Don't forget to congratulate yourself when you did a good job.
5. Remember you were successful because you chose the right strategy.

Source: Reprint permission being sought from Allyn & Bacon.

(Shannon & Polloway, 1993) to check to make sure capitalization, organization, punctuation, and spelling are correct before proceeding.

Sophisticated learners move metacognitively back and forth between the three stages—thinking and planning, writing for a while, rereading to see how they are doing, thinking of how to fix mistakes or add new information, writing again, and so on, until they are finished.

Last, they evaluate their educational decisions. Students reflects on whether the strategies they chose led to successful task completion; in this case, if the teacher approved of the book report. Evaluation also entails generalization of knowledge learned from this task. An effective learner identifies other classes that might have similar requirements and makes the connection between successful strategy use in the current situation and applicability across other academic content with like demands.

GUIDELINES FOR TEACHING STRATEGICALLY

In Table 6.3 you will find guidelines for teaching strategically, including methods for integrating strategies instruction into the curriculum. The TAKE CHARGE strategy, developed by the author, provides information useful for successfully teaching academic content using metacognitive and cognitive strategies or processes. The strategy provides a metacognitive framework for learning that the teacher can use to structure each lesson regardless of the content, highlighting that the learning process is the same whether teaching or learning math, science, or reading. The steps of TAKE CHARGE are as follows:

1. Teach both the learning process and content.
2. Authenticate the usefulness of the strategy by providing a rationale for why students should choose to use them to facilitate learning.
3. Think aloud so students can see/hear how successful thinkers operate to solve a learning problem.
4. Engage students so they learn to think aloud as they work through a problem.
5. Critical-thinking skills are developed via strategy use—teach students to self-evaluate.
6. Happiness is choosing your strategies wisely—teach students to equate success with strategy use.
7. Attitude is key—encourage students to develop a "can do" relationship with learning.
8. Reinforce the link between strategy use and success, because nothing motivates like success.
9. Goal setting is to be encouraged as a method for increasing positive learning outcomes.
10. Effort is not everything: Work smarter, not harder.

METACOGNITION IN THE CLASSROOM: THE IMPACT OF BELIEFS ON TEACHING AND LEARNING

If research indicates strategic instruction (i.e., cognitive and metacognitive) is beneficial to student learning, why do teachers generally report a lack of willingness to utilize it and other forms of differentiated instruction (e.g., Dembo & Gibson, 1984; Schumm &

TABLE 6.3 TAKE CHARGE: Guidelines for Teaching Strategically

1. Teach process and content.
   - Explicitly teach students how to learn and think critically using metacognitive and cognitive strategies.
   - To ensure student success using cognitive strategies, it is necessary to introduce the concept of strategy use in general first using a metacognitive strategy, such as SODA (see Table 6.2) or PLAN (Figure 6.1).
2. Authenticate by providing a rational for why they should choose to use strategies.
   - While we know strategic thinking accounts for the difference between academic and social success and failure, students often do not.
   - Ineffective learners by their very nature typically do not understand this, which explains why they frequently give up in frustration rather than try again. They feel they have no control over learning outcomes.
   - Demonstrate this principle by relating stories, either personal or those of others, that illustrate the point. It is important to validate strategy use.
3. Think aloud so students can see/hear how successful thinkers operate to solve a problem.
   - It makes the covert thought process accessible to students. Consider having students listen and watch as you demonstrate your thought processes. For example, you might begin with a graphic organizer to introduce a lesson on the Watergate investigation. Think aloud as you process through the lesson.
4. Engage students to think aloud as they work through a problem.
   - By having learners reflect on their thought processes aloud either during or after task completion, you will provide an opportunity to identify and correct faulty cognitions.
   - Do this whether student outcomes are successful or unsuccessful. Often students do not know how they got the correct answer, making it unlikely that will be able to repeat the success independently.
5. Critical-thinking skills.
   - Provide opportunities that facilitate analytical ability and reasoning skills. For example, ask students to keep an informal journal of their thinking as they attempt assignments. This activity will allow the students and the teacher to overtly evaluate thought processes that are generally unavailable for examination. This activity can also provide opportunities to make modifications to faulty cognitions in a timely manner.
   - In the journal, students record the process or steps they went through to complete a given assignment or task. Journaling is a formative assessment method that allows the teacher to monitor, modify, and evaluate student thinking. The teacher uses questions designed to stimulate student thinking (see Table 6.2) about their thought processes.
   - The teacher acts as a thinking coach to guide the student through a discussion of the contents of their journal.
   - Students who are experiencing academic difficulty may need to discuss their journal after each assignment to allow the teacher to correct faulty cognitions or eliminate faulty attributions before they can develop. Students learning to overcome learned helplessness, in particular, will need more support initially.
   - Formative feedback teaches students how to monitor, modify, and evaluate their thinking by scaffolding as they reflect on their thought processes. This is a critical aspect of helping students to

TABLE 6.3 *(Continued)*

become independent self-directed learners. The extra effort and time teachers spend providing formative feedback is well teaching.

6. Happiness is choosing your strategies wisely!
   - Banish frustration—teach students to attribute their success or failure to their choices rather than factors outside their control, such as a perceived lack of intelligence, bad luck, or lack of teacher support.
   - Teach students to monitor strategy use, to modify before becoming frustrated, how to avert failure, and to reinforce efficacious beliefs as a part of your strategy to retrain faulty attributions.
   - Attribution retraining is needed to end learned helplessness. It motivates and creates positive efficacious beliefs.

7. Attitude is key—encourage students to develop a "can do" relationship with learning.
   - Part of the attribution retraining process is developing and strengthening students' efficacious beliefs regarding school.
   - This is a vital step in the process of becoming a self-directed independent learner because efficacious beliefs drive behavior.
   - Students must realize they can control their own destiny by making appropriate choices.

8. Reinforce the link between strategy use and success, because nothing motivates like success.
   - Linking success with strategy use gives students control. Students who are in control no longer feel a sense of helplessness.
   - If necessary, set up a situation where students are successful—make it clear that success is attributable to appropriate strategy choices and a lack of success is attributable to nothing more than an inappropriate choice.
   - Acceptance of this premise provides for the continued development of efficacious beliefs, which in turn motivates students to put forth the effort necessary to learn.

9. Goal setting is to be encouraged.
   - It takes time to develop metacognitive proficiency—maintain students' motivation by reinforcing each successive approximation toward the goal.
   - Make learning authentic—it motivates. Encourage students to establish big goals and big dreams. Consider having students bring in photographs of people they admire, lifestyles they would like to establish, and careers of interest them. Collaboratively analyze the skills and knowledge students must acquire to reach their goals. Show them how setting goals is the way to realize their dreams; choosing the right strategies or tools is how they get there.

10. Effort is not everything: Work smarter, not harder.
    - If students or teachers are frustrated, it is likely they have made an inappropriate strategy selection and are perseverating. In all likelihood, they have forgotten to monitor and modify their plan of action. Model strategic learning for students—toss out teaching methods or learning strategies that frustrate you both and choose again!

Source: Spencer, S. (2009). Unpublished course material. Center for Pedagogy, Winthrop University.

Vaughn, 1991, 1992; Showers & Joyce, 1996; Soodak & Podell, 1993; Vaughn & Schumm, 1995)? Moreover, why have these beliefs and the accompanying educational practices not changed appreciably over the past decade despite educational reform efforts (Mittelhauser, 1998; Peterson, 2002; Schumm & Vaughn, 1991; Scruggs & Mastropieri, 1996; U.S. Department of Education, 2000)? Examination of this problem reveals that teacher beliefs more than any other factor may account for this phenomenon. In the following sections of the text, we will examine the link between teacher's beliefs, educational decision making, and metacognition.

Teachers' Efficacious Beliefs Affect Instructional Decisions

Although teachers sometimes attribute control of their behavior to external factors such as lack of time and support and so on, cognitive social learning theory and research suggest that internal factors may actually account for their professional decisions. Albert Bandura (1986) noted that people regulate effort in accordance with the effects they expect their actions to have, in which case teachers' beliefs, rather than the actual consequences of their actions, will direct their classroom behaviors. That is, teachers' efficacious and attributional beliefs regarding their ability to accommodate students with disabilities and other diverse learning needs will dictate their actions (Borkowski, 1992; Dembo & Gibson, 1984; Showers & Joyce, 1996; Soodak & Podell, 1993, 1994). The predictive quality of the relationship between efficacious beliefs, attributions, motivation, and underlying metacognitive knowledge and skills may provide an explanation of teachers' unwillingness to accept responsibility for students who are having academic difficulty (Dembo & Gibson, 1984). Understanding this relationship could not only positively affect future teacher's instructional practices but also improve student academic outcomes.

Bandura (1977, 1986) proposed that our behavior is determined by both general outcome expectancy and a sense of self-efficacy. Self-efficacy is related judgments (i.e., metacognitive self-assessments) of how well we can execute courses of action required to deal with prospective situations (Bandura, 1986). Efficacy as it pertains to teaching is conceptualized as existing along two dimensions—teaching efficacy and personal teaching efficacy (Ashton & Webb, 1982). The dimension of personal teaching efficacy measures teachers' beliefs in their personal abilities to instruct students, while the dimension of teaching efficacy measures teachers' beliefs about the ability of effective teaching in general to influence student learning (Gibson & Dembo, 1984).

The construct of self-efficacy explains teachers' behavior by establishing a relationship between teachers' educational beliefs, specifically the subconstruct personal teaching efficacy, and teacher planning, instructional decisions, and classroom practices (Pajares, 1992; Soodak & Podell, 1993; Woolfolk, 1998; Woolfolk & Hoy, 1990). To illustrate the point, if Akeem's teacher were strong in both variables of efficacy she could be expected to believe that all of her students could learn. She would realize that lack of success in the classroom is due to a mismatch between student needs and instructional demands. She would thus persist longer with students having academic difficulty, provide different types of feedback, tend to use elements of direct instruction, and respond to students in an active, assured manner (Gibson & Dembo, 1984).

Teachers with weak personal teaching efficacy and strong teaching efficacy would react very differently. If we apply Bandura's theoretical predictions we would see that even if Akeem's teacher has strong general teaching efficacy and believed all students can learn regardless of factors such as family, background, and IQ, she would not persist in the face of academic difficulty unless she believed they could perform the necessary activities (Gibson & Dembo, 1984). As you may have noted, the behaviors exhibited by Akeem's teacher resemble the phenomenon of learned helplessness found in students with learning disabilities.

That is, students with learning disabilities and teachers alike appear to give up in difficult academic situations after repeated failure accompanied by faulty attributions (i.e., inaccurate metacognitive assessment) (Soodak & Podell, 1993, 1994). For example, teachers can and do attribute the failure of students to forces outside their control (e.g., lack of training or time, student lack of intelligence, or family factors; Soodak & Podell, 1993, 1994) just as students with learning disabilities do (luck, teacher, etc.). Soodak and Podell (1993, 1994) found that 62.7% of teachers studied attributed lack of student success to problems in the home, and only 2.7% attributed learning problems to their instructional style. Teachers additionally reported that they lack the knowledge, skills, and confidence necessary to plan and implement adaptations for students who are at risk or who have disabilities (Vaughn & Schumm, 1995). However, research indicates that even when teachers do claim to be skillful in using various adaptations, they often do not use them in the classroom (Schumm et al., 1994). Why does this happen? How can we as educators use this knowledge to inform our professional practice?

Perhaps as research and theory suggest, teachers do not make adaptations and accommodations for students with diverse learning needs because they do not believe their efforts will be successful (Bandura, 1986; Gibson & Dembo, 1984). Teachers' beliefs and expectations are relevant because they directly influence the expenditure of effort, such as decision making, planning, persistence in a failure situation, and the selection of professional skills and knowledge they will acquire (Gibson & Dembo, 1984; Pajares, 1992). Thus, faulty attributions or inaccurate metacognitive assessment may account for a perceived lack of control over academic outcomes, lack of motivation, lack of persistence, and a lack of planful strategic behavior in teachers and students (Borkwoski, 1992; Soodak & Podell, 1993; Torgesen & Licht, 1983).

Successful students and teachers in general metacognitively assess or analyze classroom situations correctly. They attribute their success and/or failure to factors within their control, such as effort, advantageous choices or inappropriate choices, and planful strategic behavior. They understand how to use metacognitive knowledge and skills to solve classroom problems. They are motivated to put forth the necessary effort to act, to self-direct their learning behaviors by setting goals, monitoring, and evaluating the effectiveness of cognitive and metacognitive endeavors. They will discard an ineffective strategy in favor of one with which they have previously experienced success, given similar task demands, rather than perseverating, which can lead to lowered efficacious beliefs, faulty attributions, and learned helplessness.

WHEN TEACHERS AND STUDENTS GIVE UP: RETRAINING FAULTY ATTRIBUTIONS

Faulty assumptions about the learning process, as we have seen, can inaccurately lead individuals to mistake causality for educational actions and attribute outcomes to external forces. An external locus of control often results in a sense of powerlessness; students and teachers may feel unable to control their own academic destinies. These feelings (i.e., meta-experiences) and subsequent beliefs may lead to the development of learned helplessness, which, over time, can cause each to give up on teaching and or learning in frustration (Maier & Seligman, 1976). To break the cycle of learned helplessness and motivate students to learn and teachers to teach strategically, we must understand the problem.

Learned helplessness as it affects students and teachers is the result of faulty metacognitive regulatory activity among three components—strategic knowledge, self-regulation, and the motivational beliefs associated with strategy use (Borkowski, 1992). Individuals who have given up educationally due to learned helplessness do not understand the value of strategic behavior and therefore are not motivated to use it to solve classroom problems (Gaskins & Elliot, 1991). They do not understand the value of strategy use because they have not learned to regulate the thinking, teaching, and learning processes. The ability to do so is metacognitive in nature.

Metacognitive knowledge and skills enable us to develop an internal locus of control, wherein we realize that control over our learning is the result of combining cognitive strategy knowledge and knowledge of the metacognitive processes (Borkowski, Estrada, Milstead, & Hale, 1989). Specifically, the two types of knowledge are used procedurally, forming a mental model or schema from which to reason that being strategic is the key to successfully solving problems. This leads to an increased sense of self-efficacy, or confidence in one's ability to act in a way that will lead to goal attainment. Correctly attributed successes or failures serve to motivate both teacher and student.

When this knowledge does not develop naturally, attributions must be explicitly retrained to accurately equate academic successes with effort and the use of appropriate tools (i.e., strategic effort) rather than to luck, family, or lack of intelligence (Borkowski, 1991). Enjoyment of the learning and/or teaching process will increase when teachers and students become more metacognitively aware, attributing success to strategic events, wherein motivation increases as successes increase; motivation then acts as a catalyst, energizing the strategic processes, thus starting the cycle anew with the advent of the next problem to be solved (Brophy, 1987; Borkowski & Muthukrishna, 1992).

Attribution Retraining Methods

Attribution retraining begins by reconceptualizing the teacher's role. The teacher is no longer simply a purveyor of information; the teacher is a thinking coach (see Table 6.1). In your role as thinking coach, consider providing questions to prompt or guide student thinking that will facilitate metacognitive development. When teachers ask questions such as these, students can see overtly how experienced thinkers process information, how they approach solving an academic problem.

The TAKE CHARGE strategy (see Table 6.3) suggests that this process can be facilitated by asking students to keep a journal of their thought processes as they undertake tasks. Provide a notebook or computer on which students can record and analyze the actions they take to complete given tasks. This method provides the teacher with a valuable tool with which to monitor student thinking and attribution retraining. It provides students an opportunity to think about how they approach learning, to develop the ability to self-regulate and self-assess. As they become more proficient at thinking and develop the ability to ask themselves questions, faulty attributions are retrained, efficacious beliefs increase, and students become more confident in their abilty to succeed in the classroom, which in turn motivates them to engage in learning. In addition to the thinking journal, the TAKE CHARGE strategy offers other methods that teachers can use to promote the development of positive attributions, such as providing rationales for strategy use, thinking aloud to make covert processing accessible, and the importance of goal setting.

Last, it is important to remember to provide feedback to students and link success to strategy use. Specifically, make students aware that success is the result of appropriate strategy choices, and a lack of success is nothing more than a poor strategy choice. If a student or teacher makes a poor choice, simply choose again. Everyone makes inappropriate choices; they learn to analyze and learn from these mistakes. Making this connection for students is vital to attribution retraining. If left out, students and/or teachers may perseverate and perpetuate the negative learning cycle.

Metacognitive strategies retrain faulty attributions. Earlier in the chapter, we discussed the PLAN strategy (see Figure 6.1) and the SODA strategy (see Table 6.2). The PLAN strategy acts as a framework for learning from which all of these strategies can be integrated across all grade levels. These strategies provide teachers and students a common language and framework from which to both access and deliver academic content and social skills instruction. They are appropriate choices when selecting strategies for supporting attribution retraining. The instructional methods and cognitive theory upon which they are based can promote the acquisition, maintenance, and generalization of both content knowledge and metacognitive and cognitive strategy knowledge and skills (Borkowski, 1992; Flavell et al., 2002; Hartman & Sternberg, 1993; Spencer & Logan, 2005).

Summary

Teachers have chosen, or have been directed to use, instructional programming based on a traditional one-size-fits-all model. This method of teaching tends to foster discrete fact-based learning and dependence, which is qualitatively different from the higher-order knowledge they and others report as valuable. Thus, teachers' and students' lack of success may be due to ineffective instructional choices and ineffectual programming options—not a lack of effort, as some think.

Although ineffectual programming options may not account for all instances of lack of effort, it could account for continuing frustration with student performance, loss of efficacious beliefs, and motivation attributed inaccurately by teachers to student-centered problems. A metacognitive model of instruction could eliminate contextual mismatches that can account for student learning. An educational environment such as this takes into consideration the strengths and needs of both the teacher and the students. This model draws upon educational research and theory that indicates intellectual performance, both cognitive and metacognitive, is influenced by an interaction between the classroom environment and ones beliefs (e.g., Borkowski, 1992; Flavell et al., 2002; Hartman & Sternberg, 1993; Logan et al., 1999; Logan & Stein, 2001; Spencer & Logan, 2003, 2005).

If you understand how learning occurs, you can change it. As you have read, educators often do not know how to affect change where student learning is concerned. Teachers, just as those they teach, are not immune to metacognitive deficiencies. As professionals, we have not always learned from our mistakes; sometimes we try to solve our problems before properly identifying them. Teachers as students may perseverate, using ineffective strategies until the result is repeated failure that leaves many teachers with an unwillingness to persist in the face of demanding classroom situations. Like students, we can exhibit symptoms of learned helplessness.

Can this situation be avoided? It would seem so. Teachers are students as well as teachers, therefore, they can learn how to "think"—learn how to learn. Adequate instructional opportunities for students today and for future generations depend on all students having the opportunity to develop and apply metacognitive skills and knowledge. Our ability to learn how to solve educational problems depends on it. We must learn how to learn, so that we can teach others how to learn.

References

Ashton, P., & Webb, R. (1986). *Making a difference: Teachers' sense of efficacy and student achievement*. New York: Longman.

Atkinson, R. C., & Shiffrin, R. M. (1968). Human memory: A proposed system and its control processes. In K. W. Spence & J. T. Spence (Eds.), *Psychology of learning and motivation* (2nd ed.). New York: Academic Press.

Baker L. (1989). Metacognition, comprehension monitoring, and the adult reader. *Educational Psychology Review, 1*, 3–38.

Bandura A. (1977). *Social learning theory*. Upper Saddle River, NJ: Prentice Hall.

Bandura A. (1986). *Social foundations of thought and action: A social cognitive theory*. Upper Saddle River, NJ: Prentice Hall.

Belmont, J. M., & Butterfield, E. C. (1969). The relations of short-term memory to development and intelligence. In L. C. Lipsitt & H. W. Reese (Eds.), *Advances in child development and behavior* (4th ed., pp. 29–82). New York: Academic Press.

Borkowski, J. G. (1992). Metacognitive theory: A framework for teaching literacy, writing, and math skills. *Journal of Learning Disabilities, 25*, 253–257.

Borkowski, J. G., Carr, M., & Pressely, M. (1987). "Spontaneous" strategy use: Perspectives from metacognitive theory. *Intelligence, 11*, 61–75.

Borkowski, J. G., Carr, M., Rellinger, L., & Pressley, M. (1990). Self-regulated cognition: Interdependence of metacognition, attributions and self-esteem. In B. J. Jones & L. Idol (Eds.), *Dimensions of thinking and cognitive instruction* (pp. 53–92). Hillsdale, NJ: Lawrence Erlbaum Associates.

Borkowski, J. G., Estrada, M. T., Milstead, M., & Hale, C. A. (1989). General problem-solving skills: Relations between metacognition and strategic processing. *Learning Disability Quarterly, 12*, 57–70.

Borkowski, J. G., & Muthukrishna, N. (1992). Moving metacognition into the classroom: "Working models" and effective strategy teaching. In M. Pressley, K. R. Harris, & J. T. Guthrie (Eds.), *Promoting academic competence and literacy in school* (pp. 477–501). San Diego, CA: Academic.

Boudah, D. J., & O'Neill, K. J. (1999). Learning strategies (ERIC/OSEP Digest #E577). Reston, VA: *ERIC Clearinghouse on Disabilities and Gifted Education*. (ERIC Document Reproduction Service No. ED433 669). Retrieved January 11, 2006, from http://www.ericdigests.org/2000-2/learning.htm

Brenna, B. A. (1995). The metacognitive reading strategies of five early readers. *Journal of Research in Reading, 18*(1), 53–62.

Brophy, J. (1987). *Motivation in the classroom*. East Lansing: Michigan State University Institute for Research on Teaching.

Brophy, J. (1992). Probing the subtleties of subject-matter teaching. *Educational Leadership, 49*(7), 4–8.

Brown, A. L. (1987). Metacognition, executive control, self-regulation, and other more mysterious mechanisms. In F. E. Weinert & R. H. Kluwe (Eds.), *Metacognition, motivation, and understanding* (pp. 65–116). Hillsdale, NJ: Lawrence Erlbaum Associates.

Bruner, J. (1974). *Toward a theory of instruction*. Cambridge, MA: Harvard University Press.

Carr, M., & Jessup, D. L. (1997). Gender differences in first-grade mathematics strategy use: Social and metacognitive influences. *Journal of Educational Psychology, 89*(2), 318–328.

Ceci, S. J. (Ed.). (1985). *Handbook of cognitive, social, and neuro-psychological aspects of learning disabilities, Vol. 1.* Hillsdale, NJ: Lawrence Erlbaum Associates.

Ceci, S. J. (1989). On domain-specificity . . . more or less: General and specific constraints on cognitive development. *Merrill Palmer Quarterly, 35,* 131–142.

Crane, J. (1996). Effects of home environment, SES, and maternal test scores on mathematics achievement. *Journal of Educational Research, 89*(5), 305–314.

Dembo & Gibson, (1984). Teacher efficacy: A construct validation. *Journal of Educational Psychology, 76,* 569–582.

Dewey, J. (1997a). *Experience and education.* New York: MacMillan.

Dewey, J. (1997b). *How we think.* New York: Dover.

Dickinson, D. (2001) *Beginning literacy with language.* Baltimore: Paul H. Brookes.

Ediger, M. (2005). Struggling readers in high school. *Reading Improvement, 42,* 34.

Ehri, L. C., Nunes, S. R., Stahl, N., & Willows, D. M. (2001). Phonemic awareness instruction helps children learn to read: Evidence from the National Reading Panel's meta-analysis. *Reading Research Quarterly, 36*(3), 250–287.

Ellis, E. S. (2004). *What is the big deal about graphic organizers?* GraphicOrganizers.com. Retrieved February 5, 2006, from http://www.graphicorganizers.com/Sara/ArticlesAbout/Q&A%20Graphic%20Organizers.pdf

Felton, R. H., & Wood, F. B. (1989). Cognitive deficits in reading disability and attention deficit disorder. *Journal of Learning Disabilities, 22,* 3–13.

Fernandez-Duque, D., Baird, J. A., & Posner, M. I. (2000). Executive attention and metacognitive regulation. *Consciousness and Cognition, 9,* 288–307.

Flavell, J. H. (1971). First discussant's comments: What is memory development the development of? *Human Development, 14,* 272–278.

Flavell, J. H. (1976). Metacognitive aspects of problem solving. In L. B. Resnick (Ed.), *The nature of intelligence.* Hillsdale, NJ: Lawrence Erlbaum Associates.

Flavell, J. H. (1979). Metacognition and cognitive monitoring: A new area of cognitive-developmental inquiry. *American Psychologist, 34,* 906–911.

Flavell, J. H. (1985). *Cognitive development* (2nd ed.). Upper Saddle River, NJ: Prentice Hall.

Flavell, J. H., Green, F. L., & Flavell, E. R. (1995). Young children's knowledge about thinking. *Monographs of the Society for Research in Child Development, 60*(1) (Serial No. 243).

Flavell, J. H., Miller, P. H., & Miller, S. A. (2002). *Cognitive development* (4th ed.). Upper Saddle River, NJ: Prentice Hall.

Gaskins, I. W., & Elliot, T. T. (1991). *Implementing cognitive strategy instruction across the school: The Benchmark manual for teachers.* Cambridge, MA: Brookline Books.

Gerber, M. M. (1983). Learning disabilities and cognitive strategies: A case for training or constraining problem solving? *Journal of Learning Disabilities, 16*(5), 255–260.

Gibson, S., & Dembo, M. H. (1984). Teacher efficacy: A construct validation. *Journal of Educational Psychology, 76*(4), 569–582.

Hartman, H. J., & Sternberg, R. J. (1993). A broad BACEIS for improving thinking. *Instructional Science, 21*(5), 400–425.

Huitt, W., & Hummel, J. (2003). Piaget's theory of cognitive development. *Educational Psychology Interactive.* Valdosta, GA: Valdosta State University. Retrieved July 1, 2005, from http://chiron.valdosta.edu/whuitt/col/cogsys/piaget.html

Hunt, R. R., & Ellis, H. C. (1999). *Fundamentals of cognitive psychology* (6th ed.). Boston: McGraw-Hill.

Keeley, S. M., Browne, M. N., & Kreutzer, J. S. (1982). A comparison of freshmen and seniors on general and specific essay tests of critical thinking. *Research in Higher Education, 17,* 139–154.

Kistner, J., & Torgesen, J. K. (1987). Motivational and cognitive aspects of learning disabilities. In A. E. Kasdin & B. B. Lahey (Eds.), *Advances in clinical child psychology.* New York: Plenum.

Langley, S., Wambach, C., Brothen, T., & Madyun, N. (2004, Fall). Academic achievement motivation: Differences among underprepared students taking PSI general psychology course. *Research in Teaching in Developmental Education.* Retrieved July 1, 2005, from http://www.findarticles.com/p/articles/mi_qa4116/is_200410/ai_n9465339/pg_3

Logan, G. H. (1976). Do sociologists teach students to think more critically? *Teaching Sociology, 4*(1), 29–48.

Logan, K. R., & Stein, S. S. (2001). The research-lead teacher model: Helping general education teachers with classroom behavior problems. *Teaching Exceptional Children, 33,* 10–15.

Logan, K. R., Stein, S. S., Nieminen, P., Wright, E. H., Major, P., & Hansen, C. (1999). *The research-lead teacher model: Gwinnett county public school's model for bridging the gap from research to practice.* Retrieved November 13, 1999, from http://www.lsi.ukans.edu.jg/bluelogan.htm.

Lonigan, C. J., & Whitehurst, G. J. (1998). Relative efficacy of parent and teacher involvement in a shared-reading intervention for preschool children from low-income backgrounds. *Early Childhood Research Quarterly, 13,* 263–290.

Maier, S. F., & Seligman, M. E. P. (1976). Learned helplessness: Theory and evidence. *Journal of Experimental Psychology: General, 105,* 3–46.

Mastropieri, M. A., & Scruggs, T. E. (1997). Best practices in promoting reading comprehension in students with learning disabilities: 1976 to 1996. *Remedial and Special Education, 18*(4), 197–213.

Markman E. M. (1985). Comprehension monitoring: Developmental and educational issues. In S. F. Chipman, J. W. Segal, & R. Glaser (Eds.), *Thinking and learning skills: Vol. 2 Research and open questions* (pp. 275–291). Hillsdale, NJ: Lawrence Erlbaum Associates.

Mazzoni, G., & Nelson, T. O. (1998). *Metacognition and cognitive neuropsychology: Monitoring and control processes.* Mahwah, NJ: Lawrence Erlbaum Associates.

McDougall, P., Borowsky, R., MacKinnon, G. E., & Hymel, S. (2005). Process dissociation of sight vocabulary and phonetic decoding in reading: A new perspective on surface and phonological dyslexias. *Brain and Language, 92,* 185–203.

Meltzer, L. J. (1993). Strategy use in students with learning disabilities: The challenge of assessment. In L. J. Meltzer (Ed.), *Strategy assessment and instruction for students with learning disabilities: From theory to practice* (pp. 93–139). Austin, TX: Pro-Ed.

Meltzer, L. J., Solomon, B., Fenton, T., & Levine, M. D. (1989). A developmental study of problem-solving strategies in children with and without learning disabilities. *Journal of Applied Developmental Psychology, 10,* 171–193.

Mittelhauser, M. (1998). *The outlook for college graduates, 1996–2006: Prepare yourself.* Washington, DC: U.S. Department of Labor Bureau of Labor Statistics. Retrieved July 3, 2005, from http://www.pueblo.gsa.gov/cic_text/employ/3college/3college.htm

National Assessment of Educational Progress (NAEP). (1996). *Trends in academic progress.* Washington, DC: Author. Retrieved July 1, 2005, from http://nces.ed.gov/pubsearch/pubsinfo.asp?pubid=1999452

National Assessment of Educational Progress (NAEP). (2005). *Condition of education.* Washington, DC: Author. Retrieved July 1, 2005, from http://nces.ed.gov/programs/coe/

Neisser, U. (1967). *Cognitive psychology.* New York: Appleton-Century.

Nelson, T. O., & Narens, L. (1990). Metamemory: A theoretical framework and new findings. In G. H. Bower (Ed.), *The psychology of learning and motivation.* New York: Academic Press.

Newell, A., Shaw, J. G., & Simon, H. A. (1958). Elements of a theory of human problem solving. *Psychological Review, 65,* 151–166.

Nist, S. (1993, Fall–Winter). What the literature says about academic literacy. *Georgia Journal of Reading,* 11–18.

Otero J. C., & Campanario J. M. (1990). Comprehension evaluation and regulation in learning from science texts. *Journal of Research in Science Teaching, 27,* 447–460.

Pajares, M. F. (1992). Teachers' beliefs and educational research: Cleaning up a messy construct. *Review of Educational Research, 62,* 307–332.

Paris, S. G., Newman, R., & Jacobs, J. E. (1985). Social contexts and functions of children's remembering. In C. Brainerd & M. Pressley (Eds.), *The cognitive side of memory* (pp. 81–115). New York: Springer-Verlag.

Paris, S. G., & Winograd, P. (1990). How metacognition can promote academic learning and instruction. In B. F. Jones & L. Idol (Eds.), *Dimensions of thinking and cognitive instruction* (pp. 15–51). Hillsdale, NJ: Lawrence Erlbaum Associates.

Pierce, W. (1998). *Understanding students' difficulties reasoning: Perspectives from several fields.* Retrieved July 5, 2005, from http://academic.pg.cc.md.us/~wpeirce/MCCCTR/underst.html

Pellegrini, A. D., & Bjorklund, D. F. (1997). The role of recess in children's cognitive performance. *Educational Psychologist, 32,* 35–41.

Peterson, K. D. (2002). Positive or negative: A school's culture is always at work, either helping or hindering adult learning. *Journal of Staff Development, 23,* 3.

Piaget, J. (1972). *The psychology of the child.* New York: Basic Books.

Piaget, J. (1990). *The child's conception of the world.* New York: Littlefield Adams.

Price, E., & Driscoll, M. (1997). An inquiry into the spontaneous transfer of problem-solving skill. *Contemporary Educational Psychology, 22,* 472–494.

Randi, J., Grigorenko, E. L., & Sternberg, R. J. (2005). Revisiting definitions of reading comprehension: Just what is reading comprehension anyway and what is the relationship with metacognition? In S. E. Israel, C. Collins-Block, K. L. Bauserman, & K. Kinnucan-Welsch (Eds.), *Metacognition in literacy learning: Theory, assessment, instruction, and professional development* (pp. 149–199). Hillsdale, NJ: Lawrence Erlbaum Associates.

Reder, L. Y., & Schunn, C. D. (1996). Metacognition does not imply awareness: Strategy choice is governed by implicit learning and memory. In L. Y. Reder (Ed.), *Implicit memory and metacognition.* Mahwah, NJ: Lawrence Erlbaum Associates.

Rojewski, J. W., Schell, J. W., Reybold, E., & Evanciew, C. E. P. (2004). Perceived structure of advanced cognitive skills for adolescents with learning disabilities. *Journal of Industrial Teacher Education, 32,* 4. Retrieved July 4, 2005, from http://scholar.lib.vt.edu/ejournals/JITE/v32n4/rojewski.html#Berryman1992#Berryman1992

Schneider, W. (1998). The development of procedural metamemory in childhood and adolescence. In G. Mazzoni & T. O. Nelson (Eds.). *Metacognition and cognitive neuropsychology: Monitoring and control processes* (pp. 1–21). Mahwah, NJ: Lawrence Erlbaum Associates.

Schumaker, J. B., & Deshler, D. D. (1992). Validation of learning strategy interventions for students with learning disabilities: Results of a programmatic research effort. In B. Y. L. Wong (Ed.), *Contemporary intervention research in learning disabilities: An international perspective* (pp. 22–46). New York: Springer-Verlag.

Schumm, J. S., & Vaughn, S. (1991). Making adaptations for mainstreamed students: General classroom teachers' perspectives. *Remedial and Special Education, 12,* 18–27.

Schumm, J. S., & Vaughn, S. (1992). Plans for mainstreamed special education students: Perceptions of general education teachers. *Exceptionality, 3*(2), 81–96.

Schumm, J. S., Vaughn, S., Haager, D., McDowell, J., Rothlein, E., & Saumell, L. (1995). General education teacher planning: What can students with learning disabilities expect? *Exceptional Children, 61*(4), 335–352.

Schunn, C. D., & Dunbar, K. (1996). Priming, analogy, and awareness in complex reasoning. *Memory and Cognition, 24*(3), 271–284.

Scruggs, T. E., & Mastropieri M. A. (1996). Teacher perceptions of mainstreaming/inclusion, 1958–1995: A research synthesis. *Exceptional Children, 63*(1), 59–74.

Shannon, T. R., & Polloway, E. A. (1993). Promoting error monitoring in middle school students with LD. *Intervention in School and Clinic, 28,* 160–164.

Short, E. J., & Ryan, E. B. (1984). Metacognitive differences between skilled and less skilled readers: Remediating deficits through story grammar and attribution training. *Journal of Educational Psychology, 76*(2), 225–235.

Showers, J., & Joyce, B. (1996). The evolution of peer coaching. *Educational Leadership, 53*(6), 12–16.

Spencer, S. S., & Logan, K. R. (2003). A school based staff development model that bridges the gap from research to practice. *Teacher Education and Special Education, 26,* 51–62.

Spencer, S. S., & Logan, K. R. (2005). Improving students with learning disabilities ability to acquire and generalize a vocabulary learning strategy. *Learning Disabilities: A Multidisciplinary Journal, 13,* 87–94.

Soodak, L., & Podell, D. (1993). Teacher efficacy and student problem as factors in special education referral. *Journal of Special Education, 27,* 66–18.

Soodak, L. C., & Podell, D. M. (1994). Teachers' thinking about difficult-to-teach students. *Journal of Educational Research, 88,* (1), 44–51.

Sternberg, R. J. (1986a). Inside intelligence. *American Scientist, 74,* 137–143.

Sternberg, R. J. (1986b). *Intelligence applied.* New York: Harcourt Brace Jovanovich.

Stone, A., & Michaels, D. (1986). Problem-solving skills in learning disabled children. In S. J. Ceci (Ed.), *Handbook of cognitive, social and neuropsychological aspects of learning disabilities: Vol. I.* Hillsdale, NJ: Lawrence Erlbaum Associates.

Stone, C. A., & Conca, L. C. (1993). The origin of strategy deficits in children with learning disabilities: A social constructivist perspective. In L. Meltzer (Ed.), *Strategy Assessment and Instruction*. Austin, TX: Pro-Ed.

Swanson, H. L. (1987). Information-processing theory and learning disabilities: An overview. *Journal of Learning Disabilities, 20*, 3–7.

Swanson, H. L. (1989). Strategy instruction: Overview of principles and procedures for effective use. *Learning Disability Quarterly, 12*, 3–14.

Torgesen, J. K., & Licht, B. (1983). The learning disabled child as an inactive learner. Retrospect and prospects. In J. D. McKinney & L. Feagans (Eds.), *Topics in learning disabilities* (pp. 3–32). Baltimore: Paul H. Brookes.

Torgesen, J. K. (1993). Variations on theory in learning disabilities. In G. R. Lyon, D. B. Gray, J. F. Kavanagh, & N. A. Krasnegor (Eds.), *Better understanding of learning disabilities: New views from research and their implications for education and public policies* (pp. 153–170). Baltimore: Paul H. Brookes.

U.S. Department of Education. (2000). National longitudinal transition study-2. Menlo Park, CA: SRI International. Retrieved July 4, 2005, from www.nlts2.org/reports/2007_08/nlts2_report_2007_08_complete.pdf.

U. S. Department of Education Institute of Education Institute of Education Sciences. (2002). *The nation's report card*. Washington, DC: Author. Retrieved September 5, 2005, from http://nces.ed.gov/pubsearch/pubsinfo.asp?pubid=2003529

United States Office of Educational Research and Instruction (OERI). (2002). *Report on national literacy trends*. Retrieved July 1, 2005, from http://www.ed.gov/offices/OERI/SAI/

Vaughn, S., & Schumm, J. S. (1995). Responsible inclusion for students with learning disabilities. *Journal of Learning Disabilities, 28*, 264–270, 290.

Vygotsky, L. (1986). *Thought and language*. Boston: MIT Press.

Vygotsky, L., & Vygotsky, S. (1980). *Mind in society: The development of higher psychological processes*. Cambridge, MA: Harvard University Press.

Weaver C. A. (1995). Monitoring of comprehension: The role of text difficulty in metamemory for narrative and expository text. *Memory & Cognition, 23*, 12–22.

Wolf, M., Bowers, P., & Biddle, K. (2000). Naming speed processes, timing, and reading: A conceptual review. *Journal of Learning Disabilities, 33*, 322–324.

Woolfolk, A. (1998). *Educational psychology*. Boston: Allyn & Bacon.

Woolfolk, A. E., & Hoy, W. K. (1990). Prospective teachers' sense of efficacy and beliefs about control. *Journal of Educational Psychology, 82*(1), 81–91.

Wong, B. Y. L. (1994). Instructional parameters promoting transfer of learned strategies in students with learning disabilities. *Learning Disability Quarterly, 17*, 110–120.

Designing Instruction to Meet the Needs of All Learners: Universal Design for Learning

After reading this chapter, you will be able to:

1. Define Universal Design for Learning (UDL)
2. Discuss the reasoning behind using UDL to provide equal access to instruction
3. Explain the principles of UDL
4. Detect barriers to student learning with the LEARNS strategy
5. Apply the principles of UDL to remove barriers to learning through the use of the LEARNS strategy

INTRODUCTION

"Individuals with disabilities now have the right to a free appropriate public school education, and can expect to find educational buildings that are physically accessible to them. It remains a tragedy, however, that the curricula—the materials and methods for learning inside those building—are frequently NOT available or accessible to children with disabilities." (Rose, 2001a)

The regulations found in laws and acts of Congress (IDEIA-04, NCLB, ADA, and Assistive Technology Act; see Table 7.1) compel educators and school personnel to provide students with disabilities access to the general education curriculum whenever appropriate. To meet the requirements of the new regulations found in IDEIA-04 and NCLB, general educators and related service personnel need to employ practices that will support all students, support all students' efforts to meet state standards, and help all students pass grade-level assessments and exit exams. However, with fixed, uniform learning materials, teachers are left with the burden of individualizing instruction by providing supplementary adaptations or accommodations for student with special learning needs. Unfortunately, few teachers have either the time or expertise to adequately adapt the curriculum materials to meet the diverse needs of their students (Pisha & Stahl, 2003). Because teachers do not have time, expertise, or resources, students are not receiving the appropriate educational experience they deserves and are entitled to by law. For example, McGuire, Scott, and Shaw (2006) cited a number of studies and reports that decry the fate of many students with disabilities in our public schools. Comments quoted in their article include concerns that (a) special education is broken; (b) there is a need to prevent and forestall educational problems; (c) large numbers of students experience low academic performance, high dropout rates, and poor postschool outcomes; and (d) many general educators do not have the proper attitudes, accommodations, and adaptations in place to educate students with disabilities (p. 166).

To meet the goals of IDEIA-04 and NCLB, the general curriculum must be accessible to all students, and educators must use research-based practices that will achieve results for students who have disabilities. An accessible curriculum can be developed using the principles of Universal Design for Learning (UDL) from the onset. As teachers, we should be aware of UDL as an idea that is gaining acceptance in the educational community. The principles of a UDL curriculum were developed to meet the needs of the full range of students who are actually in our schools, students with a wide range of sensory, motor, cognitive, linguistic, and affective abilities and disabilities rather than a narrow range of students in the middle (Hitchcock & Stahl, 2003). Other groups with exceptional needs that are found in typical classrooms are students who are English language learners (ELL), at risk for school failure, and gifted or talented. In addition, special education classrooms are just as diverse as general education classrooms, and as special education teachers we are compelled to meet the needs of our students who have exceptional needs that are related to their diversity as well as the needs brought about by their disability. Universal Design in education allows educator to prepare, in advance, for these very different needs and, to the extent feasible, design and deliver instruction so as to meet those needs. The information in this chapter offers a way to plan and teach that will accomplish those goals.

As you begin this chapter about UDL, an example from architecture may be helpful in anticipation of the information to follow. Buildings built before the Americans

TABLE 7.1 Review the Laws: IDEA-04, NCLB, ADA, & AT ACT

Access to the General Education Curriculum

The Law	Law's Regulations	Reference Within the Law	Implications
IDEA-04	Adds that students with IEPs should have • Teachers who have high expectations • Ensured access to general education curriculum in the regular classroom	20 U.S.C. § 1400(c)(5)(A)	• General and special educators must take equal responsibility for supporting student's work within the general education curriculum and general education classrooms.
	• Established the National Instructional Materials Accessibility Standard (NIMAS)	20 U.S.C. § 1474(e)(2)	• Increases the ability for educators & students to access digital materials
	• Established a standard for preparing electronic files	Id. at § 1474(e)(3)(B)	• Preparation and distribution of digitized materials is standardized,
	• Established a process for preparation, delivery, and purchase of digitized instruction materials	Id. at §§ 1412(a)(23), 1413(a)(6)	making access possible regardless of the software or computer (PC vs. Mac) selected by a school.
	• Universal design—The term "Universal Design" has the meaning given the term in section 3 of the Assistive Technology Act of 1998 (29 U.S.C. 3002).	§ 602(35)	• Schools should consider the use of UDL and technology as a means to provide access to the general education curriculum.
	• To support the use of technology, including technology with Universal Design principles and assistive technology devices, to maximize accessibility to the general education curriculum for children with disabilities.	§ 611 (e)(2)(C)(v)	
	• Universal Design—The state educational agency (or, in the case of a districtwide assessment, the local educational agency) shall, to the extent feasible, use Universal Design principles in developing and administering any assessments under this paragraph.	§ 612(a)(16)(E)	

(Continued)

TABLE 7.1 Review the Laws: IDEA-04, NCLB, ADA, & AT ACT *(Continued)*

Access to the General Education Curriculum

The Law	Law's Regulations	Reference Within the Law	Implications
NCLB	• Purpose of the act is to ensure that all children have access to high quality and accessible curriculum and reach proficiency on challenging state standards.		• Schools must include students with disabilities as part of the ALL in NCLB. • Both NCLB and IDEIA-04 share requirements for raising expectations for students with disabilities.
ADA-1990	• Public schools must provide fully accessible buildings and classrooms.	Title II	• Schools must provide all students (and visitors, such as parents) equal access to classrooms within a school. • Classrooms should be built or retrofitted to allow students with disabilities full participation in that classroom.
ATA-2004	• Option A: Use 60 percent of assistive technology funds on direct aid programs, including AT reutilization, demonstration programs, alternative financing, and device loan programs. • Option B: Use 70 percent of grant funds on direct aid programs, but states are given full discretion on how to allocate funds for at least two, but up to four, of the programs listed in option A.		• Educators and students have access to Assistive Technology Projects in all 50 states. • Educators and related services providers can attend conferences and professional development opportunities provided by their state's AT project. • Students and their teachers/caregivers can borrow AT for evaluation purposes prior to purchase. • Schools in some states may be eligible for grant funds to purchase AT.

Involvement in the General Education Curriculum

IDEA-04	IEP must contain a statement of • How the student's disability affects the child's involvement and progress in the general education curriculum	20 U.S.C. § 1414(d)(1)(A)(i)(I), (II), (IV)	• The first provision: Understanding the effects of a student's disability is a first step to designing an appropriate educational program and general education

TABLE 7.1 (*Continued*)

Involvement in the General Education Curriculum

The Law	Law's Regulations	Reference Within the Law	Implications
	• Measurable annual goals that enable the student to be involved in and make progress in the general education curriculum • The program modifications or support for school personnel that will be provided for the student to be involved in and make progress in the general education curriculum		classrooms. Also includes a statement about functional performance that acknowledges that functional performance is a critical element to be measured (Karger, 2005). • The second provision: Student progress must be a part of the discussion, which implies that the student should be making progress. Again, functional goals are extended into the general education classroom, recognizing their importance for some students with disabilities (Karger, 2005). • The third provision: stresses that access must include appropriate supports and can guide teachers to consider how they can adapt instruction to enable student participation in the general education curriculum (Karger, 2005).
	The IEP team must include • The extent to which a student will not participate with nondisabled peers in the regular class • At least one regular education teacher of the student and one special education teacher of the student In addition, a student cannot be removed from the general education class simply because modification(s) to the general education curriculum is required.	20 U.S.C. § 141(d)(1)(A)(i)(V) *Id.* § 141(d)(1)(B)(ii)–(iii) 34 C.F.R. § 300.552(e)	• These three provisions, while not requiring that all students with IEPs be placed in the general education classroom, increased the obligation for schools to consider such placement and must *justify* not selecting that placement (emphasis added). • Further, the second provision clearly indicates that the teacher must be the student's regular education teacher.

(Continued)

TABLE 7.1 Review the Laws: IDEA-04, NCLB, ADA, & AT ACT *(Continued)*

Progress in the General Education Curriculum

The Law	Law's Regulations	Reference Within the Law	Implications
IDEA-04	The IEP must • Include descriptions of how student's progress in meeting annual goals will be measured & when periodic reports will be given	20 U.S.C. § 1414(d)(1)(A)(i)(III)	• IEP teams will need to agree on assessment methods to use, how often goals should be assessed, and how often to report results.
	• Be review periodically, but at least once annually; during the review, revisions must be made to address lack of expected progress, when appropriate All students with disabilities must be	*Id.* § 1414(d)(4)(A)(i), (i)(I)	• IEP teams will need to be accepting of change and flexible in choices of teaching methods, accommodations, or modification if student progress is not evident.
	• Included in all state & district assessment programs, including NCLB assessments	20 U.S.C. § 1412(a)(16)(A)	• This provision requires that students receive effective instruction in the content and held to high expectations for successful learning.
	• Given appropriate accommodations & alternative assessments, as necessary & prescribed in IEPs		• Appropriate assessments are most effective when used during instruction.
	If the student does not participate in above described assessment, the IEP must contain an explanation of why the student cannot participate & why the alternative assessment is more appropriate	*Id.* § 141(d)(1)(A)(i)(VI)	

Sources: Individuals with Disabilities Education Improvement Act of 2004. Retrieved on August 8, 2006, from (2005); Simpson, LaCava, & Graner (2004).

with Disabilities Act (ADA) had to be retrofitted to meet this law that requires all public buildings be accessible for persons with limited mobility and other physical limitations. The universal designs used to make spaces accessible included adding curb cuts for sidewalks and ramps for wheelchair users, elevators in buildings built before elevators existed, doors that can be opened by persons with limited physical stamina, and Braille labels on doors and elevators. However, many of these retrofits are architecturally unattractive and may not be fully useful to users. For example, historical and other older buildings often cannot be retrofitted to allow users to enter via the front door, and instead users might be required to enter through an alleyway or at the rear of the building. This hardly provides a warm or welcoming entrance. Other buildings have had to build ramps that interrupt the beautiful facades of the buildings and sometimes are not easily navigated due to steep slopes. Compare these retrofits to the accommodations made in buildings constructed since ADA, where access is considered in the original design of the building and needs of persons with limited mobility and strength are built into and blend with the design. After ADA was passed, architects struggled with the retrofits because they were costly in both expense and construction time—for example, finding space to add the accessible stall within the confines of an already constructed public restroom. On the other hand, architects had few problems making those accommodations in new construction. In fact, they are so seamless that most of us rarely even notice them. When was the last time you actually paid attention to the fact that a door opened automatically for you, or that you could Rollerblade down a curb cut to cross the street, or that you took advantage of the extra room in an airport restroom's accessible stall because you were pulling a carry-on bag. Thinking about UDL in construction of buildings leads us to draw two conclusions, which are presented in the UDL literature.

First, designing instructions that include accommodations is easier than retrofitting them into existing lesson plans and less costly in teacher time and effort. Second, many, if not most, accommodations benefit all students just as curb cuts benefit all walkers, moms with baby strollers, bicycle riders, and so on. To that end, we will explore the principles of UDL, benefits of using this thinking when designing learning experiences, and a strategy for applying UDL principles when planning instruction. In the next section we will define UDL, outline its history, and explain the principles of UDL established by CAST.

DEFINITION OF UDL

To begin, think about these two statements by Bowe, who is deaf, that define what he considers a disability to be:

> "Disability is something you experience, not something you are." (Bowe, 2000, p. 10)
> "Disability is an interaction between a person and an environment." (Bowe, 2000)

As you read the following two definitions of UDL, reflect about how the use of UDL would enhance the experience and interactions of persons with disabilities.

> In terms of learning, universal design means the design of instructional materials and activities that *make the learning goals achievable by individuals with wide differences in their abilities to see, hear, speak, move, read, write, understand English, attend, organize, engage, and remember.* Universal design for learning is achieved by means of *flexible curricular materials and activities* that provide alternatives for students with differing abilities. These *alternatives are built into the instructional design and operating systems of educational materials; they are not added on after-the-fact.* (emphasis added: Council for Exceptional Children, 1999)

Here is the second definition: UDL is "the design of products and environments to be usable by all people, to the greatest extent possible, without the need for adaptation or specialized design" (Mace, 1997).

AN OVERVIEW AND BRIEF HISTORY OF UDL

Rose and Meyer founded the Center for Applied Special Technology (CAST) in the early 1990s. They began to apply the concepts they knew from the architectural concepts of Universal Design and coined the term Universal Design for Learning (UDL). The CAST researchers developed electronic books and templates for eBooks with built-in features to make the books accessible to young readers with disabilities. These first efforts at creating books were published by Don Johnston Developmental Equipment (e.g., Gateway Stories and Gateway Authoring System). Eventually those prototypes evolved into the Wiggleworks literacy program, which was published in collaboration with Scholastic. This early intervention literacy program has been marketed successfully for all young children, but it contains many built features that make the program accessible to students with sensory, physical, and learning disabilities. As teachers used these early UDL materials, they noted that students without disabilities enjoyed using the electronic texts (Rose & Meyer, 2000). As the CAST researchers continued their work they saw similarities between Universal Design for access to physical spaces and their work on making instructional materials more accessible for learners. Thus they began further development of the ideas behind Universal Design for Learning.

While UDL is grounded in the principles of Universal Design in architecture, it is also supported by recent research that has allowed researchers to detect activity in human brains (Hitchcock, Meyer, Rose, & Jackson, 2002). A key idea that formed the foundation of UDL (Rose & Meyer, 2002) is that human learning is distributed across three interconnected networks in the brain: recognition, strategic, and affective networks.

Using fMRI/PET (functional magnetic resonance imaging/positron-emission tomography) scans, scientists are able to view patterns of glucose burning as these patterns light up during activities of reading such as looking at words, listening to others read, or reading aloud. During these scans, researchers found that the brain has separate parts or modules that can be rearranged, replaced, or interchanged easily as the brain processes information. Rose described the specialized processors as operating "like a well functioning ad-hoc committee" (Hitchcock, Rose, & Danielson, 2000, p. 1). During these glucose burns, activity patterns are seen distributed throughout the brain as tasks vary. Activity occurs in both hemispheres as well as the front, middle, and rear sections of the brain. Researchers noted that after a number of trials with a new task the level of the glucose burn is reduced, and if a familiar task is repeated with new information, there are lower levels of glucose burn than seen when executing a new task. Researchers discovered differences in the glucose within each subject. Hitchcock and colleagues (2000) concluded that when teachers teach isolated facts and figures they may be making learning more difficult or even compromising learning because within individual brains the functioning can vary significantly. This may explain why teachers find variances in how students with similar achievement levels learn, or why some students may do well on one learning task but not in another. Finally and perhaps most important, researchers also noticed that these glucose burns appeared to be a series of networks that attended to different tasks. Each of these networks—recognition, strategic, and affective—performs its task parallel to the others, and while they are interconnected, each is a specialized network.

The recognition networks "are specialized to sense and assign meaning to patterns we see; they enable us to identify and understand information, ideas and concepts"

(Rose & Meyer, 2002, p. 12). Recognition networks help students recognize the information to be learned. The strategic networks "are specialized to generate and oversee mental and motor patterns" thus enabling students "to plan, execute and monitor actions and skills" (Rose & Meyer, 2002, p. 12). Strategic networks allow students to apply strategies to process information. The affective networks "are specialized to evaluate patterns and assign them emotions significance; they enable us to engage with tasks and learning and with the world around us" (Rose & Meyer, 2002, p. 13). Affective networks allow students to fully engage with the learning task.

During the glucose burns discussed above, parallel processing is occurring as the brain attempts to recognize an image. As Hitchcock and colleagues (2000) explained, the brain is looking for context and content. To accomplish that, the back of our brains attempts to *recognize* the images while the front brain is determining a *strategy* for investigating. At the same time, our *affective* system is determining if this image is important to us.

Taking what they learned from their brain research one step further, Rose and Meyer determined that these three networks parallel Vygotsky's three prerequisites of learning. Vygotsky's (1978) theory states that there are three prerequisites for learning to take place. Students must be able to recognize the information to be learned, apply strategies to process information, and engage fully with the task presented. Data from the brain research reported by CAST suggest that the networks allow students to accomplish Vygotsky's prerequisites as the recognition network recognizes the information to be learned, the strategic network processes the information, and the affective network engages the students interest in the task. In the next section, we will explore how the brain research translates to using UDL in our teaching practices.

Assumptions Must Shift

UDL shifts our assumptions about teaching and learning in four fundamental ways:

1. Students with disabilities are not a separate category of learners; instead they are one of a continuum of learners, all with differences. We should not focus *only* on categorical differences, such as disabilities/nondisabled, ELL/English speakers, or at risk/gifted. When we have a limited focus we may miss many differences between learners within the categories and likewise miss similarities across categories of learners (Rose & Meyer, 2000).
2. The student is not seen as the one who must change, but rather the focus shifts from remediation or fixing students to creating a flexible curriculum with options embedded within the curriculum that accommodates learner differences. Originally our curriculum was designed to assimilate and acculturate a variety of immigrants who came to the United States into one culture with little regard for those who were not Anglo-Saxon Christians (e.g., slaves from Africa and China or Native Americans), but as our population has changed and we have invited many cultures and religions into our communities and schools, we have not changed the way we teach. We still use the printed and spoken word as the primary ways of delivering instruction and assessing learning. UDL asks us to reconsider this approach to take into account the variety of learners we teach. The UDL approach is similar to but not quite the same as a teaching approach known as *differentiating instruction*, because that approach is centered

mostly on a learning style philosophy and does not generally take learners with disabilities or the entire learning environment into account (Hitchcock & Stahl, 2003).

3. Curriculum materials should be varied and diverse, including digital and online resources, rather than centering on a single textbook or solely on print materials. We should consider the wide variety of options available to us, such as audio books, including online talking dictionaries, podcasts, video, interactive Internet sites, and so forth.

4. Teacher adjustments for learner differences should occur for all students, not just those with disabilities. Just as you and I take advantage of automated doors, curb cuts, and moving walkways, all students should be offered options for how they take in and express learning experiences.

The *central practical premise* of UDL is that a curriculum should include alternatives to make it accessible and appropriate for individuals with different backgrounds, learning preferences, abilities, and disabilities in widely varied learning contexts (see Figure 7.1). However, the *universal* in Universal Design does *not* imply *one* optimal solution for everyone, but rather it reflects an awareness of the unique nature of each learner and the need to accommodate differences, creating learning experiences that suit the learner and maximize his or her ability to progress (Rose & Meyer, 2000). Further, UDL does not imply that there is one medium for instruction but that *universal* implies multiple teaching methods and types of media (Rose & Meyer, 2000). UDL curriculums are not available for purchase because UDL is not a single method or program (see Figure 7.2) but is a way of thinking and acting when teachers plan and implement instruction (Hitchcock & Stahl, 2003).

As we discussed in Chapter 1, some teachers in both general and special education have had a deficit view of students with exceptional needs: They have seen what is "wrong" with the student or that the students with exceptional needs are the problem and then attempt to fix the "wrong" part of the student. Certainly it is important for educators to be able to recognize that a student has a disability or any other specific need—without that knowledge we would not understand what to do to eliminate the barriers found in the interaction of the student with the curriculum. Too often in the past, though, teachers have used accommodations and modifications that we have come to understand lower standards and water down the curriculum that every student should learn. Ellis (1997) suggested that accommodations and modifications that require less work (such as fewer spelling words), basing grades on effort rather than actual achievement, providing high-interest/low-vocabulary materials, or providing special content classes outside the general education classroom may seem like logical practices, but they actually limit achievement of students with disabilities. Rather than looking at the students as having the problem, teachers who use UDL look for the barriers to learning that exist in classrooms, teaching materials, and teaching methods. When these barriers are removed, learning becomes possible for a wider audience of students and lessens the need for many of the individual accommodations generally provided (Rose & Meyer, 2002). Furthermore, principles of UDL provide a framework for general and special educators as they collaborate to plan and teach in order to meet the growing diversity found in public school classrooms (see Figure 7.3).

Bowe (2000) suggested that educators can design learning experiences based on the seven principles of Universal Design used in designing accessible buildings and products.

1. **Equitable Use:** Design or find curricular materials that are accessible to all learners.
   a. Provide the same means of use for all learners; identical whenever possible; equivalent when not.
   b. Avoid segregating or stigmatizing any learners.
   c. Make provisions for privacy, security, and safety equally available to all learners.
   d. Make the design appealing to all learners.
2. **Flexibility in Use:** Design or find curricular materials that meet the widest variety of preferences.
   a. Provide a variety of ways to use the learning materials.
   b. Accommodate for right- or left-handed access and use.
   c. Provide adaptability to the user's pace.
3. **Simple & Intuitive Use:** Design or find curricular materials that avoid unnecessary complexity and are easy to use and understand.
   a. Eliminate unnecessary complexity.
   b. Be consistent with user expectations and intuition.
   c. Accommodate a wide range of literacy and language skills.
   d. Arrange information in order of its importance.
   e. Provide effective prompting and feedback during and after task completion.
4. **Perceptible Information:** Design or find curricular materials that provide information effectively to the user, regardless of conditions or the user's sensory abilities and are effective in all kinds of settings
   a. Use different modes (pictorial, verbal, tactile) for redundant presentation of essential information.
   b. Maximize legibility of essential information.
   c. Differentiate elements in ways that can be described (i.e., make it easy to give instructions or directions).
   d. Provide compatibility with a variety of techniques or devices used by people with sensory limitations.
5. **Tolerance for Errors:** Design or find curricular materials that accommodate errors by minimizing hazards and the adverse consequences of accidental or unintended actions.
   a. Arrange elements to minimize hazards and errors: Most-used elements should be the most accessible; hazardous elements should be eliminated, isolated, or shielded.
   b. Provide warnings of hazards and errors (e.g., tell students about the errors most frequently made by students in the past).
   c. Provide failsafe features (e.g., allow students to use computer with spell and grammar check; use calculators for advanced math problems).
   d. Discourage unconscious action in tasks that require vigilance.
6. **Low Physical Effort:** Design or find curricular materials that require minimal effort to use so that the device or instruction can be used efficiently, comfortably, and with a minimum of fatigue.
   a. Allow user to maintain a neutral body position.
   b. Use reasonable operating forces (e.g., automatic door openers minimize operating force; specific keyboards for persons who must type with one hand, or who need something other than QWERTY keys, do the same for students who need them).
   c. Minimize sustained physical effort.
7. **Size & Space for Approach and Use:** Design or find curricular materials that accommodate variations, and provide appropriate size and space for approach, reach, manipulation, and use regardless of user's body size, posture, or mobility.
   a. Provide a clear line of sight to important elements for any seated or standing user.
   b. Make reach to all components comfortable for any seated or standing user.

FIGURE 7.1 The Principles of Universal Design

Sources: Information from Bowe (2000); McGuire, Scott, & Shaw (2006).

c. Accommodate variations in hand and grip size.

d. Provide adequate space for the use of assistive devices or personal assistance.

McGuire, Scott, and Shaw (2006, p. 170) suggested two additional principles that would make the original principles more applicable to education.

8. **A Community of Learners:**
   a. The instructional environment promotes interaction and communication among students and between students and faculty.

9. **Instructional Climate:**
   a. Instruction is designed to be welcoming and inclusive.
   b. Teachers hold high expectations for all students.

Providing Physical Access

- Assures that classrooms, labs, and fieldwork are accessible to individuals with a wide range of physical abilities and disabilities.
- Assures that equipment and activities
  - Minimize sustained physical effort
  - Provide options for operation
  - Accommodate right- and left-handed students,
  - Accommodate those with limited physical abilities
- Assures the safety of all students

Varying Delivery Methods

- Uses multiple modes to deliver content. Alternate delivery methods, including:
  - Lecture and demonstrations by students as well as the teacher
  - Discussion, including whole and small groups as well as peer partners
  - Hands-on activities as well as project-based learning
  - Internet-based activities, such as Web Quests and using online dictionaries, podcasts, electronic textbooks
  - Fieldwork, including homework assignments in the community as well as school-sponsored field trips and outdoor activities around the school and in the community
- Assures that content is accessible to students with a wide range of abilities, disabilities, interests, and previous experiences
  - Provide printed materials that vary the degree of support. For example, teacher-made worksheet with examples completed, digital materials that can be read by text-to-speech software, and hyperlinked electronic books.
  - Provide written summaries of content delivered orally.
  - Provide printed materials early to allow the student to prepare ahead of time.

Web Pages

Should be accessible by

- Providing printed materials digitally
- Providing text descriptions of graphics presented on Web pages
- Creating printed and Web-based materials in simple, intuitive, and consistent formats that support, enrich, or assess student knowledge
- Arranging content in order of importance

FIGURE 7.2 Translating the Seven Principles Into Classroom Teaching Practices

Interaction

Encourages a variety of ways for students to interact with each other and with you. These methods may include

- In-class questions answered with raised paddle, thumbs-up, or hand on nose
- Peer groups
- Collaborative discussions
- Heterogeneous group work
- Internet-based communications (discussion boards/chat rooms)

Feedback

- Provide effective prompting during an activity and feedback after the assignment is complete.
- Prompting can be verbal or physical or visual.
- Feedback can be brief or extensive, such as in a task analysis.

Demonstration of Knowledge

Provide multiple ways for students to demonstrate knowledge. For example, as an alternative to traditional tests and papers, provide options for demonstrating knowledge.

- Project-based learning reports
- Group work reports
- Demonstrations
- Portfolios
- Dynamic assessments
- Presentations
- Experiments
- Role-plays

FIGURE 7.2 (*Continued*)

Employing Universal Design principles to fully include one group of students can generate unanticipated benefits to others. Consider this list of students who might benefit from closed captioning in videos shown in your classroom.

- Students for whom English is a second language. Often their reading skills are better than their spoken English skills.
- Students who are deaf. By reading what they cannot hear, captioning provides access to deaf students.
- Students with visual impairments. Captioning is generally not useful for students with visual impairments, but there is one exception. Students who are deaf and have low vision (i.e., they can see large print) can benefit from captioning if the captions are large enough for them to see.
- Students watching the video in a noisy environment. By reading what they cannot hear, students watching the tape in a noisy environment will benefit from captioning.
- Students who have learning disabilities. Some may comprehend material better when they both see text and hear it spoken aloud.

FIGURE 7.3 Who Benefits from UDL?

As mentioned above, three networks found in the brain inform the foundations of the UDL framework (Orkwis & McLane, 1998; Rose, 2001b):

1. Because individuals have diverse *recognition* networks, teachers should provide multiple, flexible methods of presentation. Alternative modes of presentation reduce perceptual and learning barriers. For example, important teacher demonstrations could be recorded on digital video, saved to a classroom computer, and enhanced with captions of the teacher's explanation. These videos are then made available to any student who wishes to review the demonstration for clarification or review.

2. Because individuals have diverse *strategic* networks, teachers should provide multiple, flexible methods of expression and apprenticeship. Students can respond with preferred means to accommodate for strategic and motor system barriers. For example,

   a. Paper/pencil assignments may present barriers to those who have physical or written expression difficulties; for those students, responding using a computer or voice recorder may eliminate that barrier.

   b. Oral presentation can present barriers for some students with speech, expressive language, or anxiety disorders; for these students, using a multimedia presentation format or creating a video may eliminate those barriers.

   c. Artwork can be fun for most students, but for some it is very difficult or impossible. Offering students opportunities to use digital programs such as KidPics, or PaintShop or digital libraries of clip art may eliminate this barrier.

   d. Organization of reports, essays, and notes from reading can present barriers to students with difficulty in attending and organizing; for these students, using a graphic organizer or concept map, such as Inspiration, may eliminate that barrier.

3. Because individuals have diverse *affective* networks, teachers should provide multiple, flexible options for engagement. Students' interests in learning are matched with ways of presenting and responding, which can increase motivation to meet cognitive challenges of learning.

   a. Finding the right balance of support and challenge to give a student is the key to engagement in learning activities, especially as every child has a different need for being supported or challenged. Therefore, providing varying levels of support with scaffolds and setting varying levels of challenge will allow the curriculum to be flexible enough to remove barriers for those who need them but will not be too easy for the high achievers. For example, offering *optional* bare-bones note-taking guides or graphic organizers for lectures, demonstrations, or videos will support those who have difficulty writing, attending, or organizing but will not take away autonomy from those who prefer to take notes in their own way.

   b. Generally children and youth enjoy a degree of novelty in learning experiences, but some may be more comfortable with familiar tasks and higher degrees of repetition when learning. Providing multiple levels of novelty and familiarity will support most learners. For example, when researching a topic for a report/research paper, allow students to use standard print and library resources as well as Internet searches, WebQuests, or interviews of experts (in person or via an Internet site).

c. While students in the same grade or class may be close in chronological age, they have not developed at the same rate, either physically or cognitively, and they may have cultural differences that affect learning. As a result, individuals will be attracted to different content and formats of presentation. Providing important concepts and big ideas in a variety of formats and contents will help remove barriers of development and culture. For example, provide students the choice to use graphic organizers or concept maps rather than note cards; rather than writing a book report, allow them to make a video or PowerPoint presentation or allow them to choose to discuss either the book or the life of the author and events that caused the author to write the book; or give students opportunities to chose to work in small-group work or with a single partner or to complete individual work for some activities.

d. Students may be more fully engaged in learning if they contribute to the learning process. A curriculum that allows students to contribute is often referred to as being "half full" (Orkwis & McLane, 1998, p.19). This does not mean that planning is unfinished or incomplete but that the curriculum is flexible enough to allow direct student input. For example, activities that allow for student contributions to the curriculum include project-based learning experiences, WebQuests, book clubs, and class blogs.

It is important to note, just as UDL is not one size fits all, we should not make the mistake of thinking that access to information is the same as access to learning (Rose & Meyer, 2000). UDL is more than just making the information accessible, which can be counterproductive. For example, text-to-speech readers can read to students, which is wonderful if the task is to read for content; but if the task is to learn how to decode new words, then text-to-speech software is counterproductive (Rose & Meyer, 2000). Therefore, it is important to understand the learning task goals before assuming that technology is the answer to gaining access to learning. Just as Ellis (1997) noted that some accommodations used with students who have disabilities water down the curriculum and do not actually facilitate true learning, teachers cannot assume that merely giving students access to information equals student learning. Teachers must clearly understand what goal is to be accomplished, determine what students can and cannot do, and decide what barriers exist before they can decide how to change the task to support learner differences (Rose & Meyer, 2000). The strategy presented in the next section is meant to support teachers as they consider the demographics of their students, determine what barriers to learning may be present, and plan instruction.

USING THE LEARNS STRATEGY TO PLAN UDL LESSONS

All teachers, regardless of grade or content taught, are now teaching students with diverse learning needs in their classrooms. In the previous chapters, you have read about those students and the laws, IDEIA and NCLB, that have placed an increased emphasis on inclusion of these students in general education classrooms and on teacher accountability for the learning gains of all students. The LEARNS strategy (see Figure 7.4) provides a framework for applying the principles of UDL by helping you plan instruction and use materials that support all students, while increasing student engagement and integrating the appropriate use of technology in your lessons.

	Learning Goal(s) matched to appropriate state standard	
STEP 1: Learning goal Determine the learning goals based on state standards.		
	Teaching activity	**Skills necessary to complete task or activity**
STEP 2: Note teacher **Expectations**. What must students be able to do to complete learning tasks successfully or to achieve mastery of content taught?		
STEP 3: Areas of strength and need for each student are noted.	**Note academic and/or social strengths and weaknesses with name of student(s)**	**Note general academic and social implications or ways that these problems are evident in the classroom**
STEP 4: Review Compare and contrast Step 2 and Step 3, and note major areas where any students will encounter barriers to learning if you do not make any accommodations.	**Skills necessary to complete task or activity**	**Note barriers to learning with name of student(s)**
STEP 5: Note accommodations. Determine methods, strategies, and materials that will meet most students' needs.	**Area of need with name of student(s)**	**Universal Design features that will eliminate barriers to learning**
STEP 6: Specify individual accommodations needed by students whose special needs are not met by UDL provisions.	**Unmet need with name of student(s)**	**Accommodations for individual needs**

FIGURE 7.4 The LEARNS Strategy Worksheet for Designing UDL Lesson Plans

The LEARNS strategy for planning UDL lessons uses the following six steps (see Figure 7.4):

Step 1: **L**earning goal: Determine what content will be taught.

Step 2: Note teacher **E**xpectations for lesson objective.

Step 3: **A**reas of strength and need for each student are noted.

Step 4: **R**eview and determine barriers.

Step 5: **N**ote accommodations needed.

Step 6: **S**pecify individual accommodations needed for specific students.

The LEARNS strategy is based on three assumptions. First, all instructional environments present barriers to learning. These barriers may be in the physical environment or in the instructional methods and materials used for instruction. Barriers may include the inability to *see or hear* the teacher due to seating arrangements; the inability to *use* the printed materials due to visual impairment, language difference, or reading disability; and the inability to *communicate* learning because of language difference, language disability, speech impairment, or inability to physically use instructional materials or a cognitive processing disability. These are just some of the possible barriers to learning commonly found in classrooms.

The second assumption of LEARNS is that with analysis of student needs and strengths, the tasks required to acquire knowledge and skills, and the barriers within the instructional setting and tasks, teachers can plan instruction that meets the needs of diverse students in their classroom. Once the analysis is completed, teachers can select instructional methods, materials, and accommodations that can remove barriers for more than one student and maximize students' learning opportunities. Selecting accommodations for groups of students in their classrooms will minimize the amount of time required to differentiate instruction. For example, an audio text might be used by students who are ELL as well students who are visually impaired or have a reading disability.

The third assumption of LEARNS is that by planning ahead to meet those diverse needs, teachers can reduce the amount of time required to add on accommodations. Think back to the beginning of this chapter and the discussion of adding Universal Design accommodations to existing buildings versus building the accommodations into the design of the building. The same is true for teachers who must retrofit lessons with accommodations. LEARNS can help teachers design their lessons with accommodations already in mind. This ensures building the most effective accommodations into the lesson, allowing all students opportunities to select or reject the accommodations they need, and providing equitable access to the curriculum for all students.

The LEARNS strategy was mainly designed to use the principles of UDL, but it also includes elements of differentiated instruction. These two approaches are quite similar and use many of the same principles for designing instruction. When differentiating instruction, teachers first must recognize that students have differing background knowledge, readiness, language, preferences in learning, and interests. Then, teachers plan their instruction with the intent of maximizing each student's growth and individual success by meeting each student where he or she is and assisting in the learning process (Hall, 2002). These are the same ideals held by teachers who use UDL to plan instruction, with the primary difference being that UDL users recognize that instructional environments present barriers and that these barriers must be removed.

Using the LEARNS strategy does not eliminate the continuing need for special education services; in fact, Step 6 in the strategy provides for inclusion of special education services and specialized accommodations for individual students who require them. Further, UDL is not intended to eliminate or replace special education and its related services, because even if teachers design curricula, assessments, and teaching methods that are accessible to a wide variety of students, some students with specific disabilities will continue to need the services and educational setting found in individualized special education programs (McGuire, Scott, & Shaw, 2006). There will always be the need for some specific accommodations, such as sign language interpreters for students who are deaf, speech and language services, orientation and mobility and Braille instruction, and individual instruction in basic skills, but applying the LEARNS strategy with Universal Design concepts in course planning will ensure full access to the content for most students.

Using the Steps

STEP 1: LEARNING GOAL: DETERMINE WHAT CONTENT WILL BE TAUGHT   Teachers may use several methods to determine what to teach. They may begin with a scope and sequence of a long-term instructional plan for their grade or content, use the curriculum guide provided by a textbook publisher, or have a specific skill set that needs to be taught to prepare students for other content work. Whatever the method used to determine content to be taught, the first step of LEARNS requires that content be linked to state standards, as most assessments required by NCLB are based on state standards, and therefore actual content taught should be based on the same standards.

Once the standard has been selected the teacher should determine the final learning goal(s) that will be assessed and develop each goal's learning objectives for the lesson. The final task for Step 1 is to determine the level of Bloom's Taxonomy. Determining the Bloom's level will assure that a portion of the learning experiences presented to the students is above the knowledge level so that some experiences include application and synthesis of knowledge.

STEP 2: NOTE TEACHER EXPECTATIONS FOR LESSON OBJECTIVE   In this step teachers will determine the tasks required to complete each of the lesson objectives. Complete a task analysis for each of the tasks. For example, let's assume that students are to read a book for a book report. Tasks may include reading print, taking notes, finding additional information (research skills), following a plot and understanding plot development, distinguishing characters and remembering their actions, and understanding allegories and other literary devices while reading. Then, for the writing portion of the assignment, students will need to be able to organize their thoughts about the book/author, be able to compose the report, and complete basic writing tasks such as spelling, sentence structure, and punctuation. Each of these tasks may present a barrier to any of the students in your classroom, depending on their special needs and abilities.

STEP 3: AREAS OF STRENGTH AND NEED FOR EACH STUDENT ARE NOTED   To determine the areas of strength and need for each student, we suggest completing a demographic worksheet for your class (see Chart 7.1; an example will also be provided in the instructor's manual). Information you might collect includes gender; age; race/ethnicity;

CHART 7.1 Class Demographics

ID#	Student Name	Gender	Native Language	Race	Parent Status	SES/ Lunch Status	Reading Level	Math Level	Language, Exceptionality, or Other Special Need	Other
1										
2										
3										
4										
5										
6										
7										
8										
9										
10										
11										
12										
13										
14										
15										
16										
17										
18										
19										
20										
21										
22										
23										
24										
25										
26										
27										
28										
29										
30										

socioeconomic status; reading and math competency levels; special needs, such as disability, ELL status, gifted/talented; and any other information that might be pertinent for your content area. For example, secondary teachers may want to know how students preformed in prerequisite courses (i.e., how well did the student do in Algebra I, if enrolled in an Algebra II class now?). Once these data are collected, teachers are able to see areas of concern that should be addressed, such as students who are not reading on grade level or have a disability that requires accommodations. Once this task is done, the demographics information can be used again for other planning sessions and need only be reviewed periodically to update or add new students.

STEP 4: REVIEW AND DETERMINE BARRIERS   Now the teacher is ready to compare the required tasks (Step 2) with possible areas of need (Step 3) and determine the barriers that may exist in the instructional environment. The first task here would be to look for barriers that affect more than one student. For example, one of the tasks noted in Step 2 is reading the text and teacher-made print materials. Imagine that one student has a reading disability, several other students do not read on grade level, and two students are ELL; then the teacher may assume that reading print materials presented during the lesson will present a barrier for all of these students (see Figure 7.5). In addition, if one or more students are reading above grade level or are considered gifted/talented, some of the print materials may present a barrier to higher-order thinking and advancement of their learning, so then the teacher will need to extend the learning and provide appropriate print materials for their learning abilities.

Each task in Step 2 should be reviewed so that barriers and students affected by the barrier can be determined. To facilitate the process required for Step 4, completing a Common Barriers Inventory prior to beginning Step 4 may be helpful (see Figure 7.5). In addition, this inventory will help teachers think about their classroom organization and most often used instructional groupings, materials, methods, student tasks, and student methods of response. Knowing and understanding what conditions and learning experiences exist in any classroom is essential to understanding what barriers may face students and obstruct their learning. Teachers may be unintentionally creating a barrier to learning in seating or placement of student desks near a noisy window area, in grouping of students, or in assigning a task that is difficult for students to complete. Once the teacher has determined the present conditions, possible barriers, and which students may be adversely affected by one or more barriers, the teacher is ready to note accommodations that would eliminate each of the barriers.

While this task may seem time-consuming, in most cases many tasks used in any one lesson will be repeated in lessons throughout the year. Once a teacher determines that a barrier exists for a particular task, that would be true for this task across all lessons, and similar accommodations for eliminating the barriers could be repeated across lessons and content areas. For example, if a student has difficulty writing legibly due to a specific disability, this student may have difficulty producing work that requires handwriting or drawing. Therefore, barriers could exist in language arts, social studies, math, science, art, and so forth. In many tasks found in all of these content areas, students might benefit from using a word processor to complete required tasks.

STEP 5: NOTE ACCOMMODATIONS NEEDED   At this point the teacher is ready to make decisions about ways and means to eliminate barriers found in Step 4. Let's continue

(The first item has been completed to illustrate the purpose of each column.)			
	Present Situation	**Possible Barriers**	**Students Who May Experience a Barrier Are Those Who**
Classroom organization	**Physical space** • Room designed for 20 students but 25 enrolled • West wall of windows facing the playground • Room next to a restroom • Whiteboard across the room from windows	• Size of the room and spacing of the seating • Placement of board, materials, and student seats • Teacher's voice volume • Windows, doorways, and hallway traffic	• Use wheelchairs • Have sensory impairments • Have attention impairments
	Routines		
	Climate		
	Rules		
	Other		
Instructional groupings	**Whole class**		
	Small groups		
	Individual		
	Peer mediated		
Instructional materials	**Textbooks**		
	Workbooks/worksheets		
	Trade books		
	Teacher-made handouts		

FIGURE 7.5 Common Barriers Found in Classrooms, Materials, and Curricula

Sources: Bowe (2000); Center for Applied Special Technology (CAST, 2006); Friend & Bursuck (2006); Rose & Meyer (2002).

	Present Situation	Possible Barriers	Students Who May Experience a Barrier Are Those Who
	Posters		
	Journals, newspapers, or newspapers		
	Computer		
Instructional methods used by teacher	Lecture to whole group		
	One to one		
	Group work		
	Project-based learning (group or independent)		
	Activity based		
Instructional presentation methods used by teacher	Demonstration		
	Videos		
	Audio materials (tape/ CD, includes music)		
	PowerPoint presentations		
	Chalkboard or white-board		
	Note-taking guides or handouts		

FIGURE 7.5 (*Continued*)

	Present Situation	Possible Barriers	Students Who May Experience a Barrier Are Those Who
	Images (photographs, maps, drawings, time-lines, graphs, charts, tables, etc.)		
Student tasks during instruction	Whole-class discussions		
	Small-group discussions		
	Independent reading		
	Use manipulatives		
	Independent practice of tasks		
	Homework		
Student tasks for response	Oral responses to questions		
	Oral reading		
	Handwritten work (paper/pencil tasks)		
	Drawings/diagrams/graphic organizers		
	Essays and papers (research or term)		
	Project results (reports or three-dimensional items)		

FIGURE 7.5 (*Continued*)

	Present Situation	Possible Barriers	Students Who May Experience a Barrier Are Those Who
	Project results (oral presentation)		
Student tasks outside instructional setting	Library research		
	Online research		
	Data collection		
	Interviews		

FIGURE 7.5 Common Barriers Found in Classrooms, Materials, and Curricula

with the example of print materials for the book report. Assume that you have selected a state standard that requires students read and write about a book they have read. One way to eliminate barriers presented by print is to allow students to select a book at their reading level, another is to allow students to use an audio book or a digital copy with a screen reader such as Kurzweil or allow students to read a graphic novel, and still another is to allow students to form a book club and read a book together. Suppose, however, that your students must all read the same book as might be required in middle and high school classes; then, providing audio and digital copies of the book might be most helpful. Reviewing the chapters on technology and methods for teaching specific content will provide more examples of ways to eliminate barriers to learning.

STEP 6: SPECIFY INDIVIDUAL ACCOMMODATIONS NEEDED FOR SPECIFIC STUDENTS As previously noted, the first five steps of LEARNS do not eliminate *every* barrier for *every* student. Students with disabilities may have very specific accommodations or modifications that need to be in place. For example, students with hearing impairments may need voice amplification or a sign language interpreter, while students with physical disabilities may need a special desk, preferential seating, a personal assistant, or specialized assistive technology. These special accommodations would be found on the student's Individual Education Program or related to a teacher by the special educator and would be routine for most lessons and class activities. As a teacher becomes more familiar and comfortable with UDL principles, some of these specialized accommodations also may be eliminated though use of UDL; however, teachers should not expect that all individual accommodations will or can be eliminated.

Summary

The classroom environment and learning tasks required can affect the learning of all students, but especially those with who are diverse learners with exceptional needs and, in particular, students with disabilities. Schools and teachers are guided by the laws (IDEIA-04, NCLB, ADA, and AT Act) that support inclusion of students with disabilities and assess for all students to a high-quality, accessible curriculum based on challenging state standards. Further, classrooms have become more diverse and contain students with exceptional needs, such as ELL and G/T, as well as students with disabilities. Teachers are faced with designing classrooms and instruction to meet the needs of this diverse population and helping these students meet state standards. This can seem like a daunting task, but using UDL when planning classroom design, instruction, and assessments can ease the teachers' task as they plan for instruction. While UDL is not intended to create a one-size-fits-all curriculum, understanding how students recognize information, generate and oversee mental and motor patterns, and engage with the learning task will help teachers find the barriers to learning that are present in their classroom and learning tasks. Finally, the LEARNS strategy provides a method for identifying demands of learning tasks, needs of individual and groups of students, barriers within learning tasks that will affect student learning, and accommodations. When teachers use LEARNS to plan, they avoid the need to retrofit their lessons and are able to meet the needs of most students.

This chapter began with a quote from Rose's testimony before the U.S. Senate's Appropriations Committee. Rose (2001a) made a final recommendation to the committee, which is a clarion call to all educators:

"The over-arching recommendation I make to you is that we extend the same kinds of protections now afforded to physical spaces and to information in the workplace to a new area, the most important space for our future—the learning space. Our future as a culture depends on us to make the learning spaces, those most precious spaces in the lives of our children, accessible and supportive of every single child. I believe that if we make the learning spaces of our schools accessible to all of our children, we will save both the short-term costs of mis-educating our children in the present and the long-term costs of NOT educating them in the future." (p. 67)

References

Bowe, R. G. (2000). *Universal Design in education: Teaching nontraditional students*. Westport, CT: Bergin & Garvey.

Center for Applied Special Technology (CAST). (2006). *Teaching every child*. Available at http://www.cast.org/teachingeverystudent/

Council for Exceptional Children. (1999). *Research connections (No. 5)*. Arlington, VA: Author.

Ellis, E. (1997). Watering up the curriculum for adolescents with learning disabilities: Goals for the knowledge dimension. *Remedial and Special Education, 18*(6), 326–346.

Friend, M., & Bursuck, W. D. (20090. *Including students with special needs: A practical guide for classroom teachers*. Upper Saddle River, NJ: Pearson.

Hall, T. (2002). *Differentiated instruction.* Wakefield, MA: National Center on Accessing the General Curriculum. Retrieved August 8, 2006, from http://www.cast.org/publications/ncac/ncac_diffinstruc.html

Hitchcock, C., Rose, D., & Danielson, L. (2000). *Assessing the general curriculum: Promoting a Universal Design for Learning.* Presentation at American Youth Policy Forum on Capitol Hill, Washington, DC. Retrieved on January 1, 2006, from http://www.aypf.org/fournbriefs/2000/fb110300.html

Hitchcock, C., & Stahl, S. (2003) Assistive technology, Universal Design, Universal Design for Learning: Improved learning opportunities. *Journal for Special Education Technology, 18*(4). Retrieved on June 26, 2006, from http://jset.unlv.edu/18.4/hitchcock/first.html

Hitchcock, S., Meyer, A., Rose, D., & Jackson, R. (2002). Providing new access to the general curriculum: Universal Design for Learning. *Teaching Exceptional Children, 35*(2), 8–17.

Individuals with Disabilities Education Improvement Act of 2004. Retrieved on August 8, 2006, from http://www.ed.gov/about/offices/list/osers/osep/index.html

Karger, J. (2005). What IDEA & NCLB suggest about curriculum access for students with disabilities. In D. Rose, A. Meyer, & S. Hitchcock (Eds.), *The universally designed classroom: Accessible curriculum and digital technologies.* Cambridge, MA: Harvard Press.

Mace, R. (1997). *The principles of universal design, version 2.0.* Raleigh, NC: Center for Universal Design.

McGuire, J. M., Scott, S. S., & Shaw, S. F. (2006). Universal Design and it applications in educational environments. *Remedial and Special Education, 27*(3), 166–175.

Orkwis, R., & McLane, K. (1998). A curriculum every student can use: Design principles for student access. Eric/OSEP Topic Brief. Retrieved on June 26, 2006, from http://www.eric.ed.gov/ERICWebPortal/Home.portal?_nfpb=true#x0026;ERICExtSearch_SearchValue_0=Orkwis+and+McLane&ERICExtSearch_SearchType_0=au#x0026;_pageLabel=RecordDetails#x0026;objectId=0900000b8009404d#x0026;accno=ED423654

Pisha, B., & Stahl, S. (2003). The promise of new learning environments for students with disabilities. *Intervention in School & Clinic, 41*(2), 67–75.

Rose, D. (2001a). Text of testimony before the Senate Appropriations Committee. *Journal for Special Education Technology, 16*(4). Retrieved on June 26, 2006, from http://jset.unlv.edu/16.4/asseds/rose.html

Rose, D. (2001b). Universal Design for Learning: Deriving guiding principles from networks that learn. *Journal for Special Education Technology, 16*(1). Retrieved on June 26, 2006, from http://jset.unlv.edu/16.1/asseds/rose.html

Rose, D., & Meyer, A. (2000). The concept of Universal Design. *Journal for Special Education Technology, 15*(1). Retrieved on June 26, 2006, from http://jset.unlv.edu/15.1/asseds/rose.html

Rose, D., & Meyer, A. (2002). *Teaching every student in the digital age: Universal Design for Learning.* Alexandria, VA: Association for Supervision and Curriculum Development.

Simpson, R. L., LaCava, P. G., & Graner, P. S. (2004). The No Child Left Behind Act: Challenges and implications for educators. *Intervention in School and Clinic, 40*(2), 67–75.

Vygotsky, L. S. (1978). *Mind and society: The development of higher mental processes.* Cambridge, MA: Harvard University Press.

Chapter 8

Integrating Technology to Meet Student Needs

After reading this chapter, you will be able to:

1. Recall and explain important terms related to the field of assistive technology
2. Explain who would benefit from using assistive technology devices to enhance their learning
3. Identify team members and their roles and responsibilities in developing IEPs, IFSPs, and IWRPs
4. Understand the assessment process using the SETT framework
5. Discuss how funding for assistive technology is determined and obtained
6. Evaluate the appropriate uses of hardware and software accessibility devices for communication, reading, writing, and mathematics
7. Reflect on the importance of assistive technology as a means for providing all learners access to the curriculum

Most of us have used assistive technology often without realizing it, such as when walking into a business with automatic doors or reading closed-captioned television screens in health clubs, but to people who have physical, sensory, or cognitive impairments, assistive technology is critical, as they may be unable to accomplish everyday tasks and enjoy recreational activities independently without it.

A PARADIGM SHIFT IS UNDERWAY

Educational services for students with exceptional learning needs have changed considerably since the passage of the first special education law in 1974. The way services are provided is influenced by legislation and a changing philosophy and approach to individuals with exceptional needs. This is due in part to a shift in the social consciousness of our society. Passage of the Americans with Disabilities Act (1990) played a large role in making the general public aware of the needs of persons with disabilities. As never before, we are made aware in our daily lives that there are persons with exceptional needs—when we ride our bicycle up a curb cut, note the Braille on an elevator keypad, or see real people with disabilities and actors portraying characters with disabilities on television programs such as *West Wing*, *Sesame Street*, and *Blind Injustice*. We can watch portrayals of persons with exceptionalities in movies like *Rain Man*, *What's Eating Gilbert Grape*, or *I Am Sam*, and the news media regularly call our attention to special cases of persons with special needs who have overcome great challenges or done great things. In short, we are more aware of the diversity of the human condition than in any previous time in our history.

Another important factor that has helped make people with special needs visible in our society is the inclusion movement in our schools. No doubt many readers of this text had classmates with exceptional needs during their public school experience. Your awareness and sensitivity to their needs influenced your general perceptions of persons with exceptional needs. Further, the reauthorizations of the Individuals with Disabilities Education Improvement Act (IDEA-04) and the Assistive Technology Act of 2004 demonstrate a public awareness of and willingness to meet the needs of citizens with disabilities.

All of these factors have created a shift in public and professional attitudes that has led to the growth of the independent living movement. Just as the inclusion movement worked to achieve greater access to the public schools, the independent living movement is working for greater access to information and even more inclusive practices in schools. Beyond the educational setting, it is working for equal employment opportunities and access to the same goods and services as other citizens have.

A shift in thinking about persons with special needs who could benefit from assistive technology has taken place as well. This important paradigm shift has gone from looking at the person as defective (i.e., failing to perform or as having a deficit) to looking at the person as trying to perform within a fragmented system of resources with limited access to information or a lack of fit with the environment. This technology/ecology way of thinking about persons with exceptional learning needs has been put into practice by the proponents of Universal Design for Learning (UDL) and implemented by many in the field of assistive technology. The basic premise is this: If we give the person who is attempting a task the proper tools and suitable workspace, he/she will be able to complete the task in a satisfactory manner. To make this possible, we need to be aware of the proper tools and how to make the workspace or classroom environment a user-friendly place to work and learn.

Teachers, related services professionals, administrators, and family members often think that assistive technology (AT) is only for persons with physical, sensory, or severe cognitive disabilities. An overriding purpose of this chapter is to change that way of thinking. King (1999) wrote of the constraints of AT use, that devices for a specific task are seen as only for that task, in part because we are not able to see past the obvious intended use to a personal vision for using the device. In this chapter you will be challenged to think about AT as a routine part of your teaching methods, to include AT as one of the UDL options in every lesson you plan, and to recognize that AT can be used by all students with exceptional needs, not just a select few.

DEFINING ASSISTIVE TECHNOLOGY

Who Uses Assistive Technology?

There are an estimated 44 million Americans with disabilities today. These are persons who have a limitation of activity that could make them viable candidates for AT. This composes the single largest minority group ever defined, eclipsing the elderly (37 million), Hispanics (44 million), and African Americans (37 million) (U.S. Census Bureau, 2009). Furthermore, the population is extremely heterogeneous, including persons who are young and old, rich and poor, and of any gender, race, religion, or ethnicity. In fact, there is a strong likelihood that many readers of this book may need AT in their own future.

This also means that there is a high probability that any educator at any level of schooling from early childhood care centers to the highest graduate levels may work with a person who uses AT. Most certainly, this means that teachers of the 5 million students with disabilities in P–12 public schools are likely to work with a student who uses or could benefit from AT. At this point, we have limited scientifically collected data on the actual number of school-aged AT users. As this book is being written, data collection is underway at the National Assistive Technology Research Institute (NATRI) at the University of Kentucky, but without such definitive information, it is safe to say that potentially every student with an IEP (Individualized Education Program) could use assistive technology.

What Is Assistive Technology?

Assistive technology can be a device or service that can be used as a tool by a person with a disability to achieve, maintain, or improve a function of daily life, including meeting educational goals and objectives. In addition, as educators we should remember that AT does not only mean a *device* but a *service* as well. Comparison of the AT Act of 2004 and IDEA-04 definitions of *assistive technology*, AT devices, and AT services are provided in Figure 8.1. You may note that these definitions are very similar and all define AT as any device that is assistive to a person who is trying to complete a task, whether it is a task for a daily living activity or learning.

In their discussion of what constitutes AT, Watts, O'Brian, and Wojcik (2004) pointed to disagreement in the field about including instructional applications as AT.

The following definitions are from H.R. 4278: The Assistive Technology Act of 2004 (see previous mention in Chapter 1 of this text).

Assistive Technology is defined as product, appliance, apparatus, or device utilized as an assistive technology device or assistive technology service (§3.3). **IDEA-04** does not include this definition.

An *Assistive Technology Device* is defined as "any item, piece of equipment, or product system whether acquired commercially off the shelf, modified, or customized, that is used to increase, maintain, or improve functional capabilities of individuals with disabilities" (Section 3, part 4). **IDEA-04 adds** "The term does not include a medical device that is surgically implanted, or the replacement of that device" (§300.6).

"Assistive Technology Service" means any service that directly assists an individual with a disability in the selection, acquisition, or use of an assistive technology device. Such term includes

   (A) the evaluation of the assistive technology needs of an individual with a disability, including a functional evaluation of the impact of the provision of appropriate assistive technology and appropriate services to the individual in the customary environment of the individual;
   (B) a service consisting of purchasing, leasing, or otherwise providing for the acquisition of assistive technology devices by individuals with disabilities;
   (C) a service consisting of selecting, designing, fitting, customizing, adapting, applying, maintaining, repairing, replacing, or donating assistive technology devices;
   (D) coordination and use of necessary therapies, interventions, or services with assistive technology devices, such as therapies, interventions, or services associated with education and rehabilitation plans and programs;
   (E) training or technical assistance for an individual with a disability or, where appropriate, the family members, guardians, advocates, or authorized representatives of such an individual;
   (F) training or technical assistance for professionals (including individuals providing education and rehabilitation services and entities that manufacture or sell assistive technology devices), employers, providers of employment and training services, or other individuals who provide services to, employ, or are otherwise substantially involved in the major life functions of individuals with disabilities; and
   (G) a service consisting of expanding the availability of access to technology, including electronic and information technology, to individuals with disabilities (Section 3: part 5: A-G) **IDEA-04** includes A–F with slightly different wording but similar meanings; however, the special education law does not include item G in their definition of AT service.

FIGURE 8.1 Definitions from the AT Act of 2004 Compared with IDEA-04

Sources: Information from the Council of State Administrators of Vocational Rehabilitation (2004); Mandlawitz (2006).

They included the following definition of AT: "a cognitive prosthesis that can replace an ability that is impaired" (p. 43). Further, they cited an Office of Special Education Programs letter of clarification that states "there is no defined list delineating what can and cannot be considered assistive technology" (p. 43). Thus, professionals in schools have considerable freedom when defining and selecting AT for their students' use and for instructional purposes.

Also, AT has been defined by levels, types, and categories. Levels of AT devices are distinguished between *no-tech, low-tech,* and *high-tech,* and types are applications that are *transparent, translucent,* and *opaque.* Categories are determined by the use or task performed by the device or software.

LEVELS   *No-tech* refers to items that may be used by anyone to more easily accomplish a particular task. No-tech items might include handheld magnifiers, highlighters, sticky notes, cushioned pens and pencils, book stands, and slanted clipboards. Typically, low-tech involves the application of ergonomics—that is, the science of making the space or task more comfortable for or accessible to a person. Low-tech usually refers to less complicated AT devices such as customized hand tools, work space modifications, and off-the-shelf devices such as adjustable lamps or cushioned chairs. Finally, high-tech usually refers to specialized computer software and electrical and electronic devices such as computers and handheld hardware, augmentative communication boards, and environmental control systems (see Figure 8.2).

TYPES   Technology may be considered *transparent* (King, 1999) if the device uses icons or signs that are easily understood or may be guessed. For example, the printer icon (a graphic that resembles a printer) used in virtually every word-processing program is readily understood and therefore provides transparency. A device may be *translucent* (King, 1999) if the user may be able to guess how to use it but needs some background knowledge to fully understand how to operate the device. For example, while we may guess how to use a new cell phone or digital camera, we might not be able to take advantage of all the options without reading the owner's manual and practice with special features. Finally, devices are defined as *opaque* (King, 1999) when users must be

No/Low Tech -->	Variety of pens and pencils
	Pencil grips
	Outline
	Graphic organizers
	Templates
	Prewritten words/phrases
	Dictionaries
	Spell checkers
	Thesauruses
	Electronic dictionaries
	Touchscreen
	Macros (fewer keystrokes)
	Word processor with spelling and grammar check
	Slowing the rate of the keys
	Alternative keyboards
	Alternative input devices: switches, head pointers
<--High Tech	Word prediction software
	Voice recognition software
	Speech output: screen and Web readers
	Translation to sign language or Braille output

FIGURE 8.2 AT Continuum from No/Low- to High-Technologies That Are Specifically Related to Written Expression
Source: Information from Watson (2005).

taught specific information to adequately use them. For example, the first time most of us might attempt to use a copier to make a double-sided, stapled, hole-punched booklet we would need to have specific instructions to find our way through the menu and put the paper in correctly.

CATEGORIES King (1999) and others have divided AT into 10 essential categories:

1. Augmentative and alternative communication (AAC)
2. Adapted computer access
3. Devices to assist listening and seeing
4. Environmental control
5. Adapted play and recreation
6. Seating and positioning
7. Mobility and powered mobility
8. Prosthetics
9. Rehabilitation robotics
10. Integration of technology into the home, school, community, and place of employment (p. 17)

The above list covers AT that is generally seen as being useful to persons with physical, sensory, and severe cognitive disabilities. Professionals in the field of AT also include devices and software that will also benefit persons with high-incidence disabilities. For example, the Center on Disabilities (at California State University, Northridge) include AT for persons with learning disabilities in their AT training program. Bryant and Bryant (2003), Male (2003), and others describe a variety of technologies that enhance access for all learners with exceptional needs to information and academic instruction as assistive technology. (See Table 8.1 for more information on the categories and purposes of AT.)

SELECTING ASSISTIVE TECHNOLOGY

The steps to selecting AT applications and devices include assembling the team that will make the decisions, assessing the skills and needs of the AT user, training the student and support persons, evaluating AT effectiveness, supporting student use, and, finally, determining who has financial responsibility for the purchase of selected AT. In the following section, we will look at each of these steps in more detail.

Step 1: Assembling the Team

Selecting appropriate AT solutions requires a collaborative team approach. Therefore, selecting appropriate team members is essential (see Figure 8.3 for a list of team members). This team will consider all the possibilities and determine how best to incorporate appropriate technology into the Individualized Family Service Plan (IFSP) for young children, Individualized Education Program (IEP) for school-age students, or the Individualized Written Rehabilitation Plan (IWRP) for transitioning students.

To accomplish these tasks, the team must have the full participation and mutual understanding of all members and encourage creative, inclusive solutions. For example, including the student and his family in the decision-making process is extremely

TABLE 8.1 Purposes of Assistive Technology

| Author | Purposes | |
	General	Educational
Ashton, 2000	Body support, protection, and positioning problems Communication problems Education and transition problems Environmental interaction problems Existence problems Sports, fitness, and recreation problems Travel and mobility problems	
Behrmann, 1994		Accessing reference materials Cognitive assistance Modified materials Note taking Organizational tools Productivity tools Writing tools
Beigel, 2000		Academic Communication Psychomotor Social
Blackhurst & Edyburn, 2000	Body supports, protection, and positional problems Communication problems Education and transition problems Environmental interaction problems Existence problems Sports, fitness, and recreation problems Travel and mobility problems	
D. P. Bryant, Bryant, & Raskind, 1998		Listening Math Organization/memory Reading Writing
Clinton, 1993	Cognitive and academic abilities Expressive and/or receptive language Fatigue factors Physical abilities Positioning in relation to the device Vocational potential	

(Continued)

TABLE 8.1 Purposes of Assistive Technology (*Continued*)

Author	Purposes	
	General	**Educational**
Edyburn, 2000		Academics Daily living Leisure/recreation Program accessibility Study skills
Hutinger, Johanson, & Stoneburner, 1996	Cognition Communication Motor skills Social and emotional development	
Lueck, Dote-Kwan, Senge, & Clarke, 2001	Daily living Educational Occupational Recreation and leisure Social-emotional relations	
Parette & Murdick, 1998	Assistive listening Electronic Communication Environmental access Independent living Leisure/recreation Mobility Positioning Visual	
Quenneville, 2001		Academic achievement Organization Fostering social skills
RESNA, 1992	Assistive listening Augmentative Communication Computer access Computer-based Instruction Environmental controls Mobility Physical education, Recreation, leisure, and play Positioning Self care Visual aides	

Source: Information from Watson (2005).

The following includes just some of the people who may make up the team for any AT intervention and a brief description of each role.

- **Teachers**—both special and general education teachers can contribute information on classroom setting and instructional demands, barriers to the student's academic performance, and participate in the assessment, training, and follow-up processes. Most important, however, is that they will reinforce use of the AT in their classrooms and do any reteaching that may be needed.
- **Student & family members**—should be full collaborating partners in the process of evaluating and selecting AT. Because families may not be informed about appropriate AT devices, teachers may need to educate them so that everyone is on the same page. As the user, students should be included in the selection to ensure that any devices meet their individual needs. Families can ensure that students receive support and encouragement to use or practice with the device outside the school setting. Further, families can be helpful advocates in acquiring and funding issues.

Not every school or district has an AT specialist. If the district where you work does, here is what you might expect that person to provide for the team

- **Assistive technology specialist (ATS)**—individuals trained to conduct assessments of students' needs as well as capabilities to use various AT devices and provide the training for students, family members, and teachers who will be using or supporting use of a specific device. In addition, the practitioner may collaborate with a variety of other professionals to bring information to the team during the selection and training process. These can include:
  - **Physician**—will be required to write a prescription for assistive devices that meet medical needs and must be used during the school day. This is especially true if funding is provided by an insurance company or Medicaid/Medicare.
  - **Assistive technology supplier (ATS)**—can provide commercially available assistive technology devices that require personalized fitting or special accessories, such as wheelchairs, hearing aids, eye glasses, and specialty magnifiers.
  - **Audiologist**—may be a physician or specialist who can assess needs and recommend devices for students with a hearing impairment.
  - **Designer/fabricator**—may be an AT professional or the maintenance person at the school who can build personalized accessories such as blocks to raise desks, ramps, accessible door/cabinet handles, or other features that will support student accessibility.
  - **Funding agency**—commonly called third-party payer, can assess written justification, prescription, or grant application for AT devices and services for adherence to regulations or company manual. This may be an insurance company, community organization, or Medicaid/Medicare.
- **Occupational therapist (OT)**—can provide information about the student's functional skills, including gross motor skills and muscle control of different body parts, and may provide training or adapt devices as appropriate.
- **Physical therapist (PT)**—can provide information about the student's muscle strength, range of motion, flexibility, balance, and coordination. The PT plans and implements exercises to improve physical function and trains individuals in use of assistive devices such as wheelchairs and prosthetic devices.
- **Speech language pathologist (SLP)**—can provide information about the student's speech and language problems, evaluate the potential use of communication devices, and recommend types of specialized communication aids and techniques.

FIGURE 8.3 Team Members Who Might Be Part of the AT Assessment Process

- **Social worker**—can provide information about the student's total living situation and how the use of AT may impact the culture of the family. The social worker can be a valuable resource about community organizations and resources for funding and can act as the liaison for the team.
- **Psychologist**—can provide information about the student's potential for learning and using AT.

When the student is planning or making the transition from school to employment or postsecondary education, the team may include:

- **Vocational rehabilitation counselor (VRC)**—can provide information about the student's potential to hold a job, assist with identification of tools necessary to obtain, and execute essential functions of the job. This counselor would be involved in similar ways with students who are moving to postsecondary educational settings. Most important, the VRC can include AT in the Individual Written Rehabilitation Program (IWRP) that will be used if the student plans to use VR services.

This is in no way an inclusive list of team members, as teams must be constructed to meet the needs of individual students and special circumstances. For example, in a school situation, bus drivers, media center personnel, cafeteria workers, paraeducators, and others who have daily contact with a student may need to be involved in providing information or receiving training.

FIGURE 8.3 Team Members Who Might Be Part of the AT Assessment Process (*Continued*)
Sources: Information from the Alliance for Technology Access (1996); Bryant & Bryant (2003); Center on Disabilities at California State University, Northridge (2002); Male (2003).

important to, among other things, ensure that technology use is supported. One of the keys to achieving successful technology outcomes is the use of a collaborative approach throughout the technology intervention, starting with identification of needs. When involved, students will contribute important information about their goals, interests, dislikes, priorities, and the practical aspects of their living situation. Further, by participating in this collaborative process, they share the responsibility for achieving a good match between themselves and the technology solution.

Step 2: Assessing Skills and Needs

Three assessment concepts have been identified for selection: *ecological, practical,* and *ongoing* (Bryant & Bryant, 2003).

ECOLOGICAL   Teams should consider all environments where the student performs tasks (Watts et al., 2004). In schools, examples of environments would include classrooms (self-contained or inclusion), library/media centers, science labs, occupational skills workrooms, and gymnasiums. Home environments where students might be doing homework should be considered. In the community, examples of environments would include public libraries and field trips sites. Work environments should also be considered for students in work-study programs. Finally, all extracurricular and recreational opportunities such as after-school clubs, Scouts, and sports should be considered.

Data about the student's environments should be collected from the student, family members, teachers, paraeducators, coaches, peers, and related services professionals.

Multiple means of data collection may be used, such as observation of the student interacting the environment, paper/pencil surveys and rating scales, and interviews. The key consideration is that information be collected from as many people within the student's environments as possible.

PRACTICAL Buying AT that is not appropriate because it is too difficult for the student to use or unsuitable for the environment is wasteful of time, effort, and funds. Evaluating the practical use of AT prior to purchase can decrease instances of AT abandonment. During the selection process, students and teachers need opportunities to use and personally evaluate the hardware and software being considered (Long, Huang, Woodbridge, Woolverton, & Minkel, 2003). Decision making when selecting AT must be grounded in the everyday practicality of the device within the actual environment where the student works.

Obtaining AT for pre-purchase evaluations in school settings can present practical problems, but solutions are available. Methods for obtaining AT to use in these situations include contacting state assistive technology projects and searching the Internet. State AT projects maintain demonstration labs, and most will lend AT to schools for evaluation and training purposes (see discussion of AT projects in the Funding section of this chapter). The AT specialist or district office can contact the sales department of AT suppliers and vendors regarding availability of AT for evaluation and training. Finally, some software companies offer free 30-day-trial copies on CD or for download from their Web sites.

ONGOING AT is meant to enhance users' learning experience and help them perform tasks that they might not be able to do otherwise within their environment. Therefore, as students learn and are required to demonstrate advanced levels of a task, perform new tasks, or change environments, the requirements for AT may change as well, so ongoing assessment is essential to providing optimal AT and AT services. For example, a second-grader may require only a simple calculator that performs basic mathematical calculations, but as the student advances in grade levels so do the mathematical calculations he is required to perform. At some point, a basic calculator will not meet the student's skill level or needs and a calculator that performs the functions required by new tasks must be selected. This will be true for both hardware and software that the student uses. Ongoing assessment is required to ensure that student skills and needs are known and supported.

Decision-Making Models

A variety of models for assessing and selecting AT devices exist within the AT literature (Table 8.2). Among these, we have chosen the SETT (Table 8.3) model for several reasons. One reason is that it is widely acknowledged as an excellent model (Bryant & Bryant, 2003). In addition, SETT contains the features viewed as important in the educational assessment literature, such as a comprehensive ecological approach; team problem-solving, strength-based assessment, ongoing longitudinal approach, student involvement, documentation, and student outcomes (Watts et al., 2004). Further, the SETT model includes the three assessment components we noted above (Bryant & Bryant, 2003): ecological, practical, and ongoing.

TABLE 8.2 Models for Assessing and Selecting AT

Author	Steps
Bryant & Bryant (2003)	• Consider various contexts. • Consider strengths and weakness. • Consider technology experience. • Consider technology characteristics. • Consider the person–technology match.
Cook & Hussey (2002)	Human, Activity, Assistive Technology (HAAT) model considers • The skills of the individual • The task that the person is expected to perform • The context or constraints on the activity
Harden & Rosenberg (2001)	• Conduct student observations. • Conduct student interview. • Review IEP goals. • Observe and assess the environment. • Obtain family input.
Institute for Matching Person and Technology (2002)	Matching Person and Technology (MPT) model considers • The environment • The users' preferences • Functions and features of the AT
Long et al. (2003)	• Recognize the problem. • Evaluate of the need. • Assess barriers, identify AT & AT services. • Consider AT menu. • Match AT and AT service to need. • Select AT, identify training needs. • Secure suppliers. • Secure funding for AT & AT services. • Implement AT. • Follow up.
Zabala (2002)	• Conduct intake/referral. • Identify student needs. • Identify desired outcomes. • Develop and nurture team members. • Conduct skills assessment. • Conduct device trials. • Revisit desired outcomes. • Procure device. • Begin implementation of AT. • Conduct follow-up/follow-along.

Sources: Information from Bryant & Bryant (2003); Cook & Hussey (2002); Harden & Rosenberg (2001); Institute for Matching Person and Technology (2005); Long et al. (2003); Zabala (2002).

TABLE 8.3 Using the SETT Framework to Facilitate Team Discussions

S = Skills	• What are the skills we know the student is unable to perform in all environments? • Are there other special needs? • What are the student's current abilities? • How does the student manage learning tasks now? • How does the student manage the physical environment now?
E = Environment	• What is the physical arrangement of the environment? • What setting demands are found in the environment? • What types of materials and equipment are used here? (For example, PE, math, or science classrooms have unique equipment.) • Are there accessible issues in the environment? • Are there attitudes and expectations of teacher, staff, and others that should be considered when selecting AT?
T = Tasks	• What are the instructional demands of the curriculum or teacher in each instructional situation? • What tasks occur in the student's natural environments that enable progress? • What tasks are required for active involvement in these environments?
T = Tools	Based on skills needed to perform required tasks and student's present capabilities to function in all environments: • Brainstorm possible AT applications (no, low, and high). • Select the most promising for a trial use. • Plan specifics of the trial period (including ways success will be assessed). • Collect data on success.

Sources: Information from Center on Disabilities (2002); Male (2003); Watts et al. (2004).

However, the most important feature of SETT is the collaborative nature of this framework. As discussed earlier, many professionals may be involved, each with his or her own professional points of view. SETT provides a structure that allows a diverse group to share expertise and work together to plan with the student. In an interview, Zabala, the developer of SETT (Bryant & Bryant, 2003, p. 28), reported that she asks team participants to spend the first few minutes of a meeting jotting down on sticky notes the five most important things the team should know about the student, environments where the student works or lives, and the tasks frequently required in these environments. Then Zabala invites the participants to place their sticky notes on poster paper under the appropriate heading. This activity allows the group to learn about the student quickly.

THE SETT FRAMEWORK   SETT stands for Student, Environment, Tasks, and Tools. Within the framework, individuals work collaboratively to increase the team's collective knowledge about (a) the student, (b) the environment in which AT will be used, and (c) the tasks that must be preformed in that environment and to (d) select the most appropriate tools for those tasks (see Figure 8.4 for definitions).

SETT components include, but are not limited to the following:

Skills that are typically found in general and special education environments:

- Motor
- Cognitive, including memory and attitude
- Language and processing
- Sensory

Environments where the student is typically required to perform:

- School (self-contained or inclusion)
- Community (library, field trips)
- Work (for students in transition programs)
- Recreation (Scouts, after-school clubs, PE, sports)
- Home (doing homework)

Tasks typically performed in the above environments:

- Academic tasks of reading, writing, and assessment of learning
- Use of classroom equipment and tools (pens/pencils, paper, sports equipment, art and music equipment)
- Organization (notebooks, projects, homework, work schedules)
- Participation in activities requiring spoken word
- Using research resources (library, Internet, etc.)
- Using teaching materials (handouts, textbooks, maps, etc.)
- Use of standard technology applications (keyboard, monitor, mouse, storage devices, and printers)

Tools that may be applicable:

- No-technology solutions that may work
- Low-technology tools that may work
- High-technology tools that may work

FIGURE 8.4 Definitions of SETT Components

Sources: Information from Center on Disabilities at California State University, Northridge (2002); Watts et al. (2004).

The SETT framework and the sticky-note activity provide a structure for educators, parents, and students to collaborate and discuss AT devices and services that are a given student needs. For example, the IEP team may think that the student needs to word process written work but is not sure what hardware application is best. By discussing the student's skills and capabilities to function without a computer, the places a computer will be used, and the tasks to be performed in that environment, the team can decide if a desktop, laptop, or handheld computer would best meet the student's skills and needs. This will also eliminate the purchase of an expensive device that cannot be used in all environments or is more opaque (complex) than the student can readily use. See Table 8.3 for questions that facilitate team discussions and decision making.

Step 3: Training

Giving educators and related service providers, students, and their families training and opportunities to try the AT before implementation is crucial. Such opportunities reduce the problem of underuse, misuse, and abandonment of the AT device (Long et al., 2003). In addition, when all the professionals involved understand the device, how it works, and how to use it effectively in the classroom environment, they are more likely to accept and support its use. Lack of training is a major barrier to implementation of AT in the classroom (Hutinger, Johanson, & Stoneburner, 1996; McGregor & Pachuski, 1996).

In this phase of the assessment, a good working relationship with knowledgeable vendors and suppliers is critical. These are most knowledgeable about the equipment or software and its features and your school district requirements. Further, suppliers and vendors who have working relationships with your school district will be more willing to loan items for evaluation.

Step 4: Evaluation of AT Effectiveness

The first assessments and evaluation of AT use should be performed soon after delivery of the AT device, ideally within the first month. This is a time to check that student, family, and teachers are satisfied with it and that the system is working effectively. Follow-along assessment is just as important and is a long-term commitment to the student's use of AT. Follow-along assessments should occur regularly, as often as every 2 to 3 months during the first year of AT and before each IEP meeting during the student's academic career. As noted previously, the goal of follow-up and follow-along assessments is to ensure that the AT continues to meet the student's skills and needs and is being used to the fullest potential. Throughout this period, the team can determine if additional training is needed and if the stated goals for AT use are being met.

Ongoing evaluation can help reduce the occurrence of AT device abandonment. This is a serious problem and should be a concern during the assessment and selection process. A growing body of research on the abandonment of assistive technology illustrates the complexity of the interface between a person and a device (King, 1999). One overarching factor is failure to consider the student user's preferences in AT selection. The rate of device abandonment ranges from as low as 8% to as high as 75% (Center on Disabilities, 2002). On average, about one-third of all devices are abandoned. This issue must be addressed when selecting the team. As noted earlier in this chapter, being inclusive when selecting the team maximizes acceptance of whatever AT is selected. And most certainly, it is vital to include the student user whose skills, needs, and preferences are being considered. Most of the abandonment occurs within the first year, especially within the first 3 months, as users learn relatively early whether a device works for them (Center on Disabilities, 2002). In short, ongoing and early evaluations of AT effectiveness are essential to make certain that the selected AT meets the student's skills and needs, is used to the fullest potential, and is not abandoned.

Step 5: Supporting Student Use

In Steps 1–4 we mentioned the importance of the student user's role in the selection of AT use, in particular, the importance of matching the student and the AT for skills and needs. In this section we will discuss factors that affect the use of AT and may lead to abandonment during the transitional stage to full acceptance and use of the AT. This process of becoming accustomed to using and being seen using the AT can be difficult. For example, the human factors of culture, age, gender, and literacy (King, 1999) constitute student preferences. While the student is the primary focus of AT selection, we cannot ignore the cultural beliefs and customs that may affect acceptance and use of AT.

Student preferences based on cultural beliefs and customs must be honored by not forcing students to use AT that they do not believe in or cannot accept (King, 1999). For example, devices and software that were developed for a specific age can be problematic if these are not also age appropriate for the student under consideration. Thus, software developed primarily for early-childhood or elementary-age students would not be age appropriate for an adolescent, regardless of the student's skill level. Taking the time and effort to find age-appropriate AT is essential for acceptance by the student (King, 1999). Giving careful consideration to these issues will help support students and avoid early abandonment as they become accustomed to their new AT.

Two final considerations during AT selection are service and replacement of AT that is broken or requires maintenance or updating. King (1999) suggested three measures: (1) teaching the student alternative backup methods for accomplishing the task for which the AT was being used, (2) obtaining devices that can be repaired or replaced easily, and (3) knowing the warranty policies before you purchase. Lengthy disruptions in AT use can lead to abandonment, which may exacerbate the effects of the disability and tax the recourses of a school district (Long et al., 2003).

So far in this section we have discussed assembling the team that will make AT decisions, assessing the skills and needs of the AT user, training the student and support persons, evaluating AT effectiveness, and supporting student use. The final step is the determination of financial responsibility for providing the AT.

Step 6: Responsibility for Providing AT

The sources for funding and how to access these sources are important aspects of the selecting process for all teachers to understand. Frequently students are denied AT applications and devices because school teams are concerned about costs to the school district and parents are unable to afford the device. Therefore, understanding that neither the school nor parents must be responsible for funding all AT devices needed in school settings will help in the decision process. Further, understanding the application process for third-party funding will support collaborative efforts across school, healthcare providers, and community agencies and will increase the likelihood that students will have the AT needed to have full access in school environments.

WHAT IS THE SCHOOL'S RESPONSIBILITY FOR PROVIDING AT DEVICES AND SERVICES?   Devices and services we commonly classify as AT have been within the scope of a free appropriate public education (FAPE) since the initial enactment of federal special education legislation (Pub. L. 94-142) in 1975. Further, subsequent special education laws state clearly that representatives of the school district must consider AT during every IEP and, if AT is determined appropriate, provide or pay for AT devices or services. Under special education law, schools have always been required to provide adaptive equipment, augmentative communication devices, typewriters, tape recorders, word processors, Braille versions of print materials, auditory trainers, wheelchairs, and other types of devices and services to students who need them. In addition, over the years other decisions and policy letters have established some core principles related to AT device funding, as outlined below.

According to a U.S. Department of Education (USDOE) policy letter, known as the "Goodman Letter," schools are prohibited from refusing to consider AT devices and services as part of the IEP process (National Information Center for Children and Youth with Disabilities, 1991). The USDOE established policy even though the special education law (Pub. L. 94-142) did not use the term *assistive technology*. Therefore, when IDEIA-04 added terms defining AT devices and services, no new benefits were added but existing regulations were merely clarified. In addition, these regulations made an express connection between provision of AT devices and services and three components of a FAPE—special education, related services, and supplementary aids and services (National Information Center, 1991).

The latest revision that reauthorizes and amends IDEIA-04 was signed into law in December of 2004. The 2004 reauthorization made only one change related to AT. In the definition (Sec. 602(1)(B)) of the term *assistive technology device,* the law states that a device does not include surgically implanted medical device or replacement of such a device. This exception arose in part from a concern, based on a recent due-process hearing, that school districts might be held responsible for providing cochlear implants for children with hearing impairments (Mandlawitz, 2006). No other substantial changes to assistive technology portions of the 1997 law were made in the 2004 reauthorization; therefore, all previous provisions of 1997 still apply to AT. Briefly, the law is clear that AT is not a school district option. When needed by a student with disabilities, it must be provided.

Obtaining AT Funding from Third Parties

Local education agencies are not required to fund all assistive technology devices, especially when devices are not related directly to the FAPE or are related to medical conditions. Inability to provide or obtain funding for AT devices can be frustrating for school districts, teachers, and families of students with disabilities (Erickson, 1998). Funding remains a primary deterrent to acquisition of assistive technology (Male, 2003). Therefore, it is imperative that all parties involved be aware of the laws and regulations that permit, for example, Medicaid and Medicare funds to be used for AT devices. In addition, educators and related service providers should understand how to obtain funding from sources in their community. Resolving the funding problem requires a creative and innovative collaborative problem-solving approach involving professionals, families, and the community.

MEDICAID   Recipients of Supplemental Security Income (SSI), Aid to Families with Dependent Children (AFDC), and In-Home Supportive Services (IHSS) automatically receive Medicaid. In addition, some students may qualify under one of the federal poverty-level programs (Erickson, 1998).

AT under the Medicaid program is generally classified as medical supplies, durable medical equipment or prosthetic or orthotics equipment and will require prior approval. Each state is allowed to establish a definition for medical necessity, therefore it is important to know how a given state defines the term and to be able to argue that the equipment or services needed come within the definition (U.S. Department of Health and Human Services, n.d.).

In all instances, technology and service must be considered medically necessary. A commonly used definition requires proof that the device is necessary to preserve bodily functions essential to activities of daily living or to prevent significant physical disability. Certainly, educators and families may assert that the FAPE is an activity of daily living for school-age children and youth. By contrast, items promoting comfort or well-being alone are covered only if their primary purpose satisfies the first criterion. The federal courts have determined that the question of medical necessity should be determined by the individual's treating physician, not agency personnel or even Medicaid physician consultants.

Teachers and members of IEP teams can request that families ask their health provider to determine if devices selected at the IEP meeting fall into any of the Medicaid categories of medically necessary AT. Collaboration between schools and health-care providers can improve the prospects that students receive appropriate AT needed.

MEDICARE Medicare is a federal health insurance program for aged and disabled persons. Entitlement to Medicare services is not based on an individual's financial status (Social Security Administration, 2001). Students may be entitled to benefits under Medicare if they have received 24 months of Social Security Disability Insurance (SSDI) benefits or 24 months of railroad retirement disability benefits (42 U.S.C. §426(b)) (Sheldon & Hart, 2004).

Medicare, just as Medicaid, covers AT devices and services only when necessary and reasonable for the treatment of an illness or injury or to improve the functioning of a malformed body member (see 42 U.S.C. §1395y(a)). Devices may include prosthetic devices, durable medical equipment, crutches or walkers, and wheelchairs, including power chairs, customized chairs, and power-operated vehicles such as tri-wheelers, when considered appropriate, and diagnostic tests (Part B coverage). Medicare does not cover devices that are solely for educational purposes, such as augmentative and assistive communication devices, braillers and Braille texts, and eyeglasses and contacts (U.S. Department of Health and Human Services, 2004). Physicians are responsible for completing and submitting the proper forms to the Social Security office and must establish that the requested equipment (a) is medically necessary, (b) is part of the beneficiary's course of treatment, (c) has a potential functional outcome, and (d) is the least expensive appropriate equipment available. Certainly, educators can support the physician argument that the functional outcome is a free, appropriate education. Teacher support can include observational data and samples of student work completed with and without the device. Thus, if an assistive augmented communication (ACC) device is the only means available for a student to communicate effectively, it may be considered a Medicaid benefit. In fact, every Medicare beneficiary from 1993 to 2001 was successful when appealing the Medicare decision not to fund ACC (Sheldon & Hart, 2004). Persons eligible under Medicare have the right to challenge any decision that they believe to be wrong by requesting an administrative hearing. Each state is required to provide an opportunity for the applicant to explain why he or she disagrees with a denial of requested technology. An unfavorable decision can be appealed to state or federal court.

VOCATIONAL REHABILITATION While Department of Vocational Rehabilitation (VR) services do not cover students until they have graduated from public school, vocational rehabilitation personnel may become involved with students during their transition planning process. At this time, AT should be discussed with the rehabilitation counselor and included in the student's Individualized Written Rehabilitation Plan (IWRP). Once a student has transitioned to the VR Department, AT devices and services related to postsecondary education and employment become the responsibility of that agency (Sheldon & Hager, 1997).

Private Insurance, State Resources, Foundations, and Community Organizations

PRIVATE INSURANCE Families of students who do not qualify for Medicaid or Medicare may be willing to purchase AT with their own funds or apply for funding through their private health insurance companies. Students may come to school with AT purchased by families and ask for permission to use the appliance in general education classrooms or for an accommodation permitting the appliance be written into IEP. Educators should be mindful that while families may agree to purchase AT, they may not be required or coerced to do so (Male, 2003).

STATE RESOURCES Each state and territory in the United States has an Assistive Technology Project Center funded with federal grant money from the Assistive Technology Act. These centers have up-to-date information on AT resources, including funding sources within each state. Some projects list resources available on their Web sites. These projects may also offer lending programs that allow students and teachers to evaluate an AT device before it is purchased. School personnel and persons with disabilities are able to visit their state's project center to learn and gain hands-on experiences with AT. Finally, project center personnel are invaluable resources regarding AT and welcome sharing their knowledge. (You can find your state project's Web site with an online search.)

FOUNDATIONS AND COMMUNITY ORGANIZATIONS Most major corporations and businesses, including banks, retailers, and manufacturers, have foundations that provide scholarships, grants, and awards for philanthropic purposes, including public school programs. You can find information about grants, scholarships, and gifts by visiting the corporate Web site or calling the local branch office.

Community organizations that have philanthropic missions include Shriners, Lions, Moose, and Rotary Clubs. These organizations' members may be able to access funds through their foundations. In addition, many organizations aligned with specific disabilities have foundations that provide or loan funds to purchase AT; some have programs that buy back and sell used equipment. Their Web sites list contact information as well as information about AT services they offer.

Additional sources are vendors and suppliers of AT. A number of these vendors and suppliers are provided in the resource list at the end of this chapter. While they may not supply funding, they often have information about funding sources and may offer support in applying for grants. Finally, social workers, counselors, and AT specialists in school districts may have working relationships with the foundations and organizations within a local community or state for other purposes, so they are often a good place to start when searching for funding.

Whether students qualify for AT from their school district, Medicaid, Medicare, a private organization, or a combination of funds from several sources will depend on the proactive teamwork of all parties involved in the process. To be successful, teams must collaborate on a plan to seek multiple funding sources, research information on how each organization determines funding, and who makes the funding decisions (Male, 2003). Such intensive teamwork makes close collaboration between the family, school, physician(s), funding sources, and suppliers absolutely vital. In conclusion, taking time to complete the steps necessary in forming a team, selecting appropriate AT, and obtaining funding are imperative to providing full access to the standards-based curriculum in classrooms.

AT APPLICATIONS FOR INSTRUCTION

As you learned in the beginning of this chapter, AT is rather broadly defined, making it impossible to provide comprehensive coverage of the full range and depth of the topic in one book chapter. In this section of the chapter, we will discuss the categories of AT that teachers are likely to find or need in school settings to teach content knowledge to students with exceptional needs. Examples of specific hardware and software programs will be given to illustrate what is available. Based on the mandate for teachers and students to meet state and national standards, the emphasis will be on providing AT applications that will allow students with exceptional needs full access to the curriculum and the materials used to teach that curriculum. The ultimate goal of using AT in the classroom is to support students so that they can become increasingly independent, empowered learners. Some examples of technology that are remedial and tutorial in nature may be offered if these also support content learning, but that is not the main focus. The discussion will begin with ensuring barrier-free access to computers and then move to specific AT applications for specific instructional tasks.

Barrier-Free Access to Assistive Technology

Computer access can mean the difference between success and failure in academic classes for many students with disabilities. As noted in the chapter on UDL, the first step in planning instruction should be to assess the barriers to learning found in the learning environment. In keeping with that philosophy, AT provides opportunities to remove a variety of barriers to learning, and the first barrier that should be removed to create a UDL learning environment is any barrier presented by computer hardware. Students who may encounter barriers to computer use are described below (Center on Disabilities, 2002).

- *Students with physical limitations* may not have the quality of movement in their limbs or trunks of their bodies necessary to use a standard keyboard and mouse. Some students may need a pointing device or an alternative keyboard, such as a one-handed or on-screen keyboard.
- *Students with limited cognitive abilities* may not be able to use standard computer equipment. For example, the standard keyboard has many keys that may confuse, overwhelm, or confound the student. Providing keyboards with less crowded configurations, different arrangement of the keys, keys for specific actions, or keys with simple switches may be best for some students.
- *Students with visual impairments* may not have sufficient vision to read a standard keyboard or monitor screen. Some students may need screen magnifiers, screen readers, Braille translators, and Braille printers.
- *Students with hearing impairments* may not have sufficient hearing to view Web sites with spoken language, such as videos. In fact, if they are young American

Sign Language (ASL) users, they may not have sufficient Standard English reading skills for some Web sites. In addition, some students may need on-screen captions or headphones to remove background noise.

- *Students who experience problems with receptive or expressive language processing or production (e.g., MR or LD) or who are not proficient Standard English users* will have difficulty reading or processing what they read. Some students may need voice activated-software, screen readers, or digital language translators.

What Are the Barriers to Computer Use?

As you learned in the previous chapter, access to information and learning materials is a primary goal of the UDL. Using a similar philosophy, we think of AT as an accessibility tool that provides students with exceptional learning needs access to the world of information and school curriculum and permits them to demonstrate learning and engage, interact, and communicate with others. However, although using technology while teaching can provide a richer experience, certain barriers may limit or prevent the use of computers for some students. Certain applications facilitate computer access through interface or input, output, and processing tools (see Table 8.4 for examples of these interface devices). The Center on Disabilities defines these devices as enhancements and alternatives to keyboards, mouse, monitor, or printer. Enhancing, altering, or bypassing is accomplished by hardware, software, system tools, or a combination of the three (Center on Disabilities, 2002). Information about specific applications for interface, input, and output is available from assistive technology specialists, occupational and physical therapists, vocational rehabilitation counselors, and the Internet. See Figure 8.5 for directions to find alternative input and processing that is standard on all computers.

ASSISTIVE TECHNOLOGY FOR SPOKEN COMMUNICATION

Think back over the last 24 hours and make a list of all the times and ways that you communicated with another person (or a surrogate, such as a phone answering machine). Who did you communicate with? What was the purpose of the communication? If it was formal communication, what skills did you use? If it was informal, what skills did you use? Do those skills overlap? Now consider how you might communicate if you could not use speech. Communicating is so much a part of our day that we do not even notice when we are communicating, but what about persons who do not have the physical capacity to speak, and those who cannot hear the voices of others? In this section we will discuss how AT can facilitate communication for persons with speech and hearing impairments.

What Is Communication?

This section briefly reviews information about communication that you may have learned in other courses and suggests ways to apply this knowledge when selecting appropriate AT for students.

We generally communicate in a variety of ways each day; for example, we use *expressive language* in the forms of spoken and written language, as well as gestures and facial expressions (body language). We communicate using *receptive language* when we read, listen, or interpret the body language of others.

TABLE 8.4 How Do We Interface (Input/Output) with a Computer?

Input		
Device	**Types**	**Possible Features**
Keyboards	• On-screen cursor control/pointer systems • Alternative keyboards • Voice recognition software • Eye gaze • Mind control • Switches	Physical Adjustments • Slant board • Key guards • Pads and supports • Keyless Electronic Adjustments • Sticky keys • Slow keys • Rearrange keys • Mouse keys Layouts • QWERTY • ABC • AEIOU • Frequency • Number • Custom • Right hand/left hand • Software specific • Person specific

Cursor controls and pointing systems	• Mouse
	• Trackball
	• Joystick
	• Paddles
	• Head mice
	• Touchscreen/window
	• Touchpad/glide pad
		Can
		• Control mouse speed
		• Be shaped to fit hand
		• Have more than one button
		• Be programmed with scripts and macros
		• Controlled by
		  ○ head movements
		  ○ touching monitor
		  ○ using windows

Output		
Device	**Types**	**Possible Adjustments**
Visual	Displays	• Font type • Contrast • Size
	Indicators	• Button tags • Label cues
	Hard copy	• Print formats/methods • Printers

TABLE 8.4 *(Continued)*

Input

Device	Types	Possible Features
Auditory	Software enhancement	• Text enlargement • Screen enlargement
	Feedback	• Key beep • Character echo
	Speech	• Synthesized speech • Digitized speech and sound
	Sound system	• Headphones • Hearing devices
Tactual	Braille text	• Optical to tactile
	Software enhancement	• Text to Braille • Braille-to-text-conversion

Processing

Device	Types	Methods
Rate enhancement (increase productivity rate)	Word prediction	Use software such as Co:Writer by Don Johnston.
	Abbreviation expansion	Create macros in computer software to type a word or phrase based on abbreviation typed by user.
	Word/phrase supplements	Use overlays that include words or phrase that type when one overlay key is hit.
	Macros	Use software built-in macro feature (see Tools in Word and use Help to teach you how) OR use built-in keyboard strokes to complete tasks in document.
Layout	Keyboard	Select a keyboard that is most suited to user's age, ability, and task to be completed.

The components or skills of language necessary for effective communication include the following:

- *Listening* involves obtaining meaning from what we hear. In fact, the act of listening is our ability to gain meaning from the spoken word. In other words, how many words, types of words, and types of syntactic structures can we understand?
- *Speaking* is the production of meaningful sounds such as words, including the number and types of words produced as well as the types of sentence structures used.
- *Semantics* refers to the content of language, which is the meaning and precision of the words we use. Speakers who use good semantics have a rich, deep vocabulary and are able to use complex sentence structures.

Computers that use the Microsoft operating systems have built-in accessibility tools that can be helpful to users with disabilities. These are free and can be used easily by most students who are able computer users.

To find these items:
1. Go to Start
2. Once you have opened the new window, click on All Programs (or whatever will take you to your programs).
3. Find and click on Accessories.
4. Find and click on Accessibility. At this point you should see a list of items to use.
5. Find and click the on-screen keyboard. You can use the keyboard if you open a word-processing program.
6. Open the Magnifier so that you can use it to read what you wrote.
7. Open the Narrator so that you can read what you wrote.

FIGURE 8.5 What Is on Your Computer?

- *Syntax* is refers to using the rules of a language; for example, knowing where to place adjectives and adverbs, proper use of nouns and pronouns, and so on.
- *Morphemes* are the smallest bit of language that can stand alone with their own meaning. They must be used properly to achieve semantic proficiency.
- *Phonology* is the ability to hear the sounds used in a language and to use them correctly in words. (*Phonological awareness* is the ability to identify those sounds and to manipulate them.)
- *Pragmatics* is the use of language with purpose or to achieve a purpose. We speak to request, inform, assist, greet, comfort, and a variety of other reasons.

Persons with communication disorders are not proficient enough in one or more of the above skills to communicate their needs or wishes. If the first six skills are not developed appropriately, students will not be able to accomplish the last—which is purposeful speech. Students who may encounter barriers when communicating are described below (Hallahan & Kauffman, 2003).

- *Students with limited physical or cognitive abilities* may have a communication disorder as the primary disability or secondary disability; for example, impaired speech may be a side effect of cerebral palsy, stroke, or traumatic brain injury. Other students may have communication difficulties related to autism and severe expressive language disorders.
- *Students with hearing impairments, including deaf/blind,* may not have enough hearing to understand spoken language. Further, students who have experienced hearing loss since birth may not have sufficiently clear spoken language to communicate with others. During the training and acquisition of spoken language, AT can support communication and social interactions with others.

Communication devices were among the first AT devices used in public schools and were used before regulations required AT in classrooms. The speech-language therapist and the audiologist will most likely take leading roles in assessing, selecting, and training steps in the team decision-making process. The next sections provide information about the major categories of AT available for persons with speech, language, and hearing impairments.

Augmented and Alternative Communication (ACC) Systems

While many people view speech as the only form of communication, as noted above, there are other modes of communication, including facial expressions, gestures, body language, and eye gaze. Each of us communicates our thoughts and moods via these modes as do persons who are not verbal. Educators need to observe, accept, and enhance the communication methods preferred by their students. Further, an ACC system will only be one part of an individual's communication system, and the other areas cannot be ignored (see section on unaided communication below).

The three primary functions of ACC systems are to (1) serve as a substitute for the vocal mode of communication, (2) supplement vocal communication for the person who has difficulty with formulation or intelligibility, and (c) facilitate communication with emphasis on intelligibility, output and organization, and general skills (Bryant & Bryant, 2003). We typically divide communication devices into two categories: aided and unaided. We will begin with the unaided, but the discussion of this topic will be very brief as the focus of this chapter is AT.

Unaided Communication

As you might think, *unaided communication* refers to methods that do not use external equipment or devices but use body parts, usually arms and hands. Print communication can be used with students who have learned to read and write enough language to express their needs and preferences. However, this is time-consuming and cumbersome, since this method requires paper, pencil, and a writing surface. Three common forms of unaided communication include sign language, education sign systems, and gestural language codes.

- *Sign language* is a primary communication system for persons who have hearing impairments. Recently teachers have found American Sign Language (ASL) to be useful in communicating with persons who have severe communication problems that have nothing to do with deafness, such as autism.
- *Education sign systems* were developed to improve movement from using sign language to reading Standard Written English grammar. One example of an educational sign system is Signing Exact English, which is composed of about 4,000 signs and includes common prefixes, suffixes, and inflectional endings.
- *Gestural language code* is a third form of sign language and uses finger spelling to communicate. American Manual Alphabet is the most commonly used finger-spelling system and is one of the forms of communication used by persons who are deaf and blind (e.g., Annie Sullivan taught this to Helen Keller).

Learning and teaching one of these unaided communication methods to students who use AT communication devices would serve as a backup system should the device need to be repaired or replaced.

Aided Communication

Aided communication can take one of two forms, either non-electronic or electronic. We will discuss the non-electronic briefly, again because the emphasis of this chapter is on technology.

NON-ELECTRONIC COMMUNICATION   Aids include language boards, communication books, and alphabet boards, to name a few. Often these devices are made by teachers and/or family members on a printer using communication board software or by drawing freehand symbols. Communication boards (e.g., Mayer-Johnson in the resource list in the Appendix) are designed to best meet the specific needs of the person and their modes of communication. If the person is able to spell, for example, the board may consist of the alphabet and some phrases to speed up communication. Such phrases could include "May I have a drink of water?" or "My name is Becky." Others who do not spell well may need symbols to represent ideas they are trying to communicate. These could be symbols of family members, comments, questions, wants and needs, and so on.

For individuals who need more communication messages than a single communication board will hold, another option is a communication book (e.g., see Mayer-Johnson in the resource list in the Appendix). Communication books may be constructed in a notebook with multiple pages for each communication set. For example, there might be a page each for school, home, recreation, restaurants, and other settings frequented by the user. Some books are organized by categories of speech. For example, there would be a page for people, verbs, places, and greetings. These types of communication systems require more cognitive and physical skill than a single language board.

Non-electronic communication devices should not be looked at just as a backup to an electronic system. For many, a non-electronic device is sufficient and there is no need to pursue a more expensive electronic device.

ELECTRONIC ACC SYSTEMS   Electronic communication devices range from something as simple as a two-location device that provides yes and no buttons to a device that is a fully functional laptop computer. As with all areas of AT, it is important to match the needs of the consumer to the features of the device. Providing a $7,000 multifunctional AAC device to a child who is only developmentally ready to say her name and answer yes or no questions would seem pointless. This is exactly the type of situation that can lead to abandonment, as mentioned earlier.

Any computer can serve as an augmentative communication device by installing communication software, but this type of system is not for everyone. While a laptop will enable the user to use software (such as word processing in addition to a variety of communication software), using computers in this manner can cause problems. For example, laptop computers lack the durability of most dedicated communication systems and therefore are not suitable for young children or persons whose disability may cause them to drop things. Also, computers do not respond well to spills or drool. Many AAC manufacturers test their equipment for durability and seal surfaces so that spills or drool will not affect operation.

A number of small commercially available communication devices are suitable for student use in the classroom. These devices can record words, phrases, music, different languages, and just about anything else a student might want to use. They can be simple, with one stored word or phrase, or complex, with hundreds of prerecorded words, phrases, and sentences.

The Say-It! SAM Communicator (Words+) is an example of electronic devices that use digitized speech systems. Devices using digitized speech work like tape recorders: Teachers or friends can record words, phrases, music, sound effects, and whatever else the user might want. There is little room for spontaneous communication when using these devices because all speech is prerecorded, but one advantage to these programmable devices is that they allow speech input in languages other than English.

Synthesized speech (or text-to-speech), on the other hand, allows the user to communicate spontaneously, as well as speak stored words or phrases. Although still awkward sounding in many cases, the quality of synthetic voices has improved as has the selection of voice types. Examples of voice output communication aids are the DynaVox (Sunrise Medical) and IntelliTalk 3 (IntelliTools).

Communication Devices Used by Persons Who Are Deaf

One final consideration in the discussion of communication is the ability to hear others speak. Persons with hearing impairments experience differing levels of hearing capabilities from no hearing, garbled hearing, to loss of hearing in certain tonal ranges (Friend, 2005).

Assistive listening systems (ALS) are frequently used in public schools to amplify the teacher's voice for students who are hard of hearing. You may have seen persons using these devices at theaters and during religious services or other public events. Essentially, ALS are amplifiers that bring sound directly into the ear. The speaker wears a microphone, and the listener wears headphones. Sound is transmitted wirelessly throughout the room from an antenna to the headphones. The headphones separate the sounds, particularly speech, from background noise.

Traditional hearing aids are electronic, battery-operated devices that amplify and change sound to allow for improved communication. Hearing aids receive sound through a microphone, which then converts the sound waves to electrical signals. The amplifier increases the loudness of the signals and then sends the sound to the ear through a speaker. Below we will briefly look at the most common hearing aids as well as the pros and cons for children.

- In-the-ear (ITE) hearing aids fit completely in the outer ear and are used for mild to severe hearing loss. The case, which holds the components, is made of hard plastic. ITE aids can accommodate added technical mechanisms such as a tele-coil, a small magnetic coil contained in the hearing aid that improves sound transmission during telephone calls. ITE aids can be damaged by earwax and ear drainage, and their small size can cause adjustment problems and feedback. They are not usually worn by children because the casings need to be replaced as the ear grows.
- Behind-the-ear (BTE) hearing aids are worn behind the ear and are connected to a plastic ear mold that fits inside the outer ear. Sound travels through the earmold into the ear. BTE aids are used by people of all ages for mild to profound hearing loss. Poorly fitting BTE ear molds may cause feedback, a whistle sound caused by the fit of the hearing aid or by buildup of earwax or fluid. Children typically use BTE aids because the ear molds can be adjusted easily as the child grows.

- Canal aids fit into the ear canal and are available in two sizes. The in-the-canal (ITC) hearing aid is customized to fit the size and shape of the ear canal and is used for mild or moderately severe hearing loss. A completely-in-canal (CIC) hearing aid is largely concealed in the ear canal and is used for mild to moderately severe hearing loss. Because of their small size, canal aids may be difficult for the user to adjust and remove and may not be able to hold additional devices, such as a telecoil. Canal aids can also be damaged by earwax and ear drainage. These are not typically recommended for children.
- Body aids are used by people with profound hearing loss. The aid is attached to a belt or a pocket and connected to the ear by a wire. Because of its large size, it is able to incorporate many signal processing options, but it is usually used only when other types of aids cannot be used.
- Cochlear implants are electronic devices designed for persons who have severe to profound losses of hearing. The implant bypasses the outer and middle ear by sending auditory signals directly to the inner ear, where useful information is sorted from random sounds and sent to the auditory nerve. (At present, cochlear implants are a source of controversy in the deaf community and may not be an acceptable AT device for all students who are deaf.) In the earlier section, we noted that a student's cultural beliefs may affect how he or she views or accepts AT, and this appears to be true of using cochlear implants. Some members of the deaf community are opposed to implants because they see the implants as an attempt to eradicate deafness and therefore the deaf community, but the implant providers and many parents of children who are deaf consider implants as an opportunity for their children to participate in mainstream society (National Association of the Deaf, n.d.). As a final note, this is one of the AT exceptions noted in IDEA-2004, because school districts may not be required to fund cochlear implants.

Spoken communication can be augmented and supported with a variety of AT, from an easy-to-construct and inexpensive set of pictures on a communication board to complex electronic voice output communication aids and hearing aids.

ASSISTIVE TECHNOLOGY FOR WRITTEN COMMUNICATION

Results of research on effects of word processing on the quality and quantity of P–12 student writing are mixed (Roblyer, 2003). Most differences were attributed to the researcher's choice of software, students' prior experience and writing abilities, and types of writing instruction. Use of a word-processing system appeared to have positive effects on student writing when used in the context of good writing instruction and when students were given opportunities to learn word-processing procedures prior to the research study. Therefore, understanding the writing process and providing guidance to students who experience difficulty in producing age-appropriate written products is just as important as providing the AT for the physical production of writing work.

The Writing Process

Written communication is a complex task that involves both process and mechanics. Process consists of organizing ideas gathered from research or personal knowledge (imagination for creative writing) into a coherent product. Mechanics include spelling, handwriting, punctuation, and capitalization as well as an understanding the complexities of syntax and semantics.

Many students with disabilities have a lower level of age-appropriate spelling, capitalization, and punctuation skills than their peers. Problems with basic writing skills require these students to spend a majority of their writing time on mechanics rather than acquiring the skills needed for high-level writing processes. For example, students who are not good spellers use only words that they can spell, which can lead to short sentences void of descriptive words. The same is true for sentence structures; if a student is unsure about punctuation or complex grammar constructs, she will produce short, choppy sentences. Naturally, when students expend all of their energy on the mechanics of writing, they are less likely to produce written products that demonstrate higher-level thinking about a topic or concept. Finally, students who experience difficulties with handwriting skills due to psychomotor deficits or a physical disability expend all their energies on the visual aspects of the written product, which can be physically as well as mentally exhausting.

Other students with disabilities may experience problems with planning, acquiring information, and organizing their thoughts. These are skills needed for writing the creative stories often required in elementary school or completing research papers and projects at the middle and high school levels in most content areas. Often these students are unable even to begin a project because the task seems so overwhelming to them.

There are assistive technologies available that can take away these concerns for mechanics, handwriting, and organizing skills. With appropriate AT, the product becomes the focus of the student's efforts, not the process.

Students who may encounter barriers during the writing process are described below (Hallahan & Kauffman, 2003). To construct effective writing instruction and independent practice that allows students to learn and demonstrate their knowledge, teachers should recognize barriers and plan instructional activities in which barriers are removed.

- *Students with specific writing disorders* may be referred to as having a written expression language deficit. Because writing involves several brain areas and functions, the brain networks for vocabulary, grammar, hand movement, and memory must all be in good working order. Thus, a writing disorder may result from problems in any of these areas.
- *Students with hearing impairments* may have written expression difficulties. Students who learn ASL at an early age often experience many of the same language acquisition and usage problems with Standard English as do students who are not native speakers of English (consider that ASL is their first language and Standard English is their second language).
- *Students with visual impairments* experience access problems when producing written products and usually have difficulty acquiring useful handwriting skills. They may be able to write by hand, but their ability to produce large quantities of written work may be limited. In addition, Braille users, like ASL users, may have acquisition and usage problems similar to students who are English language learners. Braille uses a series of contractions that stand for common letter combinations; this can be confusing during elementary years when students are learning both Braille contractions and the spelling of Standard English words.

- *Students with ADHD* may experience difficulties with the attention and organizational processes required to write effectively. Whether they have inattentive or hyperactivity type of ADHD, students will have difficulty maintaining attention required for planning, researching, and writing.
- *Students with physical disabilities* that limit use of their fingers, hands, and arms will experience difficulty with the physical requirements for handwriting. For example, students may have problems that limit their ability to hold conventional writing instruments, produce readable handwriting, or use handwriting for extended periods of writing required for essay questions on exams or in-class writing.

In this section we will discuss a variety of AT devices, including hardware and software, that will support learning and production of written products. Generally, these AT applications work for most of the students described above. For example, you will learn about speech recognition software that may be appropriate for students with LD, visual impairments, and physical disabilities.

One of your tasks as a member of the IEP team will be to decide which AT application would be most useful for an individual user. The IEP team should decide which specific AT application is most useful for an individual student. However, cost and availability are considerations, and several AT applications will be helpful additions to purchase AT and can support the learning of all students in your classroom. Computers and software applications have become commonplace additions in many classrooms and can remove barriers to learning for a very wide variety of students with and without disabilities.

Digital graphic organizers can help students organize their ideas or research information into a written product. Inspiration (see Inspiration in the resources section of the Appendix) is a software program that allows users to construct graphic organizers to complete a variety of tasks, and organizing a writing project is one of those tasks. Kidspiration is an option for younger users.

Word processors with auditory feedback combine a word-processor software package with a software package that reads information on the computer screen, giving users a way to independently edit and correct their work. There are several word-processing applications on the market with integrated text-to-speak capability. For example, Write OutLoud (see Don Johnston Company in the resources section of the Appendix) software reads what the user is writing as he writes, so that he may correct errors immediately. Write OutLoud To-Go is a version that is packaged with the AlphaSmart 3000 (more information is provided later in the Appendix), so students can use the computer version in the general education class or computer lab and then take the AlphaSmart version to continue the work in the resource room or at home.

Word prediction software works within any word-processing program to allow students to select the correctly spelled word. One example of this type of software is Co-Writer Solo Edition (see Don Johnston Company in the Appendix) with FlexSpell, which allows for phonetic spelling and topical dictionaries that include words from across the curriculum. Thus, it provides students with the supports they need to write what they know and what they're learning. Co-Writer can also be packaged with the AlphaSmart 3000.

Symbol-supported writing programs allow students to write stories and communicate with pictures. Writing with Symbols 2000 (see Mayer-Johnson in the Appendix) is an example of this software, which contains over 8,000 pictures to support student writing.

Speech recognition systems, also known as voice-activated software, allow students to use any word-processing or spreadsheet program to dictate information, which is then automatically converted to text. This can be an extremely useful tool for individuals who have writing difficulty, regardless of the reason. One stand-alone speech recognition application is Dragon Naturally Speaking (see ScanSoft in the Appendix). Naturally Speaking performs computer functions as well, such as opening and closing software programs, opening and saving documents, and making corrections within documents.

AlphaSmart products include the AlphaSmart 3000, Neo, and Dana. These devices are similar to laptop computers but are considerably less expensive. Each device differs in features, but all include a word processor, calculator, and spell- and grammar-check capabilities. Each allows for eight separate files to be password protected, permitting multiple users on each device. The Dana also offers wireless Internet connectivity. The Neo AlphaSmarts have an almost limitless list of uses in the classroom and for homework.

Handheld computers are portable, small enough to be held in the hand. The most popular handheld computers are those that are specifically designed to provide personal information management functions for to-do lists and to keep a calendar and address book. The Notes function of these devices can be used to take notes in class or during reading assignments.

Some students with limited hand use or eye–hand coordination problems may find the small keypad and stylus difficult to use. Add-ons such as Thumbpads and larger keyboards may be purchased to help students with word processing. Seiko has offered a solution to the small keyboard problem by replacing the keyboard with an electronic pen (see SmartPad in the resources section). The SmartPad allows handwritten notes to be uploaded into the handheld computer. Then the notes are moved to a computer for permanent storage. Software is also available that allows the notes to be edited and saved. This hardware and software offers an alternative to handwritten notes in science and mathematics classes, where drawing and labeling are frequent tasks.

Digital spellers and thesauruses can be software or stand-alone devices that allow the user to look up a word or meaning with or without speech feedback. The only prerequisite is that the user must be able to type in the word. Spellers and thesauruses are available from Franklin Electronic Publishers (for more information, see the resources section). In addition to the stand-alone spellers, most word processors have a spell- and grammar-checking function. Teaching students to use the spell checker, rather than having it turned on, helps them learn to be self-sufficient and take ownership for checking their work. Finally, Merriam-Webster offers a free online dictionary and thesaurus (http://m-w.com/). Students can look up a word and by clicking on an icon can also hear the word. However, if the word is misspelled the dictionary will provide a list of possible correct words for the student. While learning content and completing assignments, students can be working on spelling skills with one of the following programs.

- Simon S.I.O. (Don Johnston) is a spelling program that helps students sound and find out the word they want to spell.
- Show Me Spelling (Attainment Company, Inc.) teaches functional spelling of up to 500 words.

Note taking is another area of difficulty for students with attention, writing, and spelling problems. For some the processes required to attend to the teacher's words interfere with their ability to complete the task of note taking, or they become so stressed by trying to spell correctly that they miss the next thing the teacher says; or they simply can't tell what is important and should be written in the notes. One frequently use accommodation is to tape the lecture using the devices described below.

Analog/digital recorders are useful for a variety of tasks that students with exceptional needs have to complete, recording reminders or notes, recording lectures, and capturing spoken information before actually trying to write it. Full-size tape recorders have the advantage of being inexpensive, but they have the disadvantage of being bigger and bulkier to handle. Microcassette recorders are much more compact and still allow about the same amount of record time as the larger format, but this format does have disadvantages, such as difficulty finding specific points on a taped lecture and that saving recorded tapes requires storage space. Finally, tapes are easy to misplace or break.

A digital recorder uses an integrated circuit to record and hold sound. This allows for random access to the stored information as opposed to sequential access on tape-based systems we have used in the past. Digital systems enable the user to access stored information much easier and faster because recordings can be uploaded to any computer as a voice file and accessed for years to come. This also means that the student no longer needs the recorder to access the information.

Additionally, manufacturers supply software that allows the voice file to be uploaded, saved, and listened to later. This means the file can be saved to a disk or burned to a CD so the student or a transcriber can easily transport the file to any computer. Most MP3 players, iPods, PDAs, and newer cell phones also record voice files. And best of all, you can download voice files to those personal devices. No one will know if the student is listening to a lecture or music, which eliminates some of the stigma felt by students with disabilities and AT use that makes them stand out in the classroom.

ASSISTIVE TECHNOLOGY FOR READING

Reading difficulties are associated with the tasks of reading individual words, sentences, and/or paragraphs and with comprehension of what was read. Causal factors may include the inability to comprehend and organize information presented in print format, decode words, track lines on the printed page, or integrate new knowledge with previously learned knowledge.

Students who may encounter barriers when reading (Hallahan & Kauffman, 2003) are described below. Print materials are a primary source for providing information in classrooms via books, teacher-made materials, Web sites, and so on. Inability to read these materials constitutes a substantial barrier for students who have reading difficulties. Teachers should recognize the barriers presented below so that they can provide alternative ways for students to access print materials.

- *Students with specific reading disorders* may be referred to as having a visual receptive language disorder. Just as with writing, reading involves several brain areas and functions, and the brain networks for vocabulary, comprehension, organization, and memory must all be in good working order. In addition, students with auditory processing disorders may not develop the phonic awareness needed to decode unfamiliar words. A reading disorder may result from problems in any of these areas.

- *Students with hearing impairments* also may have reading difficulties. Students who learn ASL at an early age often experience many of the same vocabulary and reading comprehension problems with Standard English as do students who are English language learners (consider that ASL is their first language and Standard English is their second language).
- *Students with visual impairments* experience barriers to reading print materials. These students may need large print, Braille, or auditory sources to replace print texts and to read their computer screen and Internet materials. In addition, Braille users, like ASL users, may have some acquisition and usage problems similar to students who are ESOL. Braille uses a series of contractions that stand for common letter combinations; this can be confusing during elementary years when students are learning both Braille contractions and the spelling of Standard English words.
- *Students with ADHD* may experience difficulties with the attention and organizational processes required during the reading process. Whether they have inattentive type or hyperactivity type of ADHD, students will have difficulty maintaining attention required for decoding and comprehension, and recall tasks may be difficult. These students need help to learn methods for blocking distractions and organizing information for comprehension and recall tasks.
- *Students with physical disabilities* that limit use of their fingers, hands, and arms will experience difficulty with the physical requirements for reading, such as turning pages and taking notes. Physical limitations may impede their ability to hold conventional print materials.

We will now discuss a variety of AT devices, including hardware and software, that can remove barriers in the reading process experienced by the students described above. For example, you will learn about recorded books, electronic textbooks, text-to-speech software, and Internet resources that may be appropriate for a majority of the students noted above. The IEP team should decide which specific AT application is most useful for an individual student, but cost and availability are considerations, and several AT applications will be helpful additions to purchased AT and can support the learning of all students in your classroom.

SPELLERS, DICTIONARIES, AND THESAURUS   In the section on writing, we discussed these AT devices. These learning supports are useful for reading tasks as well because they allow students to look up words they do not know or cannot pronounce independently.

Quicktionary Pens (Reading Pens) scan a single word or a complete line of text and recognize printed fonts (6–22 point), even if the text is bold, italic, underlined, or inverted. The pen speaks and spells words and lines of text and can provide definitions. Finally, words are highlighted on a small screen as they are spoken so that the student can follow along.

Stand-alone text readers such as the Kurzweil 3000 (Kurzweil Educational Systems, Inc.) and WYNN3 (Freedom Scientific) are software programs that read whatever is presented on the screen. These packages include optical character recognition (OCR), the ability to scan printed pages and convert them into electronic text. Speech synthesis enables the scanned text to be read aloud in a variety of voices and at variable speeds. Both programs can read documents saved in word-processing programs or as PDFs and

Web pages from the Internet. They offer features that allow users to highlight text and create outlines from the highlighted text. Both contain an extensive dictionary, thesaurus, and spelling/grammar check. Each also has capabilities for electronic test taking. That is, teachers can enter digital copies of tests so that student can take multiple choice and fill-in-the-blank or answer essay questions. These are very powerful programs that promote independence and support learning for students with exceptional needs. The primary disadvantage to these programs is the cost, but once loaded on a computer multiple users can take advantage of their features.

Accessing the Internet with screen readers can be easy and free. The Technology Act requires that government agencies and federally funded companies and projects must be accessible. Several software developers who are dedicated to open-source information and Web accessibility for all readers have developed safe software for free downloads. This software (Code-it and Browse Aloud) allows users to read Web sites that have been made accessible. At this time, not all Web sites can be read in this manner, but more are being added. In addition to reading Web pages, Browse Aloud developers have created a software program that reads PDFs. (PDF Aloud: This software provides an alternative to expensive stand-alone screen readers, but it is less powerful and accurate than Kurzweil and WYNN3. For download information, see AT resources in the Appendix.)

Audio books or CDs are common AT applications for students who cannot use print materials. Audio books are available for fiction, nonfiction, and educational textbooks. Generally, the special education department in a school is responsible for ordering textbooks for students who are included in general education classes, but this can be a time-consuming process, so collaboration between teachers is essential here. There are a number of sources for audio books, and understanding the process is important for all teachers.

The Library of Congress maintains a free audio library for persons with visual and physical impairments as well as persons with a reading disability. Commercially published fiction and nonfiction books may be obtained from the Library of Congress by completing an application that requires a physician to certify the disability. Once the application is approved, books can be ordered at the user's local public library. Books are delivered and returned free of charge to the user. Students with disabilities in public schools are eligible for this free library service, but book availability is subject to the same issues as any library book. This means that novels and other books required for classroom assignments should be ordered well ahead of the need.

Educational textbooks must be acquired from other sources, as the Library of Congress does not carry textbooks. Recording for the Blind & Dyslexic, a supplier of such educational materials, had 98,000 titles in literature, history, math, and science from kindergarten through postgraduate and professional levels. If a required book is not in stock, they will record any text not in their inventory.

A special CD player is available that allows students to search textbooks and mark their place in the book. These features are especially valuable for students who are reading more than one book during the school day, but the CD player adds an additional cost to the purchase. There is a one-time application fee and a yearly membership fee for this service. For contact information and other recorded book sources, see AT resources in the Appendix.

PUBLISHER'S EDITIONS OF ELECTRONIC TEXTBOOKS   Many publishers of educational textbooks are now providing electronic editions of their print books. These are available free to any student in any school, so long as the school district has purchased the textbook for use. Some textbooks list the Web site in their text with directions for accessing the electronic version. Otherwise, teachers can contact the school principal or district purchasing agent for more information. These textbooks come with special features that include hyperlinks to word definitions (many with speech), detailed descriptions of important persons or characters, online activities and critical-thinking questions, and other supports for readers. Some even include audio and Spanish language versions. Electronic textbooks provide support and enrichment for students with exceptional needs, including readers who are English language learners and/or gifted.

Many books that are no longer under copyright restrictions are available online electronically through various Internet databases (see Reference Desk and University of Virginia Library in the resources section of the Appendix). These books may be accessed and used freely by the general public. Most can be uploaded to a computer, saved in any word-processing program or as PDFs, and read with screen readers.

Additional electronic books may be found at Web sites dedicated to a specific author, such as Jane Austen or Herman Melville (see AT resources for information to access the above databases and author Web sites). Author Web sites often provide in-depth information about the author and their books. While some electronic books available online are bare-bones text copies of books, others offer hyperlinks to character sketches, graphic organizers of plots and subplots, maps, and photos. These hyperlinked texts give students support for learning and understanding complex plot lines, character motivation, and historical perspectives needed to fully enjoy and learn from literature.

ASSISTIVE TECHNOLOGY FOR MATHEMATICS

Students who may encounter barriers to learning and performing mathematical tasks include students with learning, cognitive, sensory, and physical disabilities—in other words, students with almost any disability may experience difficulty in mathematics classes. Mathematics requires the ability to read, comprehend the meaning of, and write numbers and symbols. Students who encounter difficulties with reading and writing may, although not in every case, have difficulties reading and comprehending word problems and complex formulas in mathematics. And since math symbols express numerical language concepts, language skills are very important to math achievement. Therefore, students who are not fluent Standard English users (such as students who are visually or hearing impaired and English language learners) may experience barriers to learning and using mathematics. Students with visual perception disorders may experience difficulties detecting the differences in shapes and forms, which would affect their ability to complete advanced math curriculum such as geometry. Students may have fine and gross motor skills that present handwriting and organizational difficulties in producing mathematical work on paper. Finally, students who experience many years of school failure may engage in behaviors associated with learned helplessness and math phobias, such as avoidance or disruptions.

Teacher attitude and seeming reluctance to allow AT in mathematics classes may have a negative impact on student's achievement in this content area. For example, Edyburn (2003) noted the reluctance of teachers to allow students with exceptional needs to use calculators for mathematics calculations. Teachers who are wary of using calculators reason that such aids undermine acquisition of the discipline required for learning basic facts, operations, and algorithms (Edyburn, 2003). Two additional reasons for disallowing calculator use are the general ban on these devices in mandated standardized assessments and the bias that only work that the student can do without assistance is acceptable (Edyburn, 2003). Until we are able to change the ban on and negative perception of calculator use for students with exceptional needs, AT in this curriculum area is likely to be underused.

Calculators of all types are the primary AT support recommended for use in mathematics classes. In addition to discussing a variety of calculators, we will share several additional ways to support student work in mathematics.

Text readers and word processors may be applied to work in the math class as they are in reading and writing. For example, if the student is using an audio source to read textbooks, she could continue to use the audio source for reading the math textbook (e.g., audio books or CDs; electronic text with a screen reader). If the student is using a word processor to complete written work, that software may be transferred to working in the math class. For example, the student whose hard-to-read or illegible handwriting hinders reading his answers might keyboard answers to problems or dictate problems and answers using speech-to-text software.

Calculators come in various forms. Handheld calculators are the most common currently available tools for supporting student work in mathematics. Many of the handheld calculators have a speech feature that vocalizes both input and output through speech synthesis. Others have special features that enable the user to select options to speak and simultaneously display numbers, functions, entire equations, and results. Calculators can include a wide variety of special keyboard and screen features, including big number buttons and large keypads or display screens that are suitable for young children and individuals with visual impairments and physical disabilities requiring the use of pointers.

A variety of calculators are available on the Internet and free to users. One example is the Web site Martindale's Calculators On-line Center, where over 20,000 calculators are available. Students in high school and college-level mathematics courses would find these particularly useful because the site has calculators for advanced mathematical functions, such as those found in advance math classes like calculus. Access to calculators is very relatively easy and inexpensive. Most office and computer stores as well as many Internet sites offer calculators for sale. In addition, on-screen calculators are routinely installed on computers, PDAs, and cell phones.

Summary

In this chapter we focused on AT that permits access to the curriculum taught in most classrooms. After defining AT, we discussed the SETT method for assessing students' skills and needs and the steps to be taken to select appropriate AT. We provided information about the school's responsibility to provide AT and also discussed how to obtain funding from third parties. Finally, we discussed a variety of specific AT applications for communication, writing, reading, and math that IEP teams should consider for diverse students with exceptional needs.

References

Alliance for Technology Access. (1996). *Computer resources for people with disabilities: A guide to exploring today's assistive technology.* Alameda, CA: Harper House.

Ashton, P. (2000). Assistive technology. *Journal of Special Education Technology, 15*(1), 57–58.

Behrmann, M. M. (1994). Assistive technology for students with mild disabilities: Details ways that assistive technology can be used in the classroom for students with mild disabilities. *Intervention in School and Clinic, 30*(2), 70–83.

Beigel, A. R. (2000). Assistive technology assessment: More than the device. *Intervention in School and Clinic, 35*(4), 237–243.

Blackhurst, A. E., & Edyburn, D. L. (2000). A brief history of special education technology. *Special Education Technology Practice, 2*(1), 21–35.

Bowe, F. G. (2000). *Universal Design in Education: Teaching nontraditional students.* Westport, CT: Bergin & Garvey.

Bryant, D. P., & Bryant, B. R. (2003). *Assistive technology for people with disabilities.* Boston: Allyn & Bacon.

Center on Disabilities at California State University, Northridge. (2002). *Training workbook: Assistive technology applications certificate program.* Northridge: Author.

Cook, A. M., & Hussey, S. M. (2002). *Assistive technologies: Principles and practice.* St. Louis: Mosby.

Council of State Administrators of Vocational Rehabilitation. *Assistive Technology Act of 2004 as passed by the Senate.* Retrieved on June 15, 2005, from http://www.rehabnetwork.org/assistive_tech_Act/atact04_pass_senate.htm

Erickson, K. (1998, March). *Right to technology from Medicaid.* Paper presented at the California State University, Northridge, 1998 Conference in Los Angeles, CA. Retrieved on June 15, 2005, from http://www.dinf.ne.jp/doc/english/Us_Eu/conf/csun_98/csun98_045.htm

Edyburn, D. L. (2003). Measuring assistive technology outcomes in mathematics. *Journal of Special Education Technology, 18*(4), 76–79.

Friend, M. (2005). *Special education: Contemporary perspectives for school professionals.* Boston: Pearson Education.

Hallahan, D., & Kauffman, J. (2003). *Exceptional learners: Introduction to special education* (9th ed). Boston: Allyn & Bacon.

Harden, B., & Rosenberg, G. (2001). Bringing technology to the classroom: Challenges and considerations in including assistive technology under IDEA. *The ASHA leader, 5,* 16.

Hutinger, P., Johanson, J., & Stoneburner, R. (1996). Assistive technology applications in educational program of children with multiple disabilities: A case study report on the state of the practice. *Journal of Special Education Technology, 13*(1), 16–35.

Institute for Matching Person and Technology. (2005). *Matching person and technology.* Retrieved June 26, 2005, from http://members.aol.com/IMPT97/mptdesc.html

King, T. W. (1999). *Assistive technology: Essential human factors.* Boston: Allyn & Bacon.

Long, T., Huang, L., Woodbridge, M., Woolverton, M., & Minkel, J. (2003). Integrating assistive technology into an outcome-driven model of service delivery. *Infants and Young Children, 16*(4), 272–283.

Male, M. (2003). *Technology for inclusion: Meeting the special needs of all students* (4th ed.). Boston: Allyn & Bacon.

Mandlawitz, M. (2006). *What every teacher should know about IDEA 2004.* Boston: Allyn & Bacon.

McGregor, G., & Pachuski, P., (1996). Assistive technology in schools: Are teachers ready, able, and supported? *Journal of Special Education Technology, 8*(1).

National Association of the Deaf. (n.d.). *Deaf against technology?* Retrieved on April 14, 2006, from http://www.nad.org/site/pp.asp?c=foINKQMBF&b=180439

National Information Center for Children and Youth with Disabilities. (1991). Related services for school-aged children with disabilities. *NCIHCY New Digest, 1*(2). Washington, DC: Author.

Roblyer, M. D. (2003). *Integrating educational technology into teaching* (3rd ed.). Upper Saddle River, NJ: Merrill/Pearson Education.

Sheldon, J., & Hager, J. (1997). The availability of assistive technology through Medicaid, public school special education programs and state vocational rehabilitation agencies. Tucson: AZ: Neighborhood Legal Services, Inc. Retrieved on June 30, 2005, from http://www.nls.org/atart.htm#a%20purchase%20of

Sheldon, J., & Hart, S. (2004). *Medicare funding of assistive technology*. Tucson, AZ: Neighborhood Legal Services, Inc., & Arizona Center for Disability Law. Retrieved on June 30, 2005, from http://www.nls.org/conf2004/medicare-funding.htm

Social Security Administration. (2001). *Benefits for children with disabilities*. Washington, DC: Author. An electronic booklet retrieved on June 16, 2005, from http://www.ssa.gov/pubs/10026.html

U. S. Census Bureau. (2009). *American fact finder*. Washington, DC: Author. Retrieved on September 5, 2009, from http://factfinder.census.gov/servlet/ACSSAFFFacts?_submenuId=factsheet_0&_sse=on

U. S. Department of Health and Human Services. (n.d.). *Medicaid information for your state*. Washington, DC: Author. Retrieved on June 16, 2005, from http://www.cms.hhs.gov/medicaid/

U. S. Department of Health and Human Services. (2004). *Your Medicare benefits—10-116*. Washington, DC: Author. Retrieved on June 16, 2005, from http://www.medicare.gov/Publications/Search/Results.asp?PubID=10116&Type=PubID&Language=English

Watts, E., O'Brian, M., & Wojcik, B. (2004). Four models of assistive technology consideration: How do they compare to recommended educational assessment practices? *Journal of Special Education Technology, 19*(1), 43–56.

Watson, V. (2005). *Word processing as an assistive technology tool for improving production of written work by students with disabilities*. Unpublished master's thesis, Winthrop University. Used with permission.

Zabala, J. S. (2002). Assistive technology assessment process. *Training workbook: Assistive technology applications certificate program* (p. 25). Northridge: Center on Disabilities at California State University.

Chapter 9

Project-Based Learning

LISA HARRIS—*Winthrop University*

After reading this chapter, you will be able to:

1. Describe how PBL may be used to enable students with disabilities and other exceptional learning needs to meet curriculum standards and objectives

2. Plan PBL activities using research-based practices, including developing collaborative teams and integrating technology

3. Create appropriate assessment tools for PBL activities

4. Reflect on the possibilities for PBL as alternative assessment

5. Identify potential problems with PBL and how to avoid them

INTRODUCTION

Using projects and hands-on activities as teaching strategies is not new. Educators since John Dewey have stressed the importance of active rather than passive learning (Dewey, 1897). *Discovery learning, experiential education, problem-based learning*, and *active learning* are terms that have been used in the past to describe learning strategies similar to project-based learning (Thomas, 2000). Project-based learning (PBL) stems from these traditions and may be defined as "a teaching method in which students acquire new knowledge and skills in the course of designing, planning, and producing some product or performance" (Simkins, Cole, Tavalin, & Means, 2002, p. 2).

In PBL, students are actively engaged in doing things rather than passively learning about something (Moursund, 2006). PBL lessons

- Are central to the curriculum
- Focus on questions that drive students to encounter the central principles of a discipline
- Involve students in in-depth investigation
- Are largely student driven (Thomas, 2000)

Products and performances created through PBL are curriculum based, student centered, and often interdisciplinary. In addition, students receive frequent feedback and are allowed to revise while they learn from experience (Markham, Larmer, & Ravitz, 2003).

PBL requires the use of new knowledge and new skills to solve a problem, create a product, or design a performance. It is important to note that project-based learning goes beyond isolated hands-on activities. Thomas (2000) cautions, "if the central activities of the project represent no difficulty to the student or can be carried out with the application of already-learned information or skills, the project is an exercise, not a PBL project" (p. 3). Markham and colleagues (2003) from the Buck Institute for Education, offered the following examples of activities and projects to further make the distinction between true PBL and isolated activities.

EXAMPLE ONE

Theme: Civil War Battles

Activity: Take a field trip to Gettysburg. Write a report on the experience.

Project-based learning: Investigate the question, "How could wars be made humane?" Use Gettysburg as an example of a high-casualty battle, comparing it to other battles. Complete a portfolio, including an essay and a literary response journal, then conclude with a debate (p. 20).

EXAMPLE TWO

Theme: Sound Pollution

Activity: Listen to different sounds. Make a graph. Identify features of common sounds that are disturbing to the ear.

Project-based learning: Identify five sound pollution problems in the community. Form a task force to investigate the problems and devise technically feasible solutions for each (p. 20).

As illustrated in PBL lessons, no single activity is sufficient for answering the question, solving the problem, or locating the requested information. PBL lessons pose an overarching question that requires students to use a variety of skills to arrive at an answer (Simkins, Cole, Tavalin, & Means, 2002). Completing PBL products requires that students locate and appropriately use information from a variety of sources; make decisions about information, time management, and product development; manage resources; and present results. Students gather information from a variety of sources, decide how best to complete a project, and determine how the information will be presented. At their conclusion, projects are presented to an authentic audience, an audience consisting of more than just the teacher. Project audiences may be other students in the classroom, parents, members of the community, or individuals, classes, or organizations around the world and can take place face-to-face or virtually.

PBL project participants, goals, requirements, and audiences vary. The purpose of the project may be to understand a topic in depth, solve a problem, or present a particular point of view. Technology is often used to locate, analyze, or present information. Project-based learning activities may be completed by individuals, small groups, or whole classrooms. Railsback (2002), from the Northwest Regional Educational Laboratory, gave the following examples of PBL:

- design a living history museum or recreate an historical event; design and plan a community garden;
- develop a newsletter or Web site on a specific issue relevant to the school or community (school safety, recycling, how businesses can save energy and reduce waste);
- conduct a survey of historical buildings;
- create a book on tape for senior center or elementary school class; create a wildlife or botanical guide for a local wildlife area;
- compile oral histories of the local area by interviewing community elders;
- create an exhibit in a local museum or community center;
- produce audiotapes, videotapes, and books with historic photographs;
- produce a Web site as a "virtual tour" of the history (p. 15).

PBL AND EXCEPTIONAL LEARNERS

PBL provides opportunities to differentiate instruction to better meet the needs of all learners. Hall (2002) explained differentiated instruction as follows:

> To differentiate instruction is to recognize students varying background knowledge, readiness, language, preferences in learning, interests, and to react responsively. Differentiated instruction is a process to approach teaching and learning for students of differing abilities in the same class. The intent of differentiating instruction is to maximize each student's growth and individual success by meeting each student where he or she is, and assisting in the learning process (¶ 2).

Common elements of PBL related to differentiated instruction include:

- Multiple methods and materials are used to support instructional content. Whole class discussion, individual research, peer teaching, and small-group work may all be necessary to complete the project.

- Instruction is based on broad concepts rather than small details. Teachers can adjust the level of detail and complexity to accommodate learner diversity.
- Assessment of student growth and project progress are ongoing throughout the project.
- Instruction in project-based learning activities provides opportunities for active engagement in learning. Students are required to be active participants in knowledge creation rather than passive observers. Students can explore content of interest to them and produce products that capitalize on their individual talents (Hall, 2002).

Students with learning disabilities (LD) benefit from project-based learning when teachers closely monitor the process. This includes keeping students on task, explaining the relationship between concrete and abstract ideas, and encouraging and carefully supporting active thinking (Scruggs & Mastropieri, 2003). For example, investigations in science instruction suggest that students with LD respond positively to an inquiry-oriented approach when the teacher provides academic and behavioral supports (Scruggs & Mastropieri, 1994). Additional research suggests that "IQ, rather than learning disability status, predicted learning on constructivist, inquiry-oriented science tasks, and that most students with learning disabilities, perhaps with some additional prompting, could be expected to function adequately on such tasks" (Scruggs & Mastropieri, 2003, p. 373).

Low performing students can benefit from PBL for the same reasons: Active engagement in the learning process encourages student learning. Data from the Multimedia Project: Project-based Learning with Multimedia—in which students completed curriculum-based projects that culminated in multimedia products such as Web pages and computerized presentations—revealed that students with low academic skills and abilities benefit from PBL. Teachers participating in the Multimedia Project felt that students who benefit most from PBL are those for which traditional instructional methods don't work. "Some students clearly have more difficulty focusing on traditional paper-and-pencil tasks and are able to guide their energies more productively and demonstrate their knowledge more effectively with hands-on project-based learning" (Multimedia Project, 2000, p. 4). Similarly, teachers report that when they use PBL and technology "it is not necessarily the traditional gifted student who creates the highest quality product. Students use various talents as they work with teams to create a multimedia project, and the combination of student strengths leads to high-quality multimedia projects" (Steelman, 2005, p. 17).

Teachers from the Multimedia Project also felt that gifted and talented students benefited from PBL because it allowed them to participate in complex projects, take control of their own learning, and explore a topic in depth (Multimedia Project, 2000). Moursund (2006) suggested the following strategies for providing differentiated instruction in a PBL environment for gifted and talented students:

- In a project that makes extensive use of published materials, strongly encourage or require students to use primary resources.
- In a project that makes use of multimedia, strongly encourage or require talented and gifted students to create their own multimedia, rather than just drawing from the libraries of "canned" materials.
- Give talented and gifted students increased leeway to define their own project, with the stipulation that these projects be more challenging and comprehensive than the ones suggested by other students in the class. (p. 79)

Project-based learning can also benefit English language learners (ELL). Hands-on learning is one of the primary means of teaching content to ELLs, as seen by its inclusion in the Sheltered Instruction Observation Protocol (Echevarria, Vogt, & Short, 2008). Projects provide concrete engagement with the curriculum and can provide ELLs an opportunity to show what they know rather than tell what they know. In addition, projects can be structured in such a way that students gather information from multiple sources, not just the textbook. These other sources can reduce the language load on the ELLs. Examples of additional resources include books written on a different grade level, images, videos, and demonstrations. ELLs can also benefit from collaborative project-based learning for multiple reasons. Students benefit from being engaged in social interaction with their English-speaking peers; English is taught around content themes, giving students a chance to learn the necessary vocabulary; and students practice speaking English in smaller groups in which they may feel more comfortable as opposed to a larger audience (Chamot, & O'Malley, 1994; Kinsella, 1996; Long, & Porter, 1985; McCafferty, Jacobs, Christina, & Iddings, 2006; Scarcella, & Oxford, 1992).

When well-planned and carefully managed, PBL can assist exceptional learners in reaching academic goals. To ensure that all students benefit from PBL activities, teachers must make project goals clear, monitor the process, teach time management skills, and provide support and guidance throughout the process; otherwise, students easily get off task, mismanage time, and draw inaccurate conclusions related to the subject matter. Methods, strategies, and learner supports to assist teachers in implementing project-based learning activities with all students are described later in this chapter.

BENEFITS

Students engaged in PBL lessons employ a variety of skills to complete the project, including information literacy, higher-order thinking, and metacognitive skills. PBL lessons also motivate students to learn by actively engaging them in the learning process. PBL lessons also lend themselves to the principles of UDL (Universal Design for Learning) and collaborative learning. There is much evidence to suggest that project-based learning is an effective instructional strategy in the general education classroom (Thomas, 2000). While project-based learning as a method of teaching students with exceptionalities has not been studied extensively, there is some empirical research to support its use (Expeditionary Learning Outward Bound, 1999; Ferretti, MacArther, & Oholo, 2001; Ljung & Blackwell, 1996; Logan, Bakeman, Keefe, 1997). In addition, Ellis (2000) suggested that project-based learning benefits students with disabilities and other exceptional learning needs because it allows for differentiated instruction, capitalizes on students' strengths and talents, and fosters authentic motivation.

It is important to note that project-based learning takes much scaffolding and guidance by the teacher for all students. This is even more important for students with disabilities and other exceptional learning needs. Research shows that students with mild disabilities can master advanced content when they are provided with appropriate instruction, materials, and support (Dalton, Morocco, Tivnan, & Rawson, 1997; Feretti, & Okolo, 1996; Mastropieri, & Scruggs, 1994). An explanation of how to provide these supports in PBL lessons is discussed later in this chapter.

Information Literacy

PBL gives students a chance to work with multiple sources of information to develop a final product. In the information age, with both reliable and unreliable information just a click away, it is imperative that students learn how to evaluate and synthesize information. From making decisions at work to determining what kind of car to buy, adults are better informed when they make decisions based on accurate information. Source and information evaluation are key skills taught as part of the project-based learning process. In addition, computer skills are often taught in conjunction with project-based learning (e.g., digital cameras, spreadsheets, presentation software, digital video).

Higher-Order Thinking Skills

If tasks are designed appropriately, students will use higher-order thinking skills in multiple ways to complete PBL activities. For example, students must make many decisions, including what tasks have to be completed, who will be responsible for what part of the project, which information is needed, and how the information will be presented. Project-based learning requires students to use organizational skills beyond the organization of information. Successful completion of a PBL activity requires project management skills. With proper guidance from the teacher, students learn the skills necessary to make working in groups a positive and productive experience. Students also learn how to manage time, resources, and tasks. Scaffolding the project-based learning process to teach higher-order thinking skills is discussed later in this chapter.

Metacognition

By carefully scaffolding PBL activities and making the steps in the PBL process overt, teachers can help students learn valuable decision-making and project management skills as well as the required content. Making students aware of the learning goals, self-assess in relation to their progress toward the learning goal, understand that revision is necessary to achieve that goal, and recognize which tools are available to aid them in the process (e.g., scaffolds, peer assessments) helps students take on more responsibility for their learning and increases the likelihood of successful project completion (Barron, 1988). To ensure that all students progress through the PBL process successfully, information literacy and collaborative learning skills can be explicitly taught. Teachers should not assume that students will automatically develop these skills without guidance.

Motivation

PBL can motivate students by allowing them an active role in their own learning. Rather than listening passively to a lecture, students are required to actively engage in the learning process to produce a final product. Within project boundaries, students can pursue their own questions of interest and make decisions about how to synthesize and present information. PBL assignments that students find relevant to their own lives increase student motivation and active engagement in the project (Moursund, 1999). Thus, the research literature suggests that students learn more and remember better when they are motivated and actively engaged (Blumenfeld et al., 1991). PBL can also link content learning to real-world contexts. For example, through the Global Learning and Observations to Benefit the Environment Program (GLOBE), a worldwide network of students, teachers, and scientists working together to study and understand the global environment, students take measurements, analyze data, and participate in research in collaboration with scientists. The GLOBE program is online at http://www.globe.gov.

Universal Design for Learning

PBL offers many opportunities to provide multiple means of engagement, expression, and representation. By its nature, PBL requires students to actively engage in the learning process by completing projects that involve multiple steps and processes. Students can obtain information from a variety of sources (e.g., books, Internet, interviews, databases) and produce their own information in a variety of formats (e.g., multimedia presentation, video, theater production, written report). Students may be called upon to write scripts, outline information, draw illustrations, act out a part, or create a multimedia presentation. Finally, students demonstrate what they know by creating a product rather than taking a test.

Collaborative Learning

Engaging in PBL activities in collaborative groups has both academic and social benefits. Goals include encouraging the development of positive group relationships, developing the students' self-esteem in the process of learning, fostering collaboration in all aspects of the classroom, and enhancing academic achievement. When students interact with their peers, their participation and risk-taking behaviors are likely to increase compared to when they interact with someone they view as an authority figure or in a large-group setting (Vacca & Vacca, 1999). For example, students are more likely to offer suggestions, provide creative solutions to problems, and engage in learning behaviors that extend beyond their comfort zone when asked to do so in an environment they feel is less judgmental. Also, as students become more engaged in learning activities, they retain more information and learn valuable social skills (Vacca & Vacca, 1999).

PLANNING PBL LESSONS

Incorporating well-designed PBL lessons into the curriculum takes careful planning and requires making many decisions. A well-thought-out plan will make it easier for teachers to manage the project, anticipate setbacks, and make corrections. The topics outlined below should be considered before embarking on a PBL project.

Determine PBL Learning Goals

CONTENT GOALS To start off, Markham and colleagues (2003) suggested determining which topics in the curriculum need to be covered in depth and which ones can be covered more quickly. Topics that require a deeper understanding and are investigative in nature are more suitable to learn through PBL. While basic skills are more efficiently taught through other methods, PBL creates an authentic environment in which students apply their knowledge of basic skills (Markham et al., 2003).

Because lessons are typically broad in scope, PBL lends itself to interdisciplinary learning as well. Content and skills from diverse subject areas are integrated as necessary throughout the project construction, and students will use information literacy and writing skills to locate and organize information on the topic. For some projects, information from multiple disciplines is necessary to solve the problem. For example, a project to investigate the impact of a landfill on a community would incorporate multiple subject areas, including science, math, social studies, and language arts.

PROCESS GOALS   Learning from the process is also an important aspect of PBL. Students use problem-solving and decision-making skills when required to engage in this level of research. PBL activities require students to engage in process skills on higher levels of Bloom's Taxonomy. Examples of PBL activities at the application, analysis, and synthesis levels of Bloom's Taxonomy include the following:

- Students locate, synthesize, and interpret information from many sources and engage in many types of learning activities to retrieve information about a single subject (e.g., library research, online research, interviews, watching documentaries, going on a fieldtrip).
- Students use information to solve problems (e.g., identify the mystery substance in science, solve a riddle, use simulation software such as Oregon Trail or Sim City).

Emphasizing both content and process capitalizes on the complex nature of project-based learning. Making students aware of problem-solving, information literacy, and decision-making skills makes these processes more concrete. Students learn skills that can be generalized to other situations. Herman, Aschbacher, and Winters (1992) offered five questions to consider when determining content and process goals.

1. What important cognitive skills do I want my students to develop? (e.g., analyze issues using primary source and reference materials, use the scientific method, use different media to express what they know)
2. What social and effective skills do I want my students to develop? (e.g., appreciate individual strengths, have confidence in their abilities)
3. What metacognitive skills do I want my students to develop? (e.g., reflect on the research process they use, evaluate its effectiveness, and derive plans for improvement)
4. What types of problems do I want my students to be able to solve? (e.g., know how to do research, apply the scientific method, solve problems with no right answer)
5. What concepts and principles do I want my students to be able to apply? (e.g., apply basic principles of ecology and conservation in their lives, understand cause-and-effect relationships, and understanding what democracy is)

Design Projects That Make Real-World Connections

PBL can also help teachers make real-world connections to the content being taught in school, thereby making students realize that what they are learning is important *outside* the school environment. This in turn and helps teachers answer questions such as, "Why do we have to learn this? How does this apply to me?" Simkins and colleagues (2002) offered suggestions with examples for making real-world connections:

1. Connect through student interests. Create a "math in the real world presentation, in which students show how math is involved in their favorite hobbies and sports" (p. 35).
2. Connect through student experiences. Have students create family histories. Students in the classroom are likely to be from other states, cultures, or countries or have relatives from other states, cultures, or countries.
3. Connect through significant issues. "Many topics in the real world are particularly compelling to young people. These topics include public health, racism, poverty and the power of media" (p. 37).
4. Improve the real world. Students can research environmental issues (e.g., placement of a landfill, smog, air or noise pollution) and develop presentations to air on public access television, send to their congressional representatives, or present to the city council.
5. Relate to clients. Students develop a Web site for their parents to keep them up-to-date on school activities. Parents act as clients and students as designers. Students meet with parents to determine needs and gather feedback.
6. Interact with assessors. Bring content experts in to assess student work. Parents, retirees, and other residents in the community are possible content experts within a particular field.
7. Interact with people who know. Students interview experts to describe a historical event (WWII) or explain a concept (a career, how to plant a garden).
8. Learn adult work and life skills. Assign students a career and give them a salary. Have them develop a budget and "live" off of it for several months. Have students create an investment portfolio.

Plan the End Product

Numerous types of end products can result from PBL lessons. They include brochures, oral presentations, multimedia presentations, models, debates, plays, poems, short stories, digital videos, speeches, business plans, sculpture, producing a commercial, putting on a play, and creating a painting. The appropriate end product is determined by the content and process goals. For example, if a goal is effective public speaking, an oral presentation or debate would be part of the final product. Similarly, if the goal is to improve written communication, writing must be necessary to complete the final product. Students may also have ideas about what type of final product they want to create. One way to further involve them in the PBL process is to let them help you decide.

Determine Skills Necessary to Complete the Project

Teachers facilitate PBL by monitoring both the academic and the social aspects of collaborative PBL activities. For example, they guide students toward resources, help them solve problems, and teach collaborative learning skills. Moursund (2006) pointed out that "young children do not automatically know how to do a project. Even college students are often quite poor at budgeting their time and other resources" (p. 77). By guiding and closely monitoring students engaged in PBL, teachers ensure that both PBL content and process goals are successfully met at the completion of the project.

To determine what skills need to be taught, break the project down into the skills and experiences students need to have to successfully complete the project. Determine how much content and how many skills they already know. Determine what you will need to teach and in what order. For example, is there a certain level of content knowledge all students must have before they can engage in PBL activities? Do all students need to learn how to create a reference page? From here, you can develop a timeline for project activities and set aside time to teach new skills.

Multiple strategies may be used to teach new skills to students. One strategy is called shared knowledge (Barron, 1998). Teachers introduce new information or skills to the class as a whole before the project begins. This ensures that all students know entry-level content and have the skills necessary to start the project. Delivering important content and skill information to individuals or groups of students just as they need to learn the skills to complete new project work is another teaching strategy. Teachers can deliver instruction verbally, in writing, or in less traditional formats, such as digital video or via the Web or e-mail. If teachers know they will be delivering the same type of information over and over, it is helpful to capture that information in some reusable form so they do not have to repeat it over and over. For example, if students will be graphing data on the computer as part of the larger project, teachers can create a set of step-by-step directions to leave by the computer. Students can follow the directions to create the graph and only ask the teacher for help when they are confused or have a problem.

Most PBL lessons span a longer period of time than traditional lessons and activities. Because PBL lessons are multifaceted and require students to learn complex content and varied skills, students benefit from being reminded of the big picture. It is helpful for teachers to continually relate new information students learn over time back to the overarching big ideas being studied (Barron, 1998). (See Teaching the Process in this chapter for additional information.)

Decide if the Project Will Be Completed Individually or Collaboratively

PBL lessons can be implemented with individuals, pairs, groups, or the whole class. Consider the project goals, complexity of the final product, time frame, and availability of resources when deciding whether a project is best completed individually or collaboratively. Questions to consider include:

- On what level of Bloom's Taxonomy are the content goals?
- On what level of Bloom's Taxonomy are the process goals?
- Will it take more than one person to produce the product or performance in the specified time frame?
- Will working in teams provide a superior experience to working individually?
- Will working in teams produce a superior product than what would be produced working individually?

Develop a Timeline

PBL ranges from projects that cover a single subject and take place in the classroom to interdisciplinary projects that involve the larger community (Markham et al., 2003). PBL can be time-consuming, but a well-planned PBL lesson in which students are guided through decision making, information gathering, and time management prevents wasted time. Well-chosen PBL topics ensure that time is used to study concepts in depth rather than learning basic skills that can be taught more efficiently using other strategies. Markham et al. (2003) suggested that PBL be central rather than peripheral to the curriculum. Rather than thinking about PBL as taking time away from the regular curriculum, PBL can be used to teach the same material taught through lecture and discussion. PBL is then becomes a central method of teaching content that replaces traditional instruction (Markham et al., 2003).

Determine Resource Needs and Availability

The types of resources students need depend on the PBL product. First, teachers must ensure that students have access to quality information in a variety of formats. If students need access to the Internet to conduct research or computer software to produce the final product, the necessary resources need to be reserved. Students may need instruction on using the media center, finding and evaluating information on the Internet, or using the computer to complete the final product (Railsback, 2002). Providing materials such as flowcharts, checklists, and graphic organizers to guide students through the PBL process is also important and is discussed in more detail later in the chapter. Resource management requires careful planning to ensure that valuable time is not wasted.

Develop the Assessment

What skills will be assessed before, during, and after the PBL lesson should be determined before the project begins. PBL products and performances are substantially different from traditional paper-and-pencil assessments and are considered performance assessments. Performance assessments are more diverse than traditional assessments (Markham et al., 2003) and provide a way to assess complex outcomes associated with the highest levels of Bloom's Taxonomy: analysis, synthesis, and evaluation (Kuhs, Johnson, Agruso, & Monrad, 2001).

Assessments must be carefully designed to capture the complexity of PBL. Performance assessment using PBL can provide direct evidence of student learning. Product and presentation development is multifaceted, involves both content and process knowledge and skills, and requires students to actively use information to create something new. A student's ability to apply information and complete complex tasks can be directly, instead of indirectly, assessed (Kuhs et al., 2001). For example, the ability to conduct research can be assessed through a multiple-choice test in which students select reference materials from a list that they would use in a hypothetical situation. This is an indirect assessment of student research skills. A student selecting and then using information as applied to a PBL task is a direct assessment of research skills. (Additional information on assessment and rubric development is provided later in the Assessment section of this chapter.)

TEACHING THE PROCESS

Teachers should not assume that students possess the time management, resource management, and collaboration skills necessary to successfully complete PBL lessons. Explicit instruction in these areas teaches students valuable life skills in addition to the content knowledge addressed in the project.

Teaching Project Management

Successful completion of a PBL activity requires project management skills. With proper guidance from the teacher, students learn the skills necessary to make PBL a positive and productive experience. Providing explicit instruction on time and resource management can reduce wasted time and effort throughout the process. Having students set goals, develop a time frame, and monitor their own progress toward project completion teaches them valuable time management skills. Graphic organizers may be used to guide students in goal setting, project planning, assigning responsibility, and storyboarding. In addition, students can use checklists, weekly reports, task lists, and calendars to track progress.

Teaching Students to Work Collaboratively

Group members may come to the task with different expectations, cultural differences, work preferences, and leadership skills, thereby affecting the group dynamic. It is important for students to be aware of these issues so that they are better able to work in teams to complete a task. Johnson and Johnson (1999) outlined a group processing procedure to assess how well groups are functioning, provide feedback, and motivate student learning. Steps in the procedure include the following:

1. Assess the ability of the group to cooperatively work to complete the task through observation.
2. Provide feedback to the group on a regular basis.
3. Assist groups in forming goals and formulating plans about how they will improve their effectiveness.
4. Assess the progress of the entire class.
5. Celebrate both group and class successes.

Group Decision-Making Strategies

Teaching group decision-making strategies is important when students are working collaboratively in the PBL lesson. Understanding ways to make decisions can also reduce conflict and wasted time. Decision-making strategies include the following:

- *Authority.* Groups brainstorm and discuss ideas, but the group leader makes the final decision.
- *Majority.* Groups generate ideas and vote. The idea that receives the majority vote wins.
- *Negative minority.* After discussion, group members vote for the ideas they want to eliminate. Group members vote until there is only one idea left.

Slide	Diagram	References/Notes
1		
2		
3		
4		

FIGURE 9.1 Storyboard for a Multimedia Presentation

- *Consensus.* The group discusses an idea and modifies it until consensus is reached.
- *Using criteria.* Group members identify and agree on criteria for a project solution and then compare alternatives to the criteria.
- *Compromise.* Groups combine multiple ideas into one until a compromise is reached that is agreeable to everyone.

(University of Waterloo, 2000; Johnson & Johnson, 1997)

Johnson and Johnson (1997) suggested that effective groups employ different methods depending on six factors:

1. the type of decision to be made;
2. the amount of time and resources available;
3. the history of the group;
4. the nature of the task being worked on;
5. the kind of climate the group wishes to establish; and
6. the type of setting in which the group is working (p. 244)

Making groups aware of decision-making strategies can reduce wasted time and internal conflict.

Many premade project-planning and collaborative learning planning materials are available both in stores and on the Internet. Teachers may wish to design their own materials as well. Examples of these materials are shown in Figure 9.1 and Figure 9.2.

Task	Person Responsible	Due Date	Completed (check when completed)

FIGURE 9.2 Group Planning Guide

ASSESSMENT

Assessing the effectiveness of PBL requires both formative and summative measures. Formative assessment is used throughout the process to help students revise products, plan what to do next, and monitor progress toward the learning goals. To this end, self-assessment, peer assessment, and teacher assessment may be employed. Completed PBL products can be used as summative assessments to determine how well the student achieved the content learning goals at the conclusion of the assignment. The criteria for performance assessments are presented in the form of rubrics, which can be used in both summative and formative assessment.

The Role of Summative Assessment

Because the goals associated with PBL are generally numerous and complex, it is important to determine the main content and process skills you want students to demonstrate by the end of the project. These assessment criteria should be related to the initial learning goals that guided the PBL experience (see Planning PBL Lessons above).

Summative assessment in PBL informs both the teacher and the student about the degree to which the intended outcomes of the project have been met. Summative assessment is used to assign a grade to students and to evaluate the effectiveness of the PBL experience. Students can see how well they mastered the objectives, and teachers can use assessment results to look at both individual and whole class performance. Teachers can use assessment results to answer important questions: Are there particular skills that individual students need to continue to work on? Are there particular skills that the whole class mastered or didn't master? Answers to these questions help guide future instruction. As mentioned, PBL products and performances are assessed through rubrics.

The Role of Formative Assessment

Frequent formative assessment ensures that students and teachers do not get to the end of the project only to discover shallow products or performances, dysfunctional groups, and confused students (Barron, 1998). Formative assessment can be used to assess progress in many areas of the PBL process: skill development, time management, collaboration, and product development. Questions answered by formative assessment include these: Are students demonstrating progress in locating appropriate information necessary for the final product? Are students making adequate progress toward completing the final product? If not, why? Are they having trouble managing time? Do they have to wait too long to share resources? If the PBL project is collaborative, are the teams working well together? Is everyone contributing to the final product? Data from formative assessments inform teachers what they need to do next: refocus students, teach skills to individuals, teach skills to the whole class, bring in more resources, or adjust the time frame for the project.

Formative evaluation does not have to be conducted solely by the teacher. It is recommended that students be involved in the process. Having students monitor their own progress is another way to actively engage them in the learning process. Students may participate in self-evaluation or peer evaluation. Such involvement helps make them metacognitively aware of the steps in the learning process and provides an opportunity

Team Members: _____
_____
_____
_____

Complete this form as a team.

1. We feel . . .
   ❑ On schedule
   ❑ Behind schedule
   ❑ Ahead of schedule.
2. This week we completed . . .

3. Our next steps are . . .

4. We have questions about . . .

FIGURE 9.3 Project Status Report

for self-adjustment and self-correction. Student self-evaluation can focus on content learning and collaborative group participation, whereas student peer evaluation helps hold group members accountable and can make the teacher aware of groups in crisis. Finally, group evaluation helps groups see where they are in the process and set goals for successful project completion. Individuals and groups report progress, issues, and questions at intervals throughout the project (e.g., daily, weekly, and after specific skills are taught or milestones are passed). Teachers also monitor group progress through observation and provide feedback. Feedback along the way helps students correct inefficient methods, clear up misunderstandings, and clarify expectations. However formative evaluation is carried out, it provides valuable information about how the PBL lesson is progressing (Barkley, Cross, & Major, 2005). Rubrics, project status reports, and activity logs can be used for formative assessment in PBL. See Figure 9.3 for an example of project status report. Rubric development is described in detail below.

RUBRICS

Description

Rubrics tell students and teachers what elements of a given project or performance are the most important and how the project will be judged in terms of relative quality (Wiggins, 1998). Rubrics also make the assessment process more consistent and fair, as the teacher is assessing the same qualities for every product. Rubrics answer the following questions:

- By what criteria should performance be judged?
- Where should we look and what should we look for to judge performance success?
- What does the range in the quality of performance look like?
- How do we determine validly, reliably, and fairly what score should be given and what that score means?
- How should the different levels of quality be described and distinguished from one another? (Wiggins, 1998, p. 154)

Determining how the final product or performance will be assessed and informing students of this *before* embarking in PBL has many benefits:

- Grading criteria are established and explicitly defined.
- Both teachers and students know what is important.
- Rubrics help explain to students what is expected and show teachers what to teach.
- Students have an idea of what the final product or performance should include.
- Teachers can determine the skills students need to learn to successfully produce the final product.
- Students can use the rubric to evaluate their own and each other's work (Walvoord & Anderson, 1998).

Examples of rubrics are shown in Figure 9.4 and Figure 9.5.

Designing Rubrics

The following rubric development process has been adapted from Kuhs and colleagues (2001):

1. Determine what criteria will be assessed.
2. Decide whether to use a holistic or analytic rubric.
3. Develop rating scales.
4. Write descriptions of products at each level of the scale.

DETERMINING CRITERIA TO BE ASSESSED First, decide what elements of the product or performance are the most important. It is essential that the rubric reflect all important elements and is aligned with the learning goals already developed for the PBL project. For example, if students created a multimedia presentation to learn a specific curriculum, the corresponding rubric should assess both the accuracy and presentation of information. Both content and process must be assessed. Elaborately developed products do not necessarily contain appropriate content. When determining which elements to include, consider the following points:

- Are the criteria related to the learning goals specified for PBL?
- Are all important elements of the product or performance listed as traits?
- Do traits reflect teachable outcomes?
- Are traits observable?
- Are traits limited to a feasible number?

(Gronlund, 2003; Herman et al., 1992; Jonassen, Peck, & Wilson, 1999)

Analytic Rubric for Environmental Studies Project 11th Grade

Criteria	Excellent 100–90 points	Good 89–80 points	Satisfactory 79–70 points	Unsatisfactory 69 and lower
Presentation ___ / **40 points**	Presentation thoroughly explains the cause and effect of the environmental issue. Specific events are identified that lead to awareness of the issue, and the significance and outcomes of these events are noted. The presentation is well organized and easy for the audience to understand. Each group member provides an oral contribution.	Presentation explains the cause and effect of the environmental issue. Events are identified that lead to awareness of the issue, with some significance and outcomes of these events noted. Presentation is organized and comprehendible. Each group member orally contributes to the presentation.	Presentation attempts to explain the cause and effect of the environmental issue, although some significant pieces are missing. Identification of events that lead to awareness of the issue are included, although significance and outcomes are vague. Presentation is choppy and challenging to follow. Oral presentation was dominated by only a few members.	Presentation attempts to explain the cause and effect of the environmental issue. Fails to identify events that lead to awareness of the issue, and the significance and outcomes of these events aren't noted. Presentation lacks clarity and organization and is difficult for the audience to follow. One group member orally contributed to the presentation.
Spreadsheets ___ / **25 points**	40–36 points Spreadsheets demonstrate advanced comprehension of software. Data are organized and manipulated to illustrate trends of cause and effect of the environmental issue. No more than one error in data entry and/or calculation.	35–32 points Spreadsheets demonstrate enough comprehension to operate software. Data are organized and manipulated to illustrate trends of the environmental issue. No more than three errors in data entry and/or calculation.	31–28 points Attempts to illustrate cause and affect trends of the environmental issue but lacks adequate knowledge of software to complete assignment in a clear, organized fashion. Errors in data entry and calculations interfere with interpretation of issues.	27–0 points Spreadsheets do not demonstrate comprehension of software. Data are inaccurate, failing to illustrate cause-and-effect trends of the environmental issues. Too many errors are present to accurately interpret data.
Internet Sources ___ / **15 points**	25–23 points Eight or more sources are used. Sources are reliable, creditable, and relevant to the topic. All sources include information for complete documentation.	22–20 points Between five and seven sources are used. Sources are reliable, creditable, and relevant to the topic. Most sources include information for complete documentation.	19–17 points Between four and six sources are used. Sources appear reliable and creditable, although connection to topic is questionable. Some sources are relevant to the	16–0 points Three or fewer sources are used. Sources are not reliable, creditable, or relevant to the topic. Sources do not include enough information for complete documentation.

FIGURE 9.4 Analytic Rubric

Criteria	Excellent 100–90 points	Good 89–80 points	Satisfactory 79–70 points	Unsatisfactory 69 and lower
			topic and include information for complete documentation.	
Visuals ___ / 10 points	**15–14 points** Eight or more visuals are present. Visuals complement the presentation and enhance the message related to the environmental issue.	**13–12 points** Between five and seven visuals are present, appropriate, and relevant to the environmental issue.	**11–10 points** Two to four visuals are present, although most lack organization, clarity, and relevance to the environmental issue. Visuals distract rather than enhance presentation.	**9–0 points** No visuals are present to complement presentation.
Handout ___ / 5 points	**10–9 points** Clear and concise. Key points summarized, resources correctly documented, and possible solutions are included.	**8–7 points** Key points summarized, minimal documentation errors, and possible solutions are included.	**6–4 points** Attempts to summarize key points, although some are absent. Errors in documentation interfere with use, and few solutions are given.	**0 points** Summaries are not clear. Documentation errors are excessive. No suggestions for solutions are provided.
Activity ___ / 5 points	**5 points** Actively engages the audience and reinforces key concepts of the presentation.	**4 points** Engages the audience and reinforces key concepts of the presentation.	**3 points** Minimally engages the audience, fails to reinforce key concepts.	**2–0 points** Does not engage the audience and fails to reinforce key concepts of the presentation.
	5 points	**4 points**	**3 points**	**2–0 points**

FIGURE 9.4 Analytic Rubric (Continued)

Because PBL products are complex, it is also suggested that teachers determine what they are *not* going to assess (Kuhs et al., 2001). Assessing too many traits can be overwhelming for the teacher and the student. Too much emphasis may be placed on a less important goal if outcomes aren't prioritized.

CHOOSE A HOLISTIC OR ANALYTIC RUBRIC There are two types of rubrics: analytic and holistic. *Analytic rubrics* consist of traits, a rating scale, and descriptions of performances on each level of the scale. Such rubrics divide learning goals into individual categories and rate each category. An example of an analytic rubric is shown in Figure 9.4. *Holistic rubrics* consist of a rating scale and descriptions of products on each level of the scale. Each trait is not assessed individually, but the product is assessed overall. An example of holistic rubric is shown in Figure 9.5. Holistic rubrics are appropriate in settings where

---

Holistic Rubric for Campaign Poster
Fourth Grade Social Studies

4—Poster is attractive and easy to read. The overall message is clear through the use of a catchy slogan and three short messages regarding candidate issues. Picture of candidate is clear and portrays a positive image. The poster is done in a professional manner and contains no errors in spelling or grammar.

3—Poster is easy to read and message is clear. A picture of the candidate is included along with a slogan that is appropriate but not necessarily attention grabbing. At least two issues are included on the poster that relate to campaign message with no more than one error in spelling or grammar.

2—Poster seems disorganized in terms of appearance. It is difficult to find information about the candidate. Although a picture is included, it is not the best choice of image to portray a positive message. The slogan is too long to remember and needs to be revised in order to grab the attention of prospective voters. Only one issue related to the candidate's campaign is included on the poster. There are no more than three errors in spelling or grammar. Revision is suggested.

1—Poster is not suitable for purpose of campaign. A picture of the candidate is not included. Although words and phrases are on the poster, the connection to the candidate's campaign is questionable. There are more than three errors in spelling or grammar, making the poster difficult to read and understand. Significant revision is needed.

FIGURE 9.5 Holistic Rubric

an overall performance is rated without the need for detailed feedback, as in the case of large-scale performance assessments (Arter & McTighe, 2001). Holistic rubrics are often used when it is difficult to separate the product into discrete component parts, or when certain criteria are dependent on one another (Kuhs et al., 2001). Kuhs and colleagues provided the following example:

> Students might be asked to write a fictional story. In grading student work, the teacher would want to consider if students' writings included the major components of a story: character, setting, conflict, climax, and resolution. The potential evaluative criteria of conflict, climax, and resolution are intertwined. If an analytic rubric were used, the teacher would have difficulty scoring for the presence of a resolution when a student paper doesn't really present a conflict. (pp. 57–58)

Analytic rubrics provide more specific feedback to both students and teachers and are generally more helpful in day-to-day classroom use (Arter & McTighe, 2001).

DEVELOP A RATING SCALE A rating scale can use numbers (4, 3, 2, 1) or words (Excellent, Good, Acceptable, Inadequate) to label each level. The numerical designation, word choice, and number of levels can vary according to the purpose of the assignment, the purpose of the assessment, and the age and ability level of the student. For example, the teacher may want the assessment to reflect growth rather than complete mastery. In this case a rating scale using labels such as Accomplished, Developing, and Not Yet, may be more appropriate and perceived as less punitive by the student than A, B, C.

Site	URL	Description
RubiStar	http://rubistar.4teachers.org	RubiStar is a free tool to help teachers create rubrics.
Kathy Schrock's Guide for Educators	http://school.discovery.com/ schrockguide/assess.html	Kathy Schrock's Guide for Educators links to many sample rubrics and rubric generators.
teAchnology	http://www.teachnology .com/web_tools/rubrics	teAchnology has over 20 free rubric generators and hundreds of sample rubrics.

FIGURE 9.6 Rubric Examples and Rubric-Generating Software

WRITE DESCRIPTIONS OF TRAITS AT EACH LEVEL OF THE RATING SCALE   Both holistic and analytic rubrics describe specific traits at each level of the rating scale. It is important that descriptions of traits are understandable to students, parents, and other teachers and are free from developmental, ethnic, and gender bias (Herman et al., 1992). Trait descriptions should describe observable and measurable aspects of the trait at a given level in the rating scale. For example, in a writing assignment, what aspects of effective communication would be exhibited at the emerging level or at the excellent level?

One purpose of using rubrics to assess student work is to increase the quality of feedback. To that end, watch out for the following pitfalls. One mistake is writing trait descriptions for multiple levels of performance that are comparative in nature (Wiggins, 1998). For example, how does a clear thesis statement differ from a less clear thesis statement? What information does this give the student about how to improve? A second mistake is using unclear terms like "fairly complete" or "mostly developed."

Bloom's Taxonomy is a useful tool in developing trait descriptions. Look at the verbs associated with each level of the taxonomy to describe student performance (Markham et al., 2003). Reviewing examples of rubrics can be helpful when you are designing a rubric for your specific PBL product. Many examples of rubrics as well as rubric-generating software are available on the Internet. Figure 9.6 provides a list of some of these sites.

Negotiable Contracting

Negotiable contracting involves teachers and students negotiating (at least in part) how the student will be assessed. In this process, students help the teacher design how the product or performance will be assessed, and it is another way to involve students in the learning process and give them ownership of how they will be assessed. It is recommended once students have been actively engaged in creating products or performances rather than when they have just started.

In negotiable contracting, the teacher asks students what they consider to be important elements in the final product. These statements can be grouped together to form traits. The teacher then asks students what the traits would look like at each level of the rating scale. Students provide examples verbally or on paper. The teacher can incorporate the views of the students into the final rubric. This process can be very informative to the teacher. Students may suggest criteria that the teacher didn't think of but are important to the students. For example, the teacher may be unaware of the amount of time students have spent on a particular aspect of a project or the difficulty they had completing a particular component. Students may also leave out criteria that the teacher thinks are valuable. This could indicate that the teacher needs to review certain skills and content because the students didn't view it as important. Asking students why they left something out can be just as informative as asking why they put something in.

COLLABORATIVE LEARNING

Using collaborative groups to complete PBL lessons requires additional planning. First, teachers need to determine how to group students. In general, the size of the group depends on the nature of the project. Groups that are too large leave some members without work to do, whereas groups that are too small overwhelm group members with too much work and responsibility. For example, creating a newspaper can be completed in pairs. Producing a digital video, where groups will need a cameraperson, script writers, and actors, may require more group members. Ultimately, teachers want to be sure that each group member has a role in the project and makes an individual contribution to the final product.

Access to resources also affects group size. If resources will be shared across groups, a rotation schedule is necessary to ensure that everyone has access to the resources and that group members have other tasks to perform while they are waiting their turn. If the final product involves the use of technology, how much equipment is available will also affect group size. For example, if the school has six digital cameras and the project requires that all groups take digital photos at the same time, technology will dictate the class be divided into six groups.

Johnson and Johnson (1999) offered the following suggestions when determining group size:

1. Increase group size when physical resources are limited or you want to increase the interpersonal resources available to each group.
2. Decrease group size when you want to strengthen group cohesion and social support; strengthen individual accountability; instructional time is limited; your students are not experienced working together cooperatively. (p. 20)

Several grouping strategies can be employed to assign individuals to groups: homogeneous, heterogeneous, and shared interest. Homogeneous groups include group members that are all the same—e.g., in academic ability, in ethnicity, in gender. Heterogeneous groups on the other hand include members who are different in academic ability, ethnicity, or possess different talents. For example, each group member may possess a particular talent important for project completion, such as drawing, public speaking, and using computers. Shared-interest groups are made up of students who share a common interest in a subject. Generally, when shared-interest groups are used, students brainstorm project topics and select the topic in which they are most interested. All students who select a particular topic form a group.

Students' interests, work style, and academic strengths and weaknesses affect how they perform in groups. Studies indicate that the relationship between group performance and intellectual factors is low, but the relationship between group performance, experience, social background, interests, attitudes, and personality is high (Vacca & Vacca, 1999).

Heterogeneous grouping is generally preferred so that a variety of perspectives and skills are represented (Putnam, 1998). To group students by common interest in a topic, Simkins and colleagues (2002) suggested asking students to rank project topics according to interest and then assigning students to groups based on their first and second choices. This allows the teacher to form groups of roughly equal size and ensures that more subtopics related to the broader project topic are covered. Teachers may want to group students by areas of talent and expertise. For example, if PBL lessons require the use of technology, the teacher must be sure that each group contains at least one technology-savvy member. Teachers can rate student skills such as writing, researching, drawing, using technology, and organizing information and create groups so that important talents and skills necessary for successful project completion are represented in each group (Simkins et al., 2002). Teachers can also have students rate themselves on these skills and use the self-ratings to determine group composition.

Kagan (1998) suggested that successful collaborative learning experiences can increase student self-esteem, self-acceptance, and acceptance by others. Students can also learn to understand and appreciate diversity by working in heterogeneous groups. "Only by knowing, working, and being involved in personal interactions with members of diverse groups can students really learn to value diversity, utilize it for creative problem solving, and develop an ability to work with diverse peers" (Johnson & Johnson, 1998, p. 84). It is important to note that an initial negative impact of member diversity is common (Chatman & Flynn, 2001; Watson, Kumar, & Michaelsen 1993; Williams & O-Reilly, 1998). It takes more time for diverse groups to work effectively, but given time to learn each other's strengths and work habits, heterogeneous groups are typically more effective than homogeneous groups (Watson et al., 1993).

Group Learning Strategies

Research on how groups learn comes from the business field of organizational learning strategies. Strategies used in the corporate world can also apply to school settings. These strategies are useful when the teacher needs to incorporate skills training into PBL. For example, a teacher may need to instruct students in how to evaluate Web sites, work a piece of equipment, or analyze data. Which strategy you use depends on the goals of the PBL lesson.

CROSS-FUNCTIONAL TEAMS   Using this approach, team members are involved in more than one part of the task. This helps groups remain productive when other group members are absent. For example, two students are in charge of research and two students are in charge of a multimedia presentation of the information.

JOB ROTATION   Team members rotate jobs throughout the project so that eventually every team member has held every job. For example, each team member uses the

Internet to locate information on the topic, or each team member creates slides in a multimedia presentation.

FORMAL TRAINING   The teacher interrupts the self-directed work of the group to formally train the group on a particular skill. The teacher explains the parts of a reference, for example, or teaches a specific computer skill.

CROSS-PEER TUTORING   Team members knowledgeable in a particular area train other team members. A student who knows how to test the pH in a science experiment trains the other members of the team how to read the pH (Payne-Anderson, 1998).

JIGSAW   Students join a heterogeneous group and select a topic on which they want to become an expert. Students then leave the heterogeneous group and join an expert group. The expert group will become knowledgeable on the topic and determine how they will teach the skill to the original group members. The student will rejoin the original group. Each group member shares his/her expertise. For example, if students are completing a project on biomes, each student researches a different biomes, creates learning materials, and rejoins the group to teach their topic (Slavin, 1995).

INDIVIDUAL ACCOUNTABILITY IN THE GROUP ENVIRONMENT   Each group member is required to demonstrate specific knowledge of skills individually before the group can move on to the next part of the PBL lesson. This provides individual accountability but also fosters collaboration, as each group is responsible for teaching every group member specific content or skill sets (Barron, 1998). Assessment can be in the form of informal oral presentation, written response, or skill demonstration.

POTENTIAL PROBLEMS IN PBL

Challenges and conflicts in PBL can be better managed if teachers understand and have strategies for managing possible pitfalls.

GETTING OFF SCHEDULE   PBL lessons can get off schedule due to technical difficulties, group member absenteeism, or difficulty in finding information. Allow students an appropriate amount of time to complete projects. Students are learning from the process as well as the final product. Rushing the process will not lead to quality learning experiences. Monitor student, group, and class progress throughout the process to ensure that students are moving forward.

GROUP CONFLICT   Group members are likely to have differing opinions, work strategies, and priorities. If group members cannot negotiate a conflict settlement, a third party can work with the group to mediate the situation. A mediator is a "neutral person who helps two or more people resolve their conflict by assisting them through the steps of problem-solving negotiations so that an agreement is reached that both believe is fair, just, and workable" (Johnson & Johnson, 1999, p. 397). Both students and teachers can serve as mediators. It is important to address conflict openly to ensure that groups achieve the intended learning outcomes.

FREE-RIDER EFFECT   Slavin (1995) described the free-rider effect as occurring when some group members do all or most of the work. This can be avoided by designing PBL activities in which students are individually accountable for their learning and by closely monitoring group interaction (Johnson & Johnson, 1999; Slavin, 1995).

Summary

This chapter defines PBL and described how it can be used to meet learning objectives. Benefits of PBL include information literacy, collaborative learning, higher-order thinking skills, and UDL. PBL lesson planning strategies were outlined, and formative and summative assessment of PBL activities were also discussed. Additional information about integrating PBL across the curriculum can be found in the Appendix.

References

Arter, J., & McTighe, J. (2001). *Scoring rubrics in the classroom: Using performance criteria for assessing and improving student performance.* Thousand Oaks, CA: Corwin Press.

Barkley, E. F., Cross, K. P., & Major, C. H. (2005). *Collaborative learning techniques: A handbook for college faculty.* San Francisco: Jossey-Bass.

Barron, B. J. S. (1998). Doing with understanding: Lessons from research on problem- and project-based learning. *Journal of the Learning Sciences,* 7(3&4), 271–311.

Blumenfeld, P. C., Soloway, S., Marx, R. W., Krajcik, J. S., Guzdial, M., & Palincsar, A. (1991). Motivating project-based learning: Sustaining the doing, supporting the learning. *Educational Psychologist,* 26(3–4), 369–398.

Chamot, A. U., & O'Malley, J. M. (1994). *The CALLA handbook: Implementing the cognitive academic language learning approach. Reading,* MA: Addison-Wesley.

Chatman, J. A., & Flynn, F. J. (2001). The influence of heterogeneity on the emergence and consequences of norms in work teams. *Academy of Management Journal,* 44(5), 956–974.

Dalton, B., Morocco, C., Tivnan, T., & Rawson, P. (1997). Supported inquiry science: Teaching for conceptual change in urban and suburban science classrooms. *Journal of Learning Disabilities,* 24, 261–269.

Dewey, John. (1897). My pedagogic creed. *School Journal,* 54(3), 77–80.

Echevarria, J., Vogt, M., Short, D. (2008). *Making content comprehensible for English learners: The SIOP model.* Boston: Pearson Education/Allyn & Bacon.

Ellis, E. (2000). *Project-based learning strategies for differentiating instruction.* Tuscaloosa, AL: Masterminds.

Expeditionary Learning Outward Bound. (1999). *A design for comprehensive school reform.* Cambridge, MA: Expeditionary Learning Outward Bound.

Feretti, R. P., & Okolo, C. M. (1996). Authenticity in learning: Multimedia design projects in the social studies for students with disabilities. *Journal of Learning Disabilities,* 450–460.

Ferretti, R. P., MacArther, C. D., & Oholo, C. M. (2001). Teaching for historical understanding in inclusive classrooms. *Learning Disabilities Quarterly,* 24, 59–71.

Gronlund, N. E. (2003). *Assessment of student achievement* (7th ed.). Upper Saddle River, NJ: Pearson Education/Allyn & Bacon.

Hall, T. (2002). *Differentiated instruction.* Wakefield, MA: National Center on Accessing the General Curriculum. Retrieved February 4, 2006 from http:www.cast.org/publications/ncac/ncac_diffinstruc.html

Herman, J. L., Aschbacher, P. R., & Winters, L. (1992). *A practical guide to alternative assessment.* Alexandria, VA: Association for Supervision and Curriculum Development.

Johnson, D. W., & Johnson, R. T. (1997). *Joining together: Group theory and group skills* (6th Ed). Boston: Allyn & Bacon.

Johnson, D. W., & Johnson, R. T. (1998). Cultural diversity and cooperative learning. In J. W. Putnam (Ed.), *Celebrating diversity in the classroom: Cooperative learning and strategies for inclusion* (2nd ed., pp. 67–86). Baltimore: Paul H. Brookes.

Johnson, D. W., & Johnson, R. T. (1999). *Learning together and alone: Cooperative, competitive, and individualistic learning.* Boston: Allyn & Bacon.

Jonassen, D., Peck, K., & Wilson, B. (1999). *Learning with technology: A constructivist perspective.* Upper Saddle River, NJ: Merrill/Pearson Education.

Kagan, S. (1998). New cooperative learning, multiple intelligences, and inclusion. In J. W. Putnam (Ed.), *Celebrating diversity in the classroom: Cooperative learning and strategies for inclusion* (2nd ed., pp. 105–136). Baltimore: Paul H. Brookes.

Kinsella, K. (1996). Designing group work that supports and enhances diverse classroom work styles. *TESOL Journal,* 1(6), 25–30.

Kuhs, T. M., Johnson, R. L., Agruso, S. A, & Monrad, D. M. (2001). *Put to the test: Tools and techniques for classroom assessment.* Portsmouth, NH: Heinemann.

Ljung, E. J., & Blackwell, M. (1996). Project OMEGA: A winning approach for at-risk teens. *Illinois School Research and Development Journal,* 33, 15–17.

Logan, K. R., Bakeman, R., & Keefe, E. B. (1997). Effects of instructional variables on engaged behavior of students with disabilities in general education classrooms. *Exceptional Children,* 63, 481–497.

Long, M. H., & Porter, P. A. (1985). Group work, interlanguage talk, and second language acquisition. *TESOL Quarterly,* 19, 207–228.

Markham, T., Larmer, J., & Ravitz, J. (2003). *Project-based learning handbook: A guide to standards-focused project-based learning for middle and high schools teachers* (2nd ed.). Novato, CA: Buck Institute for Education.

Mastropieri, M. A., & Scruggs, T. E. (1994). Text versus hands-on science curriculum. *Remedial and Special Education,* 15(2), 72–85.

McCafferty, S., Jacobs, G., Christina, A., & Iddings, D. (2006). *Cooperative learning and second language teaching.* Cambridge, UK: Cambridge University Press.

Moursund, D. (1999). *Project-based learning using information technology.* Eugene, OR: International Society for Technology in Education.

Moursund, D. G. (2006). *Computers in education for talented and gifted students: A book for elementary and middle school teachers.* Retrieved February 4, 2006, from http://darkwing.uoregon.edu/~moursund/Books/TAG/TAG.html.

Multimedia Project: Project-based Learning with Multimedia. (2000, January). *Challenge 2000 year 4 evaluation report, section VIII student learning.* Retrieved online March 1, 2006, from http//:pblmm.k12.ca.us/sri/Student.htm

Payne-Anderson, J. (1998). *Center for the Study of Work Teams papers: Training and learning in teams.* Denton: University of North Texas. Retrieved July 17, 2005, from http://www.workteams.unt.edu/reports/anderson.html

Putnam, J. W. (1998). *Celebrating diversity in the classroom: Cooperative learning and strategies for inclusion* (2nd ed.). Baltimore: Paul H. Brookes.

Railsback, J. (2002). *Project-based instruction: Creating excitement for learning.* Portland, OR: Northwest Regional Educational Laboratory.

Scarcella, R. C., & Oxford, R. L. (1992). *The tapestry of language learning: The individual in the communicative classroom.* Boston: Heinle & Heinle.

Scruggs, T., & Mastropieri, M. (1994). The construction of scientific knowledge by students with mild disabilities. *Remedial and Special Education,* 14(1), 15–24.

Scruggs, T., & Mastropieri, M. (2003). Science and social studies. In H. L. Swanson, K. R. Harris, & S. Graham (Eds.), *Handbook of learning disabilities* (pp. 364–379). New York: Guilford Press.

Simkins, M., Cole, K., Tavalin, F., & Means, B. (2002). *Increasing student learning through multimedia projects.* Alexandria, VA: Association for Supervision and Curriculum Development.

Slavin, R. E. (1995). *Cooperative learning* (2nd ed.). Boston: Allyn & Bacon.

Steelman, J. D. (2005). Multimedia makes its mark. *Learning and Leading with Technology,* 32(1), 16–19.

Thomas, J. W. (2000, March). *A review of research on project-based learning.* Retrieved February 28,

2006 from http://www.bobpearlman.org/BestPractices/PBL_Research.pdf.

University of Waterloo. (2000). *TRACE tip sheets: Decision-making methods for group work*. Retrieved July 16, 2005, from http://www.adm.uwaterloo.ca/infotrac/tips/groupdecisionmaking.pdf.

Vacca, R., & Vacca, J. (1999). *Content area reading: Literacy and learning across the curriculum* (6th ed.). New York: Longman.

Walvoord, B., & Anderson, V. (1998). *Effective grading: A tool for learning assessment*. San Francisco: Jossey-Bass.

Watson, W. E., Kumar, K., & Michaelsen, L. K. (1993). Cultural diversity's impact on group process and performance: Comparing homogeneous and culturally diverse task groups. *Academy of Management Journal*, 36(3), 590–602.

Wiggins, G. (1998). *Educative assessment: Designing assessments to inform and improve student performance*. San Francisco: Jossey-Bass.

Williams, K. Y., & O'Reilly, C. A. (1998). Forty years of diversity research: A review. In B. M. Staw & L. L. Cummings (Eds.), *Research in organizational behavior*, 20, 33–140.

Chapter 10

Reading/Language Arts Instruction

After reading this chapter, you will be able to:

1. Discuss the prevalence, causes, and characteristics of reading problems
2. Describe the relationship between phonemic awareness and reading
3. Describe the elements of effective reading assessment and instruction
4. Apply the LEARN strategy to identify and select effective methods and materials for remediating reading problems based on student need

PREVALENCE, CAUSES, AND CHARACTERISTICS OF READING PROBLEMS

Prevalence

Nationally, the ability to read is valued as an important and necessary basic literacy skill. Reading has, in fact, become increasingly critical to one's academic and economic survival. In the 21st century, schools and businesses expect young people to evaluate, synthesize, and communicate complex texts, including scholarly journals, repair manuals, graphics, maps, and narratives. For these reasons, our information-rich nation requires a reading-proficient citizenry to compete globally.

In direct contrast to our nations needs, the National Assessment of Educational Progress (NAEP, 2003) reported that more than 8 million American students, Grades 4–12, were struggling to read, with only 3 out of 10 eighth-graders reading at or above grade level. When measured in 2005, reading scores show surprisingly little improvement. The National Reading Results released by the NAEP indicate that on a 0-to-500-point scale, fourth-graders' average scores were only 1 point higher, and eighth-graders scored, on average, 1 point lower in 2005 than in 2003. In fact, no state had a higher average score in 2005 than in 2003, and seven states scored lower. Despite efforts at educational reform, average scores in 2005 were only 2 points higher than those of students, in both Grades 4 and 8, when assessed in 1992 (National Assessment of Educational Progress, 2005).

Similarly, longitudinal data from the NAEP (2005) do not differ greatly from those previously reported. Out of 50 states, only 20 states reported higher average reading scores for students in Grade 4 in 2005 than in 1992, while 3 states had lower average scores. The percentage of students performing at or above basic increased in 15 states and decreased in 3 states during this 13-year period. Data collected on students in grade 8 were no more promising. When the NAEP compared student scores gathered in 2005 to those gathered in 1998, they found only three states with higher than average reading scores and eight states with lower than average scores. The percentage of students who performed at or above basic increased in 3 states and decreased in 11 states (NAEP, 2005).

The National Center for Education Statistics (1997) reported on the reading ability of students from diverse backgrounds, which constituted 35% of public school enrollment, with approximately 13% of all students speaking a language other than English at home. When broken down by ethnicity, we see that, in general, the reading failure of African American, Hispanic, limited-English speakers, and poor children ranges from 60% to 70% (NAEP, 2005). Recent reading results for students in Grade 4 indicated an upward trend, with the average 2005 scores for African American and Hispanic students increasing in comparison to their 2003 scores (NAEP, 2005). Unfortunately, this trend did not continue, nor was it maintained in Grade 8. More disturbing is the prognosis that it is unlikely to reverse in the foreseeable future.

Research clearly indicates that many children in our nation's schools are at risk for academic failure due to their inability to read proficiently. It is a problem that extends across all demographic categories regardless of ethnicity, race, gender, or socioeconomic status (NAEP, 2005). Findings suggest that 90% of students who do not learn to read well in the first grade will continue to read poorly in the fourth grade (Strickland, 2002); for most of these students, it is a trend that continues throughout their academic career (Francis, Shaywitz, Stuebing, Shaywitz, & Fletcher, 1996; Torgesen, Brooks, &

Hall, 2006). Due to the enormity of the problem and its societal implications, currently there is a national focus on programming designed to facilitate language and literacy development in children 0 to 8 years of age (NAEP, 2005).

Causes

Why do children have problems learning to read? There are a number of factors known to cause reading difficulty. Children with a history of preschool language impairment are more likely to have reading difficulty (Scarborough, 1998), as are children who do not speak English as their primary language (August & Hakuta, 1997). Children whose parents did not learn to read easily (Gilger, Pennington, & Defries, 1991), children who have attention deficit–hyperactivity disorder (Shaywitz, Fletcher, & Shaywitz, 1995), learning disabilities (Breier et al., 2003), and children who are unmotivated (Snow, Barnes, Chandler, Goodman, & Hemphill, 1991) are at risk for developing reading problems. A common denominator underlying many of these risk factors is poverty; children who grow up in poverty are more likely than their peers to experience reading difficulty (Teddlie, Kirby, & Stringfield, 1989).

Second, students also have trouble learning to read if they have a phonemic deficit. This type of deficit may manifest in a number of ways, including the limited or poor ability to sound out and/or blend sounds into words, difficulty identifying words that rhyme, difficulty identifying sounds that are the same in different words, and an inability to spell and/or sound out unfamiliar words. Phonemic deficits commonly co-occur with or underlie many of the other risk factors previously mentioned. Researchers have found that phonemic deficits can negatively affect the development of phonemic awareness and other phonological processing skills critical to the reading and writing process (Lyon, 1999, 2000).

Last, children have difficulty learning to read and write when instruction is inadequate (Moats, 2000). You will recall that teachers often unknowingly place students at risk for academic failure when they do not take into account students' differing learning needs when selecting, delivering, and designing instructional methods and materials (as noted in Chapter 2) (Hixon, 1993). Students who struggle with reading often do so because of poorly designed or delivered reading instruction and/or intervention programming (Moats, 2001; Strickland, 2002). Many teachers do not understand the process by which students learn to read, believing incorrectly that reading will occur naturally (Lyon, 1999, 2000). Research indicates, however, that for many students reading is not a natural process (Lyon, 1999, 2000). Sadly, schools are not considering this finding when they choose to teach reading using holistic programming that does not include phonetic instruction; thus, uninformed educational decisions of this type contribute to the reading difficulties experienced by large numbers of students. (Lyon, 1999, 2000; Moats, 2001; National Inquiry into the Teaching of Literacy [2005a, 2000b]; National Reading Panel, 2000).

CHARACTERISTICS

Learning to read is an enjoyable experience for many, but not all, children. Children who are having difficulty reading may exhibit one or more of the following characteristics: avoidance of reading and writing, difficulty completing assignments, difficulty reading unfamiliar words, and poor spelling. Early reading failure, if not remediated, can lead to generalized academic failure because reading plays a foundational role across all academic domains (e.g., social studies, writing, math, science). Reading failure over time can also contribute to low self-esteem, lack of motivation, and behavior problems. It is common for students to act inappropriately when they are attempting to draw attention away from their inability to read. It is a way of avoiding embarrassment. Teachers and parents often misidentify students' efforts to avoid failure as a lack of motivation or disinterest. It is not surprising that these students may choose to drop out of school once they are old enough to escape the repeated failures that accompany the inability to read.

There are instances where hard work and determination allow unskilled readers to complete high school and begin postsecondary school; tenacity alone, however, can only take them so far before the complexity and volume of reading begins to undermine their efforts. The National Center for Educational Statistics (1997) found that inefficient reading skills accounts, in part, for the failure of 43% of postsecondary students to earn a degree.

Who are inefficient readers? They can come from high-achieving homes; they can be rich or poor; they can be A students or F students; and they can be Asian, Hispanic, Caucasian, or African American. Despite their differences, people who have difficulty reading often share a common problem: They lack phonemic awareness. Research suggests that many students who experience difficulty reading may do so because they lack the phonemic awareness necessary to process, effortlessly and automatically, the sounds of the English language (Ehri, 1991). This is important because phonemic awareness contributes to the development of reading skill in several areas, specifically vocabulary, fluency, and text comprehension.

What Is a Phonemic Deficit, and How Does It Affect Reading Ability?

Educational literature and research frequently discuss phonemic awareness in conjunction with reading instruction, because research has shown that phonemic awareness can predict students' ability to learn to read, write, and spell (Lyon, 1999; Moats, 2001; Share, Jorm, Maclean, & Matthews, 1984; Ehri et al., 2001). The term *phonemic awareness* refers to the ability to focus on and manipulate sounds (phonemes) in spoken words. Phonemes are the smallest units of spoken language. In the English language, there are about 41 to 44 phonemes, depending on dialect (Ehri, 1991). There are vowel phonemes (e.g., *a, e, i, o*, and *u*) and consonant phonemes (e.g., *b, d, g, th, ch*).

Phonemic awareness makes it easier for children to become skilled readers, because they are better able to learn to read words in a variety of ways (Ehri, 1994). Phonemic awareness enhances verbal and written communication by facilitating people's ability to combine and blend phonemes into syllables and words. The word *cat*, for example, has three phonemes, /c/ /a/ /t/. Multisyllabic words such as *theater* are composed of multiple phonemes (/th/ /e/ /a/ /ter/), which are combined and blended to produce sounds that convey meaning. Phonemes in words correspond to graphemes in our writing system, making the ability to read and write inextricably related.

Graphemes can consist of one letter—for example, *S, V, T*, or *B*—or multiple letters, such as *SH, TH*, or *ING*; each represents one phoneme or sound. When students combine phonemes and graphemes to form words, they are able to convey meaning and share their thoughts with others. When students have difficulty distinguishing individual phonemes, they often have problems learning to write, spell, or read text that contains unfamiliar words. These students also frequently experience social–emotional problems as well as academic ones (Lyon, 2000; National Reading Panel, 2000).

How Do Phonemic Deficits Develop?

Deficits in phonemic awareness may develop for a number of reasons: when children do not receive sufficient exposure to oral language and early literacy interactions, heredity or family factors, because of a disability or medical condition, or from correlates associated with metacognitive deficits (Cunningham & Cunningham 2002; Pressley, 1998, 2002).

EXPOSURE   Research suggests that if children are to develop phonemic awareness and word reading skills, they must be afforded opportunities to listen to and interact with language across a variety of contexts while they are young (National Reading Panel, 2000). Children growing up without these opportunities are at risk for developing reading problems, as compared to their peers who do have such opportunities, because they may not develop the background knowledge about sounds, understand the purpose of reading or print concepts, or develop the vocabulary necessary to read.

HEREDITY   Some children experience difficulty learning to read because of heredity or family factors. There is evidence that strongly suggests that some types of reading difficulties are the result of heredity factors that lead to phonemic deficits; as many as 23% to 65% of children who have parents with a reading disability also have a reading disability (Lyon, 2000). Consequently, it may be difficult for parents, who themselves have a reading disability, to provide their children with the oral and early language interactions necessary to develop reading proficiency. This is an important point to note, because exposure to oral reading and language play, such as rhyming games, can directly affect the development of phonemic awareness (Lyon, 2000).

DISABILITY AND MEDICAL CONDITIONS   Some children have a disability, such as dyslexia, that impairs their ability to read. There is research to suggest the brains of children with reading problems attributable to dyslexia are functionally and structurally different from those of children who do not have difficulty reading (Breier et al., 2003). The study by Breier and colleagues points to abnormal sound processing that makes it difficult to distinguish between similar but different sounds—in both spoken and written form. Commonly referred to as phonological processing deficits, these deficits underlie reading problems because they cause difficulty in developing an awareness of the phonological structure of speech, a prerequisite to acquiring normal reading skills (Breier et al., 2003; McBride-Chang, 1995, 1996).

Children with speech and language impairments are also at risk for reading failure. Otitis media, for example, is an inflammation of the middle ear that may have a detrimental effect on a child's ability to read. It occurs in 76% of children at least once during the first 3 years. Undetected and untreated, chronic otitis media is thought to reduce a child's hearing during that crucial period when speech and language skills are developing. Research indicates that reduced hearing caused by otitis media has a negative impact on phonemic discrimination in children that may persist even after middle ear function returns to normal (Roberts, Rosenfeld, & Zeisel, 2004).

METACOGNITIVE KNOWLEDGE AND SKILL   Metacognitive skill levels can also impact students' abilities to read (Fielding-Barnsley, Hay, & Ashman, 2005). Research suggests that children who read well have an effective repertoire of reading strategies (e.g., phonological, word attack, and comprehension) (Schunk, 2004; Wong, Harris, Graham, & Butler, D., 2003). They use their metacognitive knowledge to gain knowledge of the reading process; they apply this knowledge by planning, monitoring their performance, recognizing the need for a strategy, searching for an appropriate strategy within their repertoire, and adapting their plan to include this information. As a result, their ability to read and process information from each reading encounter supports automaticity and reading fluency across academic and social domains.

Learning to read is complex, and beginning readers must be metacognitively proficient at coordinating many cognitive processes to read accurately and fluently. Students who are not metacognitively proficient often have trouble recognizing words, understanding the meaning of sentences and text, retaining the information they read in memory, efficiently utilizing strategies for decoding and comprehension of unfamiliar text, and monitoring the reading process. They may spend much of their time trying to recognize a word, decoding individual letters, laboriously sounding out the word, and trying to blend sounds together into something recognizable. It is understandable that these students may tire easily, frequently do not understand what they read, and are not motivated to read.

ELEMENTS OF EFFECTIVE READING ASSESSMENT

Assessment is a vital part of the educational process used by administrators and teachers alike to guide instructional planning and implementation. Documentation, examination, and analysis of a student's reading performance can enable educators to identify the student's reading strengths and weaknesses and to choose instructional accommodations when appropriate. In the next section, we will identify the skills most predictive of reading success (e.g., Ehri et al., 2001; Steubing et al., 2002).

What Can We Assess?

Reading success is often linked to a student's phonemic awareness, understanding of phonics, oral reading rate, and vocabulary. Therefore these are the skills most commonly measured by assessment instruments. Below is a summary of each.

PHONEMIC AWARENESS   Phonemic awareness is the ability to hear and produce the separate sounds, or phonemes, in spoken words. Tasks included in tests of phonemic awareness from the simplest to the most complex are as follows:

- Isolating phonemes heard at the beginning, middle, and end of words
- Blending onset rhymes to form real words

- Blending phonemes to form real words
- Deleting phonemes to form new words
- Segmenting words into phonemes by breaking a words into its individual sounds
- Adding phonemes to form new words
- Substituting one phoneme for another to form a new word

PHONICS   Phonics refers to the alphabetic principle or rules that govern the relationship between letters and their representative sounds. One must understand and use these rules to decode our language, read, and spell accurately. Assessing the ability of a student to name letters and the corresponding letter sounds is the most common method of determining if a person understands and can apply phonics rules. To measure phonetic proficiency, students are often asked to decode letters and letter combinations in an unknown or nonsense word.

ORAL READING RATE   Oral reading rate assessments measure the number of words a student can read correctly in 1 minute. These measures correlate positively with reading comprehension and tell teachers if students can understand grade-level text. Oral reading rate assessments are individually administered. It should be noted that reading rate is not the same as reading fluency. Reading fluency refers to the ability to read text quickly, accurately, and with proper expression.

VOCABULARY   Vocabulary refers to word knowledge. Students with low vocabulary tend to experience difficulty decoding and comprehending text. There are four types of vocabulary that can be assessed: listening, speaking, reading, and writing. A student's receptive vocabulary is tested through either a listening or reading task. Prior reading experience and life experiences may have a significant effect on a student's score.

How Do We Assess?

Classroom teachers may use reading assessments for screening purposes, as diagnostic tools, for progress monitoring, and for measuring outcomes. Methods for assessing reading can include standardized tests, informal tests, and curriculum-based approaches. These measures, when used appropriately, can reduce the number of students experiencing difficulty in general education classrooms and limit false referrals to special education (Foorman, 2003).

SCREENING   Screening measures are appropriate for identifying students who are at risk for reading failure by determining the adequacy of their reading skills (e.g., phonemic awareness, knowledge of the alphabet) and readiness to participate in grade-level instruction. When problems are detected, data from these tests help pinpoint specific skills deficits. In the case of first- and second-grade teachers, screening batteries recognize those students most in need of early intervention. Examples of research-based screening assessments include the Comprehensive Test of Phonological Processing (CTOPP) (Wagner, Torgesen, & Rashotte, 1999), the Peabody Picture Vocabulary Test (PPVT-3) (Dunn & Dunn, 1997), and the Dynamic Indicators of Basic Early Literacy Skills (DIBELS) (Good et al., 2002).

TABLE 10.1 Research-Based Screening Assessments

Comprehensive Test of Phonological Processing (CTOPP) • Wagner et al. (1999) • Available through: www.proedinc.com • Norm referenced	• Use in K–12 (different test forms), ages 5–6, ages 7+ Subtests include: • Phoneme deletion task • Blending words and non-words • Sound matching • Memory for digits • Non-word repetition • Rapid color, digit, letter, and object naming • Phoneme reversal • Segmenting words and non-words	• Use for screening, diagnostics, and outcome measures • Measures student performance in English only • Administered individually
Dynamic Indicators of Basic Early Literacy Skills (DIBELS) • Good et al. (2002) • Available through: dibels.uoregon.edu • Criterion referenced	• Use in K–6 • K–3: Phonemic awareness • 4–6: Reading fluency • Letter-naming fluency • Initial sound fluency Phonemic segmentation fluency • Nonsense word fluency • Oral reading fluency	• Use for screening, progress monitoring, outcome measures • Progress monitoring for Grades 4–6 only • Measures student performance in English and Spanish • Administered individually
Peabody Picture Vocabulary Test, 3rd Ed. (PPVT-3) • Dunn & Dunn (1997) • Available through: www.agsnet.com • Norm referenced	• Use in ages 2.5 through 90+ years • Vocabulary: Measures student's receptive language skills	• Use for screening, diagnostic, and outcome measures • Measures student performance in Spanish and English • Administered individually

DIAGNOSIS   Diagnostic reading assessments are used to identify a variety of reading and language skills. These tests are given after a student fails to respond to instructional interventions. Diagnostics are designed to give teachers information they can use to strategically design reading interventions for the individual students needs. Examples of diagnostic reading assessments include the Early Reading Diagnostic Assessment (ERDA) (Smith, 2000), the Lindamood Auditory Conceptualization Test (LAC) (Lindamood, 1979), and the Group Reading Assessment and Diagnostic Evaluation (GRADE) (Williams, 2001).

PROGRESS MONITORING   Assessments that monitor progress are used to determine if students are learning at an adequate rate throughout the school year. They give teachers a quick example of individual student's critical reading skills and indicate whether a student will reach grade-level reading ability by the end of the year. Many different

TABLE 10.2 Diagnostic Reading Assessments

Early Reading Diagnostic Assessment (ERDA) • Donna Rury Smith • www.harcourtassessment.com • Norm referenced • Criterion referenced	• Use in K–3 • Phonemic awareness, segmentation, and letter names. Word attack: nonsense words. Word identification: regular and irregular; reading fluency; sentence reading fluency; listening comprehension; reading comprehension: oral and silent; vocabulary: oral—picture identification; rhyming; syllables; story retell task; and concepts of print • Rapid automatic naming of letters, digits, and words	• Use for diagnostics • Measures student performance in English only • Administered individually
The Lindamood Auditory Conceptualization Test—3rd Ed. (The LAC Test) • Charles & Patricia Lindamood • www.proedinc.com • Criterion referenced	• Use in Pre-K–adult • Phonemic awareness: sound discrimination and perception and comparisons of the number and order of sounds within spoken patterns	• Use for diagnostic measure • Measures student performance in English and Spanish • Administered individually
Group Reading Assessment & Diagnostic Evaluation (GRADE) • Kathleen T. Williams • www.agsnet.com • Norm referenced	• Use for pre-K–12, postsecondary • Reading comprehension, language comprehension, decoding, cipher knowledge, lexical knowledge, phoneme awareness, letter knowledge, concepts about print, semantics (vocabulary and morphology), phonological awareness	• Use for diagnostic and progress monitoring • Measures student performance in English only • Administered individually or group

kinds of instruments are used for progress monitoring. In addition to those previously mentioned in this chapter, the chart below offers other options.

ELEMENTS OF EFFECTIVE READING INSTRUCTION

Historical Context

There are two major instructional approaches to teaching reading used in U.S. schools. The whole-language or holistic approach to reading and phonics-based instruction (Moates, 2000). It is necessary to gain a brief historical perspective to understand the state of reading instruction today.

TABLE 10.3 Instruments for Monitoring Reading Skills Progress

Gray Oral Reading Tests, 4th Ed. (GORT-4) • Wiederholt & Bryant (2001) • www.proedinc.com • Norm referenced	• Use for ages 7–18 • Oral reading measures comprehension in multiple-choice format; Fluency • Children read aloud 13 increasingly difficult passages, each followed by comprehension questions. • The test scores both accuracy and rate of reading.	• Use for screening, progress monitoring, and diagnostics • Measures student performance in English only • Administered individually
Texas Primary Reading Inventory (TPRI) • Center for Academic and Reading Skills, University of Texas–Houston Heath Science Center and University of Houston • Texas Education Agency (1998–1999) • www.tpri.org • Norm referenced	• Use in K–2 • Phonemic awareness: initial sounds, blending, segmentation, invented spelling; letter names: untimed; letter sounds: untimed; word identification: regular and irregular; reading fluency: connected text; listening comprehension; reading comprehension: oral and Q & A; and other: book and print awareness, phonemic awareness: detecting final sounds, substitution tasks, spelling, reading accuracy.	• Use for screening, diagnostic, progress monitoring and outcome • Measures student performance in English only • Administered individually only; and produces raw score and development benchmarks: developed skills or skills that are still being developed

WHOLE-LANGUAGE APPROACH TO READING

Touted as a *scientific* alternative to phonics instruction, deemed boring, the whole-language approach to reading has been widely utilized by public schools throughout the United States to varying degrees since the 1940s. It is a core component in many teacher preparation programs, instructional textbooks, and a large number of educational materials (Moates, 2000). Predicated on the belief that reading is a process that occurs as naturally as speaking, proponents of whole-language instruction propose that reading for meaning should become the goal of early reading instruction (Smith, 1994).

In the late 1980s and early 1990s, whole language was lauded as a *new* approach to reading instruction. Proponents thought children, just as adults, will read if the text is interesting. Therefore, exposing young students to print and language should be sufficient to develop their ability to read if teachers make the text interesting and if students read authentic books. Teachers need not explicitly teach reading as a process since, according to this method, they can simply guide students to construct and discover conceptual understanding of what they read. According to this theory, children make a natural leap from knowing the alphabet to reading whole words when immersed in an authentic, language-rich environment.

PHONICS APPROACH TO READING

The basis of phonics instruction is very different from that of whole-language instruction. Martin Luther developed the phonetic system of instruction in the 16th century to teach illiterate farmers to read the Latin Bible (Balmuth, 1982). He recognized that the English language and Roman alphabet do not share a one-to-one correspondence between letters and sounds, making them difficult to learn. His method made explicit the association between the 26 letters of the alphabet that support the English language and the approximately 44 sounds that serve it (Balmuth, 1982).

Phonics-based reading programs have evolved over time, gaining and losing prominence in the public schools to whole-language instruction through the years (Chall, 1989). Today, the phonics approach to reading still relies on the basics, which have changed little—teaching sound symbol associations with a code emphasis. The terms associated with phonics instruction have, however, changed somewhat over the years. Phonics may be associated with several other terms, including *explicit instruction, direct instruction*, and *systematic instruction* (Balmuth, 1982). Regardless of the term, phonics advocates believe that given the growing complexity of our language, phonics instruction is as necessary today as it was centuries ago.

CURRENT PERSPECTIVE ON EFFECTIVE READING INSTRUCTION

The *reading wars*, a term used to describe the debate between advocates of whole language and phonics, have become fierce and increasing political. Amid growing concern by parents, educators, and society with our inability to improve low reading scores, in 1997 Congress mandated the formation of a panel to review evidence-based research on reading curricula. Charged with making recommendations to improve reading instruction in the schools, the National Reading Panel (NRP) began work.

Composed of leading scientists in reading research, representatives of colleges of education, reading teachers, educational administrators, and parents, the NRP prepared to conduct a meta-analysis of more than 100,000 studies on reading research. The NRP set stringent scientific guidelines for screening studies. Given the importance of educational decisions, constituents must be confident, when considering suggestions from any study, that its validity was determined empirically rather than ideologically, as is often the case with reading (e.g., Adams, 1990; Center for the Improvement of Early Reading Instruction, 1999; Pressley, 1998; Moates, 2001).

In 2000, the National Reading Panel issued their findings, aimed at helping parents, teachers, and policy makers identify key skills and methods that consistently promote reading success. The findings of the panel support those of other investigators who assessed research on the value of instruction in phonemic awareness and phonics to reading achievement, reading fluency, and reading comprehension (e.g., National Inquiry into the Teaching of Literacy, 2005a; National Reading Panel, 2000; Torgerson et al., 2006).

Phonemic Awareness (PA) Instruction

There is solid evidence that children who have phonemic awareness skills have an easier time learning to read and spell and that teaching phonemic awareness is clearly effective for those who do not already possess the skills (e.g., Bus, & van Ijzendoorn, 1999;

Hatcher, Hulme, & Ellis, 1994; Mann, 1987; National Inquiry into the Teaching of Literacy, 2005a; Torgerson et al., 2006; Treiman, 1985). Phonemic awareness training also benefits word reading, comprehension, and spelling across groups of students (e.g., preschoolers, first-graders, older readers with disabilities who have preexisting reading problems, children from various socioeconomic levels, and students learning to spell in English). Having established the value of PA for most students, we now turn to evaluating those activities and methods best suited to developing PA.

Factors to consider when choosing activities and methods to increase children's phonemic awareness include literacy level, length of instruction, group size, and metacognitive knowledge. It is important to determine a child's level of literacy development before beginning PA instruction. A child's level of literacy development can be determined by conducting an informal assessment using activities like the ones below (Schatschneider, Fletcher, Francis, Carlson, & Forman, 1999).

- *Phoneme comparison*—Students must be able to identify the names of pictures beginning with the same sound—for example, "Tell me the first sound in *taste*." (/t/) "Can you point to the picture beginning with the same sound?"
- *Blending onset-rhyme units into real words*—Students must be able to identify the initial consonant sound or sounds that come before the vowel in a syllable. For example, /f/ is the onset in the word *fine*; /gr/ is the onset in *green*.
- *Blending phonemes into real words*—Students must be able to listen to a sequence of separately spoken sounds and combine them to form a word—for example, "What word is /s/ /k/ /u/ /l/?" (*school*).
- *Phoneme deletion*—Students must be able to recognize the word that remains when a given phoneme is deleted—for example, "What is *gland* without the /g/?"

Begin with an activity that you feel is appropriate for their level of literacy development. For a younger child or one with a disability, you may begin by having him or her identify the first phoneme in words. If the activity is too easy, move on to activities that are more difficult, being sure to progress only one level at a time. Used in this manner, the activity can serve a dual purpose as a tool for formative assessment and for instruction.

Phonemic awareness training programs vary in length; however, in one study programs in which children participated in PA instruction 5 to 18 hours per year elicited greater outcomes (Cunningham & Cunningham, 2002). Research suggests the complexity of the activity, goals, and ability levels of the students are important considerations when determining the length of instructional activities. PA instruction may be most beneficial for teaching basic alphabetic knowledge, rather than going into great depth, which could confuse and bore students. As counterintuitive as it may seem, instruction that is not as lengthy produces superior phonemic awareness with greater benefits for reading and spelling (National Reading Panel, 2000).

Teachers often wonder if they should teach phonemic awareness to the entire class at once, a small group of students, or to individual students. In general, the size of the group does not matter. All are effective and have a greater impact on student learning than no phonics instruction. However, as you might expect, small group instruction is often more effective. This may be because the teacher can individualize instruction to a greater degree, providing detailed formative feedback as needed. Students may also benefit from hearing classmates respond. Learning to read can be a risky proposition for some students with social–emotional issues related to motivation and self-confidence. These students may be more willing to participate in small-group reading activities.

While children need phonemic awareness, that is not all they need. PA develops gradually and takes time. Waiting until PA develops fully to move beyond highly decodable books can have a detrimental effect (Hiebert, 1999). Exposing children to nursery rhymes and high-frequency sight-word oriented books as a regular part of the process is an authentic instructional method that also motivates. Remember, you cannot make students learn. Students must perceive some potential benefit in participating; show them that reading is both fun and useful in and out of the classroom.

Effective Phonics Instruction

SYSTEMATIC PHONICS INSTRUCTION   There is much debate about the value of phonics instruction. Is it an effective method for teaching students to read? An extensive review of the scientific literature on teaching reading, including but not limited to that of the NRP, finds that reading programs that include phonic instruction as a component of initial instruction help children understand the alphabetic system. Phonics instruction is found to improve reading, spelling, and writing better than alternative reading programs that provide unsystematic or no phonics instruction (Ehri, 2003; Johnston, & Watson, 2005; National Inquiry into the Teaching of Literacy, 2005b; National Reading Panel, 2000; Torgerson et al., 2006).

How do you know if a reading program is providing systematic phonics instruction or nonsystematic phonics instruction? Some features of each set them apart. A program of systematic phonics instruction involves the direct teaching of a prespecified set of letter–sound relationships in a clearly defined sequence (National Reading Panel, 2000). The set includes the major sound–spelling relationships of both consonants and vowels. A systematic program of reading instruction will also provide students ample opportunities to read text and practice applying these relationships to decode words.

When selecting phonics-based reading programming, be sure to make your educational decisions based on criteria validated by research. Examples of the more popular phonics programs found in our public schools include the Orton-Gillingham Method, the Benchmark Word Identification/Vocabulary Development Program, Open Court Phonics/Reading Program, and the Reading Mastery Reading Program. Although each is very similar, they do emphasize different instructional components.

The Orton-Gillingham Method of instruction employs a multisensory approach that utilizes phonics and emphasizes learning styles. There is a reciprocal teaching component designed to increase students' ability to read for meaning and retention. Reading, handwriting, and written expression are taught via direct instruction with ongoing assessment to monitor individual strength and needs.

The Benchmark Word Identification/Vocabulary Development Program emphasizes developing phonemic awareness. Students learn key words by fully analyzing them, and then, utilizing these key words, they learn how to decode unknown words. They also learn to decode multisyllabic words by analogy as well as phonics units. This program has a strong metacognitive focus on self-directed learning.

The Open Court Phonics/Reading Program provides explicit instruction of phonemic awareness, phonics, comprehension skills and strategies, inquiry skill, and writing skills and strategies. This is a systematic approach to reading instruction in which teachers utilize a scripted format and a phonics-based basal reader.

The Reading Mastery Reading Program also features phonemic training with a specified teaching format that encourages accuracy and fluency through the use of repeated reading and partner reading. This program, like the others, provides students with individualized, specific, and immediate feedback.

NONSYSTEMATIC PROGRAMS OF PHONICS INSTRUCTION   Nonsystematic reading programs are commonly referred to as whole-word programs, literature programs, basal reading programs, or sight-word programs. These differ from systematic programs of phonics instruction in several important ways. For example, programming decisions are often based on teachers' perceptions of what students have learned and when they need to learn it rather than formal assessment data. There is limited attention paid to letter–sound relationships or learning to pronounce words by blending letters. Within these programs, vocabulary develops by teaching children sight words. There is little or no direct instruction and practice of phonics. Phonics is embedded because proponents of this method believe reading and writing skills develop when students are exposed to whole-word or meaning-based activities. Teachers act as guides, modeling language by reading aloud to students.

Although research indicates that students who receive phonics instruction outperform those who do not, phonics instruction alone does not guarantee success. To ensure reading literacy, phonics instruction must be a component of a comprehensive literacy program, not the entire program. The National Institute for Literacy (2006) suggested that 2 years of phonics instruction is sufficient for most students. In general, phonics instruction that begins in kindergarten should be completed by the end of first grade. If phonics instruction begins in first grade, it should be completed by the end of second grade (National Institute for Literacy, 2006).

It is important for student to have a clear understanding of why they should want to engage in reading activities (Cunningham & Cunningham, 2002; Downing, 1979). We, as adults, take for granted that children understand cognitively why reading is important. Children with little previous exposure to print may not be able to imagine the joy of reading a story for pleasure. Cunningham and Cunningham (2002) suggested that teaching metacognitive skills along with phonics-related activities enhances reading outcomes. Making students aware of the potential benefits associated with reading, outlining the steps necessary to read, and modeling the process necessary to achieve proficiency helps learners to develop metacognitive knowledge relative to reading.

EFFECTIVE INSTRUCTION FOR DEVELOPING READING FLUENCY

Fluency is a critical component of skilled reading. Fluent readers can read text accurately and rapidly. They read aloud with ease and appropriate expression, because they readily and reliably use punctuation to group words into meaningful grammatical units to make sense of the text. Fluent readers also have well-developed, high-speed word-recognition skills that support comprehension by freeing vital cognitive resources for interpretation. They do not have to devote time and energy to decoding words and can therefore concentrate on constructing meaning from what they read. Fluency is not, however, a static stage in reading development to be conquered. Fluency fluctuates in accord with the reader's familiarity with the words and the subject matter. Reading fluency is therefore dependent to a large degree on the student's comprehension or prior knowledge of the content.

It is not difficult to assess reading fluency, nor does it require an array of expensive protocols. There are a number of informal procedures utilized routinely by teachers to assess reading fluency. These include informal reading inventories, miscue analysis, pausing indices, running records, and reading speed calculations. Each requires oral reading of text to develop an index of fluency. Informal reading inventories, for example, require students to read grade-level passages aloud and silently. The teacher then calculates the portion of words read in the passage to determine the students reading level.

While it is a commonly agreed that fluency develops from reading practice, there is no consensus as to what form of practice best promotes its development. Instructional programs most often utilized to promote fluency include oral reading with guidance (e.g., assisted reading, repeated reading, paired reading, shared reading), silent sustained reading (DEAR, SSR, USSR, SQUIRT), and unsupervised independent reading (AR) (National Reading Panel, 2000).

EFFECTIVE INSTRUCTION FOR DEVELOPING READING COMPREHENSION

Comprehension, according to Durkin (1993) and others (e.g., NRP, 2000; Pressley, 2002), is the essence of reading. Students who comprehend what they read share three common factors. First, they have fluent letter- and word-recognition skills and above-the-word-level processing ability that allow them to read fluently (Pressley, 1998, 2002). Second, students who comprehend are metacognitively engaged while reading (Pressley, 1998). They can manipulate and coordinate a variety of reading comprehension strategies to facilitate understanding. Last, students who are adept at reading comprehension acquired the necessary skills from a teacher. This is perhaps the most critical component in the comprehension process. Alarmingly, many teachers report that they do not have the training necessary to deliver this type of instruction and find this type of teaching a challenge (e.g., NRP, 2000; Vaughn & Schuum, 1995).

Letter- and Word-Level Processes in Comprehension

At the letter level, comprehension requires the rapid and fluent decoding of unknown words, which as discussed elsewhere in this book frees up short-term memory for creating meaning (Pressley, 2002). A student who is not fluent in word recognition will spend time, energy, and valuable space in short-term memory trying to sound out words, leaving no processing room for comprehension to take place. Word recognition instruction is therefore important and necessary to comprehension (Breznitz, 1997a, 1997b; Pressley, 2002).

At the word level, vocabulary plays an important part in learning to read and is necessary to reading comprehension (Pressley, 2002). Students must understand most of the words in a text to comprehend what they read, but unfortunately, many do not. In fact, research suggests that there are a number of instructional factors that can impede vocabulary development (Ryder & Graves, 1994). Learning vocabulary words by definition alone without contextual information is often ineffective (Ryder & Graves, 1994). For example, it is often ineffective when vocabulary instruction is limited to reading the definition, writing the definition repeatedly, followed by a decontextualized discussion in which the teacher then uses the word in a generic sentence. The often-used fill-in-the-blanks, dictionary practice, flashcard practice, writing definitions, and matching terms found in basal reading manuals are not any more effective.

Existing knowledge of how best to deliver vocabulary instruction in authentic school contexts is limited, which is perhaps why teachers are relying on methods that are frequently ineffective. Recently, researchers have synthesized data on effective instructional methods for teaching vocabulary (NRP, 2000). Vocabulary words are easier for students to learn when they create a graphic representation or visual image of the new word (e.g., Tomeson & Aarnoutse, 1998). To enhance the generalization of new words, teachers can make meaningful associations, connecting the new words with those in prior knowledge (e.g., Senechal, 1997). Instruction that provides active engagement across contexts with multiple, repeated exposures to vocabulary materials is also important to comprehension (e.g., Senechal, 1997). Strategy instruction also promotes vocabulary development.

Pressley and Afflerbach (1995) found that sophisticated readers are strategic because they engage in specific metacognitive behaviors before, during, and after reading to promote comprehension (Pressley, 2002). For example, before reading, good readers will engage in self-questioning as a prereading strategy. They establish goals and read the text purposefully with a specific outcome in mind. During reading, good readers will make predictions based on prior knowledge and questions to be answered. They will attempt to construct meaning by integrating the new ideas in the text into existing schemata. They will also take notes, create mental images, or construct a graphic organizer to assist with integration; and monitor their progress toward the learning goal, modifying their strategy choices when necessary to ensure goal attainment. After reading, sophisticated learners reflect on what they read and where the information can be used and evaluate the effectiveness of their strategy choices.

STRATEGIES INSTRUCTION

Comprehension Strategies

There is a great deal of research to suggest strategy use differentiates good readers from poor readers (e.g., Gaskins & Elliot, 1991; NRP, 2000; Pressley, 2002). State standards require teachers to teach students to use reading comprehension strategies to understand and remember what they read. National, state, and classroom tests assess students' abilities to demonstrate that they can proficiently use comprehension strategies. In spite of this, students who cannot independently read and comprehend a college text continue to graduate from high schools yearly (e.g., Nist, 1993). Perhaps this is because research indicates teachers are not teaching students how to comprehend; they are only testing for comprehension (Durkin, 1981).

Teachers, as you read in Chapter 6, are themselves often metacognitively deficient and as such prone to making poor educational decisions. Studies indicate that teachers do little to teach them how to become self-regulated readers (e.g., Moates, 2000, 2001; Pressley, Wharton-McDonald, Mistretta, & Echevarria, 1998). The National Reading

Panel (2000) found that teachers often depend on ineffective or inefficient strategies to develop comprehension skill. For example, teachers often rely on students simply reading and rereading text to facilitate comprehension, with no explicit comprehension strategy instruction other than verbally prompting the students to develop necessary comprehension skills (Durkin, 1981; Pressley, 1998).

Teachers also depend heavily on basal readers for delivering reading instruction (NRP, 2000). The lessons provided by basal reading series, however, offer teachers little structure or rationales to guide their educational decisions with regard to how to provide effective skill instruction (Reutzel & Cooter, 1999). Effective reading instruction is associated more with independent teacher action than prescriptive reading instruction suggested in basal texts (Pressley, 1998; Duffy, 1993). Unfortunately, teachers are not any better prepared to act independently today than they were 20 years ago (Duffy, 1993). They are not metacognitive themselves and therefore cannot teach students to reason or deliver instruction that will develop metacognitive readers (Duffy, 1993).

While there has long been interest among researchers in what we think and how knowledge develops, teachers are infrequently taught how to choose strategies based on student need and content demands (e.g., NRP, 2000; Spencer, 1998). If you will remember from Chapter 7, The LEARNS strategy is designed to fill this void. Table 10.4 provides an example of how teachers might utilize this strategy to solve specific reading problems associated with having students conduct research on a classical or contemporary author noted for fiction or nonfiction work. The steps are as follows.

STEP 1: LEARNING GOAL: DETERMINE WHAT CONTENT WILL BE TAUGHT   Once the standard has been selected, the teacher should determine the final learning goal(s) that will be assessed and write learning objectives of the lesson for each goal.

STEP 2: NOTE TEACHER EXPECTATIONS FOR LESSON OBJECTIVE   In this step teachers will determine the tasks required to complete each of the lesson objectives. Complete a task analysis for each of the tasks. For example, let's assume that students are to read a book for a book report. Tasks may include reading print, taking notes, researching the author, following a plot and understanding plot development, distinguishing characters and remembering their actions, understanding allegories and other literary devices while reading. Then for the writing portion of the assignment, students will need to be able to organize their thoughts about the book/author, be able to compose the report, and complete basic writing tasks such as spelling, sentence structure, and punctuation. Each of these tasks may present a barrier to any of the students in your classroom depending on their special needs and abilities.

In addition to these rather obvious expectations, there may be other less obvious setting demands that can affect a student's ability to learn. They include classroom organization, instructional methods and materials, and instructional grouping demands. Each expectation should be considered in the planning process.

STEP 3: AREAS OF STRENGTH AND NEED FOR EACH STUDENT ARE NOTED   In order to determine the areas of strength and need for each student we suggest completing demographic worksheet for your class (*an example will be provided in the instructors manual*). Information you might collect includes gender, age, race/ethnicity, SES status, reading and math competency levels, special needs, such as disability, ELL status, Gifted/Talented

TABLE 10.4 The LEARNS Strategy

STEP 1: Learning goal	Learning Goal (IRA/NCTE Standard) Grades 9–12
Determine the learning goals based on state standards.	• Students read a wide range of print and non-print texts to build an understanding of texts, of themselves, and of the cultures of the United States and the world; to acquire new information; to respond to the needs and demands of society and the workplace; and for personal fulfillment. Among these texts are fiction and nonfiction, classic and contemporary works.

STEP 2: Note teacher expectations	Teaching activity	Skills necessary to complete task or activity
What must students be able to do to complete learning tasks successfully or to achieve mastery of content taught?	Conduct research on a classical or contemporary author noted for fiction or nonfiction work. Prepare a written report to present to the class.	• Locate and read a biography of an author from a reference book. • Ability to plan, organize, sequence paper • Grammatical ability, including vocabulary, spelling, punctuation • Correctly identify main ideas and important details • Write legibly without careless errors

STEP 3: Areas of strength/need	Area of need and name	Note specific ways in which these needs may manifest in a classroom and names of students to whom it applies.
	Poor/advanced reading skills:	• Inability to pick out main ideas/important details • Trouble sounding out words, difficulty with word sounds, meanings, syntax • Slow oral reading rate Difficulty connecting meaning of passages • Confuse the meaning of words • Mental fatigue and frustration
	Poor/advanced writing skills:	• Inconsistent legibility of writing due to letter formation, transposition problems • Many careless errors • Organizational problems lead to poorly planned reports and papers (lack transitions, poor sequencing) • Poor vocabulary, spelling errors, punctuation, grammar • Trouble generating ideas, awkward phrasing • Difficulty with writing tasks that require critical thinking • Write slowly, hard to form letters, lack of fluid cursive writing ability

TABLE 10.4 (*Continued*)

STEP 3: Areas of strength/need	Area of need and name	Note specific ways in which these needs may manifest in a classroom and names of students to whom it applies.
	Poor/advanced prior knowledge:	• Inexperience with topic, subject, region, concept • Lack academic or social readiness skill base • May have difficulty because has no prior exposure to the topic
	Attention problems:	• Difficulty getting started on assignments • Processes too little or too much information; can't distinguish between what is important and what isn't • Focuses too superficially or too deeply on information presented • Has difficulty connecting new information with information already known
	Poor/advance math skills	• Has trouble ordering the steps used to solve a problem • Feels overloaded when faced with a worksheet full of math exercises • Not able to copy problems correctly • May have difficulties reading the hands on an analog clock • May have difficulties interpreting and manipulating geometric configurations • May have difficulties appreciating changes in objects as they are moved in space
	Social–emotional skills deficits	• Lack of or lowered levels of motivation due to learned helplessness or lack of interest
	Sensory or motor disability	• Inability to see demonstrations, board, visual aids • May not understand concepts that require vision (e.g., colors, objects, patterns) • Inability to read print materials • Inability to move about the room freely or participate in activities that require physical movement • Inability to handle manipulatives.
STEP 4: Review	Teaching activity	Note barriers to learning and names of students to whom they apply
Compare and contrast Step 2 and Step 3, and note major areas where any students will encounter barriers	Conduct research on a classical or contemporary author noted for fiction or nonfiction work.	• May not be able to identify appropriate biography or author • May have difficulty independently locating appropriate resources on author

TABLE 10.4 The LEARNS Strategy (*Continued*)

STEP 4: Review	Teaching activity	Note barriers to learning and names of students to whom they apply
to learning if you do not make any accommodations.		• May have difficulty reading independently because of decoding, trouble sounding out words, meanings, syntax
		• Lack of vocabulary, may not know how to find definitions or read the definition or understanding of genre
	Prepare a written report with supplemental visuals to present to the class.	• May not understand the concepts or important details associated with the author
		• Physical difficulty taking notes
		• Inability to identify main ideas/important details related to author.
		• May have difficulty demonstrating understanding in this format due to motor or vision problems
STEP 5: Note accommodations	Area of need and name	Accommodations and names of students to whom they apply
Determine methods, strategies, and materials that will meet students' needs.	• May not be able to identify appropriate biography or author	• Have the class brainstorm a list of American authors from your prior readings, along with any other American authors that they would like to include. Teachers can also provide a list of preapproved biographies from which students can choose.
	• Difficulty reading independently because of unfamiliarity with vocabulary	• Provide students with a vocabulary worksheet, Franklin Speller, and online dictionary.
	• Lack of background knowledge about author or the genre	• Provide online resources such as Biography.com or Brain-Juice. These sites provide biographies and a section on each subject's most notable works or milestones.
	• Inability to identify main ideas/ important details may lead to poor note taking and an unsuccessful paper	• Provide a note-taking guide, timeline tool, or graphic organizer to facilitate student's ability to pick out important details and improve comprehension.
		• Create a research guide to instruct students in the steps necessary to successfully complete project. Provide access to approved research materials or guidance on how to evaluate a Web site.
	• May not have the necessary research skills	• For the written paper, allow use of word processor or Dragon Naturally Speaking Software.
	• May not be able to write paper by hand due to motor problems	• Allow students to demonstrate understanding in multiple ways, including creating a bio-poem, role-play, take part in an author panel discussion, suggesting a project of their own choosing.

TABLE 10.4 (*Continued*)

STEP 5: Note accommodations	Area of need and name	Accommodations and names of students to whom they apply
	• May have difficulty demonstrating understanding in this format	
STEP 6: Specify individual accommodations Identify students whose needs are not met by UDL provisions. These students may represent an instructional subgroup.	**Student names/unmet need** Jose (blind) Sharon (missing two fingers)	**Accommodations** • Provide Braille version of text or text reader • Provide student with one-handed keyboard for computer

Sources: Spencer, S., & Evers, R. (2004). Unpublished course material. Center for Pedagogy, Winthrop University.

and any other information that might be pertinent for your content area. For example, elementary school teachers may want to know how students performed in coursework at the previous grade level (i.e., how well did the student do in reading language arts in the fourth grade, if the student is in the fifth grade now). Once this data is collected teachers are able to see areas of concern that should be addressed, such as students who are not reading on grade level or have a disability that may need to be accommodated.

STEP 4: REVIEW AND DETERMINE BARRIERS   Now the teacher is ready to compare the required tasks (Step 2) with possible areas of need (Step 3) and determine the barriers that may exist in the instructional environment. For example, one of the task noted in Step 2 is reading the text and teacher made print materials and if one student has a reading disability, several other students do not read on grade level, and two students are ELL then, the teacher can assume that all of these students will need accommodations in order to read and comprehend print materials presented during the lesson. In addition, if one or more students are reading above grade level or are considered gifted/talented, the teacher will need to accommodate those students as well to extend their learning and provide appropriate print materials for their learning abilities. Each task in Step 2 should be reviewed and barriers for each determined. While this task may seem time-consuming, in most cases many tasks will be repeated in each lesson throughout the year. Once a teacher determines that a student needs accommodating for a particular barrier, that would be true for all lessons and these steps would become a routine part of every lesson planning session. See Table 10.4 for some additional examples.

STEP 5: NOTE ACCOMMODATIONS NEEDED   At this point, the teacher is ready to make decisions about possible accommodations armed with data relative to the individual needs of students in her or his classroom. If the accommodation is not successful, the first time the teacher will evaluate the choice and select again rather than continuing a strategy that is not effective, as is generally the case. The teacher can act confidently, because this process allows for possible mismatches between learner needs and classroom demands. For example, a student may be unable to identify an appropriate biography or author to research. The teacher can accommodate for this problem by having the class brainstorm a list of American authors from prior readings, along with any other American authors that they would like to include. Teachers can also provide a list of preapproved biographies from which students can choose.

STEP 6: SPECIFY INDIVIDUAL ACCOMMODATIONS NEEDED FOR SPECIFIC STUDENTS
Generally, accommodations will be successful the first time around for most students in the class. That is not to say there will not be a need for more individualized accommodations for some students. There will always be students for whom specialized services are necessary. For example, if a student is blind he or she may need a Braille reader or screen reader software.

Summary

Reading comprehension is not only a necessary component of learning to read, but academic, social, and professional success depends on it also (Stevens, Slavin, & Farnish, 1991). Yet, students graduate high schools yearly believing memorization equates to comprehension. This is not a phenomenon unique to graduating seniors; students across grade levels many times a day read but do not understand. When teachers better understand how best to teach reading using research-based instructional methods, the process and the outcome are made more effective and easier.

References

Adams, M. J. (1990). *Beginning to read: Thinking and learning about print.* Cambridge, MA: MIT Press.

August, D. A., & Hakuta, K. (Eds.). (1997). *Improving schooling for language-minority children: A research agenda.* Washington, DC: National Academy Press. Retrieved January 22, 2007, from http://books.nap.edu/openbook.php?record_id=10256&page=102

Balmuth, M. (1982) *The roots of phonics: A historical introduction.* New York: Teachers College Press.

Breznitz, Z. (1997a). Effects of accelerated reading rate on memory for text among dyslexic readers. *Journal of Educational Psychology, 89,* 289–297.

Breznitz, Z. (1997b). Enhancing the reading of dyslexic children by reading acceleration and auditory masking. *Journal of Educational Psychology, 89,* 103–113.

Bus, A. G., & van IJzendoorn, M. H. (1999). Phonological awareness and early reading: A meta-analysis of experimental training studies. *Journal of Educational Psychology, 91,* 403–414.

Breier, J. I., Simos, P. G., Fletcher, J. M., Castillo, E. M., Zhang, W., & Papanicolaou, A. C. (2003). Abnormal activation of temporoparietal language areas during phonetic analysis in children with dyslexia. *Neuropsychology, 17,* 610–621. Retrieved January 30, 2007, from http://www.vsmmedtech.com/products/meg/meg_apps/pdfs/dyslexia/abnormalactivation.pdf

Center for Academic and Reading Skills, University of Texas–Houston Health Science Center and University of Houston. (1999). *Texas Primary Reading Inventory* (4th ed.) (TPRI-4). Houston: Texas Education Agency.

Center for the Improvement of Early Reading Instruction. (1999). *Improving the reading achievement of America's children: 10 research-based principles*. Ann Arbor: University of Michigan School of Education.

Chall, J. (1989). Learning to read: The great debate 20 years later: A response to debunking the great phonics myth. *Phi Delta Kappan, 70*, 521–538.

Cunningham, P. M., & Cunningham, J. W. (2002). What we know about how to teach phonics. In S. Samuels & A. E. Farstrup (Eds.), *What research has to say about reading instruction* (pp. 87–109). Newark, DE: International Reading Association.

Downing, J. A. (1979). *Reading and reasoning*. New York: Springer-Verlag.

Duffy, G. G. (1993). Rethinking strategy instruction: Four teachers' development and their low achievers' understandings. *Elementary School Journal, 93*(3), 231–247.

Dunn, L. M., & Dunn, L. M. (1997). *The Peabody Picture Vocabulary Test, third edition (PPVT-3)*. Shoreview, MN: American Guidance Service Publishing.

Durkin, D. (1993). *Teaching them to read* (6th ed.). Boston: Allyn & Bacon.

Ehri, L. C. (1991). Development of the ability to read words. In R. Barr, M. L. Kamil, P. Mosenthal, & P. D. Pearson (Eds.), *Handbook of reading research* (Vol. 2, pp. 383–417). New York: Longman

Ehri, L.C. (1994). Development of the ability to read words: Update. In R. B. Ruddell, M. R. Ruddell, & H. Singer (Eds.), *Theoretical models and processes of reading* (4th ed., pp. 323–358). Newark, DE: International Reading Association.

Ehri, L. C. (2003). Systematic phonics instruction: Findings of the National Reading Panel. London: DfES. Retrieved December 12, 2006, from www.standards.dfes.gov.uk

Ehri, L. C., Nunes, S. R., Willows, D. M., Schuster, B. V., Yaghoub-Zadeh, Z., & Shanahan, T. (2001). Phonemic awareness instruction helps children learn to read: Evidence from the National Reading Panel's meta-analysis. *Reading Research Quarterly, 36*, 250–287.

Fielding-Barnsley, R., Hay, I., & Ashman, A. (2005) Phonological awareness: Necessary but not sufficient. In R. Bryer & K. Fiona, (Eds.), *Proceedings making meaning: Creating connections that value diversity* (pp. 63–68). Brisbane, Queensland: Australia. Retrieved February 1, 2007, from http://eprints.qut.edu.au/archive/00002175/

Foorman, B. (Ed.). (2003). *Preventing and remediating reading difficulties: Bringing science to scale*. Baltimore: York Press.

Francis, D. J., Shaywitz, S. E., Stuebing, K. K., Shaywitz, B. A., & Fletcher, J. M. (1996). Developmental lag versus deficit models of reading disability: A longitudinal individual growth curves analysis. *Journal of Educational Psychology, 88*, 3–17.

Gaskins, I. W., & Elliot, T. T. (1991). *Implementing cognitive strategy instruction across the school: The Benchmark manual for teachers*. Cambridge, MA: Brookline Books

Gilger, J. W., Pennington, B. F., & DeFries, J. C. (1991). Risk for reading disability as a function of parental history in three family studies. *Reading and Writing: An Interdisciplinary Journal, 3*, 205–217.

Good, R. H., & Good, R. A. (2002). *Dynamic Indicators of Basic Early Literacy Skills, 6th edition (DIBELS-6)*. Eugene, OR: Institute for the Development of Education Achievement.

Hatcher, P., Hulme, C., & Ellis, A. (1994). Ameliorating early reading failure by integrating the teaching of reading and phonological skills: The phonological linkage hypothesis. *Child Development, 65*, 41–57.

Hiebert, E. H. (1999). Text matters in learning to read. *Reading Teacher, 52*, 552–566.

Hixon, J. (1993). Redefining the issues: Who's at risk and why. Revision of a paper originally presented in 1983 at Reducing the Risks, a workshop presented by the Midwest Regional Center for Drug-Free Schools and Communities. Retrieved December 22, 2006, from http://www.ncrel.org/sdrs/areas/issues/students/atrisk/at5def.htm

Johnston, R., & Watson, J. (2005). *The effects of synthetic phonics teaching on reading and spelling attainment*. Edinburgh: Scottish Executive Education Department. Retrieved January 2, 2007, from www.scotland.gov.uk

Lindamood, C. H., & Lindamood, P. C. (1979). *The Lindamood Auditory Conceptualization Test (LAC)*. Allen: Texas: DLM Teaching Resources.

Lyon, G. R., (2000). Why some children have difficulties learning to read. Retrieved February 1, 2007. from http://www.readingrockets.org/articles/296

Lyon, G. R., (1999). *The NICHD research program in reading development, reading disorders and reading instruction.* Retrieved February 1, 2007, from http://www.ncld.org/content/view/524/#background

Mann, V. (1987). Phonological awareness: The role of reading experience. In P. Bertelson (Ed.), *The onset of literacy: Cognitive processes in reading acquisition* (pp. 65–92). Cambridge, MA: MIT Press.

McBride-Chang, C. (1995). Phonological processing, speech perception and reading disability: An integrative review. *Educational Psychologist, 30,* 109–121.

McBride-Chang, C. (1996). Models of speech perception and phonological processing in reading. *Child Development, 67,* 1836–1856.

Moats, L. C. (2000). *Whole language lives on: The illusion of balanced reading instruction.* Retrieved February 2, 2007, from http://www.ncld.org/content/view/524/#background

Moats, L. C. (2001). *Improving reading by preparing teachers.* Washington, DC: National Governors Association, Center for Best Practices. Retrieved February 1, 2007, from http://www.nga.org/Files/pdf/IB022401VOLUNTEER.pdf

National Assessment of Educational Progress. (2003). *Condition of education. Report of the National Center for Education Statistics.* Washington, DC: U.S. Department of Education. Retrieved January 11, 2007, from http://nces.ed.gov/nationsreportcard/reading/results2003/

National Assessment of Educational Progress. (2005). *Condition of education. Report of the National Center for Education Statistics.* Washington, DC: U.S. Department of Education. Retrieved January 11, 2007, from http://nces.ed.gov/nationsreportcard/nrc/reading_math_2005/s0002.asp?printver

National Center for Education Statistics. (1997). *Condition of education.* Washington, DC: U.S. Department of Education, Office of Educational Research and Improvement. Retrieved December 18, 2006, from http://www.euser-eu.org/ShowCase.asp?CaseTitleID=380&CaseID=785&MenuID=52

National Inquiry into the Teaching of Literacy. (2005a). *Teaching reading: Report and recommendations.* Australian Government: Department of Education, Science and Training. Retrieved December 18, 2006, from www.dest.gov.au/nitl/documents/report_recommendations.pdf

National Inquiry into the Teaching of Literacy. (2005b). *Teaching reading: A review of the evidence-based research literature on approaches to the teaching of literacy, particularly those that are effective in assisting students with reading difficulties.* Australian Government: Department of Education, Science, and Training. Retrieved December 18, 2006, from www.dest.gov.au/nitl/documents/literature_review.pdf

National Institute for Literacy. (2001). *Put reading first: The research building blocks for teaching children to read.* Retrieved January 3, 2007, from http://www.nifl.gov/partnershipforreading/

National Reading Panel. (2000). *Teaching children to read: An evidence-based assessment of the scientific research literature on reading and its implications for reading instruction.* Washington, DC: National Institute of Child Health and Human Development. Retrieved December 28, 2006, from http://www.nationalreadingpanel.org/Publications/publications.htm

Nist, S. (1993, Fall–Winter). What the literature says about academic literacy. *Georgia*

Pressley, M., & Afflerbach, P. (1995). Verbal protocols of reading: The nature of constructively responsive reading. *Journal of Reading, 11*–18.

Pressley, M. (1998). *Reading instruction that works.* New York: Guilford Press.

Pressley, M. (2002). The importance of effective early intervention. In S. Samuels & A. E. Farstrup (Eds.), *What research has to say about reading instruction* (pp. 69–86). Newark, DE: International Reading Association.

Pressley, M., Wharton-McDonald, R., Hampson, J.M., & Echevarria, M. (1998). The nature of literacy instruction in ten Grade-4/5 classrooms in upstate New York. *Scientific Studies of Reading, 2,* 159–191.

Roberts, J. E., Rosenfeld, R. M. & Zeisel, S. A. (2004). Otitis media and speech and language: A meta-analysis of prospective studies. *Journal of the American Academy of Pediatrics, 113,* 238–248. Retrieved December 27, 2006, from http://pediatrics.aappublications.org/cgi/content/abstract/113/3/e238

Ruetzel, D. R., & Cooter, R. B. (1999). *Balanced reading strategies and practices.* Upper Saddle River, NJ: Prentice Hall.

Ryder, R. J., & Graves, M. F. (1994). Vocabulary instruction presented prior to reading in two basal readers. *Elementary School Journal, 95,* 139–153.

Scarborough, H. H. (1998). Early identification of children at risk for reading disabilities: Phonological awareness and some other promising predictors. In K. Shapiro, P. J. Accardo, & A. J. Capute (Eds.), *Specific reading disability: A view of the spectrum* (pp. 77–121). Timonium, MD: York Press.

Schatschneider, C., Fletcher, J.M., Francis, D.J., Carlson, C, & Foorman, B.R. (1999). Kindergarten prediction of reading skills: A longitudinal comparative analysis. *Journal of Educational Psychology, 96*(2), 265–282.

Schunk, D. H. (2004). *Learning theories an educational perspective* (4th ed.). Upper Saddle River, NJ: Merrill/Pearson Education.

Senechal, M. (1997). The differential effect of storybook reading on preschoolers' acquisition of expressive and receptive vocabulary. *Journal of Child Language, 24,* 123–138.

Share, D., Jorm, A., Maclean, R., & Matthews, R. (1984). Sources of individual differences in reading acquisition. *Journal of Educational Psychology, 76,* 1309–1324.

Shaywitz, B. A., Fletcher, J. M., & Shaywitz, S. E. (1995). Defining and classifying learning disabilities and attention-deficit/hyperactivity disorder. *Journal of Child Neurology, 10,* 50–57.

Smith, F. (1994). *Understanding reading* (5th ed.). Hillsdale, NJ: Lawrence Erlbaum Associates.

Smith, D. R. (2000). *Early reading diagnostic assessment.* University of Oregon: Sopris West.

Snow, C. E., Barnes, W. S., Chandler, J., Goodman, I. F., & Hemphill, L. (1991). *Unfulfilled expectations: Home and school influences on literacy.* Cambridge, MA: Harvard University Press. Retrieved December 29, 2006, from http://www.nap.edu/openbook/0309068363/html/385.html

Spencer, S. S. (1998). *The effect of metacognitive knowledge on the generalization of programmatic strategy instruction.* Unpublished doctoral dissertation, Georgia State University, Atlanta.

Stevens, R. J., Slavin, R. E., & Farnish, A. M. (1991). The effects of cooperative learning and direct instruction in reading comprehension strategies on main idea identification. *Journal of Educational Psychology, 83,* 8–16.

Strickland, D. (2002). The importance of effective early intervention. In S. Samuels & A. E. Farstrup (Eds.), *What research has to say about reading instruction* (pp. 69–86). Newark, DE: International Reading Association.

Steubing, K, Fletcher, J., LaDoux, J., Lyon, G. R., et al. (2002).Validity of IQ-achievement discrepancy classifications of reading disabilities: A meta-analysis. *American Educational Research Journal, 39,* 469–518.

Teddlie, C., Kirby, P., & Stringfield, S. (1989). Effective vs. ineffective schools: Observable differences in the classroom. *American Journal of Education, 97,* 221–236. Retrieved January 18, 2007, from http://www.questia.com/.jsp

Tomesen, M., & Aarnoutse, C. (1998). Effects of an instructional programme for deriving work meanings. *Educational Studies, 24,* 107–128.

Torgesen, C., Brooks, G., & Hall, J. (2006). *A systematic review of the research literature on the use of phonics in the teaching of reading and spelling.* London: Department for Education and Skills. Retrieved January 8, 2007, from www.dfes.gov.uk/research/data/uploadfiles/RR711_.pdf

Treiman, R. (1983). Onsets and rhymes as units of spoken syllables: Evidence from children. *Journal of Experimental Child Psychology, 39,* 161–181.

Vaughn, S., & Schumm, J. S. (1995). Responsible inclusion for students with learning disabilities. *Journal of Learning Disabilities, 28,* 264–270, 290.

Wagner, R. K., Torgesen, J. K., & Rashotte, C. A. (1999). *Comprehensive Test of Phonological Processing (CTOPP).* Austin, TX: Pro-Ed.

Wiederholt, J. L., & Bryant, B. R. (2001). Gray Oral Reading Tests (GORT-4). Austin, TX: Pro-Ed.

Williams, K. T. (2001). *Group reading assessment and diagnostic evaluation.* Shoreview, MN: Pearson AGS Globe.

Wong B., Harris, K., Graham, S., & Butler, D. (2003). Cognitive strategies instruction research in learning disabilities. In H. L. Swanson, K. R. Harris, & S. Graham (Eds.), *Handbook of learning disabilities* (pp. 383–402). New York: Guilford Press.

Chapter 11

Written Literacy Requires Students to Think

After reading this chapter, you will be able to:

1. Discuss the prevalence, causes, and characteristics of writing problems
2. Describe the relationship between thinking (metacognitive) and written literacy
3. Describe the elements of effective writing instruction and assessment
4. Apply the LEARN strategy to identify and select effective methods and materials for remediating writing problems

PREVALENCE OF STUDENTS EXPERIENCING WRITING PROBLEMS

The National Assessment of Educational Progress (NEAP, 2007) findings, as described by *The Nation's Report Card*, suggest the writing skills of 8th- and 12th-grade students in most racial and ethnic groups improved in 2007 compared to earlier assessments in 2002 and 1998 (students in Grade 4 were not assessed in 2007). This is also true for student with disabilities.

The NAEP (2007) data for this population indicate an upward trend in scale scores since 1998, with average gains in writing scores for students with disabilities in the 8th and 12th grades outpacing those of students without disabilities from 2002 to 2007. Why do you think this is the case? What does this mean for classroom teachers?

While it is true that the NAEP (2007) data indicate that students with disabilities are showing improvement, they continue to score much lower than their peers without disabilities do over time. Data indicate that of the 12th-grade students with disabilities participating in the assessment, 33% scored at the basic level in 1998, 30% scored at basic in 2002, and 44% scored basic in 2007 (NAEP, 2007). During the same reporting period, students with disabilities scored at the proficient level at the alarmingly low rates of 1% in 1998, 3% in 2002, and 5% in 2007 (NAEP, 2007). To put the scores into perspective, students without disabilities during the same time period scored at the basic level 81%, 77%, and 85%, respectively, and at the proficient level 23%, 25%, and 26%, respectively.

Gains by minority students, male students, and students with disabilities seem to be narrowing previously existing achievement gaps. Nevertheless, despite these gains, overall student writing scores have remained relatively stagnant over time, with only modest increases being reported over time in either reading or writing (Applebee, Arthur, & Langer, 2006; Tachibana, 2008). The most recent NAEP (2007) writing scores data indicate 88% of all eighth graders and 82% of all high school seniors tested at the basic level on the assessment, with only a third of 8th graders and a fourth of 12th graders scoring at or above the proficient level, defined as competency over challenging subject matter. Visit the NationsReportCard.gov Web site to get a fuller understanding of the scope of the problem. I also encourage the reader to look at not only the national writing scores but those of your state as well.

Findings such as these are troubling and raise many questions. Among them, why do students continue to exhibit basic skills deficits across grade levels despite classroom instruction by highly qualified teachers? As it stands, the majority of our nation's seniors are at the basic writing level as they prepare to graduate and are only capable of demonstrating partial mastery of prerequisite knowledge and skills that are fundamental to producing proficient written work in their personal and professional lives. Are the students graduating from our schools academically and functionally illiterate? It is troubling to note that despite policy and programming changes aimed at improving student performance, employers continue to question the ability of our graduates to do so (Brady, 2003; Wolf & Hall, 2005). To solve this problem we must understand what is causing it and then seek a solution. As discussed earlier in this text, when a student is not learning there is a mismatch between students' abilities and needs and classroom demands.

CAUSES

Classroom Factors Contribute to Writing Problems

Despite advances in educational psychology, learning, and technology, how is it that students continue to perform poorly on writing achievement tests? Trends suggested by years of NAEP data (2002, 2003, 2005, and 2007) indicate one possible reason: There is not much time being spent on writing in classrooms. Nor are students being given writing for homework. NAEP (2002, 2007) data indicate two-thirds of students in Grade 8 were expected to spend only an hour or less on writing homework each week, and this number remains virtually unchanged today. In addition, NAEP data from 2002 and 2007 show that 11% of eighth graders reported they were never asked to write research reports on content they studied, and only 14% and 16%, respectively, reported that they had been asked to do so once. This may explain part of the problem in that extended writing is believed to develop the skills necessary to summarize and synthesize information, develop in-depth arguments, and in general promote the use of higher-order thinking skills necessary to become a proficient and advanced writer.

Applebee and Langer (2006) looked at trends across NAEP data and found strong patterns suggesting teachers' beliefs of what higher and lower performing students can achieve drove instructional decision making. Do you remember discussing the effects of teachers' beliefs on decision making in Chapter 6 on metacognition? Apply what you learned there here to help you better understand how these teachers' beliefs may have affected their actions and student outcomes.

Applebee and Langer (2006) also found that when they analyzed teachers' responses to questionnaires on how they teach writing that in addition to teachers' beliefs and practices there are external factors affecting the teaching of writing. In particular, time spent on teaching writing is in direct competition with standardized test preparation time. Applebee and Langer report that in some cases, the focus on high-stakes test may be shifting attention away from broad programs of writing instruction toward a much narrower focus on basic skills and how best to answer particular types of test questions.

As we know, instruction that focuses on basic skills is not an effective means of providing students with the necessary skills and abilities to become proficient writers. Teaching to the test, as has become popular in educational culture, often focuses on low-level cognitive skills such as recognition and recall, those skills needed only to read a sentence and circle or answer a factual question on a paper-and-pencil exam. However, as adults, the expectations of our daily lives and jobs require reading and writing skills beyond those with such a limited purpose. Adults in today's workforce must compose memos and write business reports, among other things, all of which require higher-order thinking. Yet, students are not being taught in many cases to read and write meaningfully. Writing taught via decontextualized *basic skills* lessons in which words and sentences are read in isolation without any authentic purpose or connection to previously learned knowledge do not engender these types of skills and knowledge. Granted, some students can and do learn to become proficient writers given these circumstances, but others do not. In particular, many students with learning and behavior disorders experience difficulty learning to write in a classroom environment that focuses on basic skills alone (e.g., Graham, Harris, & Macarthur, 2006).

INFORMATION PROCESSING, PHONOLOGICAL KNOWLEDGE, HIGHER-ORDER LINGUISTIC KNOWLEDGE, AND EXCEPTIONALITY CONTRIBUTE TO WRITING PROBLEMS

Information Processing

Writing problems may occur for a number of reasons, including information processing problems that affect the ability to develop or use higher-order linguistic knowledge and phonological knowledge related to reading. As you know, the brain functions as a storage and retrieval system whose success depends on its ability to manipulate information. In the case of language, the brain looks for patterns and consistencies, repetitions in visual input and auditory input (Kuhl, 2008). These experiences are recorded or mapped by the brain and used to make sense of what we hear and see.

The ability to discriminate between sounds in one's own language and those of other languages develops very early—in fact, babies within the first 6 months of life can differentiate between phonemes used in their language as opposed to those used in other languages (Kuhl, Conboy, Padden, Nelson, & Pruitt, 2005). It is believed that the ability to represent individual sounds, by binding them together, and storing them in a meaningful way makes it easier for the brain to perceive the phonological components of language (Tallal, 2008). These coded representations are thought to serve as the building blocks of language (Tallal, 2008).

Phonological Awareness

There is also a strong connection between reading and writing. Reading and writing are dependent on shared cognitive abilities, including phonological and memory systems. The key to learning to read and write is becoming aware that words can be broken down into smaller parts of speech called phonemes. Phonemes are a type of code used to build words for both oral and written language. Children who have trouble understanding the code are more likely to have trouble with written language. One early indicator of difficulty with this code can be trouble with word games. For example, children may have trouble understanding that the word *slate* can be decoded into the word *late* by removing the /s/ or that by replacing the /s/ with an /h/ the word becomes *hate* and conveys and entirely different meaning. Why might a student's inability to play word games signal a problem? Language, both oral and written, begins with understanding that sounds are used to form words. Sounds can be broken down and reformed into an almost infinite variety of words used to convey written and spoken meaning.

Higher-Order Linguistic Knowledge

Temporal processing deficits may explain why some children do not develop phonological awareness. When you think about it, our brains must pull together, coordinate, store, and then retrieve millions of bits of coded data rapidly and in an organized fashion if language use is to be efficient and effective. Researchers compared children who struggle with learning to talk with those who do not have difficulty learning to talk and found notable differences in the way they organized basic linguistic signals and complex auditory signals (Tallal, 2008). It is believed that children who struggle with language may do so due to temporal processing deficits that make tracking and integrating speech sounds difficult (Tallal, 2008). In essence, the brain must process large amounts of information to produce written or spoken language.

Children who have difficulty processing written and spoken language often experience problems with reading and writing in school. In addition to phonological processing deficits, the problems many students exhibit with the mechanics of writing, including spelling, handwriting, and composition, often result from verbal memory problems associated with oral language (e.g., August & Shanahan, 2006; Lennox & Siegel, 1996, 1998). Studies show that verbal working memory limitations can affect both quality and quantity of writing (e.g., Lennox & Siegel, 1996, 1998; Shanahan, 2006). For example, an overload of verbal working memory can lead to choppy writing, certain kinds of syntactic and semantic errors, and composition errors. Verbal working memory, oral language, and writing are closely related with children who have well-developed oral language doing better with writing than those who do not. In fact, research suggests that written language skill is reliant on the development of oral language.

Exceptionality

Writing well does not come easily to many people. It is a complex process with which many students, including those with learning and behavior disorders, experience difficulty (e.g., Graham et al., 2006; van den Bergh & Rijlaarsdam, 2001). Students may have difficulty with written language due to psychological processing disorders (learning disabilities), neurological problems (cerebral palsy, muscular dystrophy, and traumatic brain injury), communication (autism), intellectual (metal retardation), sensory (hearing loss), or emotional impairment (selective mutism) (American Speech-Language Association, 2008). The resultant language problems are described by a variety of terms, such as language delay and language disorder.

Students labeled as *language delayed* fail to acquire language abilities according to the usual development timetable. That is, these children's language is developing normally, in the right sequence, but at a slower rate. Children who have *language disorders*, on the other hand, are not developing language normally, which may include rate and sequence. These two terms are often used interchangeably (American Speech-Language Association, 2008).

CHARACTERISTICS OF STUDENTS EXPERIENCING WRITTEN EXPRESSION DIFFICULTY

Researchers have grouped writing problems into three broad categories: knowledge difficulties, skills difficulties, and motivation difficulties (Troia, 2002; Troia & Graham, 2003). Although students may experience writing difficulty for a number of different reasons, they will often share many of the same characteristics. Examples of student characteristics by category are as follows (Troia, 2002; Troia & Graham, 2003).

Knowledge Difficulties

- Less aware of what good writing is and how to produce it
- Limited understanding of genre-specific text structures (e.g., setting or plot elements in a narrative)
- Poor declarative, procedural, and conditional strategy knowledge (e.g., metacognitively unaware of the need to plan for writing, including goal setting, strategy use, monitoring, and modifying when it is most beneficial)
- Limited knowledge of relevant vocabulary
- Underdeveloped knowledge of word and sentence structure (e.g., phonology, morphology, and syntax)
- May have limited background knowledge on a given topic or experience difficulty accessing existing topic knowledge
- Unaware of the audience for whom they are writing or the intended function of their writing

Skill Difficulties

- Poor spelling, handwriting, and punctuation
- May be unaware of the need to reflect on or revise writing, and if they do revise they may focus on superficial aspects of writing (e.g., handwriting, spelling, and grammar)
- Limited self-regulatory ability may make is difficult to regulate thoughts, attention, and actions during the writing process

Motivation Difficulties

- Students may falsely attribute academic success to external and uncontrollable factors, such as task ease or teacher assistance.
- Students may falsely attribute a lack of academic success to limited intelligence, which they also believe is beyond their control.
- As a result, these students often give up easily, have low self-efficacy, experience learned helplessness, and are unmotivated due to repeated failure.

Learning to write is a complex process, involving the mental ability to combine multiple skills and knowledge of written and spoken language simultaneously in meaningful ways. Difficulty with the mental processes involved in the use of language, regardless of the cause, can and will affect written expression in a number of ways. To determine where students are experiencing barriers to learning, teachers can utilize a variety of assessment methods.

WRITTEN LANGUAGE ASSESSMENT

Overview

When assessing student performance, particularly those with special needs, there are legal and ethical mandates requiring educators to consider information from multiple sources and approaches. These are generally a combination of standardized or norm-referenced and curriculum-based instruments. Student achievement is typically measured relative to standards for literacy and written language set by professional organizations such as the Council for Exceptional Children (CEC) and the National Council of English Teachers (NCTE) as well as national, state, and local performance standards. An individual classroom teacher approach to assessment will, however, depend on the assessment goal, professional background, orientation, and of course abilities of the students.

When assessing written language, it is important to keep these principles in mind:

1. Collect assessment data over time from across a variety of contexts and a number of sources to increase validity.
2. Choose assessments that will measure those outcomes you wish to measure. Check to be sure the instructional goal and instrument design match.
3. Assessments and tasks must be age appropriate.
4. Perhaps most important, assessments should reflect classroom instruction if they are to be valid measures of student performance.

FORMAL TESTS OF WRITTEN EXPRESSION

Written language is by its very nature a complex process, and assessing it can be difficult. Educators use both informal and formal methods to obtain an accurate performance profile. Norm-referenced tests can provide a formal or standardized measure of written language skills that are a part of the school, state, or national standards. These tests compare student performance to other students in the school system or other more diverse populations. There are many standardized, norm-referenced test options available to educators. The choice of test depends on several factors, including the student's age and skill level, questions to be answered, and characteristics of the student. The following are some of the more widely used standardized assessments of written language.

The *Test of Written Expression* (TOWE; McGhee, Bryant, Larsen, & Rivera, 1995) is intended for use with students between the ages of 6 years, 6 months, and 14 years, 11 months. It uses two assessment methods to evaluate student's writing skills. The first method involves administering a series of 76 items that measure skills associated with writing. The second method requires students to respond to a prepared story starter and use it as a stimulus for writing an essay. The test is designed to assess student's strengths and weaknesses in areas such as spelling, vocabulary, grammar, syntax, punctuation, ideation, and sentence and story construction. The TOWE may be administered either individually or to groups of students and is reported to have good reliability and adequate validity (Taylor, 2006).

The *Test of Early Written Language*, 2nd edition (TEWL; Hresko, Herron, & Peak, 1996), is intended for use with children 3 years, 0 months, to 10 years, 11 months. The purpose of this test is to measure emergent or early writing ability. Two procedures measure writing skills including spelling, capitalization, punctuation, ideation, and sentence construction. In one, students are administered 14 items to measure general understanding of writing purposes, discrimination of verbal and nonverbal visual representational forms, and understanding of linguistic terms. In the second, students write a story from a prompt. These stories are scored for skills including ideation, vocabulary, mechanics, and spelling. The test, while valid and reliable for older students, is not recommended for children under the age of 4 (Taylor, 2006).

The *Test of Written Language*, 3rd edition (TOWL–3; Hammill & Larsen, 1996), measures contrived and spontaneous written language. The test is appropriate for students in Grades 2–12. It has eight subtests that assess contextual conventions, contextual language, story construction, vocabulary, spelling, style, logical sentences, and sentence combining. Three of the subtests measure skills including grammar, syntax, punctuation, and general composition. There are two forms of this test (A and B) to eliminate test/retest contamination between the pretest and post-test. Although this test is widely used and meets nationally recognized standards, Salvia and Yesseldyke (2007) suggested that it has limited usefulness because it lacks information concerning students with special needs.

The *Wide Range Achievement Test*, 4th edition (WRAT–4; Wilkinson & Robertson, 2006), is an individually administered test for students from 5 through 9.5 years. There are four subtests: word reading, spelling, math computation, and sentence comprehension. It is widely used as a screening test to diagnose learning disabilities in spelling (Pierangelo & Giuliani, 2006).

The *Woodcock–Johnson Tests of Achievement III* (WJ III; Woodcock, McGrew, & Mather, 2001) is a subset of *Woodcock–Johnson III*. Subtests include spelling, writing fluency, and sample writing, as well as letter–word identification, reading fluency, passage comprehension, calculation, math fluency, and applied problems. Due to the continuous-year norms of the WJ III, it is considered to be a valid and reliable source for identifying significant discrepancies in learning and guiding educational decision making (Venn, 2007).

The *Writing Process Test* (WPT; Warden & Hutchinson, 1992) is a direct measure of writing that requires students to plan, write, and revise an original composition. The WPT assesses both written product and process. The students analyze the product via a checklist and questions about their composition. The WPT gives the examiner insight into the student's metacognitive awareness of the writing process when planning recursive behaviors. The test is appropriate for students in Grades 2–12 and can be administered individually or in groups.

When determining how to assess written language, there a number of factors to consider, including the purpose of the assessment, the information needed, and how that information will be used. Standardized tests, for a number of reasons, do not generally generate the type of information that is useful for planning classroom instruction. For example, standardized tests often do not test what students are taught, often consider only one response correct, and do not allow room for students to generate answers based on their knowledge and experience (Cohen & Spenciner, 2007).

Standardized test data are, however, useful as a screening device. For example, they draw upon standardized test results to determine eligibility for special education services, measure student achievement against national norms for the purposes of establishing accountability, or determine students' admissions to institutions of higher education.

INFORMAL TESTS OF WRITTEN EXPRESSION

Formal assessments serve an important function: They allow school systems to compare the performance of large groups of students, monitor the effectiveness of programming, and make broad curricular decisions. Informal assessments differ from formal measures in that they help teachers identify student strengths and weaknesses, note particular skills that need attention, monitor student progress, and guide instructional planning, goal setting, materials selection (Venn, 2007). Moreover, informal assessments share a logical and intuitive connection with classroom instruction. They occur as a normal part of the educational process that emerges from everyday teaching and learning situations.

Teachers, for example, often utilize questioning and one-on-one interviews with students to provide them with a real-time error analysis of thought processes and strategy use. Portfolio assessment is another frequently utilized informal assessment method that offers a dynamic measure of student growth over time as opposed to the more static snapshot of ability provided by standardized assessment instruments. The advantages of the informal assessment methods are that they allow for immediate feedback and revision of teaching to accommodate learner needs and can also measure competence across a variety of cognitive levels, as defined by the revised version of Bloom's

Taxonomy of Educational Objectives (i.e., knowledge, comprehension, application, analysis, synthesis, and evaluating) (Anderson, & Krathwohl, 2001; Bloom, Englehart, Furst, Hill, & Krathwohl, 1956). The following is a list of competencies, verbs, and activities that can be used to construct assessments at each level.

- *Knowledge/Remembering Level.* At the knowledge level, the goal is to determine if the student can recall basic information and facts. Among the verbs used to construct assessment activities at this level are *define, duplicate, list, memorize, recall,* and *repeat.* To assess student ability at this level, have students write a paragraph in which they identify the main characters of a book.
- *Comprehension/Understanding Level.* At this level, the goal is to determine if the student can explain ideas or concepts. Among the verbs used to construct assessment activities at this level are *classify, describe, discuss, explain, report,* and *paraphrase.* To assess student ability at this level, have students write a report in which they describe relevant events from a field trip to the United Nations.
- *Application/Applying Level.* At this level, the goal is to determine if the student can use information in a new way. Among the verbs used to construct assessment activities at this level are *choose, demonstrate, dramatize, employ, illustrate, interpret, operate, schedule, sketch, solve,* and *use.* To assess student ability at this level, have students write a report in which they rewrite the story using the literary convention discussed in today's lesson.
- *Analysis/Analyzing Level.* At this level, the goal is to determine if the student can distinguish between relationships and different parts. Among the verbs used to construct assessment activities at this level are *appraise, compare, contrast, criticize, differentiate, discriminate, distinguish, examine, experiment, question,* and *test.* To assess student ability at this level, have students write a mock newspaper editorial in which they compare and contrast the presidency of Abraham Lincoln to that of any 20th- or 21st-century president.
- *Synthesis/Evaluating Level.* At this level, the goal is to determine if the student can make and justify a decision. Among the verbs used to construct assessment activities at this level are *appraise, argue, defend, judge, select, support, value,* and *evaluate.* To assess student ability at this level, have students write a journal entry in which you evaluate the effectiveness of the strategies they used to study for the last test.
- *Evaluating/Creating Level.* At this level, the goal is to determine if the student can create a new product or point of view. Among the verbs used to construct assessment activities at this level are *assemble, construct, create, design, develop,* and *formulate.* To assess student ability at this level, have students create a poem using the vocabulary words from the story.

These activities allow students to demonstrate a variety of skills and abilities within the dynamic context of instructional activities.

One of the most important features of informal assessment that differentiates it from standardized tests is the feedback component. Students' progress toward a given learning goal must be monitored and areas of strength or weakness assessed, so that instruction can be modified quickly to meet each student's individual needs. Remember, prompt feedback to students about their work increases the likelihood of producing meaningful changes in learning outcomes.

TABLE 11.1 Holistic Writing Rubric for Journaling Activity

Use this rubric to assess students' abilities to complete the journal activities assigned for a given lesson. Share this assessment with students prior to completing the journal-writing lesson so they will understand how they will be assessed. You can also use the rubric as a basis for discussion and feedback with each student. Each journal will be given one of three scores: E, A, or NA. The reader will write with these descriptors in mind.

Excellent	• Can easily complete process independently
	• Can pre-read and follow the writing prompts without assistance; has no more than three minor errors (mechanics, word choice, sentence structure)
	• Meets all requirements
Acceptable	• Requires some help to complete process
	• Can pre-read and follow the writing prompts with minimal assistance; has four to seven minor errors (mechanics, word choice, sentence structure)
	• Meets most requirements
Not Acceptable	• Must have extensive support to complete process
	• Does not follow writing prompts without extensive support
	• Has more than seven errors (mechanics, word choice, sentence structure)
	• Does not meet all requirements

Source: Spencer, S., & Evers, R. (2009). Unpublished course material. Center for Pedagogy, Winthrop University.

Rubrics like the one in Table 11.1 are excellent tools for grading activities such as journaling. This is an example of a holistic scoring rubric; however, they may take the form of either holistic scoring rubrics or analytical scoring rubrics. Both are useful for the analysis of students' written products or the writing processes itself (Brookhart, 1999). Holistic scoring rubrics provide a general overall impression of writing ability on one or two previously identified characteristics in a student's work. Each level describes the characteristics of a response that would receive the respective score. The disadvantage of this method is that it does not provide detailed information about specific areas of writing.

Informal assessments of student learning may also be scored using an analytic scoring rubric. This method offers an alternative to the holistic scoring rubric by providing some objectivity to evaluation of content. Teachers can choose from a general rating scale that will apply to most writing assignments, or they can design scoring scales that are specific to a given genre or text. For example, these rubrics might measure student performance as being experienced, capable, developing, emergent, pre-emergent, or experimental. Rubrics like these will allow teachers to pinpoint students' specific strengths and weaknesses and set clear performance goals.

INSTRUCTIONAL ASSESSMENT AND METHODOLOGICAL DECISION MAKING

Evaluating student work to improve learning is but one aspect of effective decision making. Teachers must also become skilled at analyzing their own expectations to determine the relationship between the setting demands of their classroom and student achievement. Standardized assessments seldom provide teachers with the type of information they need to determine where students are having difficulty with a given lesson. Misinterpretation of such data may in fact lead to a misidentification of the underlying academic problem, resulting in ineffective planning by the teacher.

While the importance of assessment data for guiding instructional decisions is clear theoretically, it is less clear to teachers from a practical standpoint how to apply this construct at the classroom level. A tool is needed that will assist teachers in determining where barriers to learning lie within their lessons before they teach them, one that can provide meaningful feedback and inform instructional planning in a timely manner. One such tool is the LEARNS strategy previously introduced in Chapter 7 on Universal Design for Learning (UDL). The LEARNS strategy for planning UDL lessons consists of six steps:

Step 1: Learning goal: Determine what content will be taught.

Step 2: Note teacher Expectations for lesson objective.

Step 3: Areas of strength and need for each student are noted.

Step 4: Review and determine barriers.

Step 5: Note accommodations needed.

Step 6: Specify individual accommodations needed for specific students.

The LEARNS strategy enables teachers to diagnose where problems lie within the curriculum. It facilitates educational planning by providing a metacognitive problem-solving framework from which to make informed instructional decisions. LEARNS will help teachers design their lessons with students' abilities in mind. Based on principles of Universal Design for Learning, LEARNS requires teachers to plan lessons recognizing that students have differing ability levels due to background knowledge, readiness, language, exceptionality, preferences in learning, inability to physically use instructional materials, or inability to effectively select and apply cognitive and metacognitive strategies.

Remember, lesson plans provided by textbooks or readily available materials from the Internet are general and can unwittingly create barriers to learning because they are not tailored to the unique needs of your students. The LEARNS strategy is a tool with which to design or revise lessons for the purpose of solving academic problems and removing barriers to learning based on students' unique needs.

Applying the LEARNS Strategy to Writing Assignments

Table 11.2 illustrates how a teacher might use the LEARNS strategy to design a writing lesson.

The following is a discussion of the LEARNS process.

Step 1: Identify a *learning goal* for the lesson you plan to teach. Learning goals typically support state or content area curriculum standards; therefore, what you are required to teach is unrelated to classroom demographics. What is the learning goal in the example?

Step 2: *Specify* expectations for the lesson. This step requires the teacher to conduct a task analysis of the writing lesson to determine how the students should

TABLE 11.2 LEARNS Strategy Lesson Plan Analysis

STEP 1: Learning goal		
	Students employ a wide range of strategies as they write and use different writing process elements appropriately to communicate with different audiences for a variety of purposes.	
Determine the learning goals based on state standards.	Students will develop and support a position on a particular book by writing a persuasive essay about their chosen title.	

STEP 2: Note teacher expectations	Teaching activity	Skills necessary to complete task or activity
What must students be able to do to complete learning tasks successfully or to achieve mastery of the content taught?	Students will examine issues of censorship as it relates to a videos, Internet, music, and books.	Understand the concept of censorship
	Students will read and evaluate books to determine biases.	• Must be able to read from book • Must be able to determine relevant features in the book that are controversial and why • Must be able to take notes
	Students must write a persuasive essay on a particular book in which they develop and support a position.	• Ability to plan, organize, sequence paper • Ability to write a grammatically correct essay • Ability to correctly identify main ideas and important details intended to persuade

STEP 3: Assess areas of strength/need	Area of need and name	Note specific ways in which these needs may manifest in a classroom and names of students to whom it applies
	Poor/advanced reading skills:	• Inability to pick out main ideas/important details • Trouble sounding out words; difficulty with word sounds, meanings, syntax • Slow oral reading rate • Difficulty connecting meaning of passages • Confuses the meaning of words
	Poor/advanced writing skills:	• Mental fatigue and frustration • Inconsistent legibility of writing due to letter formation, transposition problems • Many careless errors

(Continued)

TABLE 11.2 LEARNS Strategy Lesson Plan Analysis (*Continued*)

STEP 3: Assess areas of strength/need	Area of need and name	Note specific ways in which these needs may manifest in a classroom and names of students to whom it applies
		• Organizational problems lead to poorly planned reports and papers (lack transitions, poor sequencing)
		• Poor vocabulary, spelling, punctuation, grammar
		• Trouble generating ideas, awkward phrasing
		• Difficulty with writing tasks that require critical thinking
		• Write slowly, hard to form letters, lack of fluid cursive writing ability
	Poor/advanced prior knowledge:	• Inexperience with topic, subject, region, concept
		• Lacks academic or social readiness skill base
		• May have difficulty because has no prior exposure to the topic
	Attention problems:	• Difficulty getting started on assignments
		• Processes too little or too much information; can't distinguish between what is important and what isn't
		• Focuses too superficially or too deeply on information presented
		• Has difficulty connecting new information with information already known
	Poor/advance math skills:	• Has trouble ordering the steps used to solve a problem
		• Feels overloaded when faced with a worksheet full of math exercises
		• Not be able to copy problems correctly
		• May have difficulties reading the hands on an analog clock

TABLE 11.2 *(Continued)*

STEP 3: Assess areas of strength/need	Area of need and name	Note specific ways in which these needs may manifest in a classroom and names of students to whom it applies
		• May have difficulties interpreting and manipulating geometric configurations • May have difficulties appreciating changes in objects as they are moved in space
	Social/emotional skills deficits:	• Lack of or lowered levels of motivation due to learned helplessness or lack of interest
	Sensory or motor disability:	• Inability to see demonstrations, board, visual aids • May not understand concepts that require vision (i.e., colors, objects, patterns) • Inability to read print materials • Inability to move about the room freely or participate in activities that require physical movement • Inability to handle manipulatives

STEP 4: Review	Teaching activity skills	Note barriers to learning and names of students to whom it applies
Compare and contrast Step 2 and Step 3, and note major areas where any students will encounter barriers to learning if you do not make any accommodations.	Must be able to pick out relevant features of censorship and bias.	• Lack of background knowledge may make it difficult for some students to understand the concept of societal censorship and bias.
	• Must be able to read independently from book • Must be able to determine relevant features in the book that are controversial and why	• Lack of decoding ability may lead to slow reading rate. • Confusion about the meaning of words may make it difficult for students to distinguish between relevant and irrelevant information.
	• Must have ability to plan, organize, sequence paper	• May miss important details and not know how to sequence their narrative

(Continued)

TABLE 11.2 LEARNS Strategy Lesson Plan Analysis (*Continued*)

STEP 4: Review	Teaching activity skills	Note barriers to learning and names of students to whom it applies
	• Must have ability to write a grammatical correct essay. • Must correctly identify main ideas and important details intended to persuade	• May have difficulty with vocabulary, spelling, and punctuation • May have trouble generating ideas • Difficulty with writing tasks that require critical thinking • May write slowly, hard to form letters, lack of fluid cursive writing ability
STEP 5: Note accommodations Determine methods, strategies, and materials that will meet students' needs.	**Area of need and name** Lack of decoding ability may lead to slow reading rate. Confusion about the meaning of words may make it difficult for students to distinguish between relevant and irrelevant information. • May miss important details and not know how to sequence their narrative • May have difficulty with vocabulary, spelling, and punctuation • May have trouble generating ideas • Difficulty with writing tasks that require critical thinking • May write slowly, hard to form letters, lack of fluid cursive writing ability	**Accommodations and names of students to whom it applies** Allow the students to use books on tape or recorded materials. Provide students access to online dictionaries with pronunciation feature. • Graphic organizers or note-taking guides can also help students to distinguish between important and irrelevant information. • Provide students access to online dictionaries with pronunciation feature. Use the COPS strategy (see Table 11.5) for editing work. • Have students use the DEFENDS writing strategy (see Table 11.5) to organize thoughts, generate opinions, and produce a well-written persuasive paper. • Allow students to utilize computers to improve written product
STEP 6: Specify individual accommodations Identify students whose needs are not met by UDL	**Student names/unmet need** Miguel (ELL)	**Accommodations** • Miguel does not read English well, so allow him to listen to

TABLE 11.2 *(Continued)*		
STEP 6: Specify individual accommodations	**Student names/unmet need**	**Accommodations**
provisions. These students may represent an instructional subgroup.		materials in both his native language and English. Also provide written material in both his native language and English.
	Elsa (CP)	• Provide student with speech-to-text software such as Dragon Naturally Speaking to eliminate difficulty with writing.

Source: Spencer, S., & Evers, R. (2009). Unpublished course material. Center for Pedagogy, Winthrop University.

perform. Ask yourself, what will students need to do and what will they need to know to complete the learning tasks successfully? Begin by thinking about how you will sequence your instruction of the academic content covered in this lesson. Next, outline the instructional plan in the order in which it will be implemented. Note the instructional activities, student grouping, materials, technology, and/or resources, including the use of instructional aides, parents, or other adults in the room that you will use. Last, specify methods for monitoring and assessing student learning.

The example provided is that of a typical lesson from a grade-level textbook in which students are expected to examine issues related to censorship and bias in literature. They will produce a persuasive essay on the book of their choosing. Conduct an analysis of this task, remembering that each of the tasks in a given activity may present a barrier to any of the students in your classroom, depending on their special needs and abilities. Make a list of the specific skills and knowledge necessary to complete the assignment. Be sure to include any subskills related to the activities. This list could become extensive, so prioritize and rank in order of importance.

Step 3: Determine the *areas* of strength and need for each student. We suggest completing a demographic worksheet for your class at the beginning of each school year (see Table 11.3 for an example); it then serves as a reference for planning lessons throughout the year. Information you might collect includes gender, age, race/ethnicity, SES status, reading and math competency levels, and special needs, such as disability, ELL status, gifted/talented, and any other information that correlates highly with learning outcomes as discussed in Chapter 2 on learner characteristics. For example, secondary teachers may want to know how students preformed in prerequisite courses to be in the present class (i.e., how well did the student do in Algebra I if enrolled in an Algebra II class now?). Reading, writing, and spelling abilities, on the other hand, are not necessarily content or grade-level specific and may be relevant to many teachers. Collect additional data as needed.

TABLE 11.3 Student Demographic Sheet

ID #	First Name	Gender	Ethnicity	Race	SES/Lunch Status	Reading Level	Math Level	Exceptionality
1	Jose	M	American	Black	Regular	Low	Low	Visually Impaired
2	Tina	F	American	Caucasian	Regular	Average	Average	
3	Morris	M	American	Caucasian	Reduced	Average	Average	
4	Miguel	M	Hispanic	Mestizo	Regular	Low	Low	ELL
5	Elsa	F	Asian	Pacific Islander	Regular	High	High	Physical disability: Cerebral Palsy
6	Kisha	F	American	Black	Free	Low	Average	LD
7	Karl	M	American	Caucasian	Regular	Average	Average	
8	Daniel	M	English	Caucasian	Regular	High	Average	ADHD
9	Kendra	F	American	Black	Reduced	Average	Low	
10	Timothy	M	American	Caucasian	Free	Low	Average	
11	Gary	M	American	Caucasian	Regular	High	High	
12	Barbra	F	American	Caucasian	Reduced	High	High	
13	David	M	American	Black	Regular	Average	Average	
14	Betsy	F	American	Caucasian	Regular	Average	High	
15	Darnell	M	American	Mixed	Reduced	Low	Average	
16	Adam	M	American	Black	Free	Low	Low	
17	Martha	F	American	Caucasian	Regular	Average	Average	
18	Norton	M	American	Native Amer	Regular	Average	Average	
19	Wanda	F	Hispanic	Mestizo	Reduced	Average	Average	
20	Lori	F	American	Caucasian	Regular	Average	High	

Source: Spencer, S., & Evers, R. (2009). Unpublished course material. Center for Pedagogy, Winthrop University.

Teachers can get demographic information from a variety of sources, including IEPs, permanent records, and interviews. Once acquired, it then becomes necessary to organize the data for analysis. The authors suggest creating a spreadsheet for this purpose, which will assist with sorting information categorically. Sorting by categories makes it easier to identify factors and note patterns that might affect both individual and group performance.

The demographic data in Table 11.3 provide an example of such a table. Look at the hypothetical class represented by this table. Can you analyze the information? To assist you with the process, ask yourself the following:

- What are the unique learner characteristics associated with each category? For example, what definitional characteristics are associated with a learning disability or low SES?
- In general, which of these characteristics has a significant ability to influence learning?
- What are the types of learning problems that might be associated with each?

Once data analysis is complete, describe the patterns you find, noting how this information will guide specific instructional decisions. It may be necessary to revise your learning goal based on the results, which is what occurs in the next step of the process.

Step 4: *Review* and compare the required tasks (Step 2) with possible areas of need (Step 3) and determine potential barriers in the lesson. In the example, one of the tasks noted in Step 2 requires students to prepare a written essay on the censorship and bias. Barriers associated with this activity might include difficulty understanding concepts, identifying important details, or taking notes. These problems may be common to many students in the class, although they occur for different reasons. The ability to see barriers to learning in terms of what they share in common makes it easier to make accommodations. Once a teacher determines areas of mismatch between what a student needs and the demands of the lesson, accommodations can be chosen. Consider the elements of instruction listed in the example, such as instructional groupings, materials, methods, student tasks, and suggest possible barriers to learning in this lesson. There are many, and all may not be listed in the example.

Step 5: *Note* methods and materials that will remove barriers to learning. It is important to understand that there are many strategies and tools available to a teacher. That is not the issue. Knowing which tool to select requires expertise rather than guesswork. Look at the barriers listed in Step 5 and suggest other methods and materials that might effectively eliminate barriers to learning. You may choose from strategies in Table 11.4, where there are a variety of methods and strategies suggested for removing the barriers associated with note taking, spelling, vocabulary. In addition to these, there are many other options. One choice might be the James Madison University Learning Toolbox. It is an excellent online resource for teachers, parents, and students to see some of the many learning strategies available. Which would you choose, and why?

Step 6: *Specify* individualized instruction for students with special needs. Considering the accommodations specified in students' IEPs is a place to start, and then plan

TABLE 11.4 Writing Strategies

Strategy	Author	Steps to Implementation
WWW WHAT = 2 HOW = 2 (A story grammar strategy)	Graham, MacArthur, Schwartz, & Page-Voth (1992)	**W**ho is the main character, and who else is in the story? **W**hen does the story take place? **W**here does the story take place? **W**hat does the main character want to do? **W**hat do the other characters want to do? **W**hat happens when the main character tries to do it? What happens with the other characters? **H**ow does the story end? **H**ow does the main character feel? How do the other characters feel?
PLAN & WRITE (expository writing)	De La Paz (1997)	**P**ay attention to the prompt. **L**ist the main ideas. **A**dd supporting ideas. **N**umber your ideas. **W**ork from your plan to develop your thesis statement. **R**emember your goals. **I**nclude transition words. **T**ry to use different kinds of sentences. **U**se Exciting, interesting $100,000 words.
TREE (strategy for composing essays)	Graham & Harris (1989)	Note **t**opic sentence. Note **r**easons. **E**xamine reasons. Note **e**nding
STOP and LIST (strategies for writing a persuasive paper)	Troia & Graham (2002)	**S**uspend judgment, record ideas about each side of the topic. **T**ake a side. **O**rganize ideas into ideas you plan to use. **P**lan more as you write, remember to use the plan developed earlier. **L**ist ideas and sequence them.

for supports beyond those recommended in case they are insufficient to reach the students' learning goals. The hypothetical class depicted in Table 11.3 identifies two students with special needs that might require extra planning. They are Miguel and Elsa. The LEARNS strategy provides examples of additional supports for them. Can you suggest supplementary supports for the remaining students with exceptionalities (i.e., Kisha and Daniel)? Review the previous steps of LEARNS, reflect on what you know about the educational needs of these students, and anticipate where they might face academic barriers before making your choices.

All students will experience difficulty learning; by utilizing the principles of Universal Design, teachers build in the necessary supports sufficient to remove barriers to learning for most students when they design instruction. However, there will always be students for whom additional supports are necessary. Often these supports come in the form of programmatic lines of writing instruction. How will you decide which is most appropriate for your students?

EFFECTIVE WRITING INSTRUCTION

Historical Perspective

The traditional model of writing instruction in American schools until the 1960s was a product-oriented approach in which mechanics and grammar are emphasized over content and process. Product-oriented writing instruction gives limited attention or time to activities requiring sustained writing. Students are often expected to learn to write in isolation, with little taught about the processes or strategies involved in writing. Students are thought to be able to learn to write by reading the work of others and in so doing develop the capability to independently create similar compositions. There is often little feedback from teachers to guide the development of the skills and knowledge necessary to communicate effectively, because that is not the goal. In product-oriented models, the grade is the goal. This model of instruction fell out of favor in the 1960s but has remerged in recent years, given the focus on student outcomes and high-stakes testing. As evidenced earlier in this chapter (e.g., NAEP, 2005, 2007), national assessment data indicate that this approach to writing instruction is not proving effective.

In stark contrast to the product model, an alternative instructional model for teaching writing began to emerge in the 1960s, when researchers suggested a move toward a process-oriented, or whole-language approach. In the early years, this method of teaching writing did not involve any direct instruction; critics characterized it as an anything-goes approach that emphasized writing as a natural process. For example, teachers did not typically make specific assignments, activities were not based on specific objectives, and criteria for judging writing effectiveness were not taught. The three-stage model adopted by most involved a linear prewriting, writing, and rewriting format. It was considered unnecessary for students to receive a lot of feedback from teachers to guide their writing (Hillocks, 1984). It is not surprising that initially this approach had only minimal impact of the quality of student writing (Hillocks, 1984).

Despite early setbacks, the process model continued to evolve. Work by teachers in the San Francisco Bay Area in the 1970s led to methodological changes in the process model that were positively received. These teachers' ideas were based on the theory that the writing process could be improved by comparing how professional writers compose to how writing is taught in schools (Gray, 2000). Because of their initial efforts, a process model of writing has emerged over the past 40 plus years that combines elements of both the process and product approaches to writing instruction. Writing is no longer viewed as simply a linear process in which thinking about writing occur in a straight line, neatly resolved by the prewrite, write, rewrite format of teaching writing. Writing is the result of a mental recursive process in which the writer relies on metacognitive ability to self-regulate goal setting and guide the effective use of procedural strategies for monitoring and modifying output. Goldstein and Carr (1996) defined writing as a process requiring multiple decisions:

> "Process writing" refers to a broad range of strategies that include pre-writing activities, such as defining audience, using a variety or resources, planning the writing, as well as drafting and revising. These activities, collectively referred to as "process-oriented instruction," approach writing as problem solving (p. 1).

This approach to writing is philosophically and practically different from the product approach to writing in that composition has a social function and takes place within a meaningful literacy context. Students learn that the challenges associated with writing can be overcome with the right strategies. In this environment, students learn to take risks and collaborate with teachers and peers to produce work and evaluate it. Despite variations in how the steps of the process are taught, researchers who espouse this approach see writing as a complex problem-solving process requiring a mix of composition, mechanics, and self-regulatory skill.

Research indicates that students who apply the writing process methods tend to score higher on written products than those who do not (Dyson & Freedman, 2003). Perhaps that is why elements of the writing-process approach to teaching writing are currently mandated by many state and local school systems as the method of choice for instruction in K–12 classrooms (Patthey-Chavez, Matsumura, & Valdes, 2004). If this method is a better candidate for improving writing than the traditional method, why do NAEP (2007) writing scores remain stagnate? Cramer (2001) suggested poor implementation may be the reason.

If you will remember, earlier in this chapter NAEP (2002, 2007) data suggested that teachers are spending very little time on writing instruction. Applebee and Langer (2006) reported that in some cases, the focus on high-stakes test may be shifting attention away from broad programs of writing instruction toward a much narrower focus on basic skills and how best to answer particular types of test questions. Why are teachers doing this? Does the desire to raise test scores alone explain the phenomenon, or is it a philosophical belief that one approach is superior to the other? Research on best practices in the teaching of writing suggests there is no single approach to writing that is uniformly effective for all students (Graham & Harris, 1994, 1997). Fortunately, there are models for teaching writing available to teachers that combine effective elements of both approaches.

RESEARCH-BASED METHODS OF WRITING INSTRUCTION

Educational reform efforts have resulted in a number of innovative methods purported to increase students' writing performance. Over the years, there have been several respected reviews of the research on writing instruction (e.g., Graham & Perin, 2007; Langer & Applebee, 1987; Levy & Ransdell, 1995; MacArthur, Graham, & Fitzgerald, 2006; Smagorinsky, 2006). Perhaps one of the most powerful to date is that of Graham and Perin (2007). A meta-analysis of 142 scientific studies identifies 11 effective elements of writing instruction. Listed in order from most to least effective, they are as follows:

1. Teach writing strategies for planning, revising, and/or editing.
2. Teach rule-governed or intuitive strategies for summarizing text.
3. Teach students how to work collaboratively to plan, draft, revise, and edit their compositions.
4. State writing goals that are attainable and specific.
5. Utilize computers and word processors for writing assignments.
6. Teach students how to construct complex sentences by combining two or more basic sentences into one single sentence.
7. Teachers utilize prewriting activities designed to help generate or organize ideas.
8. Teachers employ the use of inquiry activities that require students to set goals and learn how to analyze concrete and observational data for the purpose of developing ideas and content.
9. Teaching instruction is interwoven into a number of writing activities that emphasize writing for real readers, self-reflective writing, and recursive writing.
10. Students learn to analyze good models of writing for the purpose of emulating them in their own writing.
11. Teachers teach students to view writing as a tool for learning content.

Individually, these elements do not constitute a full writing curriculum; however, when combined they can improve writing results for students, including those who are at risk due to limited English proficiency, low income, minority status, and those with disabilities (Graham & Perin, 2007). There are a number of models for teaching writing that incorporate these elements. Among the most widely adopted are the Self-Regulated Strategy Development (SRSD) model (Graham & Harris, 1994, 1997), the Strategic Instruction Model (SIM) (Deshler & Schumaker, 1988), the Early Literacy Project (ELP) (Englert et al., 1995; Englert & Mariage, 2003), and the Optimal Learning Environment (OLE) model developed by Ruiz (1995a, 1995b).

All of these models combine both the process and procedual approaches to writing as discussed earlier. These research-based approaches teach students a basic framework for planning, writing, and revising. They teach writing as a process of steps recursive in nature that provide guidelines by which to analyze material learned in the classroom for the purpose of writing personal narratives, persuasive essays, and in other genres. Each provides students with meaningful feedback that they can use to enhance self-regulatory ability. Together these components have proven successful in improving students' written work and have had a positive effect on students' self-efficacious beliefs regarding their ability to write.

Specific Methods

The Self-Regulated Strategy Development (SRSD) model (Graham & Harris, 1994, 1997; Harris & Graham, 2005), developed by Steve Graham and Karen Harris at the University of Maryland, can be used to teach spelling, reading, math, and writing. Writing, however, is perhaps the area for which it is best known. The SRSD model explicitly teaches combinations of mnemonic strategies to remind students of the steps in the writing process, prompting them to plan and reflect while composing. Strategies for writing simple opinion essays, stories, and narratives are among the family of writing strategies in the model, which facilitates planning, generating, framing, and revising text (see Table 11.4).

The SRSD model provides explicit instruction on writing, self-regulation, and content knowledge. Instruction is interactive, self-paced, and collaborative with feedback tailored to meet the needs and ablities of the individual student. There are six stages in SRSD instruction (Harris & Graham, 1992):

1. The class works together to develop and activate background knowledge.
2. The class discusses the strategy, including benefits and expectations.
3. The teacher models the strategy.
4. The students memorize the strategy.
5. The teacher and students practice using the strategy collaboratively. At this time, the teacher provides corrective feedback to promote self-regulation.
6. The students use the strategy independently while the teacher monitors and provides supportive feedback as needed.

These six instructional stages are taught along with four general strategies that promote self-regulation. The four are goal setting, self-instruction (e.g., talking-aloud), self-monitoring, and self-reinforcement. The SRSD technique directs students to utilize self-directed prompts that require them to (a) consider their audience and reasons for writing, (b) develop a plan for what they intend to say using strategies to generate or organize writing notes, (c) evaluate possible content by considering its impact on the reader, and (d) continue the process of content generation and planning during the act of writing. The fact that the self-regulatory component of the model is taught explicitly and not embedded in cognitive strategy instruction is what sets it apart from other programmatic lines of strategy instruction.

A large body of research that speaks to the effectiveness of the SRSD model has amassed over the years (e.g., Barry & Moore, 2004; Chalk, Hagan-Burke & Burke, 2005; Graham, 2006; Page-Voth & Graham, 1999; Troia & Graham, 2002). A meta-analysis of 18 research studies (Graham & Harris, 2003) found the SRSD model effective for improving the writing abililty of students with learning disabilities as well as low-, average-, and high-achieving students at both the elementary and middle school levels. In one study by De La Paz, Owen, Harris, and Graham (2000), students were taught the PLAN and WRITE expository writing strategies though the six stages cited above. Strategy use in this study proved more helpful than a rating scale and sample essay alone in preparing students for a state writing assessment. Similar results were noted by De La Paz (2001) for the PLAN and WRITE strategies when used with students who had learning disabilites and attention-deficit disorder. As with the previous study, students increased their use of plans for writing, increased essay length, and produced more quality content and better structured writing.

For additional information and an online interactive tutorial on SRSD, go to the Vanderbilt University IRIS Center home page (http://iris.peabody.vanderbilt.edu/pow/chalcycle.htm), select Resources, and then click on the Star Legacy Module labeled *Using Learning Strategies: Instruction to Enhance Learning*. The module labeled *Improving Writing Performance: A Stratgegy for Writing Expository Essays*, located under the heading Differentiated Instruction, also provides a tutorial on all stages of the model, along with activities and examples.

Since as early as 1988, the Strategic Instruction Model (SIM) of Deshler and Schumaker at the University of Kansas has sought to improve the academic and social outcomes of middle and high school students with learning disabilities. The scope of their research widened when later research indicated that many students, not just those with learning disabilities, were experiencing difficulty transitioning to upper grades. Their findings indicate that students' inabilities to learn academic content in some cases could be attributed to basic skills deficits. They also found that teachers did not as a rule address these deficiencies, focusing instead on teaching content (e.g., science, history, literature). It is not surprising, therefore, that many teachers were finding it difficult to teach subject matter.

The SIM framework for improving adolescent literacy is explained as existing along a continuum of literacy instruction (CLC) that provides increasing support to students at each of five levels (Deshler, Schumaker, & Woodruff, 2004). The *first level* is content enhancement. At this level, recognizing that mastery of content is critical for all students; teachers learn routines (e.g., lesson and unit organizers) for making the curriculum accessible to all students regardless of their literacy level.

At the *second level*, teachers are encouraged to routinely embed learning strategies instruction into all classes using large group instruction. At the *third level*, teachers are asked to provide students with more intensive and explicit strategy instruction as needed to support basic skills, such as decoding, word recognition, fluency, vocabulary, and comprehension. Beginning at the *fourth level* students who are lagging behind their peers receive intensive basic skills instruction. This may require collaboration with a literacy coach, special educator, or other professional. Last, the *fifth level* of instruction provides the most support. Students on this level receive individualized therapeutic interventions to help them learn the content. Instruction may take the form of strategic tutoring before, during, or after school.

In all, there are two basic types of interventions in the SIM framework. The first is a series of teacher-focused interventions directed at how teachers plan, adapt, and deliver content. Content-enhancement teaching routines, as specified in the first level of the CLC, guide planning and learning; direct exploration of text, topics, and details; how to teach concepts; and how to increase student performance. Content-enrichment routines are designed to help teachers reach an academically diverse group of students while maintaining the integrity of the content. They are appropriate for planning instruction in both general and special education settings. The second type of interventions in the SIM framework are student-focused interventions that provide students with strategies to learn content. As indicated by the CLC, strategies can either be taught independently or embedded into core content, depending on the level of support needed by the individual student. In all, there are over 30 learning strategies in SIM designed to improve students' skills and performance in the areas of reading, expressive writing, study skills and remembering, test taking, motivation, and interacting with others.

TEACHING LEARNING STRATEGIES

A strategy refers to a plan that specifies the sequence of actions needed to solve a given problem effectively (Ellis & Lenz, 1996, p. 24). Teaching learning strategies effectively involves following a multistep process:

1. Begin by *securing a commitment* to using learning strategies. To do this the teacher explains the benefits of learning strategies to the students. Due to faulty attributions,

many students do not realize that ineffective or inefficient strategy use underlies their academic difficulties.

2. *Determine where students are having difficulty* with the curriculum. Formal and informal assessment data discussed earlier in this chapter can be used for this purpose. Based on the analysis of the student's classroom performance, identify those areas that most need attention. It is helpful to prioritize problems according to the impact on learning.

3. *Select the learning strategy most appropriate for the job.* Table 11.5 provides examples of SIM learning strategies that researchers and teachers have used successfully to improve student writing performance.

4. *Provide a rationale* for why they should learn the strategy. Introduce the strategy to the students by reviewing previously mastered strategies and relate them to the new content to be learned. For example, "Yesterday, you learned how to use the five W's strategy. It helped you identify the characters, plot, and setting in the book *Moby-Dick*. Today, we will add another learning strategy. An attribute web is a strategy that will enable you to successfully complete the book report that is due Friday by helping you to identify important details in the story." This is a necessary step in securing participation and ensuring the information is retained in a meaningful way.

5. *Describe the strategy and model how to use it* by providing an example with which they are already familiar to limit processing demands. Model the strategy, checking off each step as you think aloud, talking the students through how you as an expert learner would use each of the steps in the strategy (e.g., "What do I do first?).

6. Provide opportunities for *guided practice*. As students work, the teacher provides feedback, prompts, and guidance. As they become more proficient, support is gradually faded.

7. During *independent practice*, the teacher continues to monitor student performance, conducts an error analysis when needed, and provides feedback and correction. The teacher can reteach or offer additional practice on any step of the strategy.

8. Last, *teach for generalization* by indicating how student success is directly related to using the correct strategy for the job. Point out where the strategy can be used in other academic situations with similar task demands. For example, an attribute web could also be helpful in writing book reports in both history and science class.

Although SIM has been taught with some success for years in schools nationally, it has failed to consistently ensure acquisition and generalization across settings (Spencer & Logan, 2005). You will remember from our discussions on metacognition in Chapter 6, that if there are to be any long-term benefits, cognitive strategies instruction depends at least in part on training at the metacognitive level as well as at the cognitive level (e.g., Flavell, 1979; Spencer & Logan, 2005). The lack of an explicitly taught metacognitive component, such as the one in the SRSD model, may be problematic. This component can, however, be added and/or supported by the use of metacognitive strategies (e.g., SODA).

The Early Literacy Project (ELP; Englert, Raphael, & Mariage, 1994 was a 4-year study that sought to improve the reading and writing literacy skills of young students

TABLE 11.5 Strategic Instruction Model Writing Strategies

Strategy	Author	Steps to Implementation
DEFENDS (strategy for writing positions)	Ellis & Lenz (1987)	**D**ecide on exact position. **E**xamine the reasons for the position. **F**orm a list of points that explain each reason. **E**xpose position in first sentence. **N**ote each reason and supporting points. **D**rive home the position in the last sentence. **S**earch for errors and correct.
PLEASE (strategy for writing a paragraph)	Welch (1992)	**P**ick a topic. **L**ist your ideas about the topic. **E**valuate your list. **A**ctivate the paragraph with a topic sentence. **S**upply supporting sentences. **E**nd with a concluding sentence, and **E**valuate your work.
COPS (error-monitoring strategy)	Schumaker, Nolan, & Deshler (1985)	**C**apitalization **O**verall appearance **P**unctuation **S**pelling
WRITER	Schumaker, Nolan, & Deshler (1985)	**W**rite on every other line, using PENS. **R**ead your paper for meaning. **I**nterrogate yourself, using COPS questions. **T**ake the paper to someone for help. **E**xecute a final copy. **R**eread your paper.

with mild impairments (e.g., learning disabilities, mental impairments, and emotional impairments). These students struggle with developing written literacy due to deficits in metacognitive knowledge and tend not to plan, monitor, or revise their written work (e.g., Englert et al., 1991; Graham & Harris, 2003; Williams, 2003). Difficulty generating ideas, words, and sentences serves to exacerbate their problems. It is no surprise these students' papers tend to be substantively different from those of their nondisabled peers in that they are shorter, poorly organized, and/or mechanically and grammatically challenged (Gersten & Baker, 2001; Graham, 2006).

ELP was among the first attempts to study the effects of a sociocultural learning theory curriculum on improving literacy outcome for this population. There are four principles underling the implementation and design of the ELP curriculum: (1) Literacy should be embedded within meaningful and authentic activities; (2) promote self-regulated learning; (3) instruction should be responsive to the needs, capabilities, and interests of the student; and (4) instruction should promote the social nature of learning by collaboratively constructing communities of learners (Englert & Mariage, 2005).

From within this framework, reading and writing skills are theorized as emerging from within the collaborative context of group meetings, employing a multitude of teaching methods to facilitate the development of literacy skills. The model included a variety of oral and written literacy activities, each serving a distinct purpose. Some of these activities include thematic units, choral reading, undisturbed silent reading, sharing chair, morning message, story response, journal writing, and author's center.

The ELP curriculum contains methods proven effective for teaching students with learning disabilities how to self-regulate the writing process. Using what Englert and colleagues (1988) call the POWER strategy, students have shown that they can learn to Plan, Organize, Write, Edit, and Revise their written work (Englert et al, 1988). The POWER strategy specifies hierarchical steps to follow when creating text. The planning stage prompts students to ask themselves, "What is my topic? Who am I writing for? And what do I already know about my topic?" The second step directs students to select and utilize pattern guides to help them organize their ideas. Patterns might include story guides for identifying the elements who, what, when, where, and why; compare/contrast guides for collecting information on a given topic; explanation guides for completing the writing process; and problem solution guides for identifying the problem, the cause of the problem, and the solution to the problem. The third step, writing, requires students to use information from the planning and organization steps to complete a first draft. Editing is the fourth step, and here students learn to self-evaluate and peer edit their drafts. Last, in the fifth step, revising, students incorporate edits and make changes or other improvements as they complete the writing assignment.

In 2004, Singer and Bashir altered POWER in an effort to help students with language learning disabilities who continued to struggle despite the support provided by the strategy. The revised strategy, EmPOWER, provides more linguistic structure by adding explicit step-by-step conversational prompts to replace the more abbreviated prompts of the original strategy. They also divided the plan step into two steps, Empower and mPLAN, in an effort to lessen the processing load and more clearly delineate the interdependent relationship of this component to the next. Their research suggests that these modifications can help to move students more effectively through the steps of the strategy, thus improving writing outcomes.

Englert and her colleagues are also interested in investigating the effects of varying support methodologies as means of improving the performance of low-achieving students. Their research (e.g., Englert, Manalo, & Zhao, 2004; Englert, Zhao, Dunsmore, Collins, & Wolbers, 2007; Englert, Wu, & Zhao, 2005) into the potential of Web-based programs to increase the writing performance of students with disabilities has yielded promising results. In a recent study (Englert, Zhao, Dunsmore,

Collins, & Wolbers, 2007), a control group and an experimental group of students were asked to plan and organize their ideas in order to write expository papers on topics of their choosing. Students in the experimental group used TELE-Web software that prompted them on how to frame their introductions based on their story maps, how to elaborate on paragraphs and details, and how to incorporate conclusions into the proper locations.

The students in the Web-based scaffolding condition produced lengthier pieces and received significantly higher ratings on traits associated with writing quality. However, the most significant improvement occurred in terms of the experimental students' abilities to produce topic sentences and to generate more topically coherent pieces overall. Their research suggests that a Web-based environment can be used successfully to scaffold aspects of the students' thinking processes and provide the necessary structure to write well, and it may in fact do so more effectively than a traditional paper-and-pencil format.

The Optimal Learning Environment (OLE) (Ruiz, 1995a, 1995b) program for English language learners (ELLs), bilingual students, and Spanish-speaking students shares much with the Early Literacy Project in that both models embrace sociocultural learning theory, a writing-as-a-process philosophy, and thematic units of instruction. In addition, each model advocates delivering instruction that is contextualized, meaningful, and purposeful to develop literacy skills. For Spanish-speaking students with learning disabilities, these instructional practices are proving to be particularly germane. Academic problems attributed to the typically decontextualized nature of the bilingual educational experience have led to low motivation and higher dropout rates among this population (CREDE, 2003; Ruiz, 1999).

The English immersion model, which is the most commonly used model of bilingual education in our nation's schools, does not provide students with native language learning opportunities. This is problematic, because without native language literacy learning, English can be more difficult. It seems the basic skills of the old language serve as a contextual bridge to the new language by making reading and writing meaningful and purposeful. Ruiz's OLE model recognizes this fundamental need, providing instruction and practice in the students' native language until the teacher feels they are ready for the transition to English.

The work of Ruiz and others has led to a set of five working principles for teaching Spanish-speaking and bilingual students with special needs how to write (e.g., Baca & Cervantes, 1998; Gallimore et. al., 1989; Graves, et al., 2000; Ruiz & Figueroa, 1995; Ruiz, Figueroa, Rueda, & Beaumont, 1992). These practices include the elements of both the ELP and OLE programs, as well as those of the most prestigious center for research in second language and literacy acquisition, the Center for Research on Education, Diversity, and Excellence (CREDE, 2003). The five principles are as follows:

Principle 1: Connect students' background knowledge and personal experiences with literacy lessons. Contextualize teaching and curriculum by tying instruction to home and community.

Principle 2: Foster the use of students' primary language in literacy lessons. Allow students to exercise a choice of language with text and during literacy events.

Principle 3: Create opportunities for students to meaningfully and authentically apply their developing oral language and literacy skills. Undoubtedly, basic literacy skills and subskills instruction, such as phonemic awareness, phonics, punctuation, grammar, and comprehension, are important components of any writing program. However, the research in second and foreign language education overwhelmingly establishes the link between meaning-driven, communicative instruction and second language and literacy development (CREDE, 2003; Ruiz, 1999). Language literacy development should be fostered through use and through purposive conversation between teacher and students, rather than relying solely on drills and decontextualized rules (CREDE, 2003).

Principle 4: Foster increased levels of interaction (oral language, reading, and writing) among students and teachers. Provide authentic reasons for students to collaborate on literacy and other academic tasks to improve ELL students' productive and receptive language skills (Gersten & Baker, 2003).

Principle 5: Engage students through dialogue, especially instructional conversation. ELL programs place a great deal of emphasis on developing communication competence. The OLE program utilizes interactive journaling for this purpose. This instructional strategy enacts the four principles of effective instruction, in that when writing in their interactive journals, students communicate with either teachers or peers on the topic of their choice and receive written responses to their journal entries. They are therefore able to bring their life experiences to the literacy event (Principle 1) to use the language of their choice (Principle 2), to exchange messages with real communicative intent with a real audience, and (Principle 3) to facilitate learning through collaborative dialogue with teacher and peers for authentic purposes (Principles 4 and 5).

In addition to the interactive journaling method, the OLE curriculum contains several strategies to facilitate the development of written literacy skills:

1. Writers workshop teaches writing as a process in the context of an authentic activity. Students learn that before producing each written product they must follow the steps of planning, writing a draft, and editing.
2. Patterned writing strategies have students read and copy key phrases.
3. Teachers provide wordless books, and students create the text.
4. Shared reading activities with predictable text lead to conversations with teachers and peers on literature from read-alouds.
5. Utilize "drop everything and read" time (DEAR) to encourage the development reading and writing literacy skills.

Summary

Students who struggle with writing share many of the same characteristics. Poor planning and revising of their work results in work that is poorly organized and shorter and typically contains irrelevant details and more mechanical errors and is weaker overall when compared to their more accomplished peers (Troia, 2005). These types of difficulties with written expression are attributable to an inability to execute and regulate the cognitive and metacognitive processes underlying writing (e.g., Graham, 2006; Graham & Harris

1997). Contrary to what many believe, simply having a plethora of writing strategies on hand is not as important as knowing when and how to use them. In short, the lack of regulatory ability can cause these students to experience more writing and motivational issues than do their peers (Pajares, 2003).

As noted, writing instruction for students with and without writing problems identify many of the same critical components of effective instruction and are congruent with the principles of effective instruction as noted in the bilingual education literature (e.g., Baker, Gersten, & Graham, 2003; Gersten & Baker, 2001; Gleason & Isaacson; 2001; Troia, 2005). While it is indeed necessary to identify research-validated instructional methods, it is but the first step. Sadly, research suggests that teachers implement few if any of them to help students who are struggling with basic writing skills (e.g., Graham & Harris, 2003). Do you know why? A review of Chapter 6 on metacognition will provide the answer to this vexing question.

References

American Speech-Language Association. (2008). *Speech and language disorders.* Retrieved September 7, 2008, from http://www.asha.org/public/speech/disorders/ChildSandL.htm

Anderson, L. W., & Krathwohl, J. (2001). *A taxonomy for learning, teaching, and assessing: A revision of Bloom's Taxonomy of educational objectives.* New York: Longman.

Applebee, A. N., & Langer, J. A. (2006). *The state of writing instruction in America's schools: What existing data tell us.* Albany: Center on English Learning & Achievement, State University of New York at Albany. Retrieved September 7, 2008, from http://www.albany.edu/aire/news/State%20of%20Writing%20Instruction.pdf

August, D., & Shanahan, T. (Eds.). (2006). *Developing literacy in second-language learners: Report of the National Literacy Panel on Language-Minority Children and Youth.* Mahwah, NJ: Lawrence Erlbaum Associates. Retrieved from http://www.cal.org/natl-lit-panel/reports/Executive_Summary.pdf

Baca, L., & Cervantes, H. (1998). *The bilingual special education interface* (3rd ed.). Upper Saddle River, NJ: Prentice Hall.

Baker, S., Gersten, R., & Graham, S. (2003). Teaching expressive writing to students with learning disabilities: Research-based applications and examples. *Journal of Learning Disabilities, 36,* 109–123.

Barry, L. M., & Moore, W. E. (2004). Students with specific learning disabilities can pass state competency exams: Systematic strategy instruction makes a difference. *Preventing School Failure, 48*(3), 10–15.

Bloom, B., Englehart, M., Furst, E., Hill, W., & Krathwohl, D. (1956). *Taxonomy of educational objectives: The classification of educational goals. Handbook I: Cognitive domain.* New York, Toronto: Longmans, Green.

Brady, R. C. (2003). *Can failing schools be fixed?* Washington, DC: Thomas B. Fordham Foundation. Retrieved September 3, 2005, from http://www.edexcellence.net/institute/publication/publication.cfm?id=2

Brookhart, S. M. (1999). The art and science of classroom assessment: The missing part of pedagogy. *ASHE-ERIC Higher Education Report, 27*(1). Washington, DC: The George Washington University, Graduate School of Education and Human Development.

Chalk, J. C., Hagan-Burke, S., & Burke, M. D. (2005). Self-regulated strategy development and the writing process for high school students with learning disabilities. *Learning Disability Quarterly, 28,* 75–87.

Cohen, L. G., & Spenciner, L. J. (2007). *Assessment of children and youth with special needs.* Boston: Allyn & Bacon.

Cramer, R. L. (2001). *Creative power: The nature and nurture of children's writing.* Boston: Addison-Wesley, Longman.

CREDE (Center for Research on Education, Diversity, and Excellence). (2003). Santa Cruz, California. Retrieved from www://crede.ucsc.edu

De La Paz, S. (1997). Strategy instruction in planning: Teaching students with learning and writing disabilities to compose narrative and expository essays. *Learning Disability Quarterly, 20,* 227–248.

De La Paz, S., Owen, B., Harris, K., & Graham, S. (2000). Riding Elvis's motorcycle: Using self-regulated strategy development to PLAN and WRITE for a state writing exam. *Learning Disabilities Research and Practice, 15*(2), 101–109.

De La Paz, S., & Graham, S. (2002). Explicitly teaching strategies, skills, and knowledge: Writing instruction in middle school classrooms. *Journal of Educational Psychology, 94,* 687–698.

Deshler, D. D., & Schumaker, J. B. (1988). An instructional model for teaching students how to learn. In J. L. Graden, J. E. Zins, & M. J. Curtis (Eds.), *Alternative educational delivery systems: Enhancing instructional options for all students* (pp. 391–411). Washington, DC: National Association of School Psychologists.

Deshler, D. D., Schumaker, J. B., & Woodruff, S. (2004). Improving literacy skills of at-risk adolescents. In D. Strickland & D. Alvermann (Eds.), *Bridging the literacy achievement gap, Grades 4–12.* New York: Teachers College Press.

Dyson, A. H., & Freedman, S. W. (1991). Writing. In J. Flood, J. Jensen, D. Lapp, & J. Squire (Eds.), *Handbook of research on teaching the English language arts* (pp. 754–775). New York: Macmillan.

Ellis, E. S., & Lenz, B. K. (1987). *Features of good learning strategies.* Retrieved November 6, 2008, from http://www.ldonline.org/ld_indepth/teaching_techniques/ellis_strategy features.html

Englert, C. S., Zhao, Y., Dunsmore, K., Collings, N. Y., Wolbers, K. (2007). Scaffolding the writing of students with disabilities through procedural facilitation: Using an Internet-based technology to improve performance. *Learning Disability Quarterly, 30,* 9–29.

Englert, C. S., Garmon, A., Mariage, T., Rozendal, M., Tarrant, K., & Urba, J. (1995). The early literacy project: Connecting across the literacy curriculum. *Learning Disabilities Quarterly, 18,* 253–277.

Englert, C. S., Manalo, M., & Zhao, Y. (2004). I can do it better on the computer: The effects of technology-enabled scaffolding on young writers' composition. *Journal of Special Education Technology, 19*(1), 5–21.

Englert, C. S., & Mariage, T. V. (2003). Shared understandings: Structuring the writing process through dialogue. In D. Carine & E. Kameenui (Eds.), *Higher order thinking* (pp. 107–136). Austin, TX: Pro-Ed.

Englert, C. S., & Mariage, T. V. (2005). The sociocultural model in special education interventions: Apprenticing students in higher order thinking. In H. L. Swanson, K.R. Harris, & S. Graham, (Eds.), *The handbook of learning disabilities* (pp. 450–467). New York: Guilford Press.

Englert, C., Raphael, T., Anderson, L., Anthony, H., Steven, D., & Fear, K. (1991). Making writing and self-talk visible: Cognitive strategy instruction writing in regular and special education classrooms. *American Educational Research Journal, 28,* 337–373.

Englert, C., Raphael, L., Fear, K., & Anderson, L. (1988). Students' metacognitive knowledge about how to write informational texts. *Learning Disability Quarterly, 11,* 18–46.

Englert, C. S., Raphael, T. E., & Mariage, T. V. (1994). Developing a school-based discourse for literacy learning: A principled search for understanding. *Learning Disability Quarterly, 17,* 2–32.

Englert, C. S., Wu, X., & Zhao, Y. (2005). Cognitive tools for writing: Scaffolding the performance of students through technology. *Learning Disabilities Research and Practice, 20,* 184–198.

Flavell, J. H. (1979). Metacognition and cognitive monitoring: A new area of cognitive–developmental inquiry. *American Psychologist, 34,* 906–911.

Gallimore, R., Tharp, R., & Rueda, R. (1989). *The social context of cognitive functioning in the lives of mildly handicapped persons.* London: Falmer Press.

Gersten, R., & Baker, S. (2001). Teaching expressive writing to students with learning disabilities: A meta-analysis. *Elementary School Journal, 101*(3), 251–272.

Gersten, R., & Baker, S. K. (2003). English-language learners with learning disabilities. In S. Graham (Ed.), *Handbook of learning disabilities* (pp. 94–109). New York: Guilford Press.

Gleason, M. M., & Isaacson, S. (2001). Using the new basals to teach the writing process:

Modification for students with learning problems. *Reading & Writing Quarterly, 17,* 75–92.

Goldstein, A., & Carr, P. G. (1996, April). *Can students benefit from process writing? NAEP facts, 1*(3). Washington, DC: National Center for Educational Statistics. Retrieved September 28, 2008, from http://nces.ed.gov/pubs96/web/96845.asp

Graham, S. (2006). Strategy instruction and the teaching of writing: A meta-analysis. In C. A. MacArthur, S. Graham, & J. Fitzgerald (Eds.), *Handbook of writing research* (pp. 187–207). New York: Guilford Press.

Graham, S. (2006). Writing. In P. A. Alexander & P. H. Winne (Eds.), *Handbook of educational psychology* (pp. 457–478). Mahwah, NJ: Lawrence Erlbaum Associates.

Graham, S., & Harris, K. R. (1989). Improving learning disabled students' skills at composing essays: Self-instructional strategy training. *Exceptional Children, 56,* 201–214.

Graham, S., & Harris, K. R. (1994). The effects of whole language on children's writing: A review of literature. *Educational Psychologist, 29,* 187–192.

Graham, S., & Harris, K. R. (1997). It can be taught, but it does not develop naturally: Myths and realities in writing instruction. *School Psychology Review, 26,* 414–424.

Graham, S., & Harris, K. R. (2003). Students with learning disabilities and the process of writing: A meta-analysis of SRSD studies. In H.L. Swanson, K. R. Harris, & S. Graham (Eds.), *Handbook of learning disabilities* (pp. 323–344). New York: Guilford Press.

Graham, S., Harris, K. R., & Macarthur, C. (2006). Explicitly teaching struggling writers: Strategies for mastering the writing process. *Intervention in School & Clinic, 41*(5), 290. Retrieved September 7, 2008, from Questia database: http://www.questia.com/PM.qst?a=o&d=5015045196

Graham, S., MacArthur, C., Schwartz, S., & Page-Voth, V. (1992). Improving the compositions of students with learning disabilities using a strategy involving product and process goal setting. *Exceptional Children, 58,* 322–334.

Graham, S., & Perin, D. (2007). *Writing next: Effective strategies to improve writing of adolescents in middle and high schools* (Carnegie Corporation Report). Washington, DC: Alliance for Excellent Education. Retrieved November 14, 2008, from http://www.all4ed.org/publications/WritingNext/WritingNext.pdf

Graves, A., Valles, E., & Prodor, C. (2000). The effects of optimal learning environment (OLE) vs. traditional instruction on compositions of bilingual students with learning disabilities. *Learning Disabilities Research & Practice, 15,* 1–9.

Gray, J. (2000). *Teachers at the center: A memoir of the early years of the National Writing Project.* Berkley, CA: National Writing Project. Retrieved September 27, 2008, from http://www.eric.ed.gov/ERICWebPortal/custom/portlets/recordDetails/detailmini.jsp?_nfpb=true&_&ERICExtSearch_SearchValue_0=ED461882&ERICExtSearch_SearchType_0=no&accno=ED461882

Hammill, D. D., & Larsen, S. C. (1996). *Test of written language* (3rd ed.). Austin, TX: Pro-Ed.

Harris, K. R., & Graham, S. (1992). Self-regulated strategy development: A part of the writing process. In M. Pressley, K. Harris, & J. Guthrie (Eds.), *Promoting academic competence and literacy in schools.* San Diego: Academic Press.

Harris, K. R., & Graham, S. (2005). *Writing better: Teaching writing processes and self-regulation to students with learning problems.* Baltimore: Paul H. Brookes.

Hooper, S., Wakely, M., de Kruif, R., & Schwartz, C. (2006). Aptitude-treatment interactions revisited: Effect of metacognitive intervention on subtypes of written expression in elementary school students. *Developmental Neuropsychology, 39,* 217–242.

Hillocks, G. (1984). What works in teaching composition: A meta-analysis of experimental treatment studies. *American Journal of Education, 93*(1), 133–170.

Hresko, W. P., Herron, S., & Peak, P. (1996). *Test of Early Writing,* second edition. Austin, TX: Pro-Ed.

Kuhl, P. K. (2008). Linking infant speech perception to language acquisition: Phonetic learning predicts language growth. In P. McCardle, J. Colombo, & L. Freund (Eds.), *Infant pathways to language: Methods, models, and research directions.* Mahwah, NJ: Lawrence Erlbaum Associates.

Kuhl, P. K., Conboy, B. T., Padden, D., Nelson, T., & Pruitt, J. (2005). Early speech perception and later language development: Implications for the "critical period." *Language Learning and Development*, 1, 237–264.

Lennox, C., & Siegel, L. S. (1996). The development of phonological rules and visual strategies in average and poor spellers. *Journal of Experimental Child Psychology*, 62, 60–83.

Lennox, C., & Siegel, L. S. (1998). Phonological and orthographic processes in good and poor spellers. In C. Hume & R. M. Joshi (Eds.), *Reading and spelling development and disorders* (pp. 395–404). Mahwah, NJ: Lawrence Erlbaum Associates. Retrieved on September 1, 2007, from Questia database: http://www.questia.com/PM.qst?a=o&d=113675485

Levy, C. M. & Ransdell, S. (1995). Is writing as difficult as it seems? *Memory & Cognition, 23*, 767–779.

MacArthur, C. A., Graham, S., & Fitzgerald, J. (Eds.). (2006). *Handbook of writing research*. New York: Guilford Press. Retrieved September 7, 2008, from Questia database: http://www.questia.com/PM.qst?a=o&d=113675485

McGhee, R., Bryant, B., Larsen, S., & Rivera, D. M. (1995). *Test of written expression*. Austin, TX: Pro-Ed.

National Assessment of Educational Progress. (2002, 2003, 2005, 2007). *The nation's report card: Writing 2007. National assessment of educational progress at grades 8 and 12*. Washington, DC: U.S. Department of Education, National Center for Education Statistics. Retrieved on September 1, 2008, from http://nces.ed.gov/nationsreportcard/pdf/main2007/2008468_1.pdf

Page-Voth, V., & Graham, S. (1999). Effects of goal setting and strategy use on the writing performance and self-efficacy of students with writing and learning problems. *Journal of Educational Psychology*, 91, 230–240.

Pajares, F. (2003). Self-efficacy beliefs, motivation, and achievement in writing: A review of the literature. *Reading and Writing Quarterly, 19*, 139–158.

Patthey-Chavez, G. G, Matsumura, L. C., & Valdes, R. (2004). Investigating the process approach to writing instruction in urban middle schools. *Journal of Adolescent and Adult Literacy*, 47(6), 642–476.

Pierangelo, R., & Giuliani, G. (2006). *The special educator's comprehensive guide to 301 diagnostic tests: Revised and expanded edition*. San Francisco: Jossey-Bass.

Ruiz, N. T., Figueroa, R. A., Rueda, R., & Beaumont, C. (1992). History and status of bilingual students in special education. In R. Padilla & A. Benavides (Eds.), *Critical perspectives in bilingual education* (pp. 349–380). Tempe, AZ: Bilingual Press.

Ruiz, N. T. (1995a). The social construction of ability and disability I: Profile types of Latino children identified as language learning disabled. *Journal of Learning Disabilities, 28*, 476–490.

Ruiz, N. T. (1995b). The social construction of ability and disability II: Optimal and at-risk lessons in a bilingual special education classroom. *Journal of Learning Disabilities, 28*, 491–502.

Ruiz, N. T., & Figueroa, R. A. (1995). Learning-handicapped classrooms with Latino students: The optimal learning environment (OLE) project. *Education and Urban Society, 27*, 463–483.

Ruiz, N. T. (1999). Effective literacy instruction for Latino students receiving special education services. *Bilingual Review, 161–164*. Retrieved November 23, 2008, from Questia database: http://www.questia.com/PM.qst?a=o&d=5001895873

Salvia, J., & Ysseldyke, J. E. (2007). *Assessment in special and inclusive education* (10th ed.). Boston: Houghton Mifflin.

Schumaker, J. D., Nolan, S. M. & Deshler, D. D. (1985). *The error monitoring strategy*. Lawrence: Center for Research on Learning, University of Kansas.

Singer, B. D., & Bashir, A. S. (2004). EmPOWER: A strategy for teaching students with language learning disabilities how to write expository text. In E. R. Silliman, R. Elaine, & L. C. Wilkinson (Eds.), *Language and literacy learning in schools* (pp. 239–272). New York: Guilford Press.

Spencer, S. S., & Logan, K. R. (2005). Improving students with learning disabilities ability to acquire and generalize a vocabulary learning strategy. *Learning Disabilities: A Multidisciplinary Journal, 13*, 87–94.

Tachibana, G. (2008). "Nation's Report Card" shows modest improvement in students' writing scores. Retrieved from http://www.nwp.org/cs/public/print/resource/2557

Tallal, P. (2008). *Neuroscience, phonology, and reading: The oral to written language continuum.* Retrieved October 9, 2008, from Rutgers University, Children of the Code Web site: http://www.childrenofthecode.org/interviews/tallal.htm

Taylor, R. (2006) *Assessment of exceptional students: Educational and psychological procedures.* Upper Saddle River, NJ: Allyn & Bacon/Pearson Education.

Troia, G. A., & Graham, S. (2002). The effectiveness of a highly explicit, teacher-directed strategy instruction routine: Changing the writing performance of students with learning disabilities. *Journal of Learning Disabilities, 35,* 290–305.

Troia, G. A. (2002). Teaching writing strategies to children with disabilities: Setting generalization as the goal. *Exceptionality, 10,* 249–269.

Troia, G. A. (2005). Responsiveness to intervention roles for speech language pathologists in the prevention and identification of learning disabilities. *Topics in Language Disorders, 25*(2), 106–119.

Van den Bergh, H., & Rijlaarsdam, G. (2001). Changes in cognitive activities during the writing process and relationships with text quality. *Educational Psychology, 21*(4), 373–385.

Venn, J. J. (2007) *Assessing students with special needs* (4th ed.). Upper Saddle River, NJ: Merrill/Pearson Education.

Warden, M. R., & Hutchinson, T. A. (1992). *Writing process test.* Chicago: Riverside.

Welch, M. (1992). The PLEASE strategy: A metacognitive learning strategy for improving the paragraph writing of students with mild learning disabilities. *Learning Disabilities Quarterly, 15,* 119–128.

Wilkinson, G. S., & Robinson, G. J. (2006). *Wide Range Achievement Test 4.* Richmond Hill, Onterio: Psycan Educational and Clinical Resources.

Williams, J. P. (2003). Teaching text structure to improve reading comprehension. In H. L. Swanson, K. R. Harris, & S. Graham (Eds.), *Handbook of learning disabilities* (pp. 293–305). New York: Guilford Press.

Wolf, M. A., & Hall, S. (July, 2005). Fighting the good fight. *T. H. E. Journal, 32,* 12. Retrieved September 3, 2008, from http://www.thejournal.com/magazine/vault/A5398.cfm

Woodcock, R. W., McGrew, K. S., & Mather, N. (2001). *Woodcock–Johnson III.* Allen, TX: DLM.

Chapter 12

Mathematics Instruction

MARY LITTLE—*University of Central Florida*

BRADLEY S. WITZEL—*Winthrop University*

After reading this chapter, you will be able to:

1. Discuss the rationale underlying changes in instruction in mathematics, including current policy, revised curricular standards, and research
2. Describe the elements of the levels of learning related to mathematics instruction
3. Describe cognitive strategies, accommodations, and resources in technology to meet the individual needs for mathematics instruction for all students
4. Identify, select, and apply the levels of learning to instructional planning, teaching, and assessing student learning for remediation of instructional problems in mathematics based on student needs
5. Explain schoolwide strategies and considerations to support the implementation of research-based mathematics instruction for students with disabilities within the context of school reforms and accountability

WHY MATHEMATICS? WHY NOW? A RATIONALE FOR CHANGE

Daily, mathematics is used throughout our lives. The ability to compute, solve problems, and apply concepts and skills in mathematics influences multiple decisions in our lives. From personal, professional, and societal perspectives, the mastery of mathematical skills of number sense, computation, and problem solving are necessary. Calculating expenditures, interpreting student progress monitoring, and developing personal financial planning all require skills in mathematics. The National Research Council (1989) said that mathematics is the "invisible culture of our age" and emphasized that mathematics is embedded in our lives in many ways: practical, civic, professional, recreational, and cultural. This is especially evident in our technology-rich society, where number sense and problem-solving skills have increasing importance, as technology (e.g., calculators, computers, software programs) enhances both the opportunities for and the demands of advanced levels of proficiency in mathematics.

Mathematics, however, is often challenging for students with and without disabilities to master. Comparison studies from recent commissions and reports have focused on student results (NCES 2004; USDOE, 2000). Students in the United States are not performing as well in math as students in many other developed countries (U.S. Department of Education, National Center for Educational Statistics, 2000). In both 1995 and 2003, U.S. fourth graders showed no measurable gain in mathematics (NCES, 2004). In fact, in the 2003 National Assessment of Educational Progress (NAEP) report, 23% of Grade 4 students and 32% of Grade 8 students scored below the "basic" level. In addition, in a recent NAEP report, only 2% of American students attained advanced levels of mathematics achievement by Grade 12 (NCES, 2006). These data regarding mathematics suggest that the standing of American students relative to their peers in 14 other countries was lower in 2003 than in 1995.

Concerns regarding the poor math performance of students with disabilities have also increased. Researchers have noted that math difficulties emerge in elementary school grades and continue as students progress through secondary school grades (Cawley, Parmer, Yan, & Miller, 1998). Wagner (1995) reported that students with disabilities typically perform two grade levels or more behind their peers without disabilities. Specifically, these students fail to achieve a sufficient conceptual understanding of the core concepts that underlie operations and algorithms used to solve problems that involve whole and rational numbers (Fuchs & Fuchs, 2001). For example, difficulty in multiplication operational facility results from not only poor recall of the multiplication facts but also poor conceptualization of the meaning of multiplication.

Researchers have posited that concerns regarding the poor math performance of students with disabilities may have increased due to several national trends (Butler, Miller, Crehan, Babbit, & Pierce, 2003). Woodward and Montague (2002) described three issues underlying recent policy changes: students' levels of performance in mathematics, impact of technology, and resulting shifts in both policy and theoretical paradigms of standards in mathematics. The following sections will provide ideas and approaches aimed at meeting the needs of students with mathematics disabilities and mathematics difficulties.

Federal Legislation

One of the most widely referenced changes in recent legislation is related to the identification of students with learning disabilities. In addition to the current test-based discrepancy formula comparing ability and achievement, the Individuals with Disabilities Education Improvement Act (IDEIA-04) includes language allowing states to enact alternate models. One often chosen by school districts is the Response to Intervention model (RTI), which calls for evidence-supported curricular interventions to remediate a student's low achievement before or in lieu of discrepancy assessment. It is beyond the scope of this chapter to debate the possible benefits and consequences of variations of this model, but it is still important to note that RTI has been much more reading focused than mathematics focused thus far (Fuchs et al., 2005). Also, most of the evidence-supported mathematics interventions that appear in research-focused journals address basic computational facts. While there is great value in improving students' computation, general education curricula and standards extend well beyond computation at every grade level. Only 12% of students with learning disabilities take courses beyond algebra (Walker & Blackorby, 1996), showing the need to extend research beyond basic facts.

The next section will discuss the impact of certain provisions in the No Child Left Behind Act of 2001 regarding access to the general education curriculum for students with disabilities.

No Child Left Behind

Four years after the 1997 reauthorization of IDEA, Congress passed the No Child Left Behind Act (NCLB), the purpose of which was "to ensure that all children have a fair, equal, and significant opportunity to obtain a high-quality education and reach, at a minimum, proficiency on challenging State academic achievement standards and State academic assessments" (20 U.S.C. § 6301). Although NCLB applies to all students, and IDEA applies only to students with disabilities, both statutes share the goal of raising expectations for the educational performance of students with disabilities and increasing accountability for their educational results. In several places in the law, NCLB makes explicit reference to IDEA. Moreover, as noted earlier, IDEIA-04 aligns a number of requirements in IDEA with those in NCLB.

NCLB focuses attention on the general education curriculum by requiring that states develop "challenging" academic standards for both content and student achievement for all children in at least mathematics and reading/language arts and, by the beginning of the 2005–06 school year, science (20 U.S.C. § 6311(b)(1)(A)–(C)). The development of standards is thus a point of intersection for the two statutes: IDEIA requires that students with disabilities have access to the general education curriculum, according to their individualized needs, while NCLB helps to define and raise the level of the general education curriculum. Universal Design for Learning (UDL) principles may be used to help meet the individual needs of students within the general education curriculum.

CHANGING STANDARDS

It is important to look at possible reasons for the decline of student performance in mathematics, as well as to consider the new federal requirements and mandates related to increased rigor and accountability for results for all students, including students with disabilities. One explanation is that mathematics instruction in the United States suffers from a "splintered vision," with curricula that focus on too many superficially taught topics in a given year (Schmidt, McKnight, & Raizen, 1997). More successful approaches, found particularly in Asian countries, tend to focus on few topics. The lessons are often devoted to the analysis of a few examples, and teachers encourage students to share different solutions to problems (Office of Educational Research and Improvement, 1998; Stigler & Hiebert, 1999).

National Council of Teachers of Mathematics

The National Council of Teachers of Mathematics (NCTM) is the largest organization for mathematics educators in the United States. Their national standards plan is highly influential, as almost every state has incorporated the NCTM national standards into their state standards (Woodward & Montague, 2002). When considering issues related to reported student results and recent revisions to federal legislation, the NCTM initiated reform efforts in math education, including a revision of the suggested math standards. As a result of published concerns about student achievement, NCTM recently revised their curriculum standards to include an increased process approach for a deeper understanding of fewer standards (NCTM, 2000). NCTM highlights the importance of giving students opportunities to use and discuss multiple representations during problem solving (NCTM, 2000). The continued focus of the revised standards (2000) on high-level conceptual learning and problem solving (Maccini & Gagnon, 2002) has been cited as being responsible for the instructional shift away from procedural practice (Goldsmith & Mark, 1999). Concerns regarding these new curriculum standards as related to the successful inclusion of students with disabilities have been raised, as there is little mention of students with disabilities in the standards (Woodward & Montague, 2002). Also, the process approach to teaching math may not meet the needs for explicit instruction needed by some students, especially students with disabilities (Hutchinson, 1993). Researchers in special education have expressed concern regarding the applicability of the mathematics standards (Chard & Kameenui, 1995; Jackson & Neel, 2006; Mercer, Harris, & Miller, 1993). Despite the conceptual push by NCTM, special education has kept its emphasis on its behavioral tradition in mathematics instructional interventions (Woodward, 2004).

As a response to the overwhelming number of grade-level mathematics standards required in some states, NCTM recently presented the Curriculum Focal Points. The purpose of the Focal Points is to narrow the emphasis to what is essential at each grade level, and they address a shift in curriculum rather than recommended instructional pedagogy. While NCTM claims that the Focal Points are designed to give school districts guidance in delivering the standards, others have claimed that the Focal Points are in conflict with current standards (Cavanagh, 2006). One of the largest changes to the 15-year-old suggested mathematics standards is the shift in importance to memorizing certain computational facts, one of the most profound areas of mathematical weakness for students with disabilities (Gersten, Jordan, & Flojo, 2005). A focus of the recently formed National Mathematics Advisory Panel is to improve performance of students with disabilities in mathematics.

Meeting the Instructional Needs of All Students in Mathematics

CHARACTERISTICS Students who demonstrated poor skills in numerical calculation abilities were described as students with dyscalculia (Johnson & Myklebust, 1967) and were eligible to receive special educational services if the instructional needs met the criteria within the category of learning disabilities (IDEA, 1975). It is estimated that between 4% and 7% of the school-age population experiences some form of mathematics-focused disability (Gross-Tsur, Monar, & Shalev, 1996). Approximately one-fourth of the students identified with learning disabilities were identified because they underperformed in mathematics (Brian, Bay, Lopez-Reyna, & Donahue, 1991). It has been found that students with learning disabilities in mathematics perform several grade levels below their general education peers (Cawley et al., 1998; Wagner, 1995), struggle in basic mathematics skills (Algozzine, O'Shea, Crews, & Stoddard, 1987), and have difficulty in problem-solving situations (Maccini & Hughes, 2000). Difficulties in mathematics are part of a larger educational concern. Students who exhibit deficits in mathematics skills also evidence social deficits such as deficiencies in self-help skills and poor organization (Rourke, 1993). In addition, students with learning disabilities are frequently characterized as having perceptual and neurological concerns that affect learning. Students with difficulties in math often have other related difficulties, such as in memory, poor calculation skills, number reversals, and difficulty understanding conceptual and/or procedural processes, especially as represented through symbols and signs (Bryant, Bryant, & Hammill, 2000; Bryant, Hartman, & Kim, 2003).

There are several factors that may interfere with learning and subsequent mastery of concepts and skills in mathematics by students with disabilities, especially learning disabilities (Ginsburg, 1997):

1. *Perceptual skills.* By definition, students with learning disabilities have difficulty with spatial relationships, distances, and sequencing. These difficulties may interfere with the acquisition and demonstration of math concepts and skills, such as estimating size and distance, and problem solving.
2. *Language.* Vocabulary and language of mathematical concepts is not only varied but also abstract. Students with difficulties and/or disabilities in the area of language may also have difficulties with understanding such mathematical concepts as *first, second, greater than,* and *less than,* as well as associated vocabulary terms such as *vertex, complementary, acute,* etc. For students who have deficits in both reading and mathematics, the difficulty with word problem solving is accentuated (Jitendra, DiPipi, & Perron-Jones, 2002).
3. *Reasoning.* Students with disabilities may not possess the abstract reasoning skills necessary for higher-level math skills development. These skills in reasoning may also present difficulties if instruction in mathematics is at the conceptual, abstract level.
4. *Memory.* Many students with learning and behavioral problems have difficulties remembering information that was presented. This is especially evident with the abstract symbols used in mathematics (e.g., minus, greater than, less than).

Given these characteristics, researchers have identified considerations for lesson design and planning, comprehensive teaching methods, various accommodations, and technology that meet the instructional needs for students with disabilities in mathematics. The next section provides an overview of current research and practical suggestions for classroom use.

Considerations for Instruction in Mathematics

RESEARCH Current legislation, reforms, and revised curriculum standards in mathematics focus attention on the research base to meet the instructional needs in mathematics for all students. Difficulties with learning mathematics occur in one or more domains and on a continuum of needs, from temporary to severe problems, which may manifest at different points in a child's learning. Given that difficulties may be encountered at different ages and in different mathematical domains, research and interventions may be appropriate at different levels and in different domains.

Research supports the use of various mathematical and metacognitive approaches to scaffold instruction of abstract concepts so that students master difficult mathematical problems (National Research Council, 1989, 2001). Current researched instructional and metacognitive strategies can be implemented to address the needs of students with and without disabilities to master content in math classes (McLeskey, Hoppey, Williamson, & Rentz, 2004).

In recent years, several reviews, research summaries, and meta-analyses have been published of the math interventions in the various math domains (e.g., basic computation, number sense, problem solving). Maccini, Mulcahy, and Wilson (2007), as well as Miller and Hudson (2007), have published reviews of mathematics interventions available for students with mental retardation and with learning disabilities, respectively. Jitendra and Xin (1997) have conducted comprehensive research on problem solving by students with disabilities. Swanson and Carson (1996) published numerous meta-analyses of intervention studies for students with learning disabilities. For a sampling of the research on instructional methods and interventions and the impact on students, see Table 12.1, as well as the citations provided. These research syntheses clearly reflect the numerous possibilities for intervention, but just which interventions are most effective for which groups of students are unclear. However, various instructional methods and intervention techniques were researched to show positive effects with students with disabilities (see Table 12.1).

Problem Solving

It has been reported that students in the United States are deficient in their mathematics problem-solving abilities (NCES, 1992). Even if students were to be more fluent in their computation abilities, they do not know when and where to utilize their talent. However, as personal debt has increased, so has consumers' inability to manage their personal finances. It is important to teach not only how to solve a mathematical sentence but how that mathematical sentence relates to things that are socially relevant to students and their future successes. For example, along with learning how to solve for fractions, it is important to have the students understand fractions as they relate to matters such as sharing, ratios, news events, and even statistical and financial formulas.

Building understanding for word problems begins with building mathematics vocabulary. Mathematics vocabulary is often considered as a separate language and must be treated much like learning any foreign language. While there is growing discussion of using mathematics terminology and language in everyday language for early childhood ages (Witzel, Ferguson, & Brown, 2007), research is still in its infancy for students at the secondary levels (see Mastropieri & Scruggs, 2007). What has been learned for most

TABLE 12.1 Summary of Mathematics Research

Author(s)	Title and Source	Components	Findings
Maccini & Hughes (2000)	Effects of a problem-solving strategy on introductory algebra performance of secondary students with learning disabilities. *Learning Disabilities Research & Practice, 15*(1), 10–21.	Algebraic thinking	All participants improved their percentage of strategy-use from baseline to instructional phases for all integer operations. Participants improved their percentage accuracy on problem representation from baseline to instructional phases in computation of integer numbers. Mean percentage accuracy scores for problem solution in addition, subtraction, multiplication, and division of integers improved from baseline well above criterion level following concrete instruction. Participants also maintained high mean percentage accuracy scores during the semi-concrete and abstract instruction. Participants' mean percentage correct maintenance measures given up to 10 weeks following the intervention was 75% for problem representation and 91% for problem solution. Participants improved the mean percentage accuracy on problem representation and solution from baseline measure to the maintenance task.
Miller & Mercer (1997)	Teaching math computation and problem solving: A program that works. *Intervention in School & Clinic, 32*(3), 185–190.	Number sense, concepts, and operations	The field-test results clearly indicate the program's effectiveness varies with a variety of students in various school settings. Results obtained from experimental research further support the instructional sequence and procedures used in the Strategic Math Series. In each of these studies, student's achievement was high and program effectiveness was demonstrated. Teachers and students involved in the field tests and research studies reported high levels of satisfaction with the program. All of the teachers reported that they would definitely use the program again.
Montague, Warger, & Morgan (2000)	Solve it! Strategy instruction to improve mathematical problem solving. *Learning Disabilities Research & Practice, 12*(2), 110–116.	Number sense, concepts, and operations	Generally, across studies, students maintained strategy use and problem-solving performance for several weeks following instruction, after which performance declined. Following a booster session consisting of a day review and another for practice, students demonstrated significant improvement.

TABLE 12.1 *(Continued)*

Author(s)	Title and Source	Components	Findings
Steele & Johanning (2004)	A schematic-theoretic view of problem solving and development of algebraic thinking. *Education Studies in Mathematics, 57,* 65–90.	Number sense, concepts, and operations	Researchers identified two qualities of problem-solving schemas that students developed as a well-connected schema and a partially formed schema. Well-connected is a complex schema that has strong connections and relationships so that it could be successfully used to generalize a particular problem situation and generalize across problems. Partially formed schema is a schema that is weak in connections and does not provide the necessary relationships to articulate generalizations across problems or oftentimes within a problem.
Xin & Jitendra (1999)	The effects of instruction in solving mathematical word problems: A meta-analysis. *Journal of Special Education, 32*(4), 207–225.	Number sense, concepts, and operations Algebraic thinking	Results of the meta-analysis indicated that word problem-solving instruction improved the performance of students with learning problems and promoted the maintenance and generalization of the skill.

students who struggle in mathematics is that explicit instruction in specific mathematics terminology is essential (Monroe & Orme, 2002). Teach terms explicitly along with incorporating terms into modeling and guided practice activities until they become part of the students' vocabulary. Once initial vocabulary knowledge is acquired, well-planned peer communication regarding the vocabulary can also increase students' correct use of mathematical terminology (Topping, Campbell, Douglas, & Smith, 2003).

Most problem-solving scenarios are portrayed in word problems, thus it is imperative to establish what helps students solve word problems. In an analysis of word-problem-solving interventions with students with disabilities, Jitendra and Xin (1997) found positive effects for teaching students representations of word problems, strategy training, optimizing the sequence of word problem questions, and computer-assisted instruction. They presented caution, though, that the strategy must incorporate elements that identify essential elements of the word problem situation.

By essential elements, Jitendra (2002) asserted that word problems can have one of three types: change, group, or comparison. A student recognizes a change strategy by a beginning set, a change set that has been lost or added, and the final set being asked for reflecting the change. The group problems show a larger set in the problem, and the other smaller sets are deduced from the problem. The comparison sets of problems present one number set and a difference, more or less, and ask for a referent set. Even if the problems in your text extend these three types, it is important for students to recognize what is being asked in the problem and to have a strategy to approach the problem.

Where to Go from Here

On the basis of these recent reviews on mathematics instruction for students with learning disabilities, the following instructional practices are recommended:

1. Instructional design and lesson planning features are effective ways to differentiate presentation methods, levels of learning, and feedback and demonstration of
   mastery to meet the individual needs of the students. It is important to set clearly
   defined curricular goals aligned with standards.
2. Instructional routines and metacognitive strategies that focus on cognitive behavioral techniques benefit students with learning and behavioral problems and actively engage the students in the learning process.
3. Monitor progress and provide effective feedback through formative assessment
   procedures throughout instruction. Make adjustments in teaching, materials,
   grouping, or other features of instruction or accommodations if students are not
   making adequate progress.
4. Computer-assisted instruction and use of the Universal Design for Learning (UDL)
   principles can provide an effective way for students with disabilities to gain access,
   become more involved, and master mathematics (Hitchcock, Meyer, Rose, & Jackson,
   2002; Rivera, Smith, Goodwin, & Bryant, 1998; Xin & Jitendra, 1999).

The following sections highlight these four research-based instructional practices
in detail.

Lesson Planning to Differentiate Instruction

Differentiated instruction is a philosophy or approach to planning and teaching based
on the premise that teachers must consider *who* they are teaching as well as *what* they are
teaching. The principles of differentiation include ongoing assessment and adjustment,
clarity of the standards and learning goals of the curriculum, use of flexible grouping,
tasks that are respectful of each learner, and instruction that stretches the learner
(Tomlinson, 1999). Differentiating the content refers to what is being taught, as well as
how students gain access to a body of knowledge. Differentiating the content starts with
the teacher having clarity about the essential understandings and goals of the curriculum
for the teaching lesson or unit. Differentiating the process refers to how a student makes
sense of the information or content. Differentiating product refers to assessments or
demonstrations of what the student knows, understands, or is able to do. Differentiating
the learning environment considers both the operation of the classroom and the more abstract climate of the classroom. It is based on a set of beliefs, guided by principles, and
may be implemented in a variety of ways. Development of a differentiated classroom occurs along a continuum. A lesson may be differentiated or a unit may be differentiated as
teachers gain proficiency toward a broader use of differentiation.

To enact differentiating instruction in the mathematics classroom, teachers need to
be efficient at several types of instruction. For example, many general mathematics educators are being prepared for investigation-oriented mathematics instruction, while
special education teachers are being prepared for more explicit behavioral approaches
to teaching mathematics. Hudson, Miller, and Butler (2006) suggested a marriage of the
two approaches. To differentiate instruction requires thorough knowledge of each student and how each student learns best. Then, to enact the most effective pedagogy, the

teacher needs to balance classroom instruction. Hudson and her colleagues suggested that if a teacher could capture the high-interest activities while incorporating explicit instructional techniques, such as advanced organizers, teacher-directed instruction, and appropriate assessment, then more students would benefit from the instruction.

Learning to differentiate instruction requires knowledge of the multiple variables that must be considered when planning lessons, implementing content, and monitoring for continuous progress and assessment. These multiple variables enhance the learning opportunities for individual students based on teacher expertise with incorporation into the lesson. The critical components of lesson design include the following:

1. Learning goal related to the specific curricular standards and lesson objectives:
   - Objectives should be written in terms of the students (not in terms of the teacher).
   - Indicate the specific observable behavior.
   - Indicate the mathematics (skill or concept) to be learned by the students as the learning goal. (Example: Students will subtract a two-digit number from a two- or three-digit number with and without regrouping.)
   - Teacher expectations related to the prerequisite skills and concepts needed by the students. The teacher may need to task analyze the activity related to the learning goal of the specific objective. During this step, materials needed for the lesson are determined. List the materials needed for the teacher and for the students.
2. Areas of strength/need related to student and lesson objectives:
   - Cognitive levels of learning or combination of levels involved in the lesson: concrete, representational, abstract, concrete–representational, representational–concrete, concrete–abstract, abstract–concrete, representational–abstract, abstract–representational, and concrete–representational–abstract (all cognitive levels at the same time).
   - Consider the specific areas of need for the individual students in relation to the learning goal and classroom tasks to be completed.
   - Review the classroom expectations for the lesson in math with the specific needs and skills of the students to determine methods, strategies, and materials to consider as accommodations.
3. Accommodations for students with disabilities and English language learners: Consider and plan for individual learning needs of the students. Knowledge about the students and lesson outcomes are important before selecting any of the accommodations. Consider other areas and ideas like the following (and those contained in Table 12.2).
   - Use a variety of classroom accommodations, such as demonstrations, manipulative materials, charts, illustrations, diagrams, maps, and filmstrips to provide visual reinforcement and to make problems more concrete instead of abstract. Use more visuals, demonstrations, and media to provide informational redundancy. Relate math problems and vocabulary to prior knowledge and background. Apply problems to real-life situations. Encourage drawings to translate and visualize word problems.
   - When necessary and possible, give additional time to complete activities (tests, quizzes, handouts, experiments). Students benefit from working at their own pace, using a dictionary to help them with vocabulary, as needed.

- Adapt activities to accommodate differences. Develop simplified worksheets that use fill-in-the blanks, multiple choice, or true/false. Highlight key information with marker. (Have students in more advanced classes do the highlighting.)
- Have students work in cooperative learning groups of three to four, or use cooperative learning strategies to maximize opportunities for language development.
- Use peer teachers, volunteers, and/or other students to provide additional assistance.

4. Instructional procedures for the lesson:
   - *Introduction* (setting the stage):
     - All procedures should be detailed to implement them.
     - Include example questions, items, and/or exercises to clarify your ideas, and include copies or drawings of assigned handouts, exercises, and/or homework.
     - Critical elements: motivate the students, cover state learning objectives, relate to prior knowledge, read children's books.
   - *Instructional input and modeling* (development of main idea): This section should include an explanation of the procedures to be employed when teaching the lesson. What will the students do, and what will the teacher do? This could include demonstrations, experiments, explorations, games, and/or others.
   - *Guided practice and check for understanding*: Students demonstrate a skill or concept, extend a concept (or apply it), work samples, and repeat operations. Teachers check for students understanding by asking questions, observing operations, and adjusting problems (continuous progress monitoring).
   - *Independent practice:* Students complete follow-up activities or practice activities. Possible activities include learning centers, experiments, explorations, games, seatwork, computers, or calculators.
   - *Concluding activity* (closure or closing remarks).

5. Evaluation or assessment procedures:
   - During the planning process, consider the methods to assess student learning of the goals for the lesson in mathematics. The questions to address include: Do you know that the students mastered the skills or concepts? What procedures were used for assessment?
   - Examples could include informal observations of the students work with manipulatives, handouts, games, portfolio, project, presentation, pre- and post-tests, and/or others.

6. Self-evaluation of the lesson:
   - This section gives an opportunity to assess the success of the lesson plan after implementation to continuously improve the lesson and learning for the students.

See Table 12.2 for the LEARNS strategy with an example of a math lesson to use for lesson planning for increased differentiation to meet individual student's instructional needs.

To incorporate a balanced approach to best practices, Hudson and colleagues (2006) suggested two instructional ideas. One is to incorporate video-based problems that allow students to interact with a relevant application of the mathematical concept or principle. There are excellent video lessons, strategies, and resources on the MathVIDS Web site (http://www.coedu.usf.edu/main/departments/sped/mathvids/index.html) that will be useful when developing lessons and identifying resources to meet

TABLE 12.2 Using the LEARNS Strategy for Math Lessons

STEP 1: Learning goal Determine the learning goals and objectives based on state standards.	**Learning Goal** The student will accurately apply trigonometric ratios to find the height of flag pole, the distance to a building, and the length of a ramp (hypotenuse).	
STEP 2: Note teacher expectations What must students be able to do to complete learning tasks successfully or to achieve mastery of content taught?	**Task or activity** • Students must measure the length to the flag pole and the angle from the ground to the top of the flag pole. • Students then compute the ratio to find the height. • For the distance to the building, they are given the height of the building.	**Skills necessary to complete task or activity** • Tests knowledge of trigonometric ratios and angles • Use a tape measure.
STEP 3: Areas of strength/need Determine students' areas of strength or need. To obtain this information, talk to and observe the students, review students' work samples, use assessment data or research, talk to previous teachers, and meet with student support team, parents, and/or special education teacher (IEP).	**Areas of need And student** Manuel can explain concepts but has difficulty with computation. Sarah works hard but becomes easily frustrated with math computations.	**Note specific ways in which these needs may manifest in a classroom and names of students to whom it applies.** He may have difficulty computing the ratios and transforming the equations to solve for what is required. She may have difficulty with fractions when reading a tape measurer.
STEP 4: Review Compare and contrast Step 2 and Step 3, and note major areas where any students will encounter barriers to learning in the lesson if you do not make any accommodations.	**Teaching activity** Tests knowledge of trigonometric ratios and angles. Use a tape measure to measure angles.	**Note barriers to learning and names of students to whom they apply** Manuel may have trouble with the necessary computation. Sarah may have difficulty reading a tape measure.
STEP 5: Note accommodations Determine methods, strategies, and materials that will meet most students' needs.	**Area of need and name** Manuel may have trouble with the necessary computation. Sarah may have difficulty with understanding fractions, which makes reading a tape measure difficult.	**Accommodations and names of students to whom they apply** Manuel—Provide a graphing calculator within stepwise procedures and ISOLATE strategy for manipulating the equation. Can also suggest using Ask Dr. Math website http://mathforum.org/dr/math/

(continued)

TABLE 12.2 Using the LEARNS Strategy for Math Lessons

STEP 6: Specify	Student names/unmet need	Accommodations
Individual accommodations needed by students whose special needs are not met by UDL provisions.	ELL student Mia	Math.com http://www.math.com/ offers resources for teaching math methods and concepts to ELL students and English speaking students.

the needs of all students in mathematics. Second, multiple classroom lessons highlight the Levels of Learning approach to teaching mathematics. This approach is researched and described in literature in mathematics and special education and includes three levels in a sequence of instruction: Concrete–Representational–Abstract (CRA) (Maccini et al., 2007; Miller & Hudson, 2007).

LEVELS OF LEARNING

Researchers have noted that math difficulties emerge in elementary school grades and continue as students progress through secondary school grades (Maccini & Gagnon, 2002; Mercer & Miller, 1992). Specifically, students often fail to achieve a sufficient conceptual understanding of the core concepts that underlie operations and algorithms used to solve problems that involve whole and rational numbers (Baroody & Hume, 1991; Hiebert & Behr, 1988).

Devlin (2000) stated that for students to understand abstract concepts more easily, it is important for them to learn precursor concepts concretely first. The National Council of Teachers of Mathematics (NCTM, 2000) has emphasized the importance of representations in the development of students' communication of mathematics ideas:

> Young students use many varied representations to build new understandings and express mathematical ideas. Representing ideas and connecting the representations to mathematics lies at the heart of understanding mathematics. Teachers should analyze students' representations and carefully listen to their discussions to gain insights into the development of mathematical thinking and to enable them to provide support as students connect their languages to the conventional language of mathematics (p. 135).

One way to simplify students' understanding of abstract concepts is to transform such complex concepts into concrete manipulations and pictorial representations. Such instruction is known as the Concrete–Representational–Abstract (CRA) sequence of instruction and is illustrated in Figure 12.1.

CRA involves utilizing manipulatives (concrete). Once the student has mastered the math concept using manipulatives, the objects are replaced with pictorial representations, such as a picture of the object (representational). This level is a critical bridge between the manipulatives and the abstract symbols (e.g., equations, algorithm), as this step builds the mental schema bridging these two levels. It is critical to develop mathematics conceptual knowledge during the representational level of learning. Finally, once the student is able to comprehend representational figures and designs, the concept uses Arabic symbols and explanations (abstract). Successful performance at the

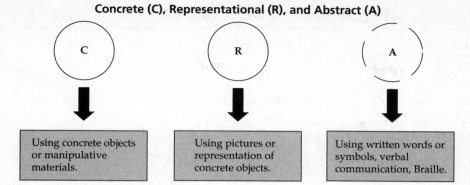

Concrete (C), Representational (R), and Abstract (A)

C	R	A

Using concrete objects or manipulative materials.

Using pictures or representation of concrete objects.

Using written words or symbols, verbal communication, Braille.

FIGURE 12.1 Learning Levels

Source: Information from Little, Kinney, & Robertson (2007)

abstract level is the goal and purpose of using CRA, as mathematics is most often expressed at this level (e.g., within text materials and assessments.)

Within CRA, each level is designed to build on the previous level to promote overall improved mathematical performance. The three levels of CRA are sequentially interrelated in that they are not independent activities but are interconnected and should not be treated as separate activities that are either hands-on, pictorial, or use abstract notation. Instead, each level prepares the student for the next level of learning (Witzel, Riccomini, & Schneider, 2008). The connections between the levels of learning are critical to bringing the student from one level to the next. For example, a concrete lesson must be designed to be easily represented pictorially and described abstractly. If the levels are not connected or designed in sequence, then the student must learn multiple ways to solve a problem without mastering any of the steps along the way. See Table 12.3 for an example of the interconnection between the learning levels within CRA.

Research in mathematics for students with disabilities and difficulties has examined the effectiveness of CRA for students learning computational facts (Miller & Mercer, 1993), place value (Peterson, Mercer, & O'Shea, 1988), basic fractions (Butler et al., 2003; Jordan, Miller, & Mercer, 1999), algebra and algebraic equations (Maccini & Hughes, 2000; Witzel, 2005; Witzel, Mercer, & Miller, 2003; Witzel, Smith, & Brownell, 2001), and geometry (Cass, Cates, Smith, & Jackson, 2003). While CRA appears to be one of the most effective mathematics intervention strategies, it also requires more teacher preparation to ensure that the same vocabulary and procedures are used at each learning level. See Table 12.3 for an example of how to implement CRA instruction with subtraction using borrowing.

METACOGNITION: STRATEGIES AND INSTRUCTIONAL ROUTINES

Metacognition refers to higher-order thinking that involves active control over the cognitive processes engaged in learning (Montague et al., 2000). Activities such as planning how to approach a given learning task, monitoring comprehension, and evaluating progress toward the completion of a task are metacognitive in nature. Metacognitive strategies include mnemonic devices, problem-solving routines, self-monitoring skills,

TABLE 12.3 Example of CRA Using Base-10 Blocks for Teaching Subtraction with Borrowing

Concrete	Representation	Abstract
43	43	43
−26	−26	−26
4 longs + 3 shorts	4 large tallies + 3 short tallies	40 + 3
2 longs + 6 shorts	2 long tallies + 6 short tallies	−(20 + 6)

Concrete	Representation	Abstract
3 longs + 1 long and 3 shorts	3 long tallies + 1 long tally and 3 short tallies	30 + 10 + 3
2 longs + 6 shorts	2 long tallies + 6 short tallies	−(20 + 6)

Concrete	Representation	Abstract
3 longs + 13 shorts	3 long tallies + 13 short tallies	30 + 13
2 longs + 6 shorts	2 long tallies + 6 short tallies	−(20 + 6)

Concrete	Representation	Abstract
1 long + 7 shorts	1 long tally + 7 short tallies	10 + 7

17	17	17

and the use of graphic organizers. Graphic organizers, such as the anchoring strategy by Bulgren, Schumaker, and Deshler (2003), are designed to assist students in representing patterns, interpreting data, and analyzing information relevant to problem solving. Figure 12.2 displays a sample graphic organizer that outlines instructional examples and non-examples to help teachers plan.

Multiplication of Fractions
Terms to teach:
1. numerator
2. denominator
3. simplify
4. improper fraction
5. mixed fraction
Preparation for Modeling Flowchart:

Examples	Explain
(a) $(\frac{1}{2}) * (\frac{3}{4}) = (1 * 3)/(2 * 4) = (\frac{3}{8})$	The process: When multiplying fractions, complete operations with numerators and denominators separately.
(b) $(\frac{5}{4}) * (\frac{2}{3}) = (5 * 2)/(4 * 3) = \frac{10}{12} = \frac{5}{6}$	Divide numerator and denominator to their simplest form.
Initiate Guided Practice	
(c) $(\frac{5}{2}) * (\frac{1}{2}) = (5 * 1)/(2 * 2) = \frac{5}{4} = 1\frac{1}{4}$	Compute an improper fraction to be a mixed fraction.
Teach what not to do and why—The Nots	
(d) $(\frac{1}{2}) * (\frac{3}{4}) = (\frac{2}{4}) * (\frac{3}{4}) \neq (1 + 3)/(4) \neq \frac{3}{8}$	Multiplication of fractions requires multiplication of both the numerator and denominator.
(e) $(\frac{1}{2}) * (\frac{3}{4}) \neq (\frac{1}{2}) * (\frac{4}{3}) = (1 * 4)/(2 * 3) \neq \frac{3}{8}$	Do not invert and multiply unless as a shortcut for dividing fractions.
Repeat Example	
(f) $(\frac{1}{3}) * (\frac{4}{2}) = (1 * 4)/(3 * 2) = \frac{4}{6} = \frac{2}{3}$	Divide numerator and denominator to their simplest form.

FIGURE 12.2 Modeling Preparation Graphic Organizer

The introduction of metacognitive strategy instruction into lessons in mathematics should not be considered an addition to the required content but rather as an array of research-based tools developed to facilitate the understanding, retention, and utilization of required course content. Metacognitive strategies allow a teacher to teach students *how to think* about what they are doing and learning. As developing learners, students should be taught these strategies to realize how they learn best. Metacognitive strategies are not only related to teaching algebraic thinking; these strategies can be used in all areas and subjects. One excellent feature of metacognitive strategies is the use of "think-alouds" for students to describe their problem solving strategies. Teachers can first model think-aloud strategies to explain reasoning of problems-solving steps and teach students how and why specific problem-solving steps are used. Teachers modeling think-alouds also allows for the introduction to mathematics vocabulary that is troublesome to students, especially those who are culturally and linguistically diverse. Other metacognitive strategies include prior knowledge prompts, advance organizers, mnemonics, and graphic/visual organizers. A sampling of metacognitive strategies is offered in Table 12.4.

There are many tools that a teacher can use with students to improve instruction. One such tool is a graphic organizer. A teacher can teach from a graphic organizer, allowing students to take notes on differences and similarities between two vocabulary terms or mathematical procedures for problem solving. The example in Figure 12.2 shows how a graphic organizer can be used to introduce a concept in relationship to previous concepts.

In addition to graphic organizers, learning strategies are also beneficial to helping students who struggle in mathematics. For example, to help students learn the associative property, teachers may teach the ASSOC strategy. In this strategy, the students learn each step successively and show each step at a mastery level before learning the next step.

A: The first step is ask if any numbers or letters are grouped by parentheses.

S: Then, see how the numbers are grouped within the parentheses.

S: Check to see if the equations have the same numerals and symbols.

O: Check that the equations have three or more numbers or symbols.

C: Make certain that each equation has only addition or multiplication symbols.

For solving simple equations, students can follow the ISOLATE strategy (Witzel, 2004).

With ISOLATE, students learn to:

I—Identify the location of the variable or unknown

S—Subtract, add, multiply, or divide parts of the expression to isolate the unknown with its coefficient and sign

O—Organize the equation to balance across the equation sign so that each operation input is completed to both sides

L—List the equations and compute

A—Arrange final calculations to isolate the unknown

T—Total both sides of the equations

E—Evaluate the answer

While strategy instruction does not simplify the information being learned, it simplifies how to learn the information. These two previous examples are mnemonics used to assist memory of the sequence and specific steps necessary to accurately solve problems in mathematics. There are many strategies that fit mathematics skills that are typically difficult to learn. It is important to find those with research support that fit the needs of your students in relation to the specific curricular goal and lesson objective.

In addition, the use of accommodations by teachers may be necessary when considering the instructional needs of students within the context of specific math curricular goals and lesson objectives. The use of accommodations does not alter the standard in mathematics or curriculum goal taught for mastery by the students. Instead, accommodations involve a wide range of techniques and support systems to assure that all students participate and demonstrate mastery of that standard in mathematics or curriculum goal.

TABLE 12.4 Samples of Evidence-Based Metacognitive Strategies

Definition	Classroom Use	Research Base
KWL Charts		
Visual, organizational tool to increase engagement in active thinking in math by: • (K) describing what is KNOWN about a topic • (W) questioning the potential learning • (L) summarizing concepts learned after instruction	As students generate their knowledge, prior knowledge and pre-assessment of a topic is conducted. Questions engage the learners in their learning. Summarizing learning provides a post-organizer and informal assessment information.	Cart & Ogle (1987)
Anticipation Guides		
Pre-teaching guide designed to activate background knowledge and build interest in content	Teacher predetermines critical information and key ideas from content and generates list of facts. Students, individually or in teams, agree/disagree with facts both before and after lessons.	Readence, Bean, & Baldwin (1985).
Mnemonic Devices		
Strategies that students and teachers can create to help students remember content. The verbal information promotes recall of unfamiliar information and content.	Teacher predetermines critical information and key ideas from content and generates list of facts. Then, through the use of a memory device from first letters, teacher creates a mnemonic. E.g.: **PEMDAS** (**P**lease **E**xcuse **M**y **D**ear **A**unt **S**ally) to remember the order of operations: Parenthesis, Exponent, Multiplication & Division (left to right), Addition & Subtraction (left to right)	Nagel, Schumaker, & Deshler (1986).

Accommodations may be considered and implemented in five general areas: instructional methods and materials, at-home assignments and classroom assessments, time demands and scheduling, learning environment, and use of special communication systems. When selecting accommodations, educators must analyze the learning needs of each student within the context of classroom and curriculum expectations. For example, a student's disability in reading affects the student's mathematics achievement when encountering word problems. Thus, if the student displays effective listening comprehension, then an appropriate accommodation would be to read aloud word problems (Johnson, 2000). In this example, reading the problems aloud enables the student to successfully participate and master the mathematics curriculum as a result of appropriate accommodations. It is important to examine the effectiveness of different accommodations in the classroom and keep a record of the student performance before using the accommodation in a high-stakes environment. Consult state and school district policies and procedures regarding the use of accommodations within the mathematics classrooms and district and state assessments.

PROGRESS MONITORING AND ASSESSMENT

Assessment is "the process of gathering evidence about a student's knowledge of, ability to use, and disposition toward mathematics and of making inferences from that evidence for a variety of purposes" (NCTM, 1995, p. 3). Furthermore, assessment tasks should match students' prior knowledge and the mathematics curriculum and instructional strategies in use as an ongoing process. In other words, the teacher should not teach one way and assess another way. Assessment should be viewed as a tool to assist the teacher design and revise instruction for the student. Within Universal Design for Learning, it is important to utilize many assessment options within the instructional environment. These considerations on assessment are reflected in the five shifts recommended by the National Council of Teachers of Mathematics (NCTM, 1995):

- Shift in content toward a rich variety of mathematical topics and problem situations and away from just arithmetic
- Shift in learning toward investigation problems and away from memorizing and repeating
- Shift in teaching toward questioning and listening and away from telling
- Shift in evaluation toward evidence from several resources and away from a single test judged externally
- Shift in expectation toward using concepts and procedures to solve problems and away from just mastering isolated concepts and procedures

There are different useful types of assessment. Various types of assessment may be used in isolation or in combination with others for the purpose of providing important information to use in instructional planning. The types of assessment included in this document are the following: objective, alternative, authentic, performance, naturalistic, achievement, standardized, and diagnostic. The following list provides a brief description of each type of assessment:

1. *Objective* assessment refers to testing that requires the selection of one item from a list of choices provided with the question. This type of assessment includes true/false responses, yes/no answers, and questions with multiple-choice answers.
2. *Alternative* assessment refers to other (nontraditional) options used to assess students' learning. When using this type of assessment, the teacher is not basing student progress only on the results of a single test or set of evidence. Some of the forms of this type of assessment include the portfolios, journals, notebooks, projects, and presentations.
3. *Authentic* assessment is a form of alternative assessment that incorporates real-life functions and applications. For students with special educational needs, this is particularly important. Students need not only to perform well on standards-based

exams, but they need to translate their learning to socially relevant aspects of their lives.

4. *Performance* assessment (often used interchangeably with authentic assessment) requires the student to complete of a task, project, or investigation; communicate information; or construct a response that demonstrates knowledge or understanding of a skill or concept.

5. *Naturalistic* assessment involves evaluation that is based on the natural setting of the classroom. It involves the observation of students' performance and behavior in an informal context.

6. *Achievement* test battery is composed of subtests of mathematics concepts and skills and usually includes technical aspects of mathematics.

7. *Standardized* assessments include content areas and provide useful information about students' mathematics skills. Their validity and reliability depend on three basic assumptions: Students have been equally exposed to the test content in an instructional program, students know the language of the test directions and the test responses, and students just like those taking the test have been included in the standardization samples to establish norms and make inferences.

8. *Diagnostic* tests are used within the diagnostic–prescriptive teaching of mathematics, which is an instructional model that consists of diagnosis, prescription, instruction, and ongoing assessment. The tests can be teacher made or commercially developed.

With the growth of the Response to Intervention (RTI) identification model, educators are asked to determine the effectiveness of their instruction and curriculum based on students' learning over a brief amount of time. To determine the effectiveness of one's instruction, a teacher administers various assessments on one or more skills to determine the growth rate of learning during the instruction and/or intervention in mathematics. While some progress-monitoring instruments are used monthly (Foegen, Jiban, & Deno, 2007), others are used weekly (Fuchs et al., 2007).

Deciding on instructional adjustments and implementing interventions can be difficult. Riccomini (2005) found that general and special education elementary teachers were able to accurately identify the mathematical error pattern of students who made repeated errors, but they did not develop interventions based on identified error pattern or needs of the students. Thus, teachers were able to determine the mathematical error but did not design an appropriate correction procedure to the help the student succeed. One thing that may help is frequent progress monitoring using the various types of assessments described in the above list. Stecker and Fuchs (2000) found that student performance increased when teachers made instructional adjustments based on individualized curriculum-based measurement data. Frequent assessment and linked instructional interventions are essential to increasing student mathematics performance.

INSTRUCTIONAL TECHNOLOGY AND COMPUTER-ASSISTED INSTRUCTION

Universal Design for Learning (UDL) is a theoretical framework developed to guide the development of curricula that are flexible and supportive of all students (Hitchcock et al., 2002; Rose & Meyer, 2000). The concept of UDL was inspired by the Universal

Design movement in architecture. This movement calls for the design of structures that anticipate the needs of individuals with disabilities and accommodate these needs from the outset. Universally designed structures are indeed more usable by individuals with disabilities, but in addition they offer unforeseen benefits for *all* users. Similarly, but uniquely, UDL calls for the design of curricula with the needs of all students in mind, so that methods, materials, and assessment are usable by all. Traditional curricula present a host of barriers that limit students' access to information and learning. In a traditional curriculum, a student without a well-developed ability to see, decode, attend to, or comprehend printed text is compelled to adapt to its ubiquity to the fullest extent.

In contrast, a UDL curriculum is designed to be innately flexible, enriched with multiple media, including assistive and augmentative technology, so that alternatives can be accessed whenever appropriate. A UDL curriculum takes on the burden of adaptation so that the student doesn't have to, minimizing barriers and maximizing access to both information and learning. Therefore, instructional needs of students can be offered in a wide variety of solutions in various curricular areas, including mathematics.

Assistive technology is legislated and described to ensure that students with disabilities receive the necessary technology support during instruction. Initially, Pub. L. 100.407, the Technology-Related Assistance for Individuals with Disabilities Act (1988), provided the definition of *assistive technology*. Through this legislation, the term *assistive technology device* means any item, piece of equipment, or product system, whether commercially off the shelf, modified, or customized, that is used to increase, maintain, or improve the functional capabilities of a child with disabilities. The needs and uses for assistive technology are necessary and used for students with more severe physical, sensory, or cognitive impairments on an individual need basis. Table 12.5 provides a brief sample of various accommodations and technology to consider when teaching mathematics to meet individual student instructional needs.

Numerous types of software programs include features specifically to support students in mathematics. *Go Solve* (www.tomsnyder.com) uses graphic organizers to help students solve math word problems, and *Classroom Suite* (www.intellitools.com) provides extensive virtual manipulatives in math. Virtual manipulatives are very useful technology tools. They support complex thinking activities, enable students to experiment with various solutions to problems, and provide a visual way to look at data. In addition, students with gross or fine-motor problems can often use virtual manipulatives easier than classroom sets of materials. *Bright Clique* (www.indivisuallearning.com) is a set of basic math manipulatives that are easy to use. *Gizmos* (www.explore-learning.com) is an extensive set of online manipulatives and virtual labs for math and science, Grades 6–12. Two additional Web sites to consult when planning and using technology in conjunction with mathematics instruction are these:

- National Library of Virtual Manipulatives—This site offers samples, resources, and lesson plans using the levels of learning and mathematics curriculum frameworks (http://nlvm.usu.edu/).
- National Council of Teachers of Mathematics—This site offers lesson plans and resources describing instructional technology in mathematics (http://nctm.org).

Graphic organizers such as *CMAP* (cmap.ihmc.us) and Inspiration (www.inspiration.com) can be used to guide students through the various steps of complex problem

TABLE 12.5 List of Sample Accommodations and Technology (*Continued*)

Target Behaviors	Accommodations (least to most intrusive)	Technology
Excessively active (Exhibits behaviors such as tapping and other distracting noises)	• Fit a foam piece on the end of student's pen or pencil to reduce the noise or disturbances to others • Utilize stress balls to reduce fidgeting	• Allow student to utilize a computer to take notes.
Verbal students (Exhibits language behaviors such as calling out, talking out of turn)	• Self-monitoring chart: Tally verbalization and set a reduction goal • Visual/nonobtrusive verbal cues/private cues	• Use whiteboards to record/show comments to teacher.
Class participation (Exhibits behaviors such as shyness, language barrier, lack of involvement)	• Pre-teach, providing advance organizer for students to preview • Cooperative learning strategies • Graphic organizers • Manipulatives	• Use whiteboards to record/show answers. • Use signals, charts, etc.
Identifying critical content (Exhibits difficulty understanding main concepts vs. facts)	• Graphic organizers • Highlight key points • Key visual cue to signal a key point during instruction	• Highlighter or highlighter tape • Videotaped review.
Motivation (Exhibits lack of interest in learning, easily discouraged, doesn't complete homework assignments)	• Offer points for participation • Emphasize achievements with frequent and specific reinforcing statements • Create opportunities for success	• Software for review activities in math • Use of math-related software programs
Note taking (Exhibits difficulty writing notes, identifying important concepts; disorganized notes)	• Provide copy of notes • Allow to listen then copy • Highlight key points • Color code • Guided notes • Graphic organizers • Skeletal notes • NCR paper • Scribe	• AlphaSmart • Tape recorder
Oral expression (Exhibits difficulty with explaining verbally answers)	• Transparencies • Whiteboards • Manipulatives	• Computers • AlphaSmart • Board maker • IntelliKeys

(continued)

TABLE 12.5 List of Sample Accommodations and Technology (*Continued*)

Target Behaviors	Accommodations (least to most intrusive)	Technology
Organization (Exhibits difficulty in taking notes, storing work and formulas; unable to remember main concepts)	• Graphic organizers • Highlight key points • Guided notes • Reference sheets • Enlarged font size • Mnemonic devices	• Kidspiration software • Inspiration software • Highlighters • Word processing
Difficulty with written expression	• Shorten length of assignment • Kinesthetic activities, such as foldables • Demonstrations through manipulatives • Oral presentations	• Taped responses • AlphaSmart

solving and multistep algorithms in mathematics. Experimental and problem-solving processes can be mapped visually to help students organize text or verbal information from simple to complex. Graphic organizers are excellent cognitive organizers for students with learning disabilities.

There are many practice and/or intervention software programs available for mathematics curricula. *FASTT Math* (www.tomsnyder.com) targets basic math fluency. Online tools such as Web-math.com provides example problem solving from general math to calculus. Each of these software programs is available to meet the specific needs for individual or groups of students. As teachers, knowledge of both the curriculum and lesson expectations as well as the specific needs of the students are necessary when universally designing a classroom for learning for all students. Table 12.6 provides several examples of students' needs within a math lesson, as well as a possible consideration and resources to use.

Therefore, advances in technology continue to benefit students with disabilities in classrooms. Both instructional and assistive (computer assisted) technology may enable special education teachers to help students with disabilities succeed in the educational environment (Edyburn et al., 2005). The definition of instructional technology is "a systematic way of designing, carrying out, and evaluating the total process of learning and teaching in terms of specific objectives, based on research in human learning and communication, and employing a combination of human and nonhuman resources to bring about more effective instruction" (Commission on Instructional Technology, 1970, p. 199). Instructional technology is essentially tools for enhancing the delivery of appropriately designed research-based instructional strategies during mathematics instruction within the classroom setting. Typically, applications of instructional technology in classrooms include media such as DVDs, video, and more complicated forms of technology such as the Internet and hypermedia. Instruction in mathematics is often enhanced through the use of technology. (The reader is encouraged to review the chapter on assistive technology in this textbook, as well.)

TABLE 12.6 Examples of Universal Access Tools to Assist Student Learning

Student Characteristics	UDL Access Tools	Resources
Antonio's mind tends to wander in math class, but he can stay on task if he has a visual representation of the lesson's concepts.	Antonio uses cognitive organizers and concept-mapping software to visually depict lesson concept.	Inspiration and Kidspiration http://www.inspiration.com
Steven is a bright student in understanding math concepts but has difficulty decoding and understanding the vocabulary contained in math problems.	Steven uses screen-reading software that translates text pages to spoken text by scanning the printed page using optical character recognition (OCR) software and listens to the text-to-audible speech.	OmniPage & OmniForm http://www.scansoft.com
Marcus understands complex math concepts at the concrete level, using manipulatives. However, his gross and fine-motor skills, as well as his in-class behaviors, limit his use of manipulatives.	Marcus uses virtual manipulatives, an extensive set of math manipulatives available online in virtual classroom labs.	Gizmos www.explorelearning.com
Susan learns her math facts but needs to develop increased accuracy and fluency with this skill.	Susan practices her math fact knowledge and recall to increase both her accuracy and speed with computer software that targets math fluency.	FASTT Math: http://tomsnyder.com
Lashawn reads and understands the math word problems but has difficulty sequencing the facts and details presented to create an equation to solve the problem.	Lashawn maps out the problem-solving process visually to use the information to solve the word problem.	CMAP: Cmap.ihmc.us

As described, technology for struggling students should not be viewed as assistive technology alone. Many forms of instructional technology may be used that benefit students' learning. For example, the use of interactive equipment and software can greatly enhance classroom instructional possibilities. The following description of a lesson set by high school teacher Emily Walker describes the many uses of technology in a mathematics class:

> *Our high school noticed that dropout rates increase if students cannot pass algebra. Because of this, we mounted an all-out effort to enable students to acquire the skills and develop the confidence needed to successfully complete algebra. One part of a multipronged effort included creating engaging, interactive lessons that show students the relevance of algebra in their everyday lives. Last year, our district purchased Promethean software, one type of interactive technology available to educators, to provide teachers with a tool for developing*

engaging lessons. For example, we developed a lesson using Promethean to help students find slope using two coordinate points. The lesson combined modeling, student interaction, video instruction, hands-on practice, and real-world application. The lesson began with a review of how to count rise over run to determine slope. We kept students active by having selected students come to the board while others used ActiveSlate. ActiveSlate is a wireless, fully integrated, mini-board that can be used at students' desks to practice the same math skill. Discussion ensued on what constitutes negative slope, positive slope, no slope, and undefined slope. Further adding to the social relevance of slope, students then observed a 9-minute video on how to calculate slope on a ski slope. In coordination with the procedures shown in the video, we practiced calculations of the change in y over the change in x. Students used personal dry-erase boards and markers to practice. The boards made it easy for teachers to quickly check the progress of students. Mistakes can be caught, erased, and corrected in a matter of seconds. The kinesthetic aspect of the boards and markers particularly appeals to the "doodlers" in the class. The lesson provides for more practice with identifying negative, positive, undefined, and no slope. The lesson culminates with photographs of slope in everyday places and a brief example of how roof pitch (slope) is calculated.

Classroom Application and Student Results

Validation research using the levels of learning is emerging in both the fields of mathematics education and special education (Witzel, 2005). For classroom teachers, program coordinators, and administrators, however, it is also critical to know that students are learning the critical concepts and objectives in higher-level mathematics as a result of professional development. Therefore, classroom teachers, math instructional coaches, and program administrators collect student data related to their math performance through the action-research process during implementation and follow-up activities of the ASK professional development (detailed below).

Action research is applied research conducted by those who want to continuously improve (Rawlinson & Little, 2005). Classroom teachers use action research because they want to improve their teaching to increase student learning. Therefore, within classrooms, the teachers themselves define the focus of the evaluation, both instruction and assessments. The three guidelines to defining evaluation are that the evaluation must be (a) related to teaching and learning, (b) something the teacher can change and (c) related to the stated instructional goals and needs of the students.

Teachers collect information about the impact of a new strategy, a new method, or procedure to determine its effectiveness. Teachers will know what works because the classroom-based research and decision making is *within* the classroom. Although various terms are used (action research, curriculum-based assessment, critical inquiry, etc.), the process of instructional decision making through the thoughtful and skillful application and evaluation of various instructional strategies is well defined. Action researchers, then, continuously self-evaluate their actions and the resulting impact of these actions on student learning. The type of action research depends on what the teacher, instructional coach, or program coordinator wants to know related to student learning. The following are two brief summaries of student impact data collected at the

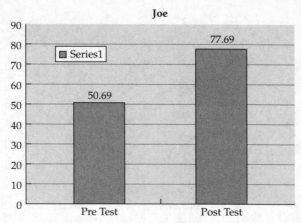

FIGURE 12.3 Algebra Success Keys Sample Comparison

math program level and one at the classroom level. Both educators used the curriculum-based school district assessments and math subtest of the Florida Comprehensive Assessment Test (comprehensive state assessment) as part of their data-collection measures of student progress.

Summer School Program: Middle School Math

A summer school program of 6 weeks was established for middle school students who scored in the two lowest levels possible out of five (1 and 2) on the Algebraic Thinking subtest of the math state assessment test (Florida Comprehensive Assessment Test, FCAT) the preceding year (2005–06 results) in this school district. In each participating educational agency, the mathematics program coordinator and the local professional developer attended professional development in a program titled Algebra Success Keys (ASK) and infused the methods, resources, and materials into the school-district-adopted curriculum during this 6-week remedial course of study in Algebraic Thinking concepts. Based on district-developed, curriculum-based assessments, students within this summer program experienced successful learning using these methods, as evidenced by their achievement on these district curriculum-based, classroom-administered measures. Data on student progress is reported in Figure 12.3.

Classroom Action Research: Grade 4

The following results of improved student performance were collected in a fourth-grade classroom of 25 students within a Title I school located in a rural school district in Florida. The fourth-grade teacher had an instructional coach assist her within the classroom, as the math students who scored the lowest on state assessment test, the Florida Comprehensive Assessment Test (FCAT), from the previous year had been administratively assigned to the classroom. The instructional mathematics coach attended the professional development in ASK and implemented lessons, strategies, and methods using the levels of learning principles 2 days each week, on average, during the school year. The chart in Figure 12.4 showing the ASK implementation of a CRA model

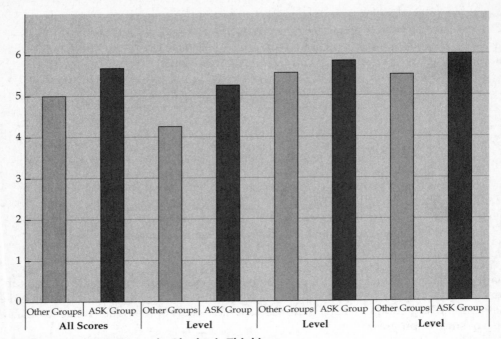

FIGURE 12.4 FCAT Scores in Algebraic Thinking

indicates that the scores of the students who were instructed using the CRA model scored higher than the students who did not receive this type of instruction. All of the students in this class, even students who scored Level 5—with Level 6 being the highest score—improved their FCAT scores in mathematics using the CRA model of instruction, as illustrated.

IMPLEMENTATION: INCLUDING STUDENTS WITH DISABILITIES IN SCHOOL REFORMS

Comprehensive school reform involves numerous stakeholders in a process of continuous improvement (Little & Houston, 2003). An important initial step is to identify a school-improvement committee to establish, articulate, and sustain the vision for high expectations for all students in mathematics within the school. The school community should be aware of and understand the vision statement and the high expectations that are being set for all students within the school. One way to do this is through active participation of staff members through meetings and committee work, at night for the community and during the workday for the staff. The main goal of the committee is to finalize the vision.

The second phase, involvement, requires that students with disabilities be actively engaged with the mathematics education curriculum. Increased numbers of students with disabilities have been attending public schools and participating in classes with students without disabilities (Nolet & McLaughlin, 2000). To illustrate the ongoing increase in student diversity, data from the U.S. Department of Education (2004) indicate that the proportion of students with disabilities with primary placements in general education increased from 33% in 1992 to 46.7% in 2001. These proportions can be expected to increase given national trends of the past three decades and IDEIA's requirement to include students with disabilities as full participants in rigorous academic and general education curriculum and assessment. The current reauthorization of IDEIA (2004) and the recent passage of the No Child Left Behind Act (2002) have placed a significant amount of pressure on school systems to provide an education in the least restrictive environment with access to the general education curriculum for students with mild disabilities (McLaughlin & Thurlow, 2003). Current practices of differentiated instruction, metacognitive strategies, levels of learning, accommodations, and technology are often implemented to address the need to involve students with disabilities with the content in general education classes (McLeskey et al., 2004).

The third phase of the process involves monitoring the progress of students with disabilities within the mathematics curriculum. The implementing regulations for IDEIA-04 described the general curriculum as the same curriculum as that provided to students without disabilities but did not elaborate further on the meaning of the term *disabilities*. The requirement in NCLB that states adopt challenging academic content and achievement standards, as well as the emphasis on a high-quality curriculum, should help define and raise the level of the general education curriculum. In addition, a number of provisions in NCLB have the potential to facilitate greater involvement in the general education curriculum—namely, the requirement that teachers be highly qualified; professional development that focuses on, for example, strategies for providing instruction to students with disabilities in regular education classes; and programs/services such as supplemental educational services.

With respect to this third phase, progress within the general education curriculum, IDEIA-04 maintains, for the most part, the obligations on the part of school districts that were introduced in IDEIA-97. These obligations, centering on the IEP (Individualized Education Program), include specification of how the student's disability affects his/her involvement and progress in the general education curriculum; IEP goals that enable the student to be involved and progress in the general education curriculum; identification in the IEP of supplementary aids and services, program modifications or supports for personnel that help the student to be involved in and progress in the general education curriculum; explanation of the extent to which the student will not participate in the regular class; and inclusion of the regular education teacher on the IEP team. These requirements are intended to engage students with disabilities as actual participants rather than passive observers in the regular education class (Malmgren, McLaughlin & Nolet, 2005). IDEIA-04 also includes a focus on functional performance and functional goals and eliminates the requirement for short-term objectives and benchmarks, except for those students who are taking assessments aligned with alternate achievement standards. IDEIA-04 includes new provisions pertaining to Universal Design for Learning (UDL) and assistive technology that should help students with disabilities have greater access in a timely manner to the print materials that are part of the general education curriculum.

Many students come to school unprepared to meet the achievement expectations inherent in the mathematics standards set forth by state departments of education. To meet these standards, the following list includes suggestions for teachers and school leaders to consider.

First, a high level of academic achievement must be established, communicated, and continuously monitored for every child based on the state curriculum standards at every grade level. State and classroom assessment data provide the continuous monitoring of impact of instruction. For students who are not achieving at expected performance levels, create a series of interventions targeted toward the needed instruction. Educators should aim their instruction at the grade-level standard rather than conclude success at the precursor skills. For example, it does little good to attempt an intervention to teach a 10th-grade student the multiplication facts when he has failed learning them for the past 7 years. Set the aim for your intervention as the grade-level standard of which the student is not succeeding.

Students struggling to meet the standards need extra assistance (Kortering, deBettencourt, & Braziel, 2005). Meet with individual teacher(s) to problem solve solutions to meet the students' needs evidenced through the continuous progress monitoring of student learning in mathematics. Convene the instructional committees (RTI, IEP, or a school and district intervention planning team) to write, review, or revise the current plans based on the current progress monitoring data. If a student already has an IEP developed, then it may be necessary to review and revise the IEP learning goals with the IEP review team. Some suggestions for interventions include additional support at home, before- or after-school programs, extra literacy assistance during the school day, peer tutoring, summer programs, or specialized programs in mathematics.

Second, follow through on enforcing high achievement expectations. Educators should be empowered to differentiate instruction to meet individual learning needs. Multiple interventions should be attempted and monitored to reach high expectations. To do so, child study teams, immediate intensive interventions, accommodations, and progress monitoring should be tried and documented to evaluate the achievement increase in students. Schedule regular meetings dedicated to monitoring the follow-through of planning and implementing instruction and interventions continuously. Revisit minutes and action plans of these child-study and intervention teams throughout the year. Provide the necessary resources, including planning time and research-based programs and materials, to address the individual student needs.

Third, communicate early and often with parents on the academic progress of their children, especially if they are not making satisfactory progress. If parents are to help their children achieve the standards, they need to know this early in the school year. Communication is essential to positively collaborating with parents and students in improving learning. The learning community at a school is fostered by honest feedback, celebrating success, and together addressing high expectations.

Also, make sure that the grading system reflects how children are performing compared to the district and state curriculum standards, as well as any IEP applied to the student. Make sure that report cards and other parent communication clearly indicate student achievement. Use a variety of forms of assessment to ensure accuracy in a child's grade placement and interventions based on assessments and progress monitoring.

Finally, with respect to accountability for progress in the mathematics curriculum, both IDEA-97 and IDEIA-04 include requirements concerning progress toward IEP goals, participation in state and districtwide assessments, and the establishment of performance goals and indicators. In the area of assessments, NCLB mandates that states must establish high-quality, yearly academic assessments for all students, including students with disabilities (with accommodations or by means of alternate assessments), and that these assessments must be aligned with state content and achievement standards. Implementing regulations for NCLB also allows for the development of alternate achievement standards for students with the most significant cognitive disabilities whose performance is based on an alternate assessment. IDEIA-04 aligns IDEA with NCLB with respect to assessments by stating that the IDEA mandate for the inclusion of students with disabilities in state and districtwide assessments includes assessments required under NCLB. Moreover, IDEIA-04 refers to the use of alternate achievement standards in several places in the statute that pertain to access to the general education curriculum. IDEIA-04 aligns IDEA with NCLB with respect to accountability by stating that performance goals should be the same as AYP (adequate yearly progress) and that performance indicators should include measurable annual goals under NCLB.

These systems are intended to increase accountability for the educational performance of all students, including students with disabilities. To accomplish these accountability goals for student learning in mathematics, teachers need time to plan, time to analyze their instruction, and time to understand data. This time can be used to determine how instruction correlates to data to ensure student learning. School leaders can coach and/or facilitate instructional coaching of teachers in this process.

Summary

Addressing school reform through research-based instruction is of great benefit to students and teachers. Accountability for improved student learning within mathematics classrooms and schools is based on student learning through the connection of the multiple considerations when planning and implementing instruction in mathematics and continuous progress monitoring through various types of assessments and action research. The active engagement of students with disabilities through the use of the revised mathematics standards, levels of learning, metacognitive strategies, accommodations, and technology improves students' achievement in mathematics understandings, concepts, and skills. Continuously monitoring student performance through various assessments and action research by teachers provides results of student learning to address instructional decisions and school accountability. Most important, however, is that actively engaging students through levels of learning, metacognitive strategies, accommodations, and technology, and actively engaging teachers through action research to inform instruction, will have the greatest impact on student learning.

References

Algozzine, B., O'Shea, D. J., Crews, W., & Stoddard, K. (1987). Analysis of mathematics competence of learning disabled adolescents. *Journal of Special Education, 21*(2), 97–107.

Baroody, A. J., & Hume, J. (1991). Meaningful mathematics instruction: The case of fractions. *Remedial and Special Education, 12*(3), 54–67.

Brian, T., Bay, M., Lopez-Reyan, N., & Donhue, M. (1991). Characteristics of students with learning disabilities: A summary of the extant database and its implications for educational programs. In J. W. Loyd, N. Nirbhay, & A. C Repp (Eds.), *The regular education initiative: Alternative perspectives on concepts, issues, and models* (pp. 113–131). Sycamore, IL: Sycamore.

Bryant, D. P., Bryant, B., & Hammill, D. (2000). Characteristic behaviors of students with LD who have teacher-identified math weaknesses. *Journal of Learning Disabilities, 33,* 168–177, 199.

Bryant, D. P., Hartman, P., & Kim, S. A. (2003). Using explicit and systematic instruction to teach division skills to students with learning disabilities, *Exceptionality, 11*(3), 151–164.

Bulgren, J. A., Schumaker, J. B., & Deshler, D. D. (2003). *The content enhancement series: the concept mastery routine.* Lawrence, KS: Edge Enterprises.

Butler, F. M., Miller, S. P., Crehan, K., Babbit, B., & Pierce, T. (2003). Fraction instruction for students with mathematics disabilities: Comparing two teaching sequences. *Learning Disabilities Research & Practice, 18*(2), 99–111.

Cart, E., & Ogle, D. (1987). K-W-L Plus: A strategy for comprehension and summarization. *Journal of Reading, 30,* 626–631.

Cass, M., Cates, D., & Smith, M., & Jackson, C. (2003). Effects of manipulative instruction on solving area and perimeter problems by students with learning disabilities. *Learning Disabilities Research and Practice, 18*(2), 112–120.

Cavanagh, S. (2006). Math organization attempts to bring focus to subject. *Education Week, 26*(4), 1–24.

Cawley, J. F., Parmer, R. S., Yan, W., & Miller, J. H. (1998). Arithmetic computation performance of students with learning disabilities: Implications for curriculum. *Learning Disabilities Research & Practice, 13,* 68–74.

Chard, D. J., & Kameenui, E. J. (1995). Mathematics instruction for students with diverse learning needs: Heeding the message of the Cheshire cat. *Focus on Learning Problems in Mathematics, 17*(2), 24–38.

Commission on Instructional Technology. (1970). *To improve learning: A report to the president and the Congress of the United States.* Washington, DC: U.S. Government Printing Office.

Devlin, K. (2000). Finding your inner mathematician. *Chronicle of Higher Education, 46,* B5.

Edyburn, D., Higgins, K., & Boone, R. (2005). *Handbook for special education technology and practice.* White Fish Bay, WI: Knowledge by Design.

Foegen, A., Jiban, C., & Deno, S. (2007). Progress monitoring measures in mathematics: A review of the literature. *Journal of Special Education, 41*(2), 121–39.

Fuchs, L. S., Compton, D. L., Fuchs, D., Paulsen, K., Bryant, J. D., & Hamlett, C. L. (2005). The prevention, identification, and cognitive determinants of math difficulty. *Journal of Education Psychology, 97*(3), 493–513.

Fuchs, L. S. & Fuchs, D. (2001). Principles for the prevention and intervention of mathematics difficulties. *Learning Disabilities Research & Practice, 16,* 85–95.

Fuchs, L. S., Fuchs, D., Compton, D. L., Bryant, J. D., Hamlett, C. L., & Seethaler, P. M. (2007). Mathematics screening and progress monitoring at first grade: Implications for responsiveness to intervention. *Exceptional Children, 73*(3), 311–330.

Gersten, R., Jordan, N. C., & Flojo, J. R. (2005). Early identification and interventions for students with mathematics difficulties. *Journal of Learning Disabilities, 38,* 291–292.

Ginsburg, H. P. (1997). Mathematics learning disabilities: A view from development psychology. *Journal of Learning Disabilities, 30*(1), 20–33.

Goldsmith, L. T., & Mark, J. (1999). What is a standards-based mathematics curriculum? *Educational Leadership, 57*(3), 40–44.

Gross-Tsur, V., Manor, O., Shalev, R. S. (1996). Developmental dyscalculia: Prevalence and demographic features. *Developmental Medicine and Child Neurology, 37,* 906–914.

Hiebert, J., & Behr, M. (1988). *Number concepts and operations in the middle grades* (Vol. 2). Reston, VA: National Council of Teachers of Mathematics.

Hitchcock, C., Meyer, A., Rose, D., & Jackson, R. (2002). Providing new access to the general curriculum: Universal Design for Learning. *Teaching Exceptional Children, 35,* 8–17.

Hudson, P., Miller, S. P., & Butler, F. (2006). Adapting and merging explicit instruction within reform based mathematics classrooms. *American Secondary Education, 35*(1), 19–32.

Hutchinson, N. L. (1993). Second invited response: Students with disabilities and mathematics education reform—Let the dialog begin. *Remedial and Special Education, 14*(6), 20–23.

Individuals with Disabilities Education Act (IDEA) Regulations (1997). 34 C.F.R. & 300.500(3)(b).

Individuals with Disabilities Education Improvement Act (IDEIA) Regulations (2004). P.L. 108–496; 48 C.F.R. & 400.500(4)(c).

Jackson, H. G., & Neel, R. S. (2006). Observing mathematics: Do students with EBD have access to standards-based mathematics instruction?

Education and Treatment of Children, 29(4), 593–614.

Jitendra, A. (2002). Teaching students math problem-solving through graphic representations. *Teaching Exceptional Children, 34*(4), 34–38.

Jitendra, A. K., DiPipi, C. M., Perron-Jones, N. (2002). An exploratory study of schema-based word-problem solving instruction for middle school students with learning disabilities: An emphasis on conceptual and procedural understanding. *Journal of Special Education, 36*(1), 23–38.

Jitendra, A., & Xin, Y. P. (1997). Mathematical word-problem-solving instruction for students with mild disabilities and students at risk for math failure: A research synthesis. *The Journal of Special Education, 30*(4), 412–438.

Johnson, D. J., & Myklebust, H. R. (1967). *Learning disabilities: Educational principles and practices.* New York: Grune and Stratton.

Johnson, E. S. (2000). The effects of accommodations on performance assessments. *Remedial and Special Education, 21*(5), 261–267.

Jordan, L., Miller, M. D., & Mercer, C. D. (1999). The effects of concrete to semi-concrete to abstract instruction in the acquisition and retention of fraction concepts and skills. *Learning Disabilities: A Multidisciplinary Journal, 9*, 115–122.

Kortering, L. J., deBettencourt, L. U., & Braziel, P. M. (2005). Improving performance in high school algebra: What students with learning disabilities are saying. *Learning Disabilities Quarterly, 28*, 191–203.

Little, M. E., & Houston, D. (2003). Comprehensive school reform. *Journal of Disability Policy Studies, 14*, 54–62.

Little, M., Kinney, M. & Robertson, S. (2007). Professional development in algebra: Improved results. *Florida Educational Leadership, 5*(1), 52–60.

Maccini, P., & Gagnon, J. (2002). Perceptions and application of NCTM standards by special and general education teachers. *Exceptional Children, 68*, 325–344.

Maccini, P., & Hughes, C.A. (2000). Effects of a problem-solving strategy on the introductory algebra performance of secondary students with learning disabilities. *Learning Disabilities Research & Practice, 15*, 10–21.

Maccini, P., Mulcahy, C. A., & Wilson, M. G. (2007). A follow-up of mathematics interventions for secondary students with learning disabilities. *Learning Disabilities Research and Practice, 22*(1), 58–74.

Malmgren, K. W., McLaughlin, M. J., & Nolet, V. (2005). Accounting for the performance of students with disabilities on statewide assessments. *Journal of Special Education, 39*, 86–96.

Mastropieri, M. A., & Scruggs, T. E. (2007). *The inclusive classroom: Strategies for effective instruction* (3rd ed.). Upper Saddle River, NJ: Merrill/Pearson Education.

McLaughlin, M. J., & Thurlow, M. (2003). Educational accountability and students with disabilities: Issues and challenges. *Educational Policy, 17*(4), 431–450.

McLeskey, J., Hoppey, D., Williamson, P., & Rentz, T. (2004). Is inclusion an illusion? An examination of national and state trends toward the education of students with learning disabilities in general education classrooms. *Learning Disabilities Research and Practice, 19*(2), 109–115.

Mercer, C. D., Harris, C., & Miller, S. P. (1993). Reforming reforms in mathematics. *Remedial and Special Education, 14*, 14–19.

Mercer, C. D., & Miller, S. P. (1992). Teaching students with learning problems in math to acquire, understand, and apply basic math facts. *Remedial and Special Education, 13*(3), 19–35.

Miller, S. P., & Hudson, P. J. (2007). Using evidence-based practices to build mathematics competence related to conceptual, procedural, and declarative knowledge. *Learning Disabilities Research and Practice, 22*(1), 47–57.

Miller, S. P., & Mercer, C. D. (1993). Using data to learn about concrete–semiconcrete–abstract instruction for students with math disabilities. *Learning Disabilities Research & Practice, 8*, 89–96.

Monroe, E. E., & Orme, M. P. (2002). Developing mathematical vocabulary. *Preventing School Failure, 46*, 139–142.

Montague , M., Warger, C., & Morgan, T. H. (2000). Solve it! Strategy instruction to improve mathematical problem solving. *Learning Disabilities Research and Practice, 15*, 10–16.

Nagel, F., Schumaker, J., & Deshler, D. (1986). *Strategic instruction model.* Lawrence, KS: Edge.

National Center for Educational Statistics. (1992). *National assessment of educational progress 1992 mathematics report card for the nation and the states* (Report No. 23-ST02). Washington, DC: Author.

National Center for Education Statistics. (2004). *Highlights from the trends in international mathematics and science study* (TIMSS) (2003). Washington, DC: U.S. Government Printing Office.

National Center for Education Statistics. (2006). *Highlights from the trends in international mathematics and science study* (TIMSS) (2005). Washington, DC: U.S. Government Printing Office.

National Council of Teachers of Mathematics. (1995). *Principles and standards for school mathematics.* Reston, VA: Author.

National Council of Teachers of Mathematics. (2000). *Principles and standards for school mathematics.* Reston, VA: Author.

National Research Council. (1989). *Every day counts: A report to the nation on the future of mathematics education.* Washington, DC: National Academy Press.

National Research Council. (2001). *Adding it up: Helping children learn mathematics.* Washington, DC: National Academy Press.

No Child Left Behind Act of 2001, Pub. L. 107–110, 115 Stat. 1425, 20 U.S.C. §§ 6301 *et seq.*

Nolet, V., & McLaughlin, M. J. (2000*). Accessing the general education curriculum: Including students with disabilities in standards-based reform.* Thousand Oaks, CA: Corwin.

Office of Educational Research and Improvement. (1998). *Attaining excellence: A TIMSS resource kit.* Washington, DC: U.S. Department of Education.

Peterson, S. K., Mercer, C. D., & O'Shea, L. (1988). Teaching learning disabilities students place value using the concrete to abstract sequence. *Learning Disabilities Research, 4*(1), 52–56.

Rawlinson, D., & Little, M. (2005). *Improving student learning through classroom action research.* Tallahassee: Florida Department of Education.

Readence, J. E., Bean, T. W., & Baldwin, R. S. (1985). *Content area reading: An integrated approach* (2nd ed.) Dubuque, IA: Kendall Hunt.

Riccomini, P. J. (2005). Identification and remediation of systematic error patterns in subtraction. *Learning Disabilities Quarterly, 28,* 233–242.

Rivera, D. P., Smith, R. G., Goodwin, M. W., & Bryant, D. P. (1998). Mathematical word problem solving: A synthesis of intervention research for students with learning disabilities. In T. E. Scruggs & M. A. Mastropieri (Eds.), *Advances in learning and behavioral disabilities* (Vol. 12, pp. 245–285). Greenwich, CT: JAI Press.

Rose, D. (2000). Universal Design for Learning. *Journal of Special Education Technology, 15*(1), 67–70.

Rose, D. H., & Meyer, A. (2002). Teaching every student in the digital age: Universal Design for Learning. Alexandria, VA: Association for Supervision and Curriculum Development.

Rourke, B. (1993). Arithmetic disabilities, specific and otherwise: A neuropsychological perspective. *Journal of Learning Disabilities, 26*(4), 214–226.

Schmidt, W., McKnight, C., & Raizen, S. (1997). Detrimental effects of reward: Reality or myth? *American Psychologist, 51,* 1153–1166.

Stecker, P. M., & Fuchs, L. S. (2000). Effecting superior achievement using curriculum-based measurement: The importance of individual progress monitoring. *Learning Disability Research and Practice, 15,* 128–134.

Steele, D., & Johanning, D. (2004). A schematic-theoretic view of problem solving and development of algebraic thinking. *Education Studies in Mathematics, 57,* 65–90.

Stigler, J., & Hiebert, J. (1999). *The teaching gap: Best ideas from the world's teachers for improving education in the classroom.* New York: The Free Press.

Swanson, H. L., & Carson, C. (1996). A selective synthesis of intervention research for students with learning disabilities. *School Psychology Review, 25*(3), 370–391.

Technology-Related Assistance Act for Individuals with Disabilities, U.S.C. 1400 et seq.

Tomlinson, C. (1999). *Differentiating instruction.* Alexandria, VA: ASCD.

Topping, K. J., Campbell, J., Douglas, W., & Smith, A. (2003). Cross-age peer tutoring in mathematics with seven and 11 year olds: influence on mathematical vocabulary, strategic dialogue and self-concept. *Educational Research, 45,* 287–308.

U.S. Department of Education. (2004). *To assure a free and appropriate public education of all children with disabilities. Twenty-fifth annual report to Congress on the implementation of the Individuals with Disabilities Education Act.* Washington, DC: Office of Special Education Programs.

U.S. Department of Education, National Center for Education Statistics. (2000). *Pursuing excellence: Comparisons of international eighth-grade mathematics achievement from a U.S. perspective, 1995 and 1999 (NCES 2001–028).* Washington, DC: U.S. Government Printing Office.

Wagner, M. (1995). Outcomes for youth with serious emotional disturbance in secondary school and early adulthood. *Future of Children, 5*(2), 90–113.

Walker, M. M., & Blackorby, J. (1996). Transition from high school to work or college: How special education students far. *Future of Children, 5*(2), 90–113.

Witzel, B. S. (2004). *Multisensory algebra guide: Operations, expressions, and equations.* Fort Mill, SC: Effective Teacher.

Witzel, B. S. (2005). Using CRA to teach algebra to students with math difficulties in inclusive settings. *Learning Disabilities: A Contemporary Journal, 3*(2), 49–60.

Witzel, B. S., Ferguson, C. J., & Brown, D. (2007). Early numeracy skills for students with learning disabilities. *LDOnline Exclusive* [Available online at www.ldonline.com].

Witzel, B. S., Mercer, C. D., & Miller, M. D. (2003). Teaching algebra to students with learning difficulties: An investigation of an explicit instruction model. *Learning Disabilities Research & Practice, 18*(2), 121–131.

Witzel, B. S., Riccomini, P. R., & Schneider, E. (2008). Implementing CRA math instruction with secondary students with learning disabilities. *Intervention in School and Clinic, 43*(5), 270–276.

Witzel, B. S., Smith, S. W., & Brownell, M. T. (2001). How can I help students with learning disabilities in algebra? *Intervention in School and Clinic, 37,* 101–104.

Woodward, J. (2004). Mathematics education in the United States: Past to present. *Journal of Learning Disabilities, 37*(1), 16–31.

Woodward, J., & Montague, M. (2002). Meeting the challenge of mathematics reform for students with LD. *Journal of Special Education, 36*(2), 89–101.

Xin, Y. P., & Jitendra, A. K. (1999). The effects of instruction in solving mathematical word problems for students with learning problems: A meta-analysis. *Journal of Special Education, 32*(4), 207–225.

APPENDIX

CHAPTER 1: RESOURCES

Annual reports to Congress are available at http://www.ed.gov/about/offices/list/osers/osep/research.html

The Carl D. Perkins Vocational and Technical Education Act is available at http://www.ed.gov/offices/OVAE/CTE/perkins.html

Gifted and talented information regarding effective teaching practices can be accessed at http://www.gifted.uconn.edu/nrcgt.html

The Individuals with Disabilities Education Improvement Act can be found at http://edworkforce.house.gov/issues/108th/education/idea/conferencereport/confrept.htm

McKinney-Vento Act information about policies and effective educational practices can be found at http://www.nationalhomeless.org

e National Center for Homeless Education offers information to assist teachers provide appropriate educational to children who experience homelessness at http://www.serve.org/nche

The National Clearinghouse for English Language Acquisition Web site provides information and additional resources at http://www.ncela.gwu.edu/

National Dropout Prevention Centers are available throughout the country to serve students with and without disabilities at http://www.dropoutprevention.org/

No Child Left Behind Act Web sites with comprehensive information about the bill are found at http://www.ed.gov/nclb/landing.jhtml and http://edworkforce.house.gov/nclb.htm

State Assistive Technology Projects can be accessed at http://www.ataporg.org/stateat-projects.asp

Workforce Enactment Act of 1998 is provided at http://www.usdoj.gov/crt/508/508law.html

CHAPTER 2: RESOURCES

Learning Disabilities

The Division for Learning Disabilities (DLD) is part of the Council for Exceptional Children and is dedicated to research and legislation for individuals with learning disabilities. Members receive *Learning Disabilities Research and Practice* and *Current Practice Alerts*. http://www.cec.sped.org/Content/NavigationMenu/AboutCEC/Communities/Divisions/default.htm

The Learning Disabilities Association of America (LDA) provides services and information to persons with learning disabilities, their parents, teachers, and other professionals. http://www.ldanatl.org/

The National Attention Deficit Disorder Association (ADDA) provides information, resources, and networking opportunities to adults with attention deficit–hyperactivity disorder (ADHD) and service providers at http://www.add.org/

The National Center for Learning Disabilities (NCLD) provides information, promotes research and programs, and advocates for policies pertaining to persons with LD. http://www.ncld.org/

The International Dyslexia Association, formerly the Orton Dyslexia Association, primarily serves professionals and families of individuals with reading disabilities. http://www.interdys.org/

Attention Deficit Hyperactivity Disorder (ADHD)

Children and Adults with Attention-Deficit Disorder (CHADD) offers support services, blogs, and conferences for professionals and families of children with ADHD. CHADD publishes *Attention* and has many regional chapters providing local support. http://www.chadd.org/

The National Dissemination Center for Children with Disabilities provides information on educational and legal rights by state as well as parent guides for attention-deficit disorder and learning disabilities. http://www.nichcy.org/

MILD MENTAL RETARDATION

The American Association on Mental Retardation (AAMR) promotes progressive policies, sound research, and effective practices and advocate universal human rights for people with intellectual disabilities. This site offers information and resources for parents, professionals, advocates, and teacher alike. http://www.aamr.org/index .html

The Association for Retarded Children (ARC) of the United States works to include all children and adults with cognitive, intellectual, and developmental disabilities in every community. http://thearc.org/

The National Fragile X Foundation: Fragile X syndrome is the most common known cause of inherited mental impairment. http://www.fragilex.org/

Parentpals.com is sponsored by Ameri-Corp Speech and Hearing. They provide information on the following subjects: ADHD, autism, deaf and hard-of-hearing issues, emotional disturbance, home-schooling, gifted students, learning disabilities, mental retardation, orthopedic impairment, other health impairment, severe and/or multiple disabilities, speech and language impairment, stuttering, traumatic brain injury, and visual impairment. http://parentpals.com/gossamer/pages/

PACER Center provides information and opportunities that lead to enhanced quality of life for children and young adults with disabilities and their families, based on the concept of parents helping parents. http://www.pacer.org/

EMOTIONAL DISTURBANCE/EMOTIONAL AND BEHAVIORAL DISORDERS

Office of Special Education Programs, U.S. Department of Education Technical Assistance Center on Positive Behavioral Interventions and Supports, provides schools capacity-building information and technical assistance for identifying, adapting, and sustaining effective schoolwide disciplinary practices. http://www.pbis.org/main.htm

About.com offers information on a variety of topics, including characteristics and educational implications of students with emotional and behavioral disorders. There are also suggestions for curricular accommodations and behavior interventions. http://specialed.about.com/cs/behaviordisorders/a/Behavior.htm

National Mental Health Information Center, Children and Adolescents with Mental, Emotional, and Behavioral Disorders. http://www.mentalhealth.org/publications/allpubs/CA-0006/default.asp

National Dissemination Center for Children with Disabilities serves the nation as a central source of information on disabilities in infants, toddlers, children, and youth. This link discusses educating students with emotional/behavioral disorders. http://www.nichcy.org/pubs/bibliog/bib10txt.htm

The Council for Children with Behavioral Disorders provides information and resources for the community, teachers, professionals, and parents. http://www.ccbd.net

The Council for Exceptional Children (CEC) offers a 1991 mini-library on behavioral disorders. Each book is brief and practitioner oriented. The books may be purchased from CEC at the address listed under List of Publishers or through the ERIC Document Reproduction Service.

COMMUNICATION DISORDERS

The American Speech-Language-Hearing Association (ASHA) is the professional, scientific, and credentialing association for more than 115,000 members and affiliates who are audiologists, speech–language pathologists, and speech, language, and hearing scientists. Teacher, parents, and students can find information here that will assist them in providing the highest quality services for people with communication disabilities. http://www.asha.org/

The National Institute on Deafness and Other Communication Disorders offers information and resources for improving the lives of people who have communication disorders. http://www.nidcd.nih.gov/

The Stuttering home page created and maintained at Minnesota State University, Mankato, is dedicated to providing information about stuttering for both consumers and professionals who work with people who stutter. It includes information about research, therapy, support organizations, a chat room for people who stutter, and conferences and other events. http://www.mnsu.edu/dept/comdis/kuster/stutter.html.

There is also a link on the site that provides a list of famous people who stutter: http://www.mnsu.edu/dept/comdis/kuster/famous/famouspws.html

The National Center for Neurologic Communication Disorders is concerned about speech and language disorders (e.g., speech and voice production, auditory and visual perception of speech, cognition, and the impairment of language function after stroke or as a result of nervous system disease). The Center has a special interest in American Indian and Hispanic cultures. The Center also operates programs that offer information dissemination to the public and continuing education for professionals through print and electronic communications links and through face-to-face meetings. http://cnet.shs.arizona.edu/

STUDENTS AT RISK

The National Institute on the Education of At-Risk Students (At-Risk Institute) is one of five institutes created by the Educational Research, Development, Dissemination, and Improvement Act of 1994. These institutes are located within the Office of Educational Research and Improvement at the U.S. Department of Education. http://www.ed.gov/offices/OERI/At-Risk/index.html

The National Center for Homeless Education provides research, resources, and information enabling communities to address the educational needs of children and youth experiencing homelessness. http://www.serve.org/nche/

The National Association for the Education of Homeless Children and Youth (NAEHCY) connects educators, parents, advocates, researchers and service providers to ensure school enrollment and attendance and overall success for children and youth whose lives have been disrupted by the lack of safe, permanent, and adequate housing. http://www.naehcy.org/

The National Poverty Center conducts and promotes multidisciplinary, policy-relevant research on the causes and consequences of poverty and provides mentoring and training to young scholars. http://www.npc.umich.edu/poverty/

LIMITED ENGLISH PROFICIENCY

The Office English Language Acquisition, Language Enhancement, and Academic Achievement for Limited English Proficient Students (OELA) provides information and resources for promoting high-quality education for limited English proficient students (LEP). http://www.ncela.gwu.edu/oela/

The Center for Applied Linguistics is a private, nonprofit organization of scholars and educators who use the findings of linguistics and related sciences to carry out activities related to language-related problems. This site offers a wide-range of databases and online resources. http://www.cal.org/

Teachers of English to Speakers of Other Languages (TESOL) is an international organization focused on teaching English to speakers of other languages. The TESOL site has information on training programs, research, ESL standards for PK–12 students, and practical applications for classroom teachers. http://www.tesol.org/

The Lab at Brown University has developed a program called Teaching Diverse Learners. This program provides teachers with information on policy, assessment, and working with parents. http://www.lab.brown.edu/tdl

JUVENILE DELINQUENCY

The National Center on Education, Disability, and Juvenile Justice focuses on assisting practitioners, policymakers, researchers, and advocates to identify and implement effective school-based delinquency-prevention programs, education and special education services in juvenile correctional facilities, and transition supports for youth reentering their schools and communities from secure care settings. http://www.edjj.org

The American Bar Association's Commission on Mental and Physical Disability Law provides materials that focus on the implementation of the Americans with Disabilities Act and other areas of mental health law. http://www.abanet.org/disability/

The National Council on Disability is an independent federal agency making recommendations to the president and Congress on issues affecting 54 million Americans with disabilities. The site provides the 2003 report, *Addressing the Needs of Youth with Disabilities in the Juvenile Justice System: The Current Status of Evidence-Based Research.* http://www.ncd.gov/

SCHOOL DROPOUTS

The National Dropout Prevention Center for Students with Disabilities (NDPC-SD) supports the national implementation of provisions of the Individuals with Disabilities Education Act (IDEA) to provide successful school outcomes for students with disabilities. http://www.ndpc-sd.org/

U.S. Department of Education School Dropout Prevention Program. http://www.ed.gov/programs/dropout/index.html

TEENAGE PREGNANCY AND SEXUALLY TRANSMITTED DISEASES

The National Campaign to Prevent Teen and Unplanned Pregnancy is an organization whose purpose is to provide national leadership and raise awareness and disseminate information and share resources about teenage pregnancy. http://www.thenationalcampaign.org/

Child Trends is a 25-year-old nonprofit, nonpartisan research organization dedicated to improving the lives of children by conducting research and providing science-based information to improve the decisions, programs, and policies that affect children and their families. http://www.childtrends.org/

SIECUS—the Sexuality Information and Education Council of the United States—has served as the national voice for sexuality education, sexual health, and sexual rights for almost 40 years. They provide technical assistance, specialized trainings and workshops, and program guidance to advance sexuality education, reproductive health, HIV/AIDS treatment and prevention programs, and advocacy efforts worldwide. http://www.siecus.org/

DEPRESSION/SUICIDE/SUBSTANCE ABUSE

Focus Adolescent Services provides information on teen and family issues related to self-destructive behaviors with links to articles and organizations on mental health and counseling that can help students at risk. http://www.focusas.com/

DisabilityResources.org provides information and resources on substance abuse and people with disabilities. http://www.disabilityresources.org/

Kids Health, a bilingual site sponsored by the Nemours Foundation, provides teenagers with information on topics such as physical and mental health, sexual health, drugs and alcohol, diseases and infection, school-related issues, and how to stay safe. http://kidshealth.org/

National Clearinghouse for Alcohol and Drug Information (NCADI) is the nation's one-stop resource for information about substance abuse prevention and addiction treatment. The resource guide provides information to assist teachers, counselors, physical therapists, and mental health professionals in their understanding and interactions with individuals with disabilities. http://www.health.org/govpubs/MS461/

CHAPTER 3: RESOURCES

The Early Childhood Research Institute on Inclusion (ECRII) was a 5-year national research project funded by the Office of Special Education Programs, U.S. Department of Education, to study the inclusion of preschool children with disabilities. The site provides research-based strategies and information on how best to promote collaboration among the various individuals involved in the inclusion process—family members, teachers, administrators—to ensure successful educational outcomes. http://www.fpg.unc.edu/~ecrii/

Learning Points Associates' Web site is a research-based site dedicated to improving educational decision making. Methods and materials are provided to assist teachers, parents, and administrators with building a foundation for school improvement based on interpreting and applying school and district data to a number of common problems—for example, after-school programming, tutorials for analyzing and interpreting data for comprehensive school improvement, professional development, math and science, and literacy. http://www.learningpt.org/

National Resource Center for Paraprofessionals serves as a comprehensive resource for teachers, paraeducators, administrators, physical and speech-language therapists, college and university stakeholders, and other educational professionals. The site offers training models, books, and other materials to facilitate recruitment, deployment, and supervision of paraprofessionals. http://www.nrcpara.org/

CHAPTER 6: RESOURCES

The Big6 promotes information literacy using a metacognitive scaffold, or an information problem-solving strategy, for teaching and reinforcing the research, problem-solving, and writing processes. http://www.big6.com/

The Foundation for Critical Thinking is a nonprofit organization that works to ensure educational reform by promoting change in education and society through the cultivation of fair-minded critical thinking. The site offers teaching strategies, learning strategies, materials, videos, professional development opportunities, and information that foster the development of self-directed, self-disciplined, self-monitored, and self-corrective thinking in K–12 students and teachers. http://www.criticalthinking.org/

The Learning Toolbox is a Web site developed by James Madison University. It provides a wide array of strategy materials appropriate for students, parents, and teachers. http://coe.jmu.edu/LearningToolbox/

GraphicOrganizers.com provides free downloadable graphic organizers and think-sheet templates. There are also free professional development materials. http://graphicorganizers.com/

The Research Cycle by Jamie McKenzie is based on over 33 years of working with teachers and media specialists to emphasize higher-level thinking, problem solving, and decision making. http://questioning.org/Q6/research.html

The Questioning Toolkit by Jamie McKenzie provides resources and suggestions for improving student's problem-solving skills using Bloom's Taxonomy. http://www.fno.org/nov97/toolkit.html

CHAPTER 7: RESOURCES

Universal Design for Learning

Review the CAST Web site at http://cast.org

- How-to tutorial for completing a barriers analysis: http://www.cast.org/teachingeverystudent/tools/curriculumbarriers.cfm
- Examples of UDL lessons and a digital copy of *Teaching Every Student in the Digital Age:* http://cast.org/teachingeverystudent

Bloom's Taxonomy

- Applying Bloom's Taxonomy: http://www.teachers.ash.org.au/researchskills/dalton.htm
- Applying Bloom's Taxonomy to the use of technology: http://education.ed.pacificu.edu/aacu/workshop/reconcept2B.html
- To learn how Bloom's Taxonomy connects to the three domains of learning: cognitive, affective, and psychomotor: http://www.nwlink.com/~donclark/hrd/bloom.html#five

To learn how to conduct a task analysis: http://classweb.gmu.edu/ndabbagh/Resources/IDKB/task_analysis.htm

CHAPTER 8: RESOURCES

State Assistive Technology Projects

The URL below links to a list for individual State Assistive Technology Projects where you can find a link for your state's project. There are 56 projects (one in each state and in DC and the U.S. territories). http://www.resna.org/taproject/at/statecontacts.html

Hardware

AlphaSmart 3000, Neo, Dana	AlphaSmart, Inc. Phone: 408/355-1000 http://www2.alphasmart.com/
Dynavox	DynaVox Technologies Phone: 866/396-2869 http://www.dynavoxsys.com/
Handheld computers	Palm, Inc. Corporate Headquarters Phone: 408/617-7000 http://www.palm.com
Intelli-Keys Intelli-Talk 3	IntelliTools Phone: 800/899-6687 http://www.intellitools.com/
BoardMaker Communication Folder and Writing with Symbols 2000	Mayer-Johnson LLC Phone: 800/588-4548 or 858/550-0084 http://www.mayer-johnson.com/
Say-It! SAM Communicator	Words+, Inc. Phone: 800/869-8521 http://www.words-plus.com/index.htm
SmartPad	Seiko Instruments USA Inc. Phone: 310/517-7700 http://www.siibusinessproducts.com/
Quicktionary Pen	Quick-Pen.com Phone: 816/942-7744 http://www.quick-pen.com/

Software

Show Me Spelling	Attainment Company, Inc. Phone: 800/327-4269 http://www.attainmentcompany.com
Co-Writer Write Out-Loud Simon S.I.O	Don Johnston Incorporated Phone: 847/740-0749 http://www.donjohnston.com
WYNN Wizard	Freedom Scientific, Learning Systems Group Phone: 888/223-3344 http://www.freedomscientific.com/LSG/products/wynn.asp
Kurzweil 3000	Kurzweil Educational Systems, Inc. http://www.kurzweiledu.com To see a video: http://www.kurzweiledu.com/k3000demo/

Writing with Symbols 2000	Mayer-Johnson LLC Phone: 800/588-4548 or 858/550-0084 http://www.mayer-johnson.com/main/
Dragon Naturally Speaking	ScanSoft http://www.nuance.com
Web Readers (free downloads)	Texthelp Systems, Inc. Phone: 888/248-0652 • Browse-Aloud: http://www.browsealoud.com/ • PDFaloud: http://www.texthelp.com/

Internet Resources

American Sign Language	American Sign Language Teachers Association http://www.aslta.org/
Calculators	Martindale's Calculators Online Center http://www.martindalecenter.com/Calculators.html
Dictionary and Thesaurus	Merriam-Webster Online http://www.m-w.com/
Signing Exact English	SEE Center http://www.seecenter.org/

Audio and Electronic Books

Audio and Braille Books	Library of Congress, National Library Service Information about services is available at your local library and at the Web site below. http://www.loc.gov/nls/
Recorded Books	Recorded Books, LLC Phone: 800/638-1304 http://www.recordedbooks.com/
Recording for the Blind & Dyslexic	RFB#x0026;D Phone: 866/732-3585 http://www.rfbd.org/
Online Electronic Books	University of Virginia E-Book Library: http://etext.lib.virginia.edu/ebooks/
Author-Dedicated Web Sites	Jane Austen: http://www.pemberley.com/janeinfo/janeinfo.html Herman Melville's *Billy Budd:* http://xroads.virginia.edu/~HYPER/bb/bb_main.html

---

Note: The above list is meant to offer a source for items mentioned in this chapter. No endorsement of any product is intended, nor should any inference be drawn because a company is not listed. Many other companies offer products that perform as well and offer similar features.

Disclaimer: Web sites in this list were available at the time the list was compiled; however, the servers or sites may not be available when you are searching. If a site is not available, try searching with Google or Bing for a new address using the organization or company name.

NAME INDEX

SUBJECT INDEX

Page numbers followed by f indicate figures; those followed by t indicate tables; those followed by c indicate charts.

A

AAMR. *See* American Association on Mental Retardation (AAMR)

About.com, 339

Academic difficulties, 120–123
case study on, 120–122

Academic learning, assessment of, 80–81

Academic literacy, defined, 122–123

ACC. *See* Augmented and alternative communication (ACC) systems

Access, to education curriculum
ADA, 154, 156t, 158–159
ATA, 154, 156t
IDEIA-04, 154, 155t
NCLB, 154, 156t

Accommodations, 318, 319–320
areas of implementation, 319
for classroom assessments, 92
LEARNS strategy, 176
selection of, 91–97
for specific needs, 94t
for teaching strategies, 92, 93, 95–97
UDL, 88
worksheet for, 93t

Accountability
in assessment, 79
in collaboration, 58
in NCLB, 10, 11

Action, in GAME strategy, 115

Activities, sampling of, 106–107

ADDA. *See* Attention Deficit Disorder Association (ADDA)

Adequate yearly progress (AYP)
accountability through, 10, 11

ADHD. *See* Attention deficit–hyperactivity disorder (ADHD)

AFDC. *See* Aid to Families with Dependent Children (AFDC)

Affective networks, 161

Aided communication, 204
electronic ACC systems, 204–205
non-electronic, 204

Aid to Families with Dependent Children (AFDC), 195

Alcohol abuse, 51

Alpha commands, 105

Alternative assessment, 320

Alternative teaching, 62

American Association on Mental Retardation (AAMR), 35, 338

American Bar Association's Commission on Mental and Physical Disability Law, 341

American Speech-Language-Hearing Association (ASHA), 339

Americans with Disabilities Act (ADA), 15, 16, 17, 77
access to education curriculum, 154, 156t, 158–159

Analog/digital recorders, 210

Analytic rubrics, 233–234f, 234, 235

ARC. *See* Association for Retarded Children (ARC)

ASHA. *See* American Speech-Language-Hearing Association (ASHA)

Assessment. *See also* specific Assessment entries
of academic learning, 80–81
accountability and, 79
classroom equilibrium and, 79
concept of, 320
content planning and, 79
of disabilities, 80

feedback, 80
laws and, 77–79
motivational incentives, 80
NCTM recommendation on, 320
of problems, 80
of progress, 80–81
of strenghts and weaknesses, 79
types of, 320–321
UDL for. *See* Universal design for learning (UDL), for assessment

Assessment, for AT selection, 188–192
concepts of, 188–189
ecological, 188–189
models of, 190t
ongoing, 189
practical, 189
SETT. *See* SETT

Assessment, of PBL. *See also* Rubrics
formative assessment, 230
in lesson planning, 227
summative assessment, 230, 231

Assessment, of reading
diagnostic, 250, 251t
methods for, 249–251
phonemic awareness, 248–249
phonics, 249
progress monitoring, 250, 251, 252t
rate of reading, 249
research-based screening, 249, 250t
screening, 249
vocabulary, 249

Assistive Technology Act (ATA), 17–18
access, to education curriculum, 154, 156t